SPECTRUM GUIDE TO
MALAWI

Camerapix Publishers International

NAIROBI

Spectrum Guide to Malawi

First published 2003 by
Camerapix Publishers International

© 2003 John Douglas and Kelly White

ISBN 1 874041 55 5

This book was designed and produced by
Camerapix Publishers International,
P.O. Box 45048, Nairobi, Kenya
Fax: (254-2) 4448926/7
Tel: (254-2) 4448923/4/5

The **Spectrum Guides** series provides a comprehensive and detailed description of each country it covers, together with all the essential data that tourists, business visitors, or potential investors are likely to require.

Spectrum Guides in print:
African Wildlife Safaris
Ethiopia
India
Jordan
Kenya
Maldives
Mauritius
Namibia
Nepal
Pakistan
Seychelles
South Africa
Tanzania
Uganda
United Arab Emirates
Zambia
Zimbabwe

Colour separations: Universal Graphics Pte Ltd, Singapore.
Printed and bound: UIC Printing & Packaging Pte Ltd, Singapore.

Publishers: Camerapix Publishers
Projects Director: Rukhsana Haq
Picture Editor: John Douglas
Editor: Kelly White
Production Editors: Roger Barnard and Jan Hemsing
Production Assistant: Azra Chaudhry
Design: Rachel Musyimi

Editorial Board

Spectrum Guide to Malawi is the latest in the acclaimed series of high-quality, lavishly illustrated and immaculately researched international Spectrum Guides to exotic and exciting destinations, cultures, flora and fauna, which were the brainchild of the late **Mohamed Amin**, who, until his untimely death in 1996 was one of the world's most respected photographers and news cameramen.

Known as 'The warm heart of Africa'. Malawi has much to offer the visitor — from uncrowded game parks to the sandy beaches of Lake Malawi, from the high Zomba plateau, with its vast forest, waterfalls and lakes, to Mount Mulanje, at 3,000 metres, the highest mountain in Central Africa.

Compared with some other African destinations, Malawi has not enjoyed a high profile in the past, but that is changing. More and more visitors are now appreciating the excellent hotels and lodges, the country's unspoilt beauty and amenities such as sailing and water sports, game parks, climbing, birdwatching and a variety of local crafts. Add to this the Dr David Livingstone heritage and the warm, warm welcome from the friendly people of Malawi, and one can see why Malawi has never been so popular.

Spectrum Guide to Malawi is the result of eight years' painstaking research by Malawi specialists, **John Douglas** and **Kelly White**, who are responsible for both the detailed text and almost all of the photographs. Both have extensive knowledge of the country, as well as being respected travel writers in their own right. This is John's fourteenth book.

Project Director, **Rukhsana Haq**, and London-based Production Editor, **Roger Barnard**, worked closely with the authors to ensure that the text not only followed the successful format of all previous Spectrum Guides, but also included some useful innovations.

Design was in the capable hands of **Rachel Musyimi** and Production Assistant **Azra Chaudry** coordinated the production of manuscripts and listings. The veteran Kenya-based author and travel writer, **Jan Hemsing**, carried out final checks for style and accuracy.

TABLE OF CONTENTS

INTRODUCTION

The Malawian Experience 13
Travel Brief & Social Advisory 14

PART ONE: HISTORY, GEOGRAPHY AND PEOPLE

The History 30
The Land 44
The People 48

PART TWO: CAPITAL AND TOWNS

Lilongwe 55
Blantyre and Limbe 70
Zomba 88
Mzuzu 92

PART THREE: PLACES AND TRAVEL

THE CENTRAL
Kasungu 100
Kasungu National Park 103
Kamuzu Academy 108
Nkhotakota Wildlife Reserve 112
Going to the Lake 118
Going West 118
Dedza 120
Going South 124

NORTH MALAWI
Viphya Plateau 128
Going to the Lake 133
Nyika National Park 135
Vwaza Marsh Wildlife Reserve 146
Livingstonia Mission 151
Going North 156

SOUTH MALAWI
Zomba Plateau 162
Lake Chilwa 174
Liwonde National Park 177
Thyolo 190
Mount Mulanje and Mulanje Town 195
Lengwe National Park 203

Majete Wildlife Reserve 207
Sucoma 211
Elephant Marsh 213
Mwabvi Wildlife Reserve 216
Going North 217

LAKE MALAWI
Mangochi 220
The Southern Lakeshore 224
Monkey Bay 236
Cape Maclear and Lake Malawi N. Park 240
Mua Mission 248
Salima and Senga Bay 254
Central Lakeshore Villages: Nkhotakota, Dwangwa, Chintheche 260
Nkhata Bay 270
Likoma Island 274

PART FOUR: SPECIAL FEATURES

Malawi's National Parks and Wildlife Reserves 279
Wildlife 285
Birdlife and Bird Habitat 303
Lake Malawi's Fish 308
Vegetation 311
Tastes of Malawi 319
Activities 322
Religion 329
Music and Dance 332
Coins, Currency Notes and Stamps 334

PART FIVE: BUSINESS MALAWI

The Economy 337
Opportunities and Investment 342
Finance 343
Incentives 344
International Connections 345
State, Parastatal and Private Organisations 345

PART SIX: FACTS AT YOUR FINGERTIPS

Visa and immigration requirements 346
Health requirements 346
Customs 346
International flights 346

Departure tax 346
Arrival by road 346
Vehicle permits 346
Driver's licence 346
Road rules and signs 346
Insurance 346
Petrol and diesel 346
Road conditions 346
Car hire 347
Public transport and taxis 347
Domestic air services 347
Currency 347
Currency regulations 347
Banks 347
Credit cards 347
Government 348
Membership 348
Languages 348
Religion 348
Business hours 348
Security 348
Communications 348
Media 348
Energy 349
Medical services 349
Medical insurance 349
Chemists and pharmacies 349
Liquor 349
Tipping 349
Clubs 349
Daylight 349
Time 349
Climate 349
English-Chichewa dictionary 350

IN BRIEF

National Parks and Wildlife Reserves 351
Waterfalls 353
Wildlife Profile 354
Animal Checklist 363
Demographic profile 368
Gazeteer 368
Museums, Monuments and Historical Sites 369
Public Holidays 371

LISTINGS

Dialling Codes 372
Air Charter Companies 372
Airlines 372
Airports 372
Banks 372
Boat Services 372
Booksellers 372
Bus and Coach Companies 372
Business Associations 373
Car Hire 373
Clubs and Societies 373
Couriers 373
Crafts and Curios 374
Foreign Diplomatic Missions 374
Galleries 374
Government Offices and Ministries 374
Horse Riding 375
Hospitals 375
Hotels and Lodges 375
Malawi Missions Aboard 377
Media 378
Museums 378
Places of Interest 378
Rail Services 378
Tourist Information Offices (International) 378
Tourist Information Offices (National) 378
Tour and Safari Companies 379
Travel Agents 379
Water Sports 379
Websites 379

Bibliography 380

INDEX   381-384

MAPS

Malawi 10
Lilongwe 54
Blantyre and Limbe 72
Zomba 88
Mzuzu 92
Central Malawi 101
Kasungu National Park 104
Nkhotakota Wildlife Reserve 114
Northern region 126
Nyika National Park 136
Vwaza Marsh Wildlife Reserve 146
Southern region 158
Zomba Plateau 160
Liwonde National Park 180
Mount Mulanje Forest Reserve 195
Lengwe National Park 204
Majete Wildlife Reserve 208
Lake Malawi 218
Cape Maclear and Lake Malawi N. Park 242
Likoma Island 275

Cover: Mt Mulanje, Malawi's highest peak.
Half-title: Fishermen in their dugout at sunset on Lake Malawi. Title page: Mount Mulanje provides a dramatic backdrop. Pages 8-9: Palm trees fringe the Shire River in Liwonde National Park.

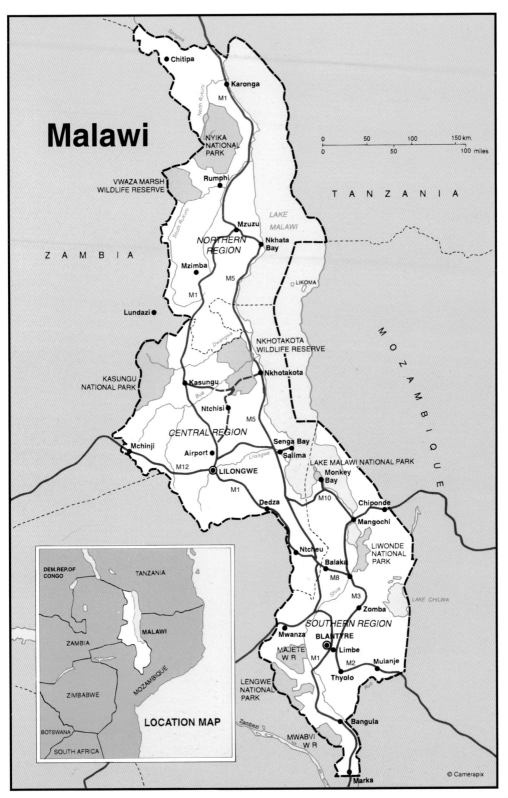

Malawi

Chitipa

Karonga

M1

NYIKA NATIONAL PARK

VWAZA MARSH WILDLIFE RESERVE

Rumphi

T A N Z A N I A

LAKE MALAWI

Mzuzu

NORTHERN REGION

Nkhata Bay

Z A M B I A

Mzimba

LIKOMA

M5

M1

Lundazi

Dwangwa

NKHOTAKOTA WILDLIFE RESERVE

KASUNGU NATIONAL PARK

Kasungu

Nkhotakota

Bua

Ntchisi

M5

CENTRAL REGION

Senga Bay

Mchinji

Airport

Lilongwe

Salima

M O Z A M B I Q U E

M12

LILONGWE

LAKE MALAWI NATIONAL PARK

M1

Monkey Bay

Dedza

M10

Chiponde

Mangochi

Ntcheu

LIWONDE NATIONAL PARK

Balaka

M8

Shire

M3

LAKE CHILWA

Zomba

SOUTHERN REGION

Mwanza

BLANTYRE

MAJETE W R

Limbe

M1

M2

Mulanje

Thyolo

Ruo

LENGWE NATIONAL PARK

Zambezi

Bangula

MWABVI W R

Marka

© Camerapix

DEM. REP. OF CONGO

TANZANIA

ZAMBIA

MALAWI

ZIMBABWE

MOZAMBIQUE

BOTSWANA

SOUTH AFRICA

LOCATION MAP

0   50   100   150 km.
0   50   100 miles

Main Routes

Descriptions of the major roads are incorporated into the 'Getting There' sections of relevant places, as detailed below

Road	Road Section	Page	'Getting There' to:
	Central Malawi		
M1	Lilongwe to Kasungu	100	Kasungu
M18	Kasungu to Nkhotakota	108	Kamuzu Academy
M7	Lilongwe to Nkhotakota Wildlife Reserve	112	Nkhotakota Wildlife Reserve
M14	Lilongwe to Salima	118	Going to the Lake
M12	Lilongwe to Zambian Border	118	Going West
M1	Lilongwe to Dedza	120	Dedza
M1	Dedza to M1/M8 Junction	124	Going South
	North Malawi		
M1	Kasungu to Mzuzu	128	Viphya Plateau
M5	Mzuzu to Nkhata Bay	133	Going to the Lake
M1	Mzuzu to Rumphi turn-off	135	Nyika National Park
M1	Rumphi turn-off to Chitimba	151	Livingstonia Mission
M1	Chitimba to Tanzania Border	156	Going North
	South Malawi		
M3	Blantyre to Zomba	162	Zomba Plateau
M3	Zomba to Liwonde	177	Liwonde National Park
M3	Mangochi to Liwonde	178	Liwonde National Park
M8	M1/M5 Junction to Liwonde	183	Liwonde National Park
M2	Blantyre to Thyolo	190	Thyolo
M2	Thyolo to Mulanje	195	Mulanje
M1	Blantyre to Lengwe National Park	203	Lengwe National Park
M1	Lengwe National Park to Mozambique Border	213	Elephant Marsh
M1	Blantyre to M1/M8 Junction	217	Going North
	Lake Malawi		
M10	Mangochi to S128 Junction	240	Cape Maclear & Lake Malawi NP
M10	S128 Junction to Mua Mission	248	Mua Mission
M5	M1/M8 Junction to Mua Mission	250	Mua Mission
M5	Mua to Salima	254	Salima & Senga Bay
M5	Salima to Chintheche	260	Central Lakeshore Villages
M5	Chintheche to Nkhata Bay	270	Nkhata Bay

Road Distances (in km)

	Lilongwe	Balaka	Bangula	Blantyre	Dedza	Karonga	Kasungu	Liwonde	Mangochi	Mchinji	Monkey Bay	Mua	Mulanje	Mzuzu	Nkhata Bay	Nkhotakota	Nsanje	Rumphi	Salima	Thyolo	Zomba
Balaka	204																				
Bangula	441	253																			
Blantyre	311	123	130																		
Dedza	84	120	357	227																	
Karonga	586	715	952	822	670																
Kasungu	121	325	562	432	205	466															
Liwonde	234	30	246	116	150	745	355														
Mangochi	263	93	317	187	213	729	368	71													
Mchinji	109	313	550	420	193	596	131	343	372												
Monkey Bay	225	155	379	249	256	691	330	133	62	334											
Mua	154	95	332	202	189	620	259	125	109	263	71										
Mulanje	392	204	211	81	308	903	513	197	268	501	330	283									
Mzuzu	360	489	726	596	444	226	240	519	503	370	465	394	677								
Nkhata Bay	381	452	689	559	465	273	287	482	466	447	428	357	640	47							
Nkhotakota	191	262	499	369	275	453	126	292	276	257	238	167	450	227	190						
Nsanje	490	302	49	179	406	1001	611	295	366	599	428	381	775	738	548						
Rumphi	429	558	795	665	513	167	309	588	572	439	534	463	746	69	116	296	844				
Salima	98	157	394	264	182	564	203	187	171	207	133	62	345	338	301	111	443	407			
Thyolo	350	162	169	39	266	861	471	155	226	459	288	241	42	635	598	408	218	704	303		
Zomba	284	80	196	66	200	795	405	50	121	393	183	175	147	569	532	342	245	638	237	105	

11

The Malawi Experience

Ex Africa semper aliquid novi. (There is always something new out of Africa.) So wrote Pliny the Elder almost two thousand years ago. For many who think they know their Africa, a discovery of Malawi is not only something new but a delightful surprise.

One of Africa's smaller countries, Malawi is a hidden treasure. So long seen as not quite East Africa, not quite Southern Africa, the country tended to be ignored by the tourists who flocked to those regions' better known destinations. Malawi was left to evolve slowly, to avoid the worst excesses of mass tourism and to retain its very African character.

Unlike many of its neighbours, Malawi was not seen during the colonial era, lasting over half a century, to be a place of mass settlement. Trade, yes, estate farming, yes, but not a place to settle. Significantly, it began its colonial history as the British Central Africa Protectorate and at no time did the number of European residents dominate either numerically or in cultural influence. Again unlike her neighbours, Malawi today is still very obviously African.

Achieving independence in 1964, the country's development was in the hands of Dr Hastings Banda for three decades. His policies never truly embraced the notion that tourism could be a vibrant and valuable sector of the country's economy. Indeed, some of the petty restrictions he placed on visitors were a positive deterrent.

Since its emergence in 1994 as a multi-party democracy, Malawi, the warm heart of Africa, has begun to come out from the shadows and is taking its rightful place as one of Africa's most attractive holiday destinations. Its developing and changing economy is also allowing the country to be seen as a place to do business and to invest in the future.

As more visitors begin to flow into Malawi, they are discovering the truth of the claim that this is Africa's most beautiful country. Nature has been generous to this land set in the great cleft that is East Africa's Great Rift Valley. Here is central Africa's highest peak, Mount Mulanje. Dominating the north-west of the country is the unique plateau of Nyika. To the east is Africa's third largest and most beautiful lake, Lake Malawi, an inland tropical sea. Despite its diminutive size (by African standards) the diversity of landscapes is quite breathtaking.

Unlike so much of the continent where the scenery has grandeur but, in truth, is often monotonous, the scene in Malawi is ever changing. Even on a short journey the variety is evident: high plateau, mountain peaks and riverine lowlands, vast tracks of forest, grasslands and plantations of sugar and tea, and always the Lake with its fringe of golden sands. Little wonder that the scene as viewed from the Zomba Plateau was described as "the best in the whole of the British Empire".

The nine game parks and reserves are a joy to visit with none of the queues of four-wheel drive vehicles all intent on viewing the same herd of buffalo or a pride of lions at a kill. No, here is game viewing and tracking as it should be with the sense of adventure that comes with the knowledge that numbers of tourists are deliberately kept at levels which ensure exclusivity.

As the market for adventure tourism grows, Malawi is satisfying the demand for something more that the laze and gaze vacation that characterised many people's holidays in the past. Climbing, hiking, cycling, horse riding and a host of water-sports are among the growing range that is available. Whether as a backpacker or a seeker after luxury, Malawi can satisfy the needs and desires of all its visitors.

But Malawi is more than scenery, fauna and flora. A country is its people and travel should be about making new friends. The sobriquet "the warm heart of Africa" is not a marketing slogan. It is reality. Malawians are the most friendly people you could meet anywhere in the world. The warm heart will welcome as you make your discovery of something new in Africa.

Opposite: Children's faces reflect Malawi's warm heart.

Travel Brief and Social Advisory

Getting there

By air
Most international visitors will arrive at Lilongwe International, a small but smart and relatively efficient airport. The alternative for regional flights is Blantyre's Chileka Airport which also has domestic connections with Lilongwe scheduled to link up with the capital's international flights.

A limited number of airlines currently provide Malawi's intercontinental flights. British Airways flies direct from Europe whilst other airlines connect through the main regional hubs. KLM/Kenya Airways use Nairobi, Virgin Atlantic/Air Malawi and South African Airways use Johannesburg, Air Zimbabwe uses Harare and Ethiopian Airlines uses Addis Ababa. Routes throughout southern and eastern Africa (and connections beyond) are offered by Air Malawi, Air Zimbabwe, Ethiopian Airlines, South African Airways and Air Tanzania. These airlines have offices in Lilongwe or Blantyre and many also have desks or representation in the foyer of the Le Méridien Capital Hotel in Lilongwe. Alternatively, Air Malawi may act as general sales and handling agents.

When leaving the country by air, a tax of US$20 per person is levied. Vouchers are purchased in the airport entrance hall but must be paid for in US dollars.

By road
There are a number of main entry points to the country by road. Entry from Mozambique can be at Mwanza on to the M6 (if arriving via the infamous Tete Corridor), at Marka on to the M1, at Muloza on to the M2 and at Chiponde east of Mangochi. From Tanzania entry is across the Songwe River, north of Iponga, on to the M1 and from Zambia at Mchinji on to the M12 or west of Chitipa, joining the M9. Border posts should be open from 06.00 to 18.00. To bring a car into Malawi, a temporary import permit (TIP) is required if a *carnet de passage* is not held. The border post will oblige for a small fee, and can also arrange third party insurance, which is compulsory.

By bus
International coach services operate to and from Harare, Lusaka and Dar es Salaam. The Trans Zambezi Express connects Blantyre with Johannesburg three times a week.

Getting around

By air
Air Malawi's scheduled domestic services currently connect Lilongwe, Blantyre, Mzuzu, Karonga and Club Makokola (southern lakeshore).

Proflight Air Services link the main towns with the lakeshore and the national parks. There are no scheduled flights but there are regular departures and fixed prices for particular routes. Specific individual requirements will also be accommodated. Locations served include the following: Lilongwe, Salima (central lakeshore), Club Makokola (southern lakeshore), Mvuu (Liwonde National Park), Mzuzu, Chelinda (Nyika National Park), Likoma Island, Chintheche (northern lakeshore), and Mfuwe (Luangwa Valley, Zambia).

By road
Travel by road is the ideal way to see much more of this relatively small country and its ever-changing and beautiful scenery. The road network stretches for some 28,000 kilometres (17,500 miles) with major highways linking the main destinations. Roads are single carriageway (even 'M' roads) and traffic volumes are low. However, the standard of the surfaces is variable and can sometimes be poor. The main towns and major routes have tarmac roads, though only the most recently built or upgraded roads have consistent surfaces. Older tarmac can be the most dangerous. Initially appearing reasonable, drivers lulled into a high speed may be confronted suddenly by

Above: Most minor roads are untarred and dusty in the dry season.

unavoidable potholes. Alternatively, when most of the tarmac has gone, occasional resistant mounds provide the hazard.

Minor rural links and routes in national parks and wildlife reserves are dirt roads. Many can be quite acceptable, if decidedly dusty when dry. No great speed is attainable but a consistent surface allows a steady pace. Drivers still need to be very alert — a seemingly regular corrugated earth road may deteriorate without much warning into a sand trap. Rains and surface water cause greater problems, particularly on slopes. When wet, roads become muddy skid-pans; having dried, the remaining channels and potholes provide obstacles. Four-wheel drive is needed for the wet season on many of these roads, and even in the dry season some may be impassable by saloon car. It is not simply the added traction offered by four-wheel drive, but the higher ground clearance which is needed to traverse the most severe undulations.

There are very few cars on the roads and few instances of indiscipline so driving is straightforward. Malawians drive on the left and the use of safety belts is mandatory.

There are two main speed limits — 80 kilometres (50 miles) per hour on main roads and 60 kilometres (38 miles) per hour in towns and villages. Except on new tarmac, these can rarely be exceeded anyway. The older tarmac can allow such speeds to be reached in stretches but possible hazards (potholes or raised mounds) dictate caution and some sections may have to be carefully negotiated at a very slow pace. An average speed of 60 kilometres (38 miles) per hour over a long journey on these surfaces is a good achievement. Even relatively consistent earth roads are unlikely to allow speeds above 50 kilometres (30 miles) per hour because of the constant jarring of the often corrugated surface, and hazards like holes, rocks and sandy patches.

Limits are even applied to the national parks and wildlife reserves but these roads are often no more than rough tracks.

Other road users can also prove problematical. Most vehicles encountered will be in poor states of repair and slow. Pick-up trucks bursting with 'passengers', over-laden bicycles, ox-carts, loose livestock and pedestrians can all appear in the road

15

without much warning. If choosing to overtake, they should be given as wide a berth as possible at a sensible speed.

Occasionally, small branches are placed on the road to indicate a hazard ahead, usually a breakdown. Not as easy to spot as red triangles, they are sometimes left in the road after the vehicle has moved on.

After dark is not a time to drive as there is no road illumination outside the towns and lighting on other road users is limited. Recovery from breakdown is also even less likely.

Petrol and diesel are available in most towns or large villages, though it is best to keep the tank as full as possible at all times in case of shortages.

By being alert to the road surface problems, driving in Malawi with its few cars is actually relatively straightforward. Even if unfortunate enough to get stuck on a remote earth road, willing helpers will quickly appear.

There are some police road blocks on Malawi's roads, particularly near to borders and on major routes. Though all vehicles should stop, tourists are usually waved on without delay.

The limited road signs indicate towns and distances but rarely road numbers. Signposts are not guaranteed even at major junctions so it is important to keep a close eye on the map to anticipate turnings.

The 1992 Tourist map at a scale of 1:1,000,000 is the most widely used, though its availability is now dwindling (try the tourist offices). The Department of Surveys also produces a 1:1,000,000 relief map which shows more of the minor roads; and sets of 1:250,000 maps at K750 per sheet (the country is covered in ten sheets). Separate town plans of Lilongwe, Blantyre, Mzuzu and Zomba should also be available. All maps can be bought from the sales offices of the Department of Surveys in Blantyre, open Monday to Friday 07.30 to 12.00 and 13.00 to 16.00.

Some road numbers have changed over the years and some maps and literature encountered may show old ones. However, Malawians do not think in terms of either road numbers or road names. Mention a place and you will be shown where to go,

ask what road you are currently on and few will know.

Car hire

Hire cars are available but prices are high and standards can sometimes cause concern. Pre-booked cars can be collected at Lilongwe International Airport, Chileka Airport (Blantyre) or from the main hotels. Sales desks are also found at these locations, as well as offices in Lilongwe and Blantyre.

Hire is available on a 'per kilometre' rate or with unlimited distance. If touring the country, it is easy to achieve the necessary average daily journeys (100 to 200 kilometres/60 to 120 miles) to make unlimited distance the most economic. Chauffeurs are also available at a not unreasonable price, though costs rapidly increase if travelling away from the town of hire.

A full driver's licence is required and a minimum age of 25 with two years driving experience may be asked for. Drivers will have to be properly insured and a variety of cover is available. The standard cover is third party but the driver remains liable for damage due to road conditions. Since unsurfaced roads are likely to be unavoidable, extra care should be taken.

Most of the cars will have a few 'superficial' problems: cracked windows; creased wings; missing wing mirrors. It is worth checking out the vehicle — at least for a spare tyre, simple tool kit and red emergency triangles (which the police at checkpoints are increasingly asking to see). The usual selection of car 'groups' is available. Air-conditioning should be considered if driving on dirt roads to allow windows to be shut and keep the dust out. Four-wheel drive will be needed if travelling on the worst roads.

Hitch-hiking and taxis

For hitch-hikers there are numerous *matola* cars or pick-up trucks which pack themselves full of passengers for a small charge. These are either drivers doing the journey anyway (possibly returning from a delivery job) or they are purpose driven to collect passengers. These creaking, overloaded vehicles are cheap and quite common. Because of this form of transport, most

Above: Many bridges on minor roads require careful driving.

people offering a lift to hitchhikers will expect a small payment.

In the main towns, a very small number of taxis operate, most easily found at the large hotels.

By bus

The bus network is quite extensive and reasonably comfortable and efficient. Shire Bus Lines is the main operator, running a variety of services. They are based on Masauko Chipembere Highway in Blantyre, with offices at the bus stations in main towns. For journeys between the regional capitals, the different services offer a choice but the cheaper they get, the more stops there are and the longer it takes.

Coachline connects Blantyre, Lilongwe and Mzuzu non-stop up to four times daily. Blantyre to Lilongwe takes four-and-a-half hours or less and costs around K800. (Blantyre to Mzuzu costs around K1500). All journeys can be booked and have steward service, drinks and snacks, air conditioning and a washroom. *Expressline* and *Speedlink* can also be booked and connect the regional capitals. However, there are more

stops and alternative routes with one or two departures daily. *Intercity* services expand the network to lesser towns but are slower, stopping at most stages, though also cheaper (less than K300 for Blantyre to Lilongwe).

Southern, Central and *Northern Countryside* services cover local routes within each region and *Cityline* urban/suburban networks are based in the three capitals.

The buses and coaches are regular and reasonably reliable, though road conditions on rural routes can cause problems. The large bus stations in the regional capitals have detailed timetable information.

Numerous minibuses also cover local routes, sometimes complementary to the Shire Bus Lines services, sometimes as the only option. If there is no main service and no minibuses, *matola* (see page 16) may be the only choice.

By boat

The *mv Ilala* passenger ferry boat operating on Lake Malawi offers much more of an experience than simply getting from A to B.

Named after the village in Zambia where David Livingstone died, the *Ilala* travels

Above: Small pickups, *matola*, are loaded with people and goods.

between Monkey Bay in the south and Chilumba in the north, stopping regularly in between. The north-south journey takes approximately three days, with the round trip operating on a weekly schedule. Comfortable cabins are available and vehicles can be carried. The owner's cabin boasts its own toilet, bath and shower, while six standard cabins (four double and one single) share facilities. Three meals a day, snacks and drinks are served. Since the boat still primarily serves the local population any trip is a real experience of the everyday hustle and bustle, noises and smells. There is also the lake itself with its colourful fish and fishermen, secluded white sand bays, fishing villages seemingly inaccessible over land, high cliffs where no road can reach the shore, and its hippos and crocodiles. For speed, take the Lakeshore Road; for experience, take the ferry.

There is a published schedule but departures and arrivals are not always on time. Stopping points between Monkey Bay and Chilumba, include Chipoka, Nkhotakota, Likoma Island and Nkhata Bay, as well as some on the Mozambiquan shore.

Tickets can be bought from the Malawi Lake Services booking office at the Monkey Bay jetty, or through Ulendo Safaris (see Listings). Booking is especially important for the cabins and re-confirmation close to the time of departure is advisable. Cabin rates include bed and breakfast and range from US$10 for short sections in a standard cabin to US$125 in the owner's cabin for the complete round trip. Foot passengers can join the first class deck for US$3 to US$30, depending on the length of journey, or travel economy with the local people.

Although vehicles can be taken on the *Ilala*, it may be safer to have your car driven to your disembarkation point (car hire companies will arrange this). Cars can be loaded and unloaded at Monkey Bay, Chipoka, Nkhata Bay and Chilumba.

The *Ilala's* sister ship, the *mv Mtendere* operates as back up but is smaller with no cabin accommodation.

By train
There is a limited rail network in Malawi, largely used for freight. At times a passenger car is attached to the rear of the

Above: Accommodation in Kasungu National Park has been up-graded.

freight train but the service is slow, with stops at every station. It is rarely used by international travellers.

By bicycle

A number of tour operators and lodges offer bicycles for hire and this can be a surprisingly effective way of touring the country. Because of Malawi's compact size and ever changing scenery, even a day spent travelling by this slow method will contain considerable variety and interest. The roads and tracks impassable by saloon car can be traversed by mountain bike, though the more rugged landscapes will provide challenging riding.

Organised tours

Malawi has a good supply of local safari operators who can assist with any or all elements of a required tour, as well as offering their own scheduled packages (see Listings).

Where to stay

The modest number of international visitors means that there is not an abundance of top grade accommodation but also that it is not difficult to find vacancies in most places. The main town hotels maintain good facilities and service — managing to enhance the attractive and positive local characteristics rather than being characterless 'five stars'. The up-market lodges and inns now found in the tourist areas (including the national parks) are now establishing good reputations. There is also now a growing range of mid-market establishments which offer very pleasant places to stay at a sensible budget.

Le Mérdien now has the management contract for the only real chain in the country (in Lilongwe, Blantyre, Mzuzu, on Zomba Plateau and at the lakeshore) and many properties are being upgraded. Many independent establishments are family-owned and run with few now remaining under government control.

In the regional capitals, the top hotels mainly host business travellers so

Above: The Imperial Hotel in Lilongwe has character at a modest price.

functionality, comfort and efficiency are paramount. For the areas attracting genuine tourists, setting, charm and leisure facilities are seen as more important — enhancing the 'experience' of the stay. Where the location is the important factor these are altogether simpler establishments with accommodation tending to be in the form of chalets or rondavels, rather than high rise blocks.

Town hotels are unlikely to be fully booked unless there is a particular conference or international football match. The resort hotels are more popular so booking comfortably ahead of time is advisable. Written confirmation of any accommodation booking should be obtained wherever possible. It is also worth re-confirming close to your departure date. Lower grade accommodation is rarely worth pre-booking except in the most popular tourist areas. Contact is difficult and it is rare to arrive and not find a vacancy.

The following summaries indicate the standards of accommodation. Bed and breakfast rates are given for single/double in US dollars and exclude the current government surcharges applied to all accommodation and meal bills (10 per cent service charge and 10 per cent tax).

Regional capitals

The top-range hotels (US$160/190 or more) offer very comfortable rooms with en suite bathrooms, air-conditioning and satellite TV. There is a choice of restaurants, bars and sporting facilities. The hotel foyers house tour operators, airline contacts and sales outlets.

There are fewer facilities in the smaller mid-range hotels (US$70/90), with air-conditioning and TV not standard in all rooms. However, these often have greater local or colonial character.

Budget accommodation (US$1 to 10 per person) is primarily used by the local population with facilities rarely extending beyond a bed and a shared bathroom (even running water may not always be available). This may be no great hardship but it is often combined with dirty living areas and poor sanitation. However, there are also some establishments specifically targeted to the international backpacker market, rather than to the local market. Availability is rarely a problem and all are very cheap.

Above: The tents at Chembe Lodge are spacious and comfortable.

There are a number of old colonial sports clubs usually offering camping sites (US$1 to 5 per tent) and a host of additional facilities — restaurant, bar, snooker table, swimming pools, tennis courts and golf courses. They are full of character and characters though can show their age.

Tourist areas
Top-range hotels (around US$120/160) provide for extremely comfortable and relaxing stays in places of natural beauty. There are fans in preference to air conditioning and television is rightly viewed as being a disturbance. A stay can be as active or inactive as the guest desires.

Mid-range establishments (around US$40/70) are Malawi's current growth sector. Facilities may be fewer and service levels reduced but the settings remain very attractive and many are very charming and homely, with a good range of activities available. There will be a restaurant and en suite rooms. Though not offering quite the air of high luxury of the top range, these mid-market lodges benefit from the pride and attention to detail that comes with being owner-run.

Budget accommodation (US$1 to 10 per person) is usually of a slightly higher standard than that in the regional capitals and the settings do provide some compensation for the shortcomings.

Sports clubs (around US$5 per person) in the more out of the way areas have chalets on offer, though self-catering is usual.

National parks and wildlife reserves
Private safari camps (US$60 to US$270 per person) offer all inclusive stays with organised safaris and restaurant meals. Accommodation ranges from large tents for those who wish to self-cater, through rondavels and cottages to luxury permanent en suite 'tents' and lodges. At the very top level there is no shortage of luxury and pampering.

Camps run by the Ministry of Tourism, Parks and Wildlife (US$5 per person), where they remain, consist of simple huts, permanent tents or campsites with extremely limited facilities. Bedding, food, and in some cases, cooking equipment, need to be taken by the visitor, whilst sanitation is at its most simple. However, with their settings

Above: Tented accommodation can be luxurious.

and rudimentary facilities, they do offer a 'real Africa' experience. Accommodation should be pre-booked through the Ministry.

Camping

Camping in Malawi is relatively easy and straightforward. Campsites can be found all along the lakeshore, in the main towns and even in the national parks. Standards vary but there are many with very well maintained facilities, the best examples being those associated with a neighbouring upmarket establishments. Malawi is a relatively densely populated country with towns and villages rarely separated by vast distances so getting provisions usually presents little difficulty. Most fuels are available, except Coleman fuel.

General Information

The people

At the 1998 census Malawi's population was 9.9 million with an annual growth rate of two per cent. Because the country is relatively small (Zambia covers six times the area yet has a smaller population), this creates one of the highest densities in Africa of 105 per square kilometre (272 per square mile).

All the indigenous groups have a common Bantu origin, with only one per cent non-African. The Maravi (Chewa) have a majority, whilst Lomwe, Yao and Ngoni are the other main groups. Though there is rarely any great ethnic tension, regional groupings were reflected in the recent parliamentary election with each of the administrative regions (Northern, Central and Southern) voting differently. Instances of armed conflict in Malawi's history are rare and the friendliness of all Malawians is renowned. A genuine welcome and beaming smile are extended to all visitors everywhere.

The greatest part of the population (85 per cent) remains rural, living largely in traditional villages of simple huts. There are few towns of any size, and the regional capitals account for most of the urban population. Blantyre in the Southern Region has half a million people and is the economic centre of the whole country. The Southern Region also has Zomba, the site of the country's university and, formerly, its parliament. Lilongwe, capital of both the Central Region and the country, is actually Malawi's second largest city. Mzuzu is the Northern Region's capital and commercial centre but is still relatively young.

The national language is Chewa (or Chichewa — literally 'language of the Chewa'), with Nyanja, Yao and Tumbuka (common in the north) the next most used local languages. English is the official language and is widely used, particularly in the commercial sector, as the primary language. English speakers experience few problems of communication.

Eighty per cent of the population is Christian with the Church of Central Africa Presbyterian the strongest in the country. Muslims account for 13 per cent, squeezing indigenous beliefs to a small minority. The election of a Muslim president by the majority Christian electorate illustrates the lack of religious tension.

Approaching 80 per cent of Malawians devote their working day to agriculture, mostly at a semi-subsistence level on small-holdings. Maize, pulses, groundnuts, rice and livestock are farmed, and there is a great deal of fishing along Lake Malawi.

Safety
Malawi is a comparatively safe country and travellers rarely feel concerned about their own safety or the security of their belongings. However, it is always wise to be discreet with items of value and protective with your money. In some of the more remote places of interest, signs at parking places will warn not to leave valuables unattended. These should be heeded as far as is practical and valuable items which can't be carried are safest locked in the boot of a car.

Every residential or business property worth its salt has at least one uniformed security guard. It is not entirely clear whether crime figures are low because of the deterrent of the guards everywhere, or because there can be no criminals since everyone is too busy at work — in security! Sadly, residential burglaries have increased in recent years.

Wild animals away from the national parks and wildlife reserves pose very little real danger. Large predators have in-

consequential populations and most will retreat if disturbed. The animal which reputedly causes most deaths in Africa is the hippo, whose dash to the safety of water will make no concession to anything in its path. Trampling by a 1500 kilogram (3300 pound) beast is likely to be fatal. The Shire River and Lake Malawi have large hippo populations but local people will warn those who wander into areas where hippos are known to be.

There are venomous snakes in Malawi but they will retreat rather than attack, unless cornered. Statistically, the risk is tiny. Wearing boots when walking through concealing undergrowth is a sensible added protection and medical advice should be sought as soon as possible if bitten. If possible, the snake should be killed and taken to the doctor to ensure correct species identification for treatment.

Weather
Malawi has an exceptionally pleasant climate. Across the three seasons of cool dry (May to August), hot dry (September to mid-November) and hot wet (mid-November to April), the range for average temperatures is only from 15° to 30°C (60°-80°F). There is unlikely to be a day without sunshine, and rain is pretty limited. Regional variations are provided largely by relief and the influence of the Lake and ensure that cooler or warmer weather, depending upon your preference, can always be found somewhere.

Clothing
Laws no longer prevent women wearing trousers, or skirts above the knee, nor is the length of men's hair or width of their trousers still a matter of concern for immigration officials. The weather mainly determines clothing and informality is the norm. For casual day wear, little more than T-shirts and shorts or light dresses are required. Trousers and jerseys may be necessary on rare cooler days, in the evenings and on the high plateaux. Those on safari will also need to wrap up warm for morning and evening excursions, especially if driving in open-topped vehicles.

It is sensible to wear a hat, sun creams

Above: An African doctor's stall in Lilongwe's walled market.

and sunglasses to guard against the intense sun, and trousers can provide useful protection from vegetation and insects when walking through the bush. In national parks and wildlife reserves it is also customary to wear dull, natural colouring (greens and browns) to prevent standing out from the vegetation. Camouflage jackets are discouraged as the military overtones may cause misunderstandings. A pair of reasonably sturdy boots is an advantage when walking through the bush.

Even in the best hotels formal dress for dinner is rarely necessary, though the top Blantyre restaurants may insist upon a tie for men.

Health

It is most important that travellers consult their doctor or a travel clinic to obtain the latest advice on immunisations. In the UK, Germany and Australia, there are medical advisory services for travellers abroad (MASTA in the UK and Australia, MEDIDAR in Germany) which also are extremely helpful for initial guidance.

At present, the following immunisations should be up to date before entering Malawi: polio, tetanus, typhoid fever and hepatitis A. Yellow fever immunisation is not required, but Zambia is in the old yellow fever endemic zone, so anyone arriving from Zambia should have an immunisation certificate. Cholera and rabies are limited and vaccination is usually only recommended for those at particularly high risk.

There is genuine risk from **malaria** in much of Malawi so prophylactics should be taken. Due to some chloroquine resistance, mefloquine (Lariam) is usually recommended (despite the current debate over potential side effects). Any course of tablets should be started well in advance of a trip to provide a check for possible side effects; and should be continued for four weeks after returning home since malaria usually takes a week or two to incubate. Whatever the prophylactic, travellers should ALWAYS OBTAIN PERSONAL ADVICE BEFORE EMBARKING UPON ANY COURSE OF TABLETS.

Initial symptoms of malaria include headaches, dizziness and flu-like aches and pains. If these are experienced any

Above: The President endorses a campaign to improve public awareness.

time during a visit, or up to a year after returning, a doctor should be seen immediately (making them aware of the possibility of malaria).

Sleeping sickness is transmitted by the tsetse fly and there is no immunisation. The national parks and wildlife reserves are areas of greatest risk though only a limited number of tsetse flies actually carry the disease and programmes of eradication mean genuine risk is very small. The disease is treatable.

With sleeping sickness and malaria, it is important to avoid being bitten. Use of repellents and keeping the skin covered is especially important in high risk areas near standing water or when walking through vegetation. Mosquitoes pose even more of a problem as dusk falls so greater vigilance is required. During the night sleeping areas should be sealed as effectively as possible to prevent insects entering. A mosquito net over the bed is a wise additional precaution, particularly on the lakeshore and in areas of wilderness.

Bilharzia (schistosomiosis) is a parasitic worm infection which, though now treatable, can lead to long-term illness. The disease can be contracted simply by entering freshwater rivers, streams and lakes. The bilharzia parasite enters the water via human urination or defecation and then uses snails as intermediate hosts, before returning to the water as a larva which enter the human body again through the skin. Immediate symptoms are irritation of the skin where the larva has entered. Months later fever or malaise will occur and, eventually, abdominal pain and passing of blood.

The level of bilharzia in Lake Malawi is presently a matter of some contention. Recent media reports, especially in the UK, have greatly exaggerated the risk of bathing in Lake Malawi, without ever actually having tested the waters. For the disease to be present there must be reeds (the habitat of the snails), coarse sand, still water and regular usage of the water by an infected local population. The reality is that this combination of environmental factors rarely occurs at the main lakeshore hotels. To their credit, establishments like Nkopola Lodge, Club Makokola, and Livingstonia Beach Hotel have been involved in reed clearance programmes as well as assisting internationally run health programmes in local villages. Risk at these hotels is therefore virtually non-existent. A medical research team from Denmark is in the process of testing the lakeshore for bilharzia and early results are extremely encouraging as most hotels and lodges are clear. Areas where the required environmental factors combine may still have bilharzia and should be avoided for bathing. This includes Cape Maclear, though an eradication programme was begun in 1998. There is also risk in other bodies of fresh water except the fast-moving rivers and streams on the mountains and plateaux.

If choosing to swim in lakes or rivers, dry yourself with a towel thoroughly and vigorously immediately on leaving the water. The larvae die quickly away from water and are also unlikely to survive such a rub down. Bilharzia can also now be easily countered with the drug praziquantel and many ex-patriate residents choose simply to swim where they please and take their tablets.

Latest figures show over 15 per cent of Malawi's adult population is infected with the **HIV** virus so sensible precautions should be taken whenever body fluids are concerned.

In cases of accident or medical problems, some travellers may feel more confident in having their own sterile medical pack with them.

Photography

There are many wonderful photographic subjects in Malawi. A complete stock of film and any equipment required should be taken as little is available and locally purchased film may be out of date. Hotel foyer shops are the most likely sources for film though the range will be limited and the prices high. Processing should be carried out on returning home. Precautions should be taken against exposing equipment to the full glare of the sun for too long. Similarly, unsheltered parked cars will overheat very quickly so should not have equipment left in them. The other hazard is dust. Travelling on the earth roads, if the windows are open (which will be necessary if the vehicle does not have air conditioning), equipment should be carefully stored to prevent covering by dust.

Most Malawians will happily pose for photographs though it is always polite to ask permission first. Children will be over keen to get into shots and usually pose unnaturally. They may ask for money but will not become agitated if none is forthcoming.

There are still bans on photographing anything with 'security' overtones, including airports, radio transmitters and official state residences. Wherever there are uniformed guards it is wise to keep the camera out of sight and first make a polite enquiry. The response will always be friendly, even if in the negative. The restriction applies to major bridges, though pictures from the bridge may be permitted.

The middle of the day is best avoided as a time to photograph due to the intense sunlight which creates problems of contrast and can result in washed out pictures. The softer light and shadows of early morning and late afternoon make pictures much more interesting. Because the haze of moisture and particles in the air builds up through the day, the early hours offer the best opportunities for landscape pictures.

When to go

Many travellers to Malawi avoid the wettest months (December to March) because of the restrictions on travel and game viewing. Road surfaces deteriorate in the rains, making road travel hazardous. Vegetation grows to obscure game viewing and the widespread water supply means that the animals are not forced to gather at limited dry season water sources.

However, the wet season does create a more lush landscape which attracts even greater numbers and species of birds to the country. January and February are particularly good months in this regard, as well as being the best time to see orchids at Nyika, Viphya and Zomba. Another flowering season is that of the aloes, which occurs during May and June at Nyika, Dedza, Zomba and Mulanje. Highlights for Lake Malawi include the ultra-light fishing tournament in April and the Lake Malawi

500 Kilometre Yachting Marathon, the longest freshwater sailing event in the world, for eight days in early July.

On safari
Game viewing in Malawi is often referred to as 'safaris as they used to be'. There are many animal species though few large populations but Malawi is much more about experience than tick lists. There are no queuing minibuses here, rather small, lone groups travelling through the bush (see Malawi's National Parks and Wildlife Reserves, Part Four)

National flag
Malawi's flag has three horizontal stripes of black, red and green. The black stands for the people of Africa and contains a red rising sun motif signifying the dawn of freedom. The red band signifies the blood of the martyrs of African freedom while the green represents the evergreen nature of Malawi.

National bird
The Malawi national bird is the fish eagle.

National motto
Unity and Freedom

National anthem
O God bless our land of Malawi,
Keep it a land of peace.
Put down each and every enemy,
Hunger, disease, envy.
Join together all our hearts as one,
That we be free from fear.
　　Bless our leader, each and everyone,
　　And Mother Malawi.

Our own Malawi, this land so fair,
Fertile and brave and free.
With its lakes, refreshing mountain air,
How greatly blest are we.
Hills and valleys, soil so rich and rare,
Give us bounty free.
Wood and forest, plains so broad and fair,
All beauteous Malawi.

Freedom ever, let us all unite,
To build up Malawi.
With our love, our zest and loyalty,
Bringing our best to her.
In time of war, or in time of peace,
One purpose and one goal.
Men and women serving selflessly,
In building Malawi.

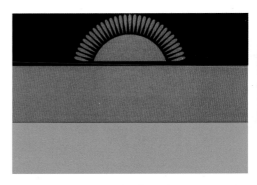

Above: The Malawi Coat of Arms. Top: Malawi's flag. Left: The national bird: a fish eagle.

PART ONE: HISTORY, GEOGRAPHY AND PEOPLE

A SLAVE CARAVAN.

Above: The nineteenth century saw the slave trade along Lake Malawi at its worst.
Opposite: A village shelters below one of Malawi's splendid *inselbergs* or mountain islands.

The History

Early Man

The East African Rift Valleys have revealed the earliest hominids and it is likely that Malawi's lakeshore supported such life close to the evolutionary split between the ancestors of humans and chimpanzees 5-6 million years ago. However, the earliest remains found on Lake Malawi's northern shore are of *Homo Rudolfensis,* dated at 2.5 million years old.

Early Stone Age sites (50,000 to 10,000 years ago) are few in number; the main concentrations are found on raised beaches of Lake Malawi's north-west shore. They reveal hunter-gatherer groups who used tools to make wooden implements from the trees of their thickly forested environment.

Through the middle to late Stone Age, settlement became more widespread and skeletal remains, particularly in the Mzimba district, have led to the identification of *Nachifukan* man — short and robust with a mixture of negro, Bushman and Caucasian characteristics. The rock art of this period has distinct geometric drawings, in contrast with the bushman art of animals and people elsewhere in southern Africa. Malawi's late Stone Age cultures remained as woodland hunters but also developed basic vege-culture. They were dominant in the country from 8000 BC through to AD200, continuing to survive in isolated pockets right up to the fifteenth century. There have even been stories of some being seen in the last 200 years.

Iron Age

The earliest Iron Age remains date from AD220, the beginning of successive waves of Bantu peoples moving south through Africa.

Though not a distinct ethnic group genetically speaking, a commonality in language linked the Bantu, who originated from the Congo area. The movements of this linguistic group lasted until the fifteenth century and brought iron working techniques, livestock and seed for cultivation into many areas of Malawi. The largest migrations didn't occur until after the twelfth century and throughout this time, the existing Batwa inhabitants (the *Kafula,* descendents of the *Nachifukan*) were left to roam and hunt, probably keenly accepting the new innovations of the Bantu.

The most significant movement in Malawi's history was around the sixteenth century. It was at this time that another large group of Bantu entered from the north-west and established themselves in Malawi, where their descendants still remain. The group is often collectively known as Maravi. However, the complexities of chiefdoms and tribes mean that many names are associated with the Maravi — usually described as sub-groups. The commonality was again based on language with all sub-groups speaking dialects of fundamentally the same language. Some of their beliefs included that a footprint in the Dzalamyama hills, south-west of Lilongwe, was made by man's first ever worldly steps, making this the site of Creation. They also believed that certain animals had mystical protective powers and so hunting was limited. The name Maravi has associations with fire, deriving possibly from the image of lake sunsets or from iron smelting fires introduced into the country at that time. For many years this was a well organised federation of groups covering an area from the Zambezi north to a point half-way along Lake Malawi's western shore. A distinct tribe, the Tumbuka, had by then entered Malawi to the north of the Maravi.

The two significant groups to emerge from the Maravi migration were the Nyanja and Chewa. The Chewa are modern Malawi's most numerous group, providing the national language of Chichewa (chi means language). It should be noted that Maravi, Chewa and Nyanja are titles which have, at different times, had varying definitions and changing degrees of importance (for both people and language).

With the Nyanja to the far south, the Chewa on the Central African Plateau and the Tumbuka to the north, for many centuries Malawi experienced slow, steady

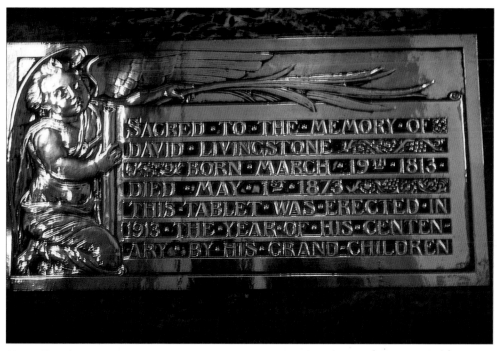

Above: This monument to David Livingstone is in Blantyre's St Michael and All Angels church.

expansion of settlements, cultivation and iron production.

Invasions and the Slave Trade

The nineteenth century witnessed great turmoil with invasions from neighbouring areas and Europe, and the arrival of the slave trade.

For many centuries, Arab traders had been establishing city-states along Africa's east coast. Largely dealing in ivory and slaves, there gradually developed an Arab-influenced African culture called Swahili. As demand increased, so the Swahili-Arabs moved further and further inland, setting up trading posts and gathering slaves. Slave trade routes were established from the coast to the interior which crossed Lake Malawi. Along the lake's western shore, towns such as Karonga, Nkhotakota, Salima and Mangochi began life as Arab trade centres (primarily for slaves). Islam was thus introduced to the area, and the present-day mosques are evidence of its lasting influence. The Arabs were quite prepared to trade with any tribe which could supply slaves and they found one recently arrived in Malawi — the Yao.

As the Yao originated from more coastal areas (near the Tanzania/Mozambique border) and had migrated through Mozambique to Malawi, they had contact and trade with the Arabs for many years. Through the early nineteenth century they established themselves as the dominant tribe in the Shire Highlands area. Initially there had been trade with the existing peaceful Nyanja, but this had soon turned to capture and murder to fuel the slave trade. Their ability to obtain firearms from the Arabs vastly aided their decimation of the local populations.

The horrors of the slave trade are well documented. The destructive effect on local populations was massive. Raids to capture slaves involved much slaughter initially in the villages and the subsequent boat journey accounted for more lives. The crossing of the Lake by dhow could take twenty-four to forty-eight hours with slaves in the most cramped and suffocating conditions. Even on the final march to the coast, those too weak to carry loads would be murdered. Each of Lake Malawi's trade centres had thousands of slaves pass through annually

32

and it is estimated that in the mid-nineteenth century 80,000 to 100,000 Africans a year were killed or sold as slaves by the Arabs and their partners.

In the 1830s another aggressive tribe arrived in Malawi — the Ngoni. Originally a Zulu group which had been forced from South Africa by King Shaka, they had migrated northwards, become Ngoni and decided to settle in central Malawi. Now classified as 'war-like pastoralists', the Ngoni remained proud warriors intent on overcoming local tribes. However, rather than sale into the slave market, the Ngoni preferred to assimilate tribes whose land they captured. This primarily affected the Chewa of central Malawi who were peaceful with no organised structure to allow them to repel such an onslought. Some Chewa did manage to fortify their settlements (remains exist in Kasungu National Park) whilst others fled to the more inaccessible areas of the country.

This policy of assimilation has resulted in many of Malawi's modern-day chiefs being able to trace their lineage back to the original Ngoni, while the majority of people in the chiefdom are actually Chewa.

Livingstone and The Missions

In 1858 Dr David Livingstone was sent by the British Government to open up explorative trade routes to the African interior. The effect this one man had on Malawi cannot be overestimated, his actions paving the way for the development of the country. Under the patronage of the Prime Minister, Lord Palmerston, Livingstone became British Consul at Quelimane, with instructions to make contact with the chiefs of the interior. He was essentially a humanitarian intent on making Europeans understand Africans as fellow human beings. With support from the church and the crown, he aimed to spread Christianity and commerce as counter measures to the slave trade.

Livingstone visited the Malawi area a number of times, first setting eyes on Lake Malawi (which he named 'Lake Nyasa') in September 1859. His talks in Britain prior to his departure had resulted in the establishment of the Universities' Mission to Central Africa (UMCA) and so, in 1861, Livingstone was joined by a UMCA party led by Bishop Mackenzie. Intent on setting up a mission station, they had tried other deep-water routes, but were blocked each time. This included the Zambezi where the Cabora Bassa rapids were the stumbling block. They eventually turned up the Shire River and, finally established a station at Magomero. Their twin battles against the Yao slave traders and the malaria which infested the area were relatively short-lived. Mackenzie himself died in April 1862 and his replacement, Bishop Tozer, re-located the station twice before retreating from Malawi in 1876.

Livingstone, meanwhile, had returned with Dr Kirk to the Shire and carried his boat round its worst cataracts (beginning at the Kapichira Falls in the present-day Majete Wildlife Reserve), reaching Lake Malawi in September 1861, some two years after he had first viewed its waters. They continued north to Nkhotakota and Bandawe, where Livingstone continued on foot to Nkhata Bay while Kirk sailed to Usisya. Not only was this as far north as they reached, but they were also deceived into believing the lake's most northerly point to be further south than was the reality.

Livingstone made another attempt to reach Lake Malawi via the Rovuma River, through Mozambique but this proved impossible some 150 miles short, leaving the Shire confirmed as the only river route to Lake Malawi. The 1863 attempt to take the *Lady Nyasa* boat to the lake was recalled before making it round the Shire cataracts but Livingstone pressed on in a smaller vessel and then on foot, ultimately reaching Nkhotakota and Kasungu. He returned to the UK in 1864 and only passed by the southern limit of Lake Malawi on his final African journey in 1866.

The Zambezi Expedition is sometimes seen as a failure, not least because Livingstone had successfully opened up

Opposite: The Livingstonia Mission was the brainchild of Dr Robert Laws.

deep-water routes which simply enabled the extension of slaving activities. However, there is no doubt that the geographical knowledge gained, and the establishment of the new route which cut across the traditional slaving ones, did much to pave the way for the eventual abolition of the slave trade.

The main period of mission establishment came after Livingstone's death in 1874. The Church of Scotland and the United Free Church of Scotland both came to Malawi and the first Livingstonia Mission was established at Cape Maclear on the southern lakeshore in 1875 by Dr Robert Laws. A year later a mission station was opened in the Shire Highlands. It was named after the town of Livingstone's birth near Glasgow in Scotland — Blantyre. Dr Laws travelled around Lake Malawi in the steamship *Ilala*, visiting the north-west shore in 1878 and 1879 to establish contact with the Ngoni. Eventually Laws re-located the Mission to Bandawe, enabling even stronger relations with the Ngoni. Plagued with disease, the site at Cape Maclear famously cost many missionary lives (their graveyard can still be visited) lasted only five years and resulted in just one African convert. The Livingstonia Mission was to move one final time before settling in its present site on the Khondowe Plateau above Lake Malawi's northern shore.

After retreat to Zanzibar, the UMCA finally returned to Malawi under the Reverend Johnson. This time they set up first on Likoma Island (1885) before expanding to Nkhotakota and Mangochi. Likoma has a strategically important position close to the Lake's eastern shore (now Mozambique). The missionaries were able to use their steamer, the *Chauncy Maples*, in the battle against the slave trade, intercepting Arab dhows.

As well as helping to fight the slave trade, the missions introduced schooling, new agricultural and medical techniques and other practical skills. They also encouraged trade in goods as European businessmen were attracted to the area. The Livingstonia Central African Mission Company was set up in 1878 though it soon changed to a more straightforward 'African Lakes Company'. Run by the Moir brothers from Edinburgh, it quickly established a position as the dominant trading force of the region. The company became known as Mandala in Africa (meaning 'reflected pools' — a reference to the spectacles worn by one of the brothers) and still exists, as do some of its original buildings in Blantyre.

A British Protectorate

In 1883 a British consul, Captain Foot RN had been accredited to the Kings and Chiefs of Central Africa. This was something of a pre-emptive move to deter German and Portuguese claims to this area of the African interior and to safeguard the missions and the developing trade. There was, though, no military protection and so slave trading continued unchecked and the settlers, in reality, remained at the mercy of the local people. Despite numbering only around thirty in the mid-1880s, this small group of missionaries and traders began campaigning to have the land declared a British Protectorate. Initial requests were turned down but eventually, after the petitioning of 11,000 Scottish churchmen, the request was successful. On 21 September 1889, John Buchanan, the acting Consul, declared the Kalolo and Shire regions under British Protection. Earlier that year, Harry Johnston had been appointed Consul to Mozambique and the Interior and Buchanan's declaration happened while Johnston was travelling the area to forge alliances with the local chiefs. Johnston had the support of Cecil Rhodes, who had also agreed to finance the Protectorate to the tune of an annual £10,000. The negotiations were intended to enable both the British and Rhodes' British South Africa Company to gain a further stronghold.

Ratification of the area of the 'British Central African Protectorate' came in 1890 and 1891. The northern border was agreed with Germany as part of a larger agreement involving Heligoland in the North Sea. To the south and east, the initial arrangement with the Portuguese extended the territory as far south as the Zambezi River but, in a trade-off with lands south of the Zambezi, the present-day border was agreed in 1891. To the west, the arrangements were all British. Rhodes had grand designs to extend the influence of his British South African

Above: Circa 1887, slave trader Mlozi at his Karonga stockade. Top: The ivory store at Mandala in 1885.

Above: 1889: The original Mandala House, home of the manager of the African Lakes Company.
Top: At the lake's southern end, the first Livingstonia Mission at Cape Maclear.

Company to include present-day Malawi. However, the African Lakes Company, now established in the new Protectorate, wanted little to do with Rhodes. In the final agreement, the watershed between the Luangwa-Zambezi system and the Lake Malawi catchment was used as a boundary. The British South African Company would have its charter extended to cover the lands to the west (present-day Zambia) but the lands east of the watershed would remain under the jurisdiction of the British Government (which would also retain a level of control over the Company's territory). And so, the borders of present-day Malawi were finalised. These borders paid scant attention to the existing tribal territories and so many groups found themselves split between the colonial powers. The Nkonde were in both German and British territories, the Tumbuka in both British government and British South African Company areas and, to the south, many tribes were divided by the British and Portuguese.

As well as the arrival of Harry Johnston and the first declaration of the Protectorate, 1889 had also witnessed the discovery of a navigable channel through the Zambezi from the Indian Ocean, opening up a clear line of communication directly into the Protectorate. In addition, Johnston had negotiated a truce between the African Lakes Company and the slave traders in Karonga.

The African Lakes Company operated a steamer on Lake Malawi and had an important station at Karonga. This town on the northern lakeshore was the terminal of the proposed Stevenson Road linking Lakes Tanganyika and Malawi. A Swahili-Arab slave trader called Mlozi was also based at Karonga and the two operations were in constant conflict.

The British, however, had a policy of no slave trading and knew that the only way to govern successfully was to disarm the traders. Harry Johnston, a very tough man and a clever negotiator, set out to rid Malawi of slavery. In January 1891 a force of Sikh and Zanzibari soldiers arrived to support Johnston and he travelled the country to inform the chiefs that slavery must stop. If they failed to heed his words, the soldiers were called into play.

In September 1895, Johnston completed the successful 'clearance' of the Yao slaving chiefs in the south of the country. Just two months later, came the killer blow. He sailed from the southern lakeshore to launch a surprise attack on Mlozi's stockade at Karonga. The attack was a success and Mlozi was tried by the local Nkonde chiefs and hanged. The very last engagement in the war against slavery came in October 1899. Though by now Alfred Sharpe had replaced Johnston as Commissioner, it is the latter who will rightly be remembered as being most responsible for cementing British rule and eradicating slavery.

Johnston had eventually come to believe that large-scale settlement was the wrong course of action. The area available was too small and the local population, with rights to a fair share of the land, was too large. He did not allow settlers' land claims to be unfair to the Africans and his methods of administration were little liked by the missionaries. His unpopularity among the British was made complete by disagreements with Rhodes, who was increasingly frustrated at still having little to show for his support of the Protectorate. Though Cecil Rhodes never visited Malawi, his brother did, eventually dying and being buried by the banks of the Shire, in the present-day Majete Wildlife Reserve.

Alfred Sharpe had been deputy to Johnston, responsible for establishing the judicial and fiscal procedures. He eventually became Commissioner in 1897 and his markedly different character meant he was generally liked by both Europeans and Africans.

The colonisation of Malawi was complete. It had successfully eradicated slavery and had been much less oppressive in nature than other areas of Africa. Both the edifying influence of the Scottish missionaries and the enlightened views of Harry Johnston can claim influence in this regard.

In 1907, the Protectorate gained a new name, Nyasaland, the lake land.

Inequalities and Discontentment

Plantation crops for export were to be the mainstay of the economy. John Buchanan had bought land in the Shire Highlands

Above: St Michael and All Angels church dates from the 1890s and the days of the early Scottish missionaries.

which was ideal for coffee, though a fall in prices in 1901 turned efforts first to cotton and then to tobacco — today Malawi's primary crop. Peasant farmers now also saw commercial opportunities, growing cotton and selling surplus food stocks for small profits. However, it was settler companies which were to dominate. Most were agriculture-based, with the main three being A.C. Bruce Estates, the British Central Africa Company and the British East Africa Company. The Imperial Tobacco Company established a factory at Limbe in 1908. These European traders and agriculturists made their profits on the backs of poorly paid and heavily taxed local labour. A system know as *thangata* was operated whereby the local 'tenant' farmers were forced to provide labour to the planters in return for having the use of their land. It was a highly resented arrangement with most local farmers, as a result, unable to tend properly to their own crops.

With the country only a protectorate and lacking in the mineral resources of the other colonies in the region, settlement,

investment and development were limited. The economy would undoubtedly have benefited from the completion of the railway link to the coast begun in 1902. Unfortunately, though the Blantyre to Port Herald (Nsanje) section was finished in 1908, the Zambezi was bridged only as late as 1935. As well as restricting trade, the railway had placed a huge financial burden on Nyasaland. With a weak economy, native Malawians began to see that there were better opportunities elsewhere and labour migrated to the mines and farms of South Africa and Southern Rhodesia (Zimbabwe). Unsurprisingly, discontent in Nyasaland with the British administration was increasing.

Beginning to emerge was an educated African elite. Not only could they easily identify and understand the injustices of the current regime, but they were able to articulate and communicate. Perhaps the first to speak out was a Tonga, Elliot Kamwana. He attacked the policies of both the Government and the missions, who still retained a bias against complete education and ordination of Africans. Not surprisingly, the authorities were unhappy and his arrest and deportation followed in 1909.

A further element of contention came with the advent of the First World War. Africans were conscripted to fight battles for a cause which was not theirs. The King's African Rifles had been formed in 1902, the result of an amalgamation of two Nyasa battalions of the Central African Rifles (founded in Zomba, 1895). Nearly 20,000 Malawian soldiers became a primary force in World War I campaigns, supported by ten times as many porters. A more positive World War I story concerning Malawi was that the Lake witnessed the first naval battle of the War. The British Governor received news of the outbreak of war before his German counterpart and so was able to send a gunboat, the *Gwendolen*, to destroy the German *Hermann von Wissmann* whilst still on its slipway.

The injustices prevalent in Nyasaland at this time were clearly recognised by the Reverend John Chilembwe, whose actions were to make him the first martyr of the move to independence. Born a Yao in 1871, Chilembwe had studied theology in the United States of America, returning to Nyasaland to establish a truly African mission, the Providential Industrial Mission (PIM) at Chiradzulu. His intention was to improve the lot of the Africans, primarily through education, and by challenging the inequalities perpetrated by the settlers. He spoke out against conscription and *thangata* but his protests fell on deaf ears within the Administration. An unfortunate geographical co-incidence meant that the PIM was a neighbour of the Bruce estate at Magomero, site of the first Anglican mission to Malawi in 1861. The estate was managed by William Jervis Livingstone, a man with a reputation as a stern and brutal master. Livingstone's cruelty to his labourers was known to the British government but no action taken. Eventually, Chilembwe took matters into his own hands, targeting Livingstone in his attack against the injustices of colonial rule.

The 'Chilembwe Rising' began on Saturday 23 January 1915 with just three organised attacks. Livingstone was speared in his bed and then beheaded. His assistant was also killed but all women and children were spared. An attempt to steal arms from Mandala in Blantyre largely failed and a local Ngoni guard was inadvertently killed. Livingstone's head was displayed on a pole at Chilembwe's service the next morning but suppression began immediately. Chilembwe was soon on the run, eventually shot dead in the Mulanje district on the Mozambique border on 3 February 1915.

A subsequent Commission of Inquiry did recommend improvements in the well-being of Africans but this was ignored as the settlers preferred to interpret events simply as one of the dangers in educating Africans.

Though short-lived and unsuccessful in changing the attitudes of the British, the rising was a significant event in sowing the seeds of rebellion.

The Move to Independence
Secular leaders began to emerge, forming local representative bodies which acted as pressure groups within the limits imposed by colonial rule, rather than causing direct conflict. The first of these 'Native Associations' (now known as 'African Voluntary Associations') was formed in Karonga in 1912. The Government, though, operated district administration through the Native Authorities of the headmen and chiefs, a less educated and easier manipulated group. The Native Associations, who felt that they were more representative of the local people, were largely ignored by the Government. However, they did serve to heighten political consciousness across the country.

In May 1944 the various local Associations united into the Nyasaland African Congress (NAC). Though one of the reasons for its formation was to speak out against proposals to amalgamate Nyasaland with the Rhodesias, the NAC took a while to gain any momentum.

Nyasaland's Africans were completely opposed to any closer association, particularly with Southern Rhodesia. Many had experience of working there and knew of the dominance of the settlers and the various legalised forms of discrimination. They feared that they would effectively become ruled by Southern Rhodesia. There would be an even more extreme bias in favour of the white Europeans, and the chances of independence under African rule would be diminished.

Despite opposition on many fronts, the Federation of Nyasaland and the Rhodesias was imposed in October 1953. The Malawians were incensed at the British Government and the NAC began to gain popular support. They established a policy of non-violent resistance to the federation but the campaign was abandoned as a failure in January 1954. The popularity of NAC waned and, increasingly disillusioned with the 'old guard', a new breed of leaders emerged. This group of younger men, including Henry Masauko Chipembere, Dunduzu Chisiza, Orton Chirwa and Kanyama Chiume, were more dynamic, wanting to fight for freedom and independence. They did, however, recognise that the NAC needed a charismatic talisman, an older figurehead. In 1957, they contacted Dr Hastings Banda, at that time living in Ghana. He returned home on 6 July 1958 as the new leader of the NAC and the hope of a nation.

No great detail is known about Banda's ancestry or childhood and though the 'official' year of Banda's birth was 1906 it is generally accepted that 1898 is more accurate. He left Malawi in 1915, expelled from his mission education at Livingstonia. It is reputed that he walked to Johannesburg to find work, stopping off on the way in Southern Rhodesia. With the help of black American missionaries, he moved to the USA in 1925, where he gained a Doctorate of Medicine. In 1938 he went to Britain, obtained a British Medical Licence, and set up in practice. Banda supported his homeland financially and his house provided a focus in London for African nationalist leaders of countries vying for independence. In 1953, Banda left England after becoming involved with a married woman, moving to Ghana before finally returning to Nyasaland.

The NAC found its teeth. Better organisation and broader recruitment, coupled with Banda's speeches around the country, led to mass public support. The country became highly charged and a series of strikes, demonstrations and riots resulted in the declaration of a State of Emergency on 3 March 1959. A number of Malawians were killed in exchanges, the NAC was banned and hundreds were imprisoned, including Banda at Gwelo in Southern Rhodesia. However, a commission of enquiry into the disturbances, headed by Judge Devlin, was sympathetic to the nationalist activities and critical of the autocratic colonial Government. Banda was released from prison after a year and immediately became leader of the new Malawi Congress Party (MCP), founded by Orton Chewa and Aleke Banda as a replacement to the NAC.

In 1960, a conference in London called by the Colonial Secretary, Iain Macleod, established a new constitution. The Legislative Council was to have directly elected members and the MCP won all the lower-roll seats in the elections on 15 August 1961. Banda, and three other MCP members became Ministers in the Government headed by the colonial governor, Glyn Jones. A second London constitutional conference took place in November 1962. The new constitution would pave the way for full independence. In 1963, the Federation came to an end and Nyasaland was self-governing, with Dr Banda as Prime Minister.

On 8 July 1964 the newly named independent country of Malawi came into being.

Banda's Malawi

Within months, there were troubles for the new regime. The younger men who had invited Dr Banda to return to Malawi as their leader were by now becoming increasingly dismayed by his autocratic style. They had needed an authoritative figure to be seen to wield absolute power, in the way of a tribal chief, but Banda seemed to have taken things too far. He was dismissive of the abilities of those he referred to as 'my boys', undermining their ministerial positions by dealing directly with senior (mainly white) civil servants. He was also making unilateral decisions to pursue a number of policies with which the younger men were opposed. Malawi, alone amongst its recently independent neighbours, maintained relations with the apartheid regimes south of the Zambezi and the Portuguese-governed Mozambique. Banda refused immediate Africanisation of the civil service, preferring to wait until

Above: Mikuyu Jail. President Banda locked up his most important prisoners in this block.

there were Africans trained enough to take over from the whites in the senior positions. He also turned down US$18 million in aid from the Communist Chinese Government and introduced a bill to allow detention which was a clear infringement of civil liberties.

Colin Cameron, the only European Cabinet member, resigned over the Detention Bill, whilst others took their grievances over these policies to Banda. Having initially offered to resign, Dr Banda changed his mind and on 8 Spetember 1964, he dismissed three Cabinet Ministers (including Orton Chirwa) and a Parliamentary Secretary. Three others resigned in sympathy and Henry Masauko Chipembere also resigned on his return to the country from Canada. Exile or death were the fates of many who had fought so hard for independence. Chipembere led a brief armed resistance but he was soon forced to flee the country. The rebellion had simply made Banda suspicious of Cabinet members and so he further strengthened his own position, and turned Malawi into a virtual police state.

On 6 July 1966, Malawi became a republic and Dr Banda was elected its first President. It was also in this year that Malawi became, by an act of Parliament, a one-party state. People without MCP membership cards were barred from markets and refused entry to clinics. In 1971 another law meant that the country was now ruled by "His Excellency the Life President Ngwazi (saviour) Dr H Kamuzu Banda".

Dr Banda's position and his grip on the country were re-inforced by a number of loyal groups. The League of Malawi Youth taught unity, loyalty, obedience and discipline, acting as the eyes and ears of the MCP. At their core was the elite Malawi Young Pioneers who were trained to spread modern agricultural practices. However, it was the security branch for which the MYP was famous. Members had similar, if not superior powers to those of the police and they were widely feared. The League of Malawi Women were largely a propaganda weapon, appearing at all gatherings attended by Banda, performing patriotic songs and dances.

Some argue that Banda's initial policies

Above: Democracy arrives and with it a Civil Service strike, Lilongwe 1995.

should have benefited the country. There was expertise worth retaining amongst the whites and few neighbouring countries truly developed as they hoped by pursuing complete Africanisation. However, it was his methods of rule which were open to criticism. Detentions, brutal oppression and tight media censorship were not ideal ways to advance a country. Journalists and politicians deemed to be speaking against Banda found themselves exiled, detained, and even murdered. He introduced restrictive legislation including laws dictating dress and preventing conversations about politics, family planning and even his age. He also made personal financial gain from a very poor country. Banda's iron grip did hold the country 'stable' and his pro-white and non-socialist position brought him favour from western governments, unquestioning of the domestic policies and human rights record of a rare ally in central Africa. However, Banda now seemed more interested in his own personal gain and vanity and Malawi and its people suffered badly from his self-aggrandizement.

Two other influential figures also emerged. 'Mama' Kadzamira was Banda's 'official hostess' and, with her uncle John Tembo, wielded such power that it was sometimes debated as to whether Tembo and Kadzamira, rather than Banda, were the real rulers of Malawi.

A New Democracy

The ending of the Cold War and the changes in South Africa weakened Banda's position. On 8 March 1992 a pastoral letter by Malawi's Catholic bishops was read out in churches across the country, and was faxed to the BBC in London. Detailing Banda's abuses, this was the first widespread criticism of the his regime. The bishops were placed under house arrest but, spurred on by a number of underground political pressure groups, Malawians began to express their pent up feelings in protests and riots. International condemnations finally came and foreign aid was suspended.

Banda had little option but to allow a referendum on electoral reform. In March 1993 Malawians voted for a change to multi-party democracy. Any unfair influence Banda attempted to exert on the electorate was nullified and 17 March 1994 witnessed Malawi's first truly democratic election. The results had regional bias. The MCP won in the Central Region, the Alliance for Democracy (AFORD) in the north but, more significantly, the United Democratic Front (UDF) took the heavily populated Southern Region, so winning the overall election. Their leader, Dr Bakili Muluzi, became Malawi's new president. He was sub-sequently re-elected for a second term in 1999.

Under Muluzi, Malawians enjoy a genuine freedom of speech and a free press. Other restrictive laws have also been repealed and economic reforms are being brought in to lift the country from its position of poverty. However, accusations of corruption in the new government are rife and there is a certain degree of discontentment amongst a poverty-stricken population now able and willing to express its feelings.

In 1995 a civil service strike over pay coincided with the trial of Dr Banda for involvement in the deaths of three cabinet ministers and an MP (just a few of many who died during Banda's rule in unexplained car crashes). Eventually, the trial (Banda was found not guilty) had to be suspended temporarily to concentrate police resources on the strike, but not before the armoured car carrying the ex-president from the courthouse encountered marching protesters in Blantyre. The singing and dancing continued without violence. As usual, the over-riding good nature of the Malawians shone through.

Above: His Excellency Dr Bakili Muluzi, President of Malawi.

The Land

Malawi is a landlocked country in the southern hemisphere. Its position is variously described as southern, central or eastern Africa. However, though it definitely lies within the southern half of the continent, and just to the east of centre, it is far from the southernmost tip and has no eastern coastline with the Indian Ocean. Malawi lies between latitudes 9° and 17° south and longitudes 32° and 36° east, bordered by three countries: Tanzania to the north and east, Zambia to the west and Mozambique to the east, south and west.

An area of some 118,000 square kilometres (46,000 square miles) — one fifth is Lake Malawi — makes Malawi one of the smallest countries in the region. Its neighbour, Zambia, occupies over six times the area. Malawi is similar in size to Cuba or about half that of the United Kingdom. At approximately 900 kilometres (560 miles) long and varying widths never more than one third of its length, the country is clearly elongated north-south along the line of the Rift Valley in which lies Lake Malawi.

One of Malawi's great attractions is its diversity of natural landscapes. A valley of the Great Rift System of East Africa forms the basis of Malawi's geography, running the entire length of the country. Much of its floor is occupied by the inland sea, Lake Malawi, the remainder consisting of the lakeshore plains and the Lower Shire Valley. Some towering escarpments mark the edges of the Rift Valley, reaching up to the Central African Plateau. The broad plains of the plateau and highlands which rise from them provide the rest of Malawi's varied landscapes.

Most of the country's land lies on the Central African Plateau between the altitudes of 500 metres (1600 feet) and 1500 metres (5000 feet). However, the highlands touch 3000 metres (10,000 feet) and the Rift Valley floor descends almost to sea level. These variable altitudes and landscape types are matched by changes in vegetation.

The natural features also help to mark Malawi's international boundaries. Part of the border with Tanzania runs down the eastern shore of Lake Malawi whilst that with Mozambique continues along a line through the centre of the lake. On the higher ground to the west, the borders (with Zambia and Mozambique) largely follow the watershed which separates the rain catchment area of Lake Malawi and the Shire River from that of the Zambezi River.

The Rift Valley

The Rift Valley floor stretches the length of the country, varying in width from 40 to 90 kilometres (25 to 56 miles). Lake Malawi occupies most of it, with a maximum length of 585 kilometres (364 miles) and width of 80 kilometres (50 miles) making it the third largest freshwater lake in Africa (eleventh in the world). Its surface lies 474 metres (1555 feet) above sea level but with the lowest sections of the lake floor below sea level, the waters reach depths greater than 700 metres (2300 feet). This magnificent feature is the main focus of Malawi. Fish-filled waters, fertile areas on the lakeshore plains and golden tourist beaches help to support the country's population.

The Rift Valley width is rarely much greater than that of the lake so there is little room for lakeshore plains. In north Malawi the lakeshore is characterised by high cliffs which mark the edge of the Rift Valley, some descending from the Viphya Highlands on the Central African Plateau straight into the waters of the lake. The Ruarwe Scarp between Nkhata Bay and Livingstonia is over 1500 metres (5000 feet) high. In central Malawi there are plains but only up to a width of 25 kilometres (16 miles). Back from the rocky, sandy or reed-lined shore, there are floodplains and lowland woodlands as well as dambos — broad, shallow depressions along drainage lines which are often dry but may flood in the rains. With areas of high fertility, much land is agricultural, including large-scale commercial crops such as sugar, cotton and rice.

Above: The lush Henga Valley seen on the way to the Livingstonia.

Lake Malawi drains to the south into the Shire River which then flows for some 480 kilometres (300 miles) along the Rift Valley floor before leaving Malawi at its southern tip. The upper valley is relatively flat and the river broad once it has left Lakes Malawi and Malombe. The river then makes its main descent — down spectacular rapids and falls known as the Murchison Cataracts. After passing through the series from Mpatamanga Gorge to the Kapichira Falls, the river begins to broaden again along its lower reaches. The entire Lower Shire Valley lies below 150 metres (500 feet) and the land to the sides of the wide river is used for cultivation of commercial crops, including sugar cane. Elephant Marsh stretches east from the river, a semi-permanent marsh covering some 440 square kilometres (170 square miles).

The transition from Rift Valley floor up to the Central African Plateau is characterised by a series of dramatic escarpments: from Ruarwe in the north to the Thyolo Escarpment climbing steeply from the flat Lower Shire Valley. Some are cut by rivers, producing deep and spectacular gorges such as the Luweya Gorge south-west of Nkhata Bay. Deciduous *Brachystegia* woodland is characteristic of the escarpments and cultivation is limited to timber and a few subsistence crops.

Lake Malawi National Park protects lake waters and shorelands at Cape Maclear while Liwonde and Lengwe National Parks and Majete and Mwabvi Wildlife Reserves all cover areas of the Shire Valley. The Nkhotakota Wildlife Reserve spans the ascent from the lakeshore plains to the Central African Plateau.

The Central African Plateau

Most of the areas of Malawi on the Central African Plateau consist of plains lying between 500 metres (1600 feet) and 1500 metres (5000 feet). Often fairly flat or gently undulating, they are punctuated by numerous steeply rising hills called inselbergs. Though sometimes flanked by dambos, many of the rivers which gently cross the plains are dry for most of the year.

The natural vegetation on the plains is

deciduous woodland — *Brachystegia*, *Acacia* or *Combretum*. However, much has been thinned or cleared for cultivation. Tobacco is commercially the most important crop but maize is also grown. Cattle, sheep and goats are reared, particularly on the dambos.

In south Malawi, the Phalombe Plains (flanked by the Shire Highlands) east of the Rift Valley are also the site of Malawi's second largest lake, Chilwa. Kasungu National Park lies on the plains of central Malawi while Vwasa Marsh Wildlife Reserve occupies an area on the Mzimba Plains in the north.

The Highlands

Rising from the Central African Plateau are a number of spectacular highland areas with cool fresh air and clear mountain streams. Climbing away from the drier plains, the thinner woodland is replaced by heaths, montane grassland and evergreen forests. Tea, coffee and timber are grown on plantations in these elevated locations.

South Malawi has the best known highlands — Mulanje Massif and Zomba Plateau. The former is a massive wilderness plateau of syenite granite rising from the Phalombe Plains. It has a number of peaks, including the highest in both the country and the whole of central Africa: Sapitwa, at 3000 metres (10,000 feet). Zomba Plateau is not as high, but none the less impressive. It is slab-like with a gently undulating plateau top which is accessible by road. The Dedza-Kirk Highlands extend the rise from the Rift Valley on its western edge between Blantyre and Lilongwe. The Dowa Highlands in central Malawi north of Lilongwe have their most notable peaks at Dowa and Ntchisi, where there is a forest reserve. The Viphya Highlands — undulating hills swathed in evergreen forests — stretch north-south in north Malawi and reach the edge of the Rift Valley. Finally, in north Malawi is the Nyika Plateau, a rolling whaleback grassland plateau unique in Africa. Much of this highest and most extensive high plateau surface in central Africa is gazetted as the Nyika National Park.

The Climate

Weather in Malawi is rarely oppressive and pleasant conditions can be found at all times of the year. Strictly, Malawi has three seasons: cool dry *(masika)* from May to August; hot dry *(malimwe)* from September to mid-November and hot wet *(dzinja)* from mid-November to April. However, the first two are usually merged, leaving a straightforward distinction between dry and wet. It is also true that recent years have witnessed something of a shift of the wet season with the rains beginning later. Landscape controls create further regional variations and differences can occur on a very small scale. It is not uncommon for Limbe and Blantyre to experience contrasting conditions even though they are only a few kilometres apart.

The 'neutral' time is the heart of the dry season from June to August. Rainfall is negligible and average temperatures are at their lowest — a pleasant 15°-20°C (60°-70°F). Days are warm with clear skies and brilliant sunshine, though nights are relatively cool. The only interruption is a light rain or low mist on high ground known as the *chiperone* (also *chiperoni*). Its name comes from a mountain in Mozambique where the mist is first spotted from Malawi on its largely northerly path. Blantyre and Limbe are often affected by the worst of the conditions, which can last for a number of days. The dry season also suffers from dust particles disturbed from the earth surfaces to become trapped in a low-level haze. This is compounded by smoke from pre-emptive burning intended to prevent uncontrolled bush fires — a practice now discouraged.

From September to November temperature and humidity increase while south-easterly winds bring in moist air. Average temperatures peak in November between 20°C and 30°C (70°-80°F) and the first rains appear as short sharp thunder-storms. These occur in the south and mark the beginning of the wet season. However, initially they die out before rains spread across the whole country,

Above: Storm clouds threaten Nyika Plateau.

The 'main rains' fall from December to March, entering the country from the north. These also occur only in short bursts. Air temperatures begin to decrease very slightly as the rains continue.

April and even May do witness rains but the falls are increasingly less frequent and lighter. Temperatures also decrease more rapidly as the heart of the dry season is approached.

Lake Malawi's prevailing wind is south-easterly, the *mwera*. This blows strongest during July, the month of the Lake Malawi Yachting Marathon. During the build up to the wet season, however, there is a change of direction and the more northerly *mpoto* takes over. Winds become variable and unpredictable through the rainy season. With such a vast lake, it is not surprising that, though rare, large storms and high swells can occur.

Regional Variations

The low lying lakeside areas are hotter than the higher plains, with average daily temperatures of 26°C (79°F) even in June. The southern lakeshore also receives very little rain (750-900 millimetres/30-35 inches per year). With an average of nine hours of sunshine in the dry season and even seven hours in the wet, this is perfect weather for the beach resorts.

In the Lower Shire Valley maximum temperatures of 37°C (98°F) are not uncommon in the hottest months and, combined with the high humidity, make conditions rather uncomfortable.

The Central African Plateau is slightly cooler but remains fairly dry on the broad plains. The highlands rising up from the plateau, however, have a profound effect on the weather patterns. Temperatures are pleasantly cooler with annual averages as low as 18°C (65°F) and even the potential for frosts in the dry season. These uplands stimulate rainfall, raising levels on nearby plains and lakeshore areas as well as the highlands themselves. While Mulanje unsurprisingly experiences rainfall of over 2000 millimetres (80 inches) in a year; due to its proximity to the Viphya Highlands and Nyika Plateau, so too does Nkhata Bay down on the lakeshore.

The People

The 1998 census put Malawi's population at 9.9 million with an annual growth rate of 2 per cent. The average population density is one of the highest in Africa at 105 per square kilometre (272 per square mile). However, even within the small area that Malawi covers, the population is not evenly spread, displaying a clear north-south divide. Densities in some Southern Region districts top 300 per square kilometre (777 per square mile) while much of the Northern Region has fewer than 50 people per square kilometre (80 per square mile).

The greatest part of the population (85 per cent) remains rural, living largely in traditional villages of simple huts. It is a very basic existence. Most people gain their water from wells or boreholes and nearly all use firewood as their main source of energy. Semi-subsistence agriculture on small-holdings is the primary occupation of Malawi's rural population.

Urban settlements are limited in size and number. Only the regional capitals and Zomba are of any size, accounting for most of the urban population. Blantyre and Zomba are in the Southern Region. The former is the economic centre of the whole country, with half a million people and the latter was the old colonial capital and is the site of the old parliament. Lilongwe, capital of both the Central Region and the country, is actually Malawi's second largest city. Mzuzu, the Northern Region's capital is still relatively young but growing rapidly as a commercial centre.

Economically, Malawi is one of the poorest countries in the world. There is an over-dependence on agriculture and even in this dominant sector, much is at a subsistence level. Of the commercial activity, tobacco dominates, accounting for three quarters of export earnings. It is grown on small-holdings as well as the larger estates. The plantations of tea, coffee and sugar make up all but ten per cent of the rest of the earnings.

Maize, pulses, cotton, groundnuts, rice and livestock are farmed, and there have been partly successful attempts at diversification into such crops as peppers, chillies and roses. There is, of course, a great deal of fishing along Lake Malawi.

Manufacturing contributes very little to the economy. It is limited to import-substitute products in light industries.

This dependence on agriculture, and particularly tobacco, is a weakness which the Government aims to correct. Adverse weather conditions and fluctuations in a single commodity market (which is in global decline) have disproportionate effects on the people and the economy.

For many, tourism may provide an answer. This industry is currently growing as international travellers become less wary about visiting. Numbers are on the increase as Malawi's natural attractions and friendly people become better known. Improvements in infrastructure are still required though, to maintain the growth.

All Malawi's indigenous groups have a common Bantu origin. The Chewa have a majority, whilst Lomwe, Yao, Nyanja, Ngoni, Tonga, Tumbuka, and Nkonde are the other main groups. Though there is rarely any great ethnic tension, political voting does usually reflect the regional distribution of the groups. Instances of armed conflict in Malawi's history are rare and the friendliness of all Malawians is renowned. A genuine welcome and beaming smile are extended to all visitors everywhere. Malawi was only a British Protectorate where settlement was always limited. As a result, its present day non-African population (mainly Europeans) accounts for just one per cent of the population.

Since the missionaries were the first Europeans to arrive in Malawi, it's not surprising that eighty per cent of the population is now Christian. The Church of Central Africa Presbyterian is the strongest in the country. Muslims account for 13 per cent, leaving only a small minority sticking to the indigenous beliefs.

Dancing, usually to the beat of the drum,

Above: Young herders along the road south of Lilongwe. Top left: An itinerant barber does his work in the shade of a tree. Top right: Bananas for sale at Nkhata Bay.

Right: Weddings are important occasions when everyone's invited.
Below: Tiny fish for sale. Learning to be a salesman starts at an early age.

is an important social element across Malawi. Performers often wear straw clothing and striking masks. The variations in the dances are fundamentally tribal. Best known is the Gule Wamkulu, performed by the Nyau of the Chewa. The Nyau are revered figures of spiritual significance. Membership is by initiation only. The Ngoni dances betray their Zulu warrior ancestry — stirring affairs associated with battle and hunting. Yao dances also have military associations but are more recent in origin. Many Yao served with the King's African Rifles and so the dances draw on military marches for inspiration. As well as the traditional music and dance found around the country, Malawi boasts a number of highly thought of modern musicians.

PART TWO: CAPITAL AND TOWNS

Above: Malawi's old Parliament building in Zomba, the former capital.
Opposite: Considerable investment has gone into ambitious building programmes in Lilongwe.

Lilongwe

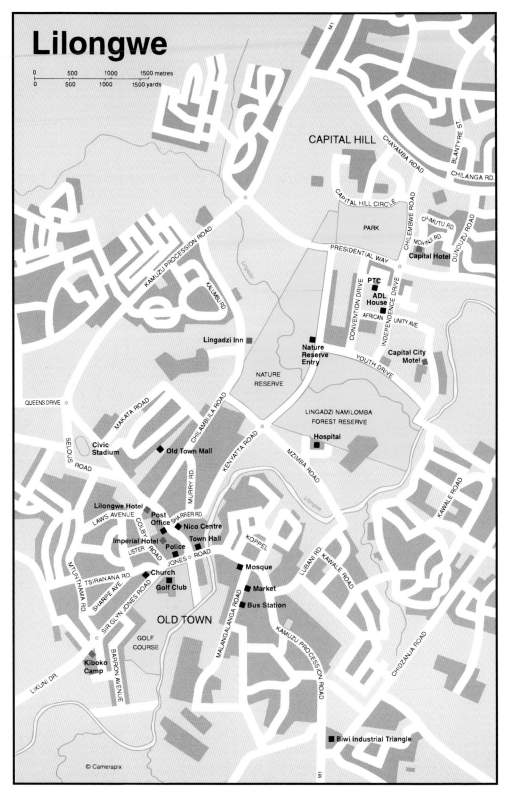

0 500 1000 1500 metres
0 500 1000 1500 yards

CAPITAL HILL

CHAYAMBA ROAD
BLANTYRE ST.
CHILANGA RD.
CAPITAL HILL CIRCLE
CHILEMBWE ROAD
CHIMUTU RD.
MCHINJI RD.
DUNDUZU ROAD
PARK
PRESIDENTIAL WAY
Capital Hotel
CONVENTION DRIVE
PTC
ADL House
AFRICAN
INDEPENDENCE DRIVE
UNITY AVE
KAMUZU PROCESSION ROAD
KALUMBULA RD.
Lingadzi
Lingadzi Inn
Nature Reserve Entry
YOUTH DRIVE
Capital City Motel
NATURE RESERVE
LINGADZI NAMILOMBA FOREST RESERVE
QUEENS DRIVE
MAKATA ROAD
CHILAMBULA ROAD
KENYATTA ROAD
MZIMBA ROAD
KAWALE ROAD
Hospital
SELOUS ROAD
Civic Stadium
Old Town Mall
MURRY RD.
Lingadzi
Lilongwe Hotel
LAWS AVENUE
COLBY
SHARRER RD.
Post Office
Nico Centre
Imperial Hotel
LISTER
ROAD
Police
Town Hall
JONES ROAD
KOPPEL
LUBANI RD.
KAWALE ROAD
MTUNTHAMA RD.
TSIRANANA RD.
Church
SHARPE AVE.
Golf Club
Mosque
SIR GLYN JONES ROAD
Market
MALANGALANGA ROAD
Bus Station
OLD TOWN
KAMUZU PROCESSION ROAD
CHIDZANJA ROAD
GOLF COURSE
BARRON AVENUE
Kiboko Camp
LIKUNI DR.
M1
Biwi Industrial Triangle

© Camerapix

54

Lilongwe

Lilongwe, the regional and national capital, lies in the shallow valley of the river from which it takes its name. The town is unusual in many ways. Firstly, it comprises two very distinct settlements: the modern **Capital City** and the **Old Town**. Secondly, even the Old Town has only a short history. Its population in 1900 was just a couple of dozen. Thirdly, the Capital City is a largely artificial creation not explained by natural growth.

Driving south along the M1 it would be possible to be unaware of the modern Capital City which now lies to the north of the original settlement. Only the rather broad avenues leading off to the east will have hinted that there is more to be seen. For the Old Town, the M1 is its high street — a busy and rapidly changing thoroughfare.

There is evidence of settlement hereabouts from palaeolithic times but the modern settlement owes its early growth to the agricultural development of the region and its position as an important bridging point over the **Lilongwe River**. At the centre of the old town the river is incised and a high bridge carries the M1 across what is almost a gorge. As trade increased and the African Lakes Company moved into the area, Lilongwe became the nodal centre of the Central Region.

Old Town and Capital City are contiguous but distinct. Residential areas, too, are clearly defined in numbered districts. Only in the heart of the Old Town is there really a mix of the commercial, industrial and residential.

In stark contrast with the very African character of the Old Town is the rather soulless Capital City. Lilongwe, not officially a town until 1947, achieved municipality status in 1966 and, an inspiration of Dr Banda (born a few miles to the north) was declared national capital of the Republic in 1975.

The Capital City, apart from its well laid out residential districts, is best described as a scattering of very modern, sometimes grand, buildings apparently set down at random in an almost park-like landscape.

More high-rise buildings are still under construction. Broad avenues with large flower-bedded roundabouts add to the impression of spaciousness. The main roads are lined with flowering trees and bushes, jacaranda, acacia and poinsettia providing splashes of colour in different seasons.

All this has been achieved at a cost. Planned in the mid-1960s, building started at the end of that decade and capital city status was achieved on the first day of 1975. Most of the finance has come from outside Malawi, especially from South Africa. Whether the extravagances of the concept of a major modern city can be justified is a matter for history but the population has grown by one thousand per cent, rising towards half a million, in the last ninety years.

Above: The basket-like architecture of Malawi's reserve bank.

Above: More new buildings are springing up in Lilongwe Old Town. This is the New Building Society headquarters.

Getting there

From Blantyre:	311km/193miles	M1
From Mzuzu:	360km/224miles	M1

The north-south artery of Malawi, the M1, passes through Lilongwe and links the city to the other regional capitals of Blantyre and Mzuzu. The M12 to the west links with the M1 in the northern part of Old Town and the M14 to the east joins the M1 near the northern outskirts of the city. Many visitors to Lilongwe and to the country itself arrive by air at Lilongwe International Airport. The airport has international flights as well as being the hub for the national air network. To get into town from the airport is to follow the link road out to the M1 and then turn right along the M1. The distance to the town is 26 kilometres (16 miles).

When to go

Lilongwe enjoys a pleasant climate throughout the year. The rainy season is between December and March but rainfalls are not high.

Where to stay

There is a variety of hotels and budget accommodation in Lilongwe, as well as two camp sites, one at the Lilongwe Golf Club and another, with a choice of accommodation, nearby. At least two new up-market hotels are projected for Lilongwe. One is to be near the golf course and another will include a casino.

Le Méridien Capital Hotel

The leading hotel is undoubtedly the Capital, managed by Le Méridien since 2000. Its low-rise buildings and the fact that it has a garden setting with plenty of trees make it a bit difficult to locate but look for the signs to the right on Chilembwe Road soon after the turn off from Presidential Way in Capital City. From the airport, turn off the M1 into Chayamba Road and follow the signposts.

The hotel was built in the mid-1970s and was beginning to show its age a little, but a room refurbishment programme has been carried out. Service is as good as most in Malawi and the clientele is largely business-men or visitors associated with the large

Above: In the dry season, the bed of the Lilongwe river becomes a pathway.

range of overseas aid organisations for whom Lilongwe seems something of a magnet. The standard rooms (there are also some suites) have picture windows looking out onto the gardens or the shrub-filled courtyard around which the hotel wings are grouped. Each has a TV set and is air-conditioned. The hotel has pleasant swimming pool with refreshment bar although the sun disappears behind the buildings rather early in the afternoon. A games room and two squash courts (bring your own racquets) complete the recreational facilities.

Meals are served outside on the terrace, beside an ornamental pool at the end of the inner court, in the adjacent La Mimosa coffee shop and in the main, relatively more expensive, Tidya restaurant. The conference facilities are good.

There's ample secure parking and a range of lobby shops including car hire (Silver and Sputnik), airline desks (Air Malawi and SAA), Lifupa Lodge (Kasungu National Park) booking office, a bookshop, a pharmacy, a beauty parlour and hair salon, a travel bureau and two gift shops. There is also a new business centre. The Capital is unlikely to let you down if you want comfortable, quiet and trouble-free, but expensive, accommodation.

Sunbird Lilongwe Hotel

In contrast with the Capital, the Old Town's main establishment, the Lilongwe Hotel, is far less international and more African both in appearance and in its clientele. It is set back a little from the M1, to the right, soon after entering the Old Town from the direction of the airport. The standard of the rooms and service has greatly improved in recent years. There is air conditioning, television and a telephone in all the rooms and the hotel is more slickly run. Family chalets are at the back of the hotel, near the swimming pool. This is another of Le Méridien's management acquisitions.

A coffee-shop-cum-restaurant, including à la carte, is much frequented by local well-to-do families and business people. However, the former top-class restaurant, the Malingundi, is currently closed with no immediate prospect of re-opening. It is to be hoped that the new management are able to reinstate what was one of the best places to eat in town. On site services include a Times bookshop, a business centre, hairdresser and travel agent.

There is a lively bar off the car park, to the right of the hotel entrance. Guests used to complain about the noise but a wall separates it from the hotel and some see it as a positive attraction.

Lilongwe Hotel offers good quality accommodation, with plenty of atmosphere, but may seem expensive.

Imperial Hotel
The Imperial reopened in 1999 with a complete facelift and refurbishment. Situated in the centre of Old Town, on the left of Mandala Road up from the post office, it is very attractively priced with a range of accommodation. Its bar is very popular in the evenings, particularly with the ex-pat community. At the back is a small restaurant, parking and a garden. It may not be quietest place to stay but it's full of life and very conveniently sited for the markets and shops of Old Town.

Sunbird Lingadzi Inn
Between Capital City and the Old Town is the Lingadzi Inn. Coming from the airport the hotel is reached by taking the next turning to the left, off the M1, after the roundabout leading to Presidential Way. This is Chilambula Road and the hotel is on the left.

This hotel caters largely for Malawians. Its thirty-six rooms are simple and without air-conditioning but do have showers. A restaurant serves simple food and there are two bars. The gardens are well kept and there is plenty of space for car parking.

The hotel is functional, clean and comfortable but not to be compared with the Capital or the Lilongwe, although it is under the same management.

Kalikuti Hotel
Travelling along the M1 out of Lilongwe towards Blantyre, to the left of the road, is the Kalikuti Hotel. It is on the edge of town and signposted off the main road. Although not very old, the hotel has a well-used look. Like all hotels in Lilongwe it is low-rise but its appearance is rather spoilt by its setting.

There are two standards of room. Rather more expensive "VIP" accommodation provides the luxury of a carpet, a shower

fitment and the promise of a TV.

The hotel is attractively priced and its modest restaurant provides cheap meals with good service. The hotel attracts large gatherings of townsfolk when it puts on entertainment, mostly at weekends.

Capital City Motel
This small hotel is a little off the beaten track but offers simple, low cost accommodation. It is situated on a road off Youth Drive, which itself is a turning off Kenyatta Road almost opposite the entrance to the Nature Sanctuary. Most of the rooms are en suite and there is a restaurant. Lodges and suites are also available.

Kiboko Camp
An alternative to the facilities offered by the Golf Club, those looking for a camping site will find that Kiboko Camp is conveniently located on the edge of Old Town. Both the Golf Club and Kiboko are on the left of Sir Glynn Jones Road which is a turning off the main roundabout on the M1 in Old Town. The Golf Club is reached first but, further on, Kiboko Camp is almost hidden behind a high fence. Kiboko offers camping, chalets and dormitory rooms. The Dutch company running Kiboko also organises safari tours not only around Malawi but also into the neighbouring countries.

Where to eat
All the hotels mentioned have restaurants which cater for non-residents. In addition there are a number of independent restaurants. In Old Town is **Modi's** which serves a variety of dishes, while **Huts**, on the other side of the main M1 near to the Lilongwe Hotel, specialises in curries. **DB's Bistro** below the Imperial Hotel is often crowded — always a good sign. The attractive **Bohemian Café** is close by, part of Land and Lake Safaris' operations. The new **Mamma Mia** restaurant, cake shop and bar is in the Old Town Mall. On Tsiranana Avenue is the **Ivy Restaurant**.

In the City, the popular **Golden Dragon** Chinese restaurant is behind the British Council Library. Two other eating places in the City Centre are the **Koreana** and the **Causerie**. Both serve a variety of dishes

Above: Lilongwe's Old Town is seeing a surge of new shopping and office blocks.

but the former specialises in East Asian food.

Sightseeing
Old Town

From the north and the airport, Malawi's central highway, the M1, goes through the heart of the Old Town. This same road is Lilongwe's link with Blantyre and the south.

Much of the Old Town can be seen from the M1. The road (presently called Kamuzu Processional Road) enters the Old Town from the direction of the airport as it descends on a winding path towards the river. The road is fringed with a jumble of commercial and industrial buildings which continue southwards to the river crossing. Storm drains separate the road from footpaths which in daylight hours are crowded with people from outlying villages and from the town. Near the beginning of the Old Town is the **Lilongwe Hotel**, on the right-hand side of the road, half hidden behind trees and its own car park.

A very new block of shops and offices has been opened near the junction of the main M1 road, the Kamuzu Processional Road,

and Chilambula Road. This is almost opposite the Lilongwe Hotel. Called the **Old Town Mall**, it is home to **Ulendo Safaris**, Malawi's largest tour company and agents for a number of operations including the *mv Ilala*. There is also a restaurant and a range of shops. Bookworm includes a branch of **Central Africana** (see Blantyre) and there are **craft shops** selling Mua Mission carvings (at inflated prices) and Dedza pottery. This new shopping centre is especially attractive to visitors. New building elsewhere in Old Town includes some smart new apartments in an enclosed area near the Ivy Restaurant.

Towards the bottom of the hill is the hub of the Old Town where all available services are found. Leading off the M1, at the traffic lights, is Sharrer Road, and immediately right is the **bus station** and the offices of **Shire Bus Lines**. The **post office** is near a corner to the right of the M1 behind the open-air **craft market**. On the left, a few blocks up from the post office in Mandala Road, are **Land and Lake Safaris** and **Makomo Safaris**. These companies both offer a range of tours and holiday packages as well as being able to cater for individual travellers. The imposing

59

Above: Fresh bread is worth queuing for in Old Town, Lilongwe. Below: Plenty of shoes. Especially if you like red!.

office of the **New Building Society** is on the opposite side of the road.

There are **petrol stations** on the left of the M1, going south, and the **banks** are here too. On a service road, parallel to the main road and near to the junction with Mandala Road, is a **car hire** company.

The main **Kandodo supermarket** is near the post office and craft market above the level of the M1. On the opposite side of the road, in wonderful contrast, is the modern **Nico Centre**. Here is a branch of the **Times Bookshops** and a bank. Seeming somewhat out of place, the smart shops attract few of the townsfolk.

Down the hill on the M1 beyond the craft market there is a roundabout. A right turn here is Sir Glynn Jones Road. Five hundred metres up this road and a turning to the left leads to the 18-hole **Lilongwe Golf Club**. Built in the 1930s, partly on the site of an abandoned hospital, the club allows daily membership and there are sports facilities including tennis, swimming and bowls as well as a small camping site.

Bearing left at the same roundabout is to

Above: Spoilt for choice: Old Town Lilongwe's craft market.

stay on the M1 and to go towards the river. On the left of the road is the **Old Town Hall**. Its simple, dated architecture is in complete contrast with the grandiose public buildings of Lilongwe City. The **Lilongwe River** is crossed by a narrow bridge high above a rather untidy-looking small gorge. In the droughts which so plagued the country in recent years, the river becomes little more than a trickle. The river valley is used by local people as a short cut into the centre of the Old Town. With river levels low, the path broadens almost to embrace the river channel itself and enterprising traders lay out their goods on the river bank for sale to passers-by. When the river rises, there is always laundry to be done.

As the M1 goes southwards from the central hub of the Old Town (left at the roundabout at the bottom of the hill), the road bridges the river then passes alongside what is the **Asian Quarter** (left). Not surprisingly, shops line the roads. There is a bakery, tailors sitting at their ancient Singer sewing machines and shops selling all manner of bits and pieces from bicycle wheel spokes to dry batteries. If a shop hasn't got what you want

they will be able to tell you where you might get it. Much trading takes place on the pavement in front of the shops. Further south, behind the shops and to the left of the road there are a number of small industrial works and yet more shops. This is part of the rather grandly named **Biwi Industrial Triangle**.

Craft Market

Near the post office, under the shade of trees and on a raised section of roadway above the level of the M1, is the craft market. Goods for sale are neatly laid out on the ground but so closely packed that it is impossible to tell where one trader's wares end and another's begin. Knots of would-be sellers sit gossiping or brushing black shoe polish into their wooden carvings (to simulate ebony) until the arrival of an easily distinguishable visitor is a signal for immediate action. Young men, only some of whom have actually made the goods, descend on the visitor like flies on a piece of raw meat. However, all the bartering is very good natured and good fun. Most of the items for sale are wood and stone carvings of variable quality but there are also paintings

61

Left: Pyramids of tomatoes but don't choose the one at the bottom. Below: City suits, but who buys?.

Above: Buckets can be made to order.
Left: Meat for sale may encourage vegetarianism.

Above: Lilongwe's Walled Market is a place not to miss.

and basketware. Traditional chiefs' chairs and small three-legged folding tables are popular buys as are lamp standards, toys and animal figures. All make good presents or souvenirs if you have the space to carry them. Goods should be carefully inspected for flaws and bargaining should be ruthless. It is usually evident when the rock bottom price has been reached. With the exception of Blantyre, there is really little difference in the price of craft goods throughout Malawi. The best guide is quality.

Walled Market

Just a little way up the hill in the Asian Quarter, a right turn off the M1, at traffic lights, is Malangalanga Road. Turn immediately right again for the mosque but just a hundred metres or so up Malangalanga Road is what is arguably Lilongwe's most interesting and exciting attraction: the old "walled market". During the latter days of the Banda regime, customers needed a Malawi Congress Party membership card in order to enter the market. Today all are welcome and the number of traders as well as customers has so increased that the

market now spills over in every direction as an extramural extension.

The market is a mixture of order and chaos. Each stall is neatly laid out with its wares carefully arranged but the general impression is one of total confusion. As in markets the world over, competing traders occupy adjacent stalls. Thus there are areas for vegetables, concentrations of fish sellers and so on. Vegetables are laid in neat rows, piled into pyramids and arranged like some wonderfully dressed army on parade. Live chickens, fly-blown meat and malodorous fish, gleaming steel buckets and watering cans, all vie for space inside the walled square. Colgate toothpaste and second-hand shoes and clothes, nuts and bolts and coir matting, the choice is yours. But who does buy all those ill-shaped city suits? In one corner there is even a witch doctor's (sin'ganga) stall, its narrow entrance almost obscured by the pages from magazines which decorate the exterior. In another corner men sit quietly playing the ever popular bawo or have a game of draughts using bottle tops. Close by, clothes are pressed with a flat iron which has been heated on a fire.

Right: Newspapers are sold to motorists from the roadside.

Apart from all the shoppers and the traders, tinkers work inside the market adding the sounds of hammer on metal to the general hubbub of animated conversation and the cries of the stall-holders. This is definitely a place not to miss on even the shortest stay in Lilongwe.

Capital City

To reach the Capital City from the airport turn off left from the M1 down Chayamba Road, at the northern limits of Lilongwe, then turn right into Chilembwe Rd. This is the location of the **Capital Hotel**.

Alternatively, and more directly, take the next major left turn at a roundabout, as the M1 gently descends. This is Presidential Way. From the Old Town to the Capital City, either retrace the M1 back towards the airport and turn right into Presidential Way or make for the traffic lights just up from the craft market and turn off here (right when travelling north). Continue past the bus station and follow Kenyatta Road which links with Presidential Way, the new town's main highway.

The Capital City is the name given to the modern town which arose largely due to the acquisition of its status as the country's capital. In contrast with Old Town, the city is all modern, high-rise, and mostly shiny, white buildings. The roads are broad tree-lined avenues. The roundabouts are like gardens. Smart, clean and tidy it is. A typical African city it isn't. It could be anywhere but the Malawians are proud of it. Like London's Docklands, it is part of the town but somehow semi-detached.

Two roads, Independence Drive and Convention Drive, leading to the south off Presidential Way, form the boundaries of the **City Centre**, the hub of this part of Lilongwe. Here is the main shopping area and the National Bank. In the crescentic **ADL House**, are **British Airways**, **Manica Travel**, a **video shop** and a **dentist**. **Central Africa Wilderness Safaris (CAWS)** used to be in ADL House but has recently moved. They are now opposite the Nature Sanctuary (see page 66) in the Risnowsty Filling Station complex. A multitude of services in **Centre House** include **Soche Tours and Travel**, **DHL**, a **pharmacy**, **clothes shops**, a **hairdresser** and **café**. Nearby is the **post office** and large branches of **PTC** and **Central Bookshop**.

Not far away is the **National Library** and most of the **embassies** are in this area, between Convention Drive and Kenyatta Road. The old French Embassy now houses the **Ministry of Tourism, Parks and Wildlife**. The **British Council** building, recently reprieved, is near the main shsopping centre. Its library provides internet access.

To the north of Presidential Way, on rising ground, is Capital Hill, the site of most of

the **government offices**. Again the concept is grandiose but well planned. Access is a circular road off Chilembwe Road which, in turn, links Chayamba Road to Presidential Way. Only those on official business will be admitted through the gates to the complex.

When Malawi's first President died in 1997 he was buried in Lilongwe. **Dr Banda's tomb** was a rather sad looking resting place in parkland just off Presidential Way. Early in 2001 however, his successor, President Muluzi, decreed that a more fitting tomb should be built on Capital Hill. The design of the tomb has yet to be decided but this was a generous gesture to a former opponent.

The most striking of all the buildings in Capital City is that of the **State House** which stands on a hill at the eastern end of Presidential Way. This was just one of Dr Banda's palaces, although he never lived there, and its future was uncertain at the end of his regime. Various plans were mooted for its use: hotel, conference centre or, a new parliament building if the Members could be persuaded to move from Zomba. They have been so persuaded and the parliament now sits there.

The road close to the palace is generally forbidden to the public who must view it from afar. However, tours of the building are sometimes arranged by Ulendo Safaris. It remains a relic of the pre-democracy era and a monument to vulgarity, closely resembling a 1930s Hollywood spectacular film set. Much of the ornate furnishing and fittings have apparently "disappeared" since Dr Banda's downfall. Gold painted carved balustrades, velvet curtaining and automatic sprinklers for the roof garden were some of the extravagances.

Lilongwe Nature Sanctuary
Much of the land on which Lilongwe is built was once a game reserve and something of the wilderness remains. But today there is just one rather small Nature Sanctuary. This is found to the west of Kenyatta Road, the main link between the Old Town and the new City. Frankly it is somewhat disappointing. Some caged and rather pathetic looking animals are to be seen near the entrance: leopard and hyena, but there is little else. Trails, poorly signposted, enable the visitor to walk down towards the Lingadzi River through mixed woodland which once covered the whole of the area now occupied by the town. A single visit might reveal little more than a few monkeys, two or three birds and some butterflies. For the small entrance fee perhaps one should not expect more and it has to be admitted that the walk and the forest are a pleasant enough diversion of an hour or so.

To be fair, the purpose of the sanctuary is now largely as an educational centre for local school children and should not be seen as, primarily, a tourist attraction. Entry costs K30 with children at half price. There's a small café outside the sanctuary. A cultural village is planned for Lilongwe and it may be sited near the sanctuary.

Tobacco Auctions
To the north of Lilongwe, just off the M1, is the town's vast tobacco auction floor in the **Kanego Industrial Estate**. During the auction season, approximately May to mid-October, it is possible, without appointment, to visit the floors and witness the auctions. Simply announce yourself as a visitor and someone's sure to take pleasure in showing you round.

It is an experience not to be missed. To observe the procession of buyers following the auctioneer through the various lots of tobacco, is to enter another world. Everything seems to go on at a breakneck speed, from the sale of the tobacco to its being whisked away by sprinting porters.

The best time of the day to make a visit is early morning. By noon it may all be over.

Lilongwe International Airport
Most international visitors fly in to Lilongwe Airport, which lies some 26 kilometres (16 miles) north of the town.

The airport is modern, clean and generally efficient. Opened in 1982, it is really much larger than its present traffic requires and its size and appearance may well mislead the first-time visitor into harbouring expectations which will not be fulfilled.

On touching down, passengers will probably be met by a bus but occasionally will have to tramp across the apron to the terminal building. Customs and immigration rarely cause delays and the arrivals concourse leads directly to the car park and exit roads. In the concourse is a variety of services including a bank and the offices of car hire companies and Malawi tour companies. Unfortunately there can be no guarantee that all of these will be functioning, although the arrival of an international flight will usually see some action. If being met by car, there is a large car park immediately outside the terminal. Taxis should be available but there is no fixed fare so it is wise to negotiate before hiring. The state of the vehicle is no guide to the price likely to be asked. Alternatively, if ordered in advance, the Capital and Lilongwe Hotels will arrange a pick-up. If using a Malawi tour company, they will meet visitors at the airport.

Leaving the airport one realises its location is in the middle of nowhere. A good tarmac road leads to the M1 and a right turn on to this takes one into Lilongwe. The M1 is well surfaced and maintained but is no wider than is necessary for two vehicles to pass safely. Unfortunately, most of the lamp standards have been stolen! This had been the only rural road with street lighting.

Before reaching the capital, some of the industrial development north of the city can be seen to the left of the M1 and it is here that there is a junction with the M14, to Salima and Senga Bay, as well as a crossing of the railway line to Zambia. Otherwise the journey is without distinction.

Above: Gardens at the Capital Hotel. Left: Small-holder farmers' fertilizer plant. Top: Capital City, Lilongwe, characterised by its late-twentieth century architecture.
Following pages: Between the towns, picturesque villages enjoy an unchanging way of life.

Blantyre and Limbe

The present day conurbation, of over half a million, comprises the older town of Blantyre and the somewhat younger settlement of Limbe. Blantyre, named after the birthplace in Scotland of **Dr David Livingstone**, has its origins in the choice of its site by a party of Scots missionaries led by a certain **Henry Henderson** in 1876. Prior to the arrival of this group just four small villages occupied the shallow basin in the Shire Highlands. Choice was partly influenced by the presence of streams flowing from the surrounding peaks. To the south, and closest to the town, is **Mount Soche** (1533 metres/5030 feet), to the north stands the Sleeping Man peak of **Ndirande** (1612 metres/5288 feet), while in the north-west **Michuru** rises to 1473 metres (4833 feet). The first European missionaries used abandoned African huts for shelter and their choice of site led to the establishment of Blantyre as a trading centre as the **African Lakes Corporation** set up its headquarters here. The **Moir brothers**, from Glasgow, arrived in 1878 and opened their first store in 1879. With encouragement from local people, who welcomed the protection the Europeans could give from raids by the **Ngoni** people from the north, trade flourished. Another Scot, **James Stewart** began to lay out the streets (simple tracks) which are still seen today in the road pattern of central Blantyre. Within twenty years of the coming of Henderson, there were permanent houses, stores and roads. Asian traders, especially concentrated now in Limbe, began to settle there.

It's interesting to note that Blantyre was a recognisable town when Johannesburg and Nairobi were hardly villages.

Limbe stole a march on Blantyre when, in 1907, it was linked by railway to Nsanje (then Port Herald). At the time the Limbe station was built there was, remarkably, no town and hardly any settlement. Two years later so much growth had occurred that it was declared a township. In fact, the railway link between Malawi and the Indian Ocean coast in Mozambique (Nsanje to Beira) was not fully opened until 1922. This section is currently out of use through flood damage.

The two towns, Blantyre and Limbe, form a single unit yet retain their own identities. While Blantyre is clearly the more important, with most of the civic buildings and greater European characteristics, Limbe is more than just a suburb, having its own shopping area, market, and commercial activity. Together they are the unrivalled centre of Malawi's economic development.

Blantyre is more able to cope with the needs of visitors, with the best hotels and most of the shops and offices the traveller may wish to use. Despite its geographical size, everything likely to be required by visitors will be found within or on the edges of the original triangle of roads laid out by Stewart. These are Glyn Jones Road, Victoria Avenue and Haile Selassie Road: an area of less than one square kilometre. Despite this apparent compactness, there is much to be seen around the town, in Limbe and in the surroundings of the conurbation.

Getting there
From Lilongwe: 311km/193miles   M1

Blantyre is the hub of south Malawi. The M1 on the western side and the M3/M2 on the eastern side provide for excellent north-south access. Many visitors will arrive by air at Chileka Airport just 13 kilometres (8 miles) out of town. The Chelika road towards town and then the M1 form the route. There are also international services into the airport but these are regional, not inter-continental. There are regular flights to and from Johannesburg and Harare.

When to go
As so often in Malawi the best time to visit Blantyre is the dry season; perhaps best of all are the months of September and October when the jacaranda is in bloom.

Opposite: Basketware is for sale on the pavements of Blantyre.

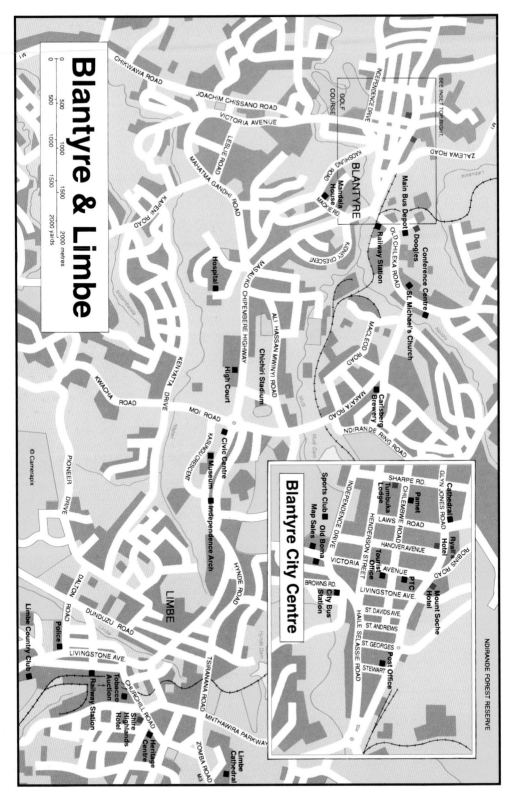

Blantyre & Limbe

0 500 1000 1500 2000 yards
0 500 1000 1500 2000 metres

© Camerapix

Blantyre City Centre

CHIKWAWA ROAD
JOACHIM CHISSANO ROAD
VICTORIA AVENUE
GOLF COURSE
INDEPENDENCE DRIVE
ZALEWA ROAD
M1
SEE INSET TOP RIGHT

LESLIE ROAD
MAHATMA GANDHI ROAD
KAPENI ROAD
KASKUNS ROAD
MACKIE RD.
BLANTYRE
Mandala House
Main Bus Depot
Doogles
Conference Centre
OLD CHILEKA ROAD
Railway Station
St. Michael's Church
KIDNEY CRESCENT

Hospital
MASAUKO CHIPEMBERE HIGHWAY
ALI HASSAN MWINYI ROAD
Chichiri Stadium
High Court
MACLEOD ROAD
MAKATA ROAD
Carlsberg Brewery
NDIRANDE RING ROAD

KWACHA ROAD
KENYATTA DRIVE
MOI ROAD
KASUNGU CRESCENT
Civic Centre
Museum
Independence Arch

PIONEER DRIVE
DALTON ROAD
DUNDUZU ROAD
HYNDE ROAD
LIMBE
LIVINGSTONE AVE.
Police
Limbe Country Club

CHURCHILL ROAD
Tobacco Auction
Railway Station
Shire Highlands Hotel
Heritage Centre
TSIRANANA ROAD
MNTHAWIRA PARKWAY
ZOMBA ROAD
M3
Limbe Cathedral

NDIRANDE FOREST RESERVE

Blantyre City Centre (inset)
Sports Club
Old Boma
Map Sales
INDEPENDENCE DRIVE
SHARPE RD.
Tumbuka Lodge
Panel
CHILEMBWE ROAD
GLYN JONES ROAD
ROBINS ROAD
Cathedral
Ryall's Hotel
LAWS ROAD
HENDERSON STREET
HANOVER AVENUE
VICTORIA
Tourist Office
PTC
Mount Soche Hotel
BROWNS RD.
City Bus Station
LIVINGSTONE AVE.
ST. DAVIDS AVE.
ST. ANDREWS
ST. GEORGES
HAILE SELASSIE ROAD
STEWART
Post Office

Above: The Le Méridien Mount Soche Hotel.

Where to stay

There is a greater diversity of accommodation here than anywhere else in Malawi. Because of the commercial importance of the city it may be wise to book ahead. For smaller hotels and resthouses it is best to enquire at the Tourist Office because these tend to change hands (and standards) rather rapidly. The legendary (with backpackers) **Doogles** is the best known of the budget accommodation and is located just one hundred metres beyond the main bus station on **Mulomba Place**. In late 2002 a new full service luxury hotel, **The Legacy-Blantyre**, will open on Independence Drive. With 142 rooms, it will cater particularly for business visitors and for conferences and conventions. Surprisingly, two more luxury hotels are being considered. If all these go ahead, Blantyre will be in danger of having surplus accommodation.

Le Méridien Mount Soche Hotel

This is currently the best hotel in Blantyre-Limbe. It has long been in competition with Ryall's (see page 74) but in terms of efficiency and service it must take the leading place.

It is situated on the edge of the triangle, on Glyn Jones Road by the junction with Victoria Avenue. It could not be more conveniently placed for the traveller and the businessman. There are two car parks, at front and rear. Security is good.

Rooms are air-conditioned and have en suite bathrooms. Standard rooms may be a little small by international standards but are quite well furnished and include TV sets, refrigerators, a safe and tea-and coffee-making facilities. The best views are from rooms at the back of the hotel. Looking out over the hotel's garden and small swimming pool, the eye is caught by the conical **Nyambadwe Hill** standing just to the west of Ndirande mountain.

In mid-1997 and again in 2001, the hotel was used as the venue for a major southern Africa Heads of State conference. Two upper floors were completely rebuilt internally with new suites being created. These changes have been followed by others. The top floor, including the famed Michuru restaurant, is destined to become an executive floor. The main restaurant has been allocated space on the ground floor and the reception area has been revamped. The hotel can claim to have gone up a star.

Above: A view towards Blantyre city from Ndirande mountain.

A coffee bar-cum-restaurant, called Gypsy's is at street level on the front of the building and food and drink can be had in the lounge and on the terrace. There is a separate bar which is always well patronised.

In the reception area, there is a Times bookshop and a business centre where Shire Bus Lines can be booked. On the first floor are offices of KLM/Kenya Airways.

This is a good quality hotel with much to commend it.

Protea Ryall's Hotel

Ryall's is just a stone's throw from the Mount Soche. Continue up Glyn Jones Road beyond the junction with Victoria Avenue and, in a hundred metres or so, Ryall's stands at the corner of Glyn Jones and Hanover Avenue. It is said to be the oldest hotel in Malawi still offering accommodation. It is managed by the South African group, Protea Hotels.

A completely new hotel is growing up in the gardens of the old. Much of the original hotel will remain but the new wing will raise the standard of Ryall's to that of the highest in Blantyre. The architecture is classical in style and the new bedrooms are particularly

well equipped, catering for business visitors.

The old hotel is not being totally demolished and some of its historic sections are likely to be retained for the foreseeable future. The main restaurant, called the '21 Restaurant' (the hotel was opened in 1921) has always had a good reputation. Gentlemen arriving for dinner without a tie used to be provided with one of the sort of design that meant it was unlikely they would forget a second time. Alas, the tie rule seems to have been abandoned. The name may be all that's left when the new 70-seater restaurant is completed. There is to be a new cocktail bar, lounge and swimming pool. Meeting facilities and a business centre are also to be built.

Shire Highlands Hotel

The Shire Highlands, another Protea-managed establishment, is in Limbe on Churchill Road near to the tobacco auction house. Like its counterpart in Blantyre, Ryall's, it has character but to rival that hotel or the Mount Soche, considerable modernisation is needed. However, its rooms are comfortable and if a colonial atmosphere appeals then the Shire Highlands is a good choice. The

Above: The morning mist rises from the hills beyond the Mount Soche Hotel gardens.

character is still there, including a smart reception area with a fountain at the foot of the staircase. Rooms are en suite and the terrace and garden, with swimming pool, are attractive.

Tumbuka Lodge
Tumbuka is a homely sort of a place. There are just six en suite bedrooms in a building retaining all the outward appearances of a colonial bungalow. Situated on Sharpe Road, near the corner with Chilembwe Road and behind a reed fence, the lodge is set in its own neat garden. It is much favoured by business clients. Breakfast is the only meal regularly provided but other meals can be arranged.

Alendo Hotel
For novel alternative accommodation there is the Institute of Tourism's establishment, previously known as the Hotel Training School. It has sixteen single (with big, "room-for-two", beds) and double rooms. The rooms are not air-conditioned but they do have television and a refrigerator. There is a simple restaurant. It's hard not to be aware that this is a training school but it's reasonably priced and quite

acceptable. It is located on the left side of Chilembwe Road just down from Victoria Avenue.

Where to eat
There is a good selection of restaurants and cafés in Blantyre but Limbe is better known for its Indian establishments. It is possible to eat from a wide variety of national dish menus from Chinese to Italian.

In the heart of Blantyre's triangle is the Italian **L'Hostaria** on Cilembwe Road. It has a good reputation and is often crowded. The **Hong Kong Restaurant** is a convenient and attractive Chinese alternative to hotel food if staying at Ryall's or the Mount Soche because it's a stone's throw from both on the corner of Robins Road and Glyn Jones Road. Again, it is very popular which is usually a good sign.

An attractive place to take a light meal or simply a cup of coffee as a break from sightseeing is the **Shire Maky** café on Laws Road by the junction with Chilembwe Road. It has a regular and loyal clientele. The **Royal Taj**, unsurprisingly, serves Indian dishes. It is located on Livingstone Avenue in the heart of the triangle just up from Central Bookshop.

Rather different is The Green House, or **Greens,** a restaurant serving mostly European dishes and run by the O'Connor family. Situated in Sunnyside, a district of Blantyre favoured by the ex-pat community, it has a local readymade clientele. Sunnyside, where there is also the well-known **St Andrew's School,** is reached by going out of town down Victoria Avenue. The district is beyond the Sports Club and on the right of the main road.

Sightseeing

Blantyre and Limbe, together with their satellite townships and suburbs, cover a large area with their centres lying about six kilometres (four miles) apart. The two central districts are compact and townships, such as Chilomoni and Ndirande, are distinct and separate. East of Blantyre and north of the connecting road to Limbe is a large industrial and commercial district. Limbe's industrial sector is altogether smaller and more compact, contiguous with the retail area.

A good road, the Masauko Chipembere (previously Kamuzu) Highway, links the centres of Blantyre and Limbe.

The easiest way to move around this quite large city is by car, although Blantyre's central triangle is within walking distance of the Mount Soche and Ryall's hotels. A hire

Hotel. The main **post office** is on Glyn Jones Road near the junction with the M1 to Lilongwe and on the corner of Stewart Street. **Petrol stations** are on both Glyn Jones and Haile Selassie roads and there's a new large service station at the junction of these two roads. **Air Malawi,** which also acts as agent for other airlines, has offices up Robins Road, a short distance up from the Mount Soche Hotel and behind the Old Mutual building. **British Airways** have offices on Victoria Avenue in Unit House and in Ryall's Hotel on Hanover Avenue while **South African** and **Ethiopian Airways** are at the corner of Haile Selassie Road and Stewart Street in Nico House. A turning off Victoria Avenue, on the right going down hill, is Chilembwe Road. On the left of this road are the offices of **Soche Tours and Travel**. On the other side of the road is **Computer World** which provides access to the internet at K120 for twenty minutes. It is open all week including Saturdays but there is often a long wait for its limited facilities.

What were the headquarters of the Ministry of Tourism on the left of Victoria Avenue going down from the Mount Soche Hotel, is now simply the **Tourist Office**. On the opposite side of the road are **Avis Car Hire** and the offices of the **Department of Immigration**. Over-the-counter sales of maps are found at the **map sales office** of the Survey Department. This is located just outside the triangle at the crossroads of Victoria Avenue, Independence Drive and Haile Selassie Road. Look for the Old Town Hall and the Survey Department is on the other side of the road. Both buildings date from colonial times. If purchasing maps, there is a useful series at a scale of 1:250,000. Ten sheets cover the country but they cost K750 each.

Near the Old Town Hall and off Haile Selassie Road is the city **bus station**. The main **bus depot** is on Chileka Road on the way to St Michael and All Angels Church. The offices of **Shire Bus Lines** are on the main road to Limbe almost opposite the National Stadium.

car or taxi (easy to arrange through hotel reception) will allow a fairly comprehensive view in the course of a day.

If driving in Blantyre-Limbe, you will encounter the heaviest traffic in the country. However, people still use the roads as footpaths from time to time and the standard of driving is not high. The size of the conurbation means that some sort of map or town plan is useful (obtainable from the Tourist Office, the map sales office or the Central Bookshop.

As with shopping, most services are available in or near Blantyre's central triangle. There are **banks** at the lower end of Victoria Avenue as well as opposite the Mount Soche

Above: Victoria Avenue, one of the streets forming Blantyre's central triangle.

The old **Apollo Cinema** has been turned into a shopping mall. At one time there were rumours of a reopening but no longer.

The range of services is rather more limited in Limbe but Churchill Road has a string of **banks** and **petrol stations**. Perhaps Limbe's most useful services are those offering repairs to anything from shoes and clothing to cars.

Shopping

Blantyre-Limbe offers a variety of shopping that is otherwise absent in Malawi. A walk around the triangle of roads in central Blantyre will lead to most of the shops a visitor might need. Walking down Victoria Avenue from the direction of the Mount Soche and Ryall's hotels, there is a **PTC** supermarket a little way down on the left. Here and for some distance down the street and into a side turning, the pavement is littered with curios for sale. Whether deliberately or not, the goods restrict and slow down anyone walking and the traders exploit the opportunity to accost the would-be passer-by. Haggling over price is the order of the day.

A particular attraction is the **Central Africana** shop and gallery in an arcade off Victoria Avenue just down from Glyn Jones Road. There are displays of antiquarian books, maps and pictures. It is well worth a visit if only to browse in this very tastefully appointed gallery. It is in a class above almost anything else in Blantyre.

A little further down the hill in Victoria Avenue was an excellent curio shop but, sign of the times, it is now a mobile telephone shop. The company which owned the curio shop, **Gangecraft**, is still in business and its goods can be purchased from its workshop out at Bvumbwe on the road out to Thyolo. Towards the bottom of the Avenue is a **Kandodo** store which rivals the PTC in price and variety.

Turning into Haile Selassie Road leads to a great range of small stores selling cloth, as well as clothing and providing a range of services. Most of these stores are run by Blantyre's strong Asian community.

Continuing up the third side of the triangle, Glyn Jones Road, brings one to the main **post office** and, nearby, another curio shop, **Safari Curios**. The standard of craftsmanship is high but the prices reflect this and there is not much encouragement to bargain. Also

Above: Emerald House, a modern block on Blantyre's Haile Selassie Road.

along Glyn Jones Road is a variety of other shops including a quite good sports store and Chibisa House, scene of disturbances in the late-1995 Civil Service strike.

It is worth exploring inside the triangle. On Livingstone Street is the **Central Bookshop**, a gem. The range of the stock is remarkable and there is always a fascinating collection of books on Malawi and other parts of Africa as well as Ladybird children's books from the UK. Maps are also on sale and there is a small café attached to the shop. The roads in the triangle are named after the patron saints of England, Scotland and Wales, and it's here you'll find two or three **restaurants** which often serve meals at least as good as those available in the hotels.

Shopping in Limbe is not directed towards visitors, all the same it is just the place to buy those everyday items like an extra holdall for the curios. The two parallel roads in central Limbe, Livingstone Avenue and Churchill Road, are packed with shops and shoppers. Largely owned by the Asian community, this is an area where long opening hours are common. An interesting diversion is **La Caverna Art Gallery**. It is up from the Shire Highlands Hotel behind the Chiperoni Blankets building.

There are two major **markets**, one in Blantyre and one in Limbe. Neither is as attractive or exciting as the walled market in Lilongwe. The more alluring is Limbe's, near the junction of Dalton and Dunduzu Roads. It is best approached by turning right after the roundabout at the end of the dual carriageway leading into Limbe from Blantyre. Blantyre's market is reached by turning down Kaoshiung Road leading off Haile Selassie Road and the triangle. Both markets are more remarkable for their atmospheres than their goods.

Historical Buildings

The original heart of Blantyre was at the lower end of Victoria Avenue, at its junction with Haile Selassie Road and Independence Drive. The **Old Boma** is here, at one time the Town Hall. It is a small white building, erected in 1903 and, unfortunately, is now neglected and sad-looking. Nearby is the **Old Library** but most of the old buildings have been replaced by characterless modern high-rise structures.

To reach **Mandala House** from the triangle, turn down Kaoshiung Road off Haile Selassie Road as though going towards the market. Continue up the rise of the road after it has bridged the Mudi River and the brick-built house is on the left.

Mandala House is believed to be the oldest house in Malawi. Built in 1882, it was the country's first two-storey building. The building, apart from the re-roofing done as long ago as 1890, is little changed in general appearance from the original. The word Mandala is traced back to one of the **Moir brothers**, John, who founded the **African Lakes Corporation** (originally called the Livingstonia Central African Company). His spectacles were likened to two 'reflecting pools' (*mandala*). The word became synonymous with the company itself. African Lakes are still active as a company in Malawi and their proud history shows them to have been the country's equivalent of the East India Company in the early days of trade in this part of the world.

The house is still used as offices but the public are freely admitted. It is hard not to feel an intruder as one wanders in and out of private offices and among the photocopiers, but no one seems to mind. There are plans to put a cultural village in the grounds.

A Blantyre landmark is **St Michael and All Angels** church. To find the church go down Glyn Jones Road to the clocktower round-about. Instead of carrying straight on to Limbe, turn left under the railway bridge to continue up Chileka Road. The red brick and white cupola church is on the left.

St Michael's, dedicated in 1891, was the work of one of the early Scottish missionaries **David Clement Scott**. Recalling that he had no training in either architecture or building, it is a truly remarkable testament to the endeavours of all those associated with the mission. Scott had to learn the art of brick-making and then pass it on to just a handful of local men who were engaged in the building. Only the more specialist work was completed by skilled tradesmen from Scotland.

Sadly, the church today is in urgent need of repointing and attention to minor structural defects. The same is true of the separate clocktower. Two plaques are worth seeking out. Near the high altar is a brass memorial

to David Livingstone, a gift to the church by his grandchildren in 1913, the hundredth anniversary of his birth. Outside the church another gives, in detail, Blantyre's geographical position and this marks the point which all Malawi's surveying took as its reference.

The mission buildings and school stand close by, nearer the road than is the church.

Museums

The **Museum of Malawi** is small but full of interest. To reach it, take the Limbe road out of Blantyre and go past the modern **Chichiri** (formerly Kamuzu) **Stadium** (on the left) to the roundabout. This stadium saw the inauguration of Malawi's current president, Dr Muluzi, in May 1994. At the roundabout, turn right and then immediately left behind the fine modern **Civic Centre** and into Kasungu Crescent. The museum is on the left. Exhibits, in and outside the building, give an insight into the country's culture and history.

There are interesting collections outlining the natural and cultural history of Malawi. An exhibition depicts *Man in Malawi* through the ages with various displays and references to the times of Livingstone and the slave trade as well as to current tribes. Outside are steam engines. There is a small kiosk selling drinks and cakes.

The museum is officially open every day, including Sunday, from 08.00 to 17.30. There is no charge to go in but there is a donations box.

The **Heritage Centre's** buildings are clustered around a courtyard and are located just down the road from the Shire Highlands Hotel in Limbe. Although called the Heritage Centre, it is in fact home to three separate bodies.

One is the **Malawi Wildlife Society**, dedicated to conservation and education. This worthy institution, although desperately short of funds, works to educate the young about their environment and to fight what must seem a difficult battle against the steady destruction of Malawi's rich natural heritage. Among the projects they are concerned with are translocations and animal counts. The Society's offices are here and welcome contributions to assist their work. They also have a well-stocked shop in the Centre which, among other items, sells books about Malawi's wildlife including its own

Above: Mandala House in Blantyre. Said to be Malawi's oldest surviving house. Top: Blantyre's Boma, the Old Town Hall.

Above: The modern headquarters of the Malawi Development Corporation in Blantyre.

journal, *Nyala*. There is also a good library but it closes at 16.00. Access to the shop and to the Society's office is between 08.00-12.00 and 13.30-16.00 Monday to Friday and 08.30-12.00 on Saturdays.

Next to the Wildlife Society are the offices of the **Society of Malawi**. This august body includes among its aims the promotion of "interest in literary, historical and scientific matters among all races in Malawi". It publishes a journal and occasional papers and welcomes overseas membership. The office and the Society's library are open on Mondays 14.00-16.00 and Fridays 08.30-11.30, or by appointment.

The third occupant of the complex is a fascinating **Transport Museum**. Unfortunately there is little comprehensive information about the exhibits which date mostly from the early colonial period.

Sports Clubs

Both Blantyre and Limbe have sports clubs. The social activities are at least as important as the sporting.

The **Blantyre Sports Club** is located off Independence Drive, a turning off Victoria Avenue down by the Old Boma. It offers short-term or daily membership and has good facilities for golf, tennis and squash. There's also a very pleasant swimming pool and a restaurant, the Copperbowl. It offers a quiet retreat from the bustle of the town centre as well as a venue for a reasonably priced dinner.

The **Limbe Country Club** is conveniently located near an exclusive housing area which provides most of its members. To reach the club from Blantyre take the main road to Limbe. Once in Limbe, continue on this road, now Livingstone Avenue, until just beyond a large tobacco processing factory (left).

The club, similar to that in Blantyre, admits temporary members. It is quite well cared for and equipped with facilities for tennis, bowling and squash. It is possible to park a camper van here overnight.

Papermaking Education Trust

On Chelembwe Road, to the right coming out of the triangle, between Laws Road and Sharpe Road, is PAMET — the Papermaking Education Trust. This excellent project aims to promote the recycling of paper and papermaking from such unusual materials

Above: The tobacco auction floor at Limbe. Following pages: Blantyre's Independence Arch on the road linking Blantyre to Limbe.

as elephant droppings and banana leaves. The skills are taught here and widely appreciated in a country short of funds to purchase paper. Much of the output from PAMET goes to schools which themselves have started their own projects. Elephant dung paper is, appropriately, exceptionally strong.

Visitors are welcome but it may be best to telephone first. A wide range of handmade papers is on sale at the Trust.

Tobacco Auction Floor

It is possible to visit the tobacco auction floors in Limbe during the selling season: late April to early September. Although casual callers may be admitted (get there early in the day) it is wiser to telephone in advance.

To reach the auction floor from Blantyre, take the main road (Masauko Chipembere Highway) out from the central triangle, via Glyn Jones Road, as for the museum. Instead of turning off at the roundabout, continue along the dual carriageway, under Independence Arch and bear right at the next roundabout. Continuing on the main road brings one to central Limbe. At the beginning of the shopping area turn left and continue up Churchill Road. The auction floors are a few hundred metres on the right.

The vast quantities of tobacco leaf, the speed of transactions and the skill of the buyers are quite remarkable. Almost at a sprint, groups of buyers pass down the lines of tobacco-filled sacks each weighing 60 kilograms (132 pounds). Their bids are made to the auctioneer who accompanies them. Quickly they distinguish between the grades: yellow or gold or green. It takes seven years to train an auctioneer, they are well paid and, according to popular belief, die young from high living in the off-season.

As the tobacco is sold, porters run with loaded trolleys down narrow lanes between the bags. The porters' speed puts into danger anyone stepping into a lane in this vast hall without first looking carefully. Tobacco can endanger your health in quite a different fashion here. The auction house can handle 4500 bales a day and the finished dealings are completed before the next day's trading begins. This is quite remarkable given that sums well into seven figures of US dollars change hands.

Above: Women gather to collect water in the township of Ndirande.

With over seventy per cent of Malawi's foreign trade being in tobacco a visit to the auction floor makes an interesting and educative experience. Cigarettes are, not surprisingly, extremely cheap in Malawi but the growers bemoan dwindling trade with Europe and, instead, have turned to China which favours strong tobaccos.

Carlsberg Brewery

The Carlsberg Brewery in Blantyre is the company's largest in Africa. It is particularly famous for its lager, the so-called "green", because of the colour of the labels on the bottles. There's also a brown ale and a stout. The brewery runs conducted tours and visitors don't come away thirsty. It is necessary to book before going on a tour.

To reach the brewery from central Blantyre take the main road out towards Limbe, the Masauko Chipembere Highway, and turn up, left, into Makata Road as you pass the Chichiri Stadium on the same side of the Highway. Carlsberg are some way up Makata Road, on the right, and it really is a case of "you can't miss it".

Blantyre's Mountains

The three mountains which ring the basin in which lies the city of Blantyre-Limbe all offer excellent views of the surrounding countryside and of the town. Of these, Soche has no easy road access and will involve something of a climb. Michuru is more accessible and has a range of marked trails but Ndirande has perhaps the most to offer the visitor on a relatively short stay in Blantyre.

A visit to **Michuru** should be seen as at least a half-day excursion with a full day plus picnic making more sense. Immediate access is by Glyn Jones Road up from the Mount Soche Hotel, past the Old Mutual building. Turn right at St Paul's church, just beyond Ryall's Hotel, and then almost immediately left into Michuru Road. This bears round to the right and goes through the outskirts of **Chilomoni** township. After bridging a small stream continue for another six kilometres (four miles) until a sign to a parking place is reached. Turn off here. The total distance is about eight kilometres (five miles) and the last five kilometres or so is on a poor track which can be difficult after the rains.

There are a number of poorly marked

walking trails from the car park. If leaving a car here it must be locked and all personal belongings put into the boot. The whole of Michuru Mountain is a conservation area and wonderfully wild with a variety of antelope, baboons, monkeys and, so it is said, leopard, hyena and jackal. It is possible to reach the summit and enjoy splendid views from 1473 metres (4833 feet). Alternatively the mountain offers solitude and time for reflection in a totally unspoilt wilderness. For the keen walker this comes close to heaven.

Ndirande, which from a distance looks like a sleeping man, has a triple attraction. It is easy to get to, offers outstanding views and allows one to see something of the township of the same name. To reach the mountain turn left at the clocktower junction at the bottom of Glyn Jones Road on to the Chileka Road past St Michael's church and turn right into Ndirande Ring Road immediately after passing Blantyre Girls School (right). The road swings round and behind the township and, as it does so, an untarred road leads up the mountain. The winding road is not good but just about passable for a car, although a four-wheel drive with high clearance is advised. Once through thin pine forests and at the top of the *Sleeping Man* the views from 1612 metres (5288 feet) are spectacular. From one viewpoint all Blantyre is laid out at the foot of the mountains, from another the view is to the Shire Valley and Zomba Mountain.

Again, if leaving the car, do not leave personal belongings in sight.

On the journey back downslope you are likely to encounter groups of women and children with great headloads of firewood making for the township. From high up the sprawling settlement can be seen — and heard. Instead of driving straight through the township, it makes an interesting excursion if you stop and wander around. The town, now a suburb of Blantyre, developed in the 1870s and '80s from a group of villages that sought the protection of the Scottish mission. It is now a maze of poorly maintained streets with an exceptionally high population density. Although Ndirande gives a very good insight into the life of the average township dweller it has to be said that this is an area where caution should be exercised. Photography is certainly not recommended. A visitor may sense an air of resentment rather than raw hostility but it is a place to see this aspect of the city in contrast to its more westernised parts.

Chileka Airport

Until the building of Lilongwe's modern international airport, Chileka was Malawi's most important aviation node. It continues to handle domestic traffic and southern African international routes but most international flights land at Lilongwe.

Blantyre's airport is just 13 kilometres (8 miles) from the centre of the town. Access is good. To reach the airport from the triangle, travel down Glyn Jones Road away from the Mount Soche Hotel and turn left into Chileka Road at the Clocktower. This road leads directly to the airport. Alternatively, use the M1.

Malawi's domestic air services are well used, especially between Lilongwe and Blantyre and advance booking is advisable.

The airport is small and simple although, in aviation terms, it is well equipped. The terminal building was renovated for the SADC conference visitors in 2001. Taxis are usually available or can be summoned on arrival. A fare should be agreed before hire but it should be around US$ 12 into town.

Zomba

The town is a colonial creation, a place chosen as much for its beauty as its convenience. Discovered by missionaries, the initial site was on the **Mulunguzi** which is the major river draining Zomba Plateau. The river provided ample fresh water in all seasons and its power was used to drive a mill. By 1885, the colonial administration had been persuaded of the importance of the place and a residency was built on the slopes of the plateau. From there it was possible to keep an eye on the slave trade which was routed to the east of the mountain, on the plains west of **Lake Chilwa**. In 1891 Zomba became the capital. This pre-eminent status was retained throughout the colonial era and into independence until, in 1975, the bureaucracy outgrew the small town and moved to the grand buildings of the rising new city of Lilongwe. However, Parliament continued to sit at Zomba until almost the end of the century.

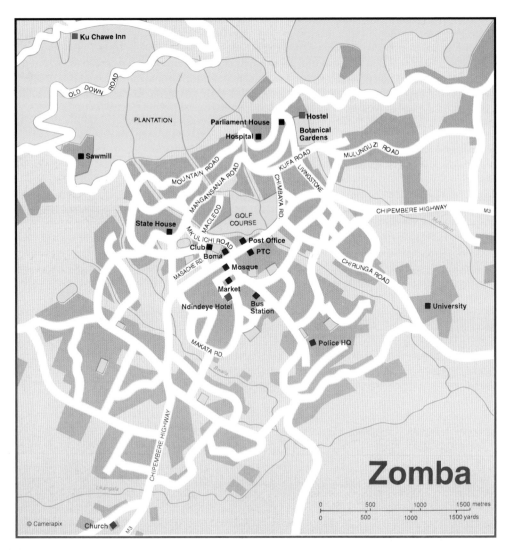

Getting there

From

Blantyre: 66km/41miles   M3
Lilongwe: 284km/176miles   M1, M8, M3

Zomba is easily reached whether from Blantyre or Lake Malawi, via the M3 which passes through the town, or from Lilongwe using the M1 and the M8 for the first part of the journey. All the approach roads are well surfaced and traffic is not heavy except in the environs of Blantyre.

When to go

Zomba's climate is pleasant throughout the year. Rainfalls are affected by the proximity of the high plateau but not so much as to make the town somewhere to avoid, even in the wet season.

Where to stay

There is little more than simple accommodation available in resthouses in Zomba town, including the **Ndindeya Motel**. However, a new hotel, the **Masongola**, is in the old Parliament area. This 51-room property includes the 1885 home of the first Commissioner, Sir Harry Johnston. It has seen many changes and, until recently, was a university hostel. It is now a mid-market hotel with en suite rooms and a restaurant.

Many visiting Zomba choose to stay on the plateau (see below) where there is a choice from the famous **Le Méridien Ku Chawe**, a pleasantly sited forest lodge, and a camping site.

Sightseeing

Zomba was the home of Malawi's parliament (until it followed its civil service to Lilongwe) and country's university town. The main access road, the M3, skirts the edge of the town and visitors to the plateau see little of the settlement until they look down from the summit. To the left of the M3 leading into the town from Blantyre is a rather fine **Catholic Church** with a separate bell-tower. Its beautiful garden setting is enhanced by a backdrop of the towering Zomba Mountain.

Along the main road is a range of services: Asian-run shops, two small **supermarkets** including a PTC , a **bank**, a **post office** and a number of **petrol stations**. However, the

Above: War Memorial to the King's African Rifles.

lively **market** area and the greater number of shops are down Namiwawa Road, almost opposite the road to the plateau. It is said to be one of the best markets in the country because visitors find it especially friendly.

On the eastern side of the town are some of Zomba's more interesting buildings. To the south of the M3, clearly marked, is the **University**, formerly Chancellor College. Set in beautiful gardens, it has a mix of old and splendid modern buildings including a Great Hall of which it is justly proud. Much of the campus can be seen by driving round its roads but a visitor wishing to make a closer inspection should call at the College office. To the north of the M3, up Livingstone Road, are the former **parliament buildings**. The old and new parliament buildings contrast in style with the older (green) structure being the more interesting. The are

Right: Zomba town, a bird's-eye view from the plateau.

not open to the public but many of the fine **old colonial offices** can be seen, often set in pleasant, well-designed gardens. Some of these are now incorporated into the university. Nearby is a small **Botanical Garden**, worthy of a visit and Harry Johnston's old **Residency**. The latter is now a hotel. **Harry Johnston** was the first Commissioner of the British Central African protectorate and it was he who chose Zomba as the administrative capital.

To the south of the turning off the M3 marked to the Ku Chawe Inn, and on the same side of the road, is the **Cobbe Barracks** of the Malawi Rifles complete with its own vegetable gardens. The prominent World War I memorial in the form of a **Clocktower** still bears the inscription KAR (**King's African Rifles**). This proud regiment's battle honours are displayed on the notice board at the entrance to the barracks although no mention is made of their part in the quelling of the **Chilembwe Rising**. Zomba's cemetery contains a number of war graves including that of a German officer.

On the other side of the M3 to the barracks is the town's **hospital**. Anyone with an interest in medicine in the developing world might well take a look here; there is always a welcome for the genuinely concerned. The term out-patient takes on a slightly different meaning as women sit in the heat of the sun awaiting their turn for their babies to be weighed. Other would-be patients gather outside in the hope that treatment will be forthcoming. The simple blue and white buildings are woefully inadequate.

To the left of the road leading towards the plateau top and the Ku Chawe Inn is the **Gymkhana Club**, a wonderful relic of colonial days both in its concept and its architectural style. The present building dates from 1923 but looks as though it has been carefully whitewashed only the day before yesterday. The club owns a nine-hole golf course, somewhat reminiscent of that at Mzuzu but the polo ground has not seen a match for some

years now. Visitors can use the golf course, squash and tennis courts: apply at the club.

Further up this same road is the **State House**. It can be seen through the gates but access is forbidden. This is a pity because the building, although extended, dates from 1898 and was originally the house of the Consul General. It was one of many residences of the President but is no longer used for this purpose and an alternative function is to be found. It may be sold.

There is an attractive little **teashop** and **curio store**, Caboodles, near the northern exit from the town, on the M3 (left of the

road before coming to the river). This is well worth a visit. Apart from cakes and toasted sandwiches there are a few 'European luxuries' — mostly toiletries — on sale.

Zomba used to be famous for the manufacture of fishing flies but recently fly tying has given way to sewing the casings of footballs.

North out of Zomba, about 15 kilometres (9 miles) is the notorious **Mikuyu Jail** where Dr Banda incarcerated many of his political prisoners. To reach the jail the turning off the M3 is about five kilometres (three miles) north of central Zomba. It is signposted, to the right, to Mikuyu and Lake Chilwa. After about 12 kilometres (7 miles) a marked turn to the left, on to a poor road, leads to the jail after three kilometres.

Mikuyu Jail is now something of a memorial to its former inmates and is open for public viewing. There is a VIP section which housed the high profile prisoners. Speaking with men now in prominent positions in government and the professions, it is extraordinary how many spent time locked up in Mikuyu. It's even more remarkable when you've seen the awfulness of the conditions.

Mzuzu

It was only in 1960 that Mzuzu took over from Mzimba as the capital of the Northern Region. At that time it was relatively small with a population of only 7-8000. By 1980 the number had trebled and in the next decade further growth doubled its size. It continues to grow at a rate of between seven and ten per cent each year, causing acute housing problems and seeing the accretion of large new residential areas on the town's periphery. The present population is a massive 75,000.

Mzuzu's communications with the outside world are all relatively modern. Even the road out to Lake Malawi (M5) is less than forty years old and few regular services linked the town with the rest of Malawi until quite recently. There remains something of a sense of isolation in the town.

Mzuzu is little more than a market centre for its immediate surroundings. Set in a shallow depression at the northern limits of the **Viphya Highlands**, the town has all the appearances of a completely unplanned settlement. Apart from the two main arterial routes, the M1 and the M5, the roads within the town, many in a poor state of repair, twist and turn through a jumble of low-rise buildings. Much of the central area has the air of a pioneer town of uncertain future. Little seems to have the stamp of permanence. It is often difficult to tell if one is looking at a partly finished construction or one which has recently collapsed.

Mzuzu has none of the grandeur of Lilongwe's Capital City or bustling activity of its Old Town. This is no Blantyre or Zomba. Rather it is a somewhat scruffy, oversized village, unsuccessfully trying to live up to its designation as a city which it achieved in 1985.

The town's redeeming feature is its central position. For all its shortcomings it is undeniably the obvious place from which to make excursions into the surrounding

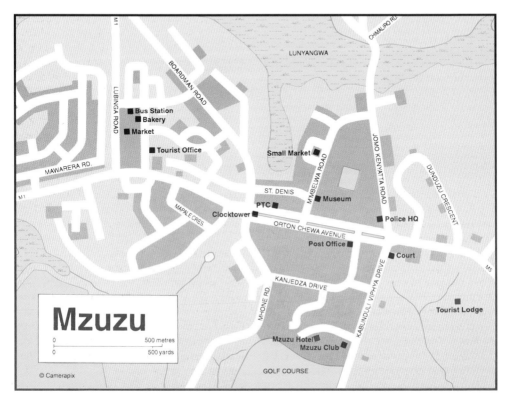

Mzuzu

© Camerapix

countryside, the **Nyika National Park** and the **Vwaza Marsh Wildlife Reserve**.

Getting there

From Blantyre:	596km/370miles	M1
From Lilongwe:	360km/224miles	M1

Visitors to the north may well choose Mzuzu as their base from which to explore the area. The town is the capital of the Northern Region and it is well served by roads. In fact it is at the T-junction of the M1, the country's main north-south highway, and the M5, the Lakeshore Road, which enters the town from the east. The M1 gives access to Lilongwe and Blantyre to the south, while northwards it continues via **Karonga** to **Mbeya** in neighbouring Tanzania. Travel by air is less convenient. There are scheduled flights from Lilongwe with Air Malawi and Proflight Air Services also use Mzuzu as a hub but there are no international flights.

Some improvement is likely in the future if the planned new airport is built. At present, Mzuzu's airport is classified as domestic and located on the very edge of the built-up area, close to the M1 leading north. The new airport is intended to have international status.

When to go

Mzuzu has some high rainfalls in the wet season. From December to April monthly figures range from 180 to 225 millimetres (7 to 9 inches). The rest of the year is quite dry and temperatures are moderated by altitude.

Where to stay

Accommodation is limited in north Malawi and much is low grade. Except for the Mzuzu Hotel, it is probably best initially to contact the local Tourist Office in the town. There are numerous small hotels and guesthouses but they quickly fill with business clients. One hotel has the main drains running under the corridors and a missing inspection cover could cause a problem as you step out of your room. Camping is possible at the **Mzuzu Club** and the Tourist Lodge.

Sunbird Mzuzu Hotel

One of the few hotels in the town with any pretensions to cater for international travellers, the Mzuzu Hotel is easily reached by turning off the M5 at the only roundabout in town and taking the pot-holed Viphya Drive, signposted to the hotel. The building is easily seen two hundred metres or so on the right.

This modern two-storey hotel, managed by Le Méridien, is set in well kept gardens and there is adequate and safe parking. Beyond reception an impressive staircase leads to the sixty rooms. All the rooms have en suite bathrooms but only about half are air-conditioned. In Mzuzu's upland climate the latter facility is of little consequence for much of the year.

This is a well appointed business-type hotel of a quite acceptable standard. There is a small shopping arcade and drinks are served in the Kaningina Bar. Perhaps the biggest flaw is the slow service in the Nyika Coffee Shop. What was once the main restaurant is now a function room, frequently booked for private parties by the local well-to-do. Mzuzu's remote location may mean that items shown on the menu are "off" for days at a time. Residents have access to the Mzuzu Club's tennis and golf.

Makuzi Lodge

A welcome addition to good quality accommodation in Mzuzu is the new Makuzi Lodge run by the same family who own Makuzi Beach, a lodge on the central lakeshore. There are just six very reasonably priced en suite rooms. It's worth booking ahead of a visit.

To find the lodge take the M5 as though going to Nkata Bay. At the top roundabout, while still in town, take the left turn down the tarred road past St John's Hospital. When the tar ends, carry on for about 200 metres and then turn right into Three Bridges Road. The lodge is signposted from here and is a little way along the road.

Mzuzu Tourist Lodge

This is government-run and offers very simple accommodation in ten rooms with shared bath-room facilities. Meals, other than breakfast, have to be arranged and you may be expected to provide your own food although a cook can be employed. The resthouse is used to train staff for the hotel trade and they give willing if painfully slow and unsure service. The location of the resthouse is clearly

Above: Mzuzu Hotel is the premier accommodation in the town.

signposted on the M5 (left) as you first enter the town from Nkhata Bay. There is also a camping site

Where to eat
Other than the hotels and the Club, there are few other options when it comes to restaurants. However, the **Tropicana Restaurant**, behind the PTC store is inexpensive if not especially exciting.

Sightseeing
The M5 forms the town's high street, Orton Chewa Avenue, a broad stretch of road which includes a central reservation planted with bushes. Entering the town from the direction of Nkhata Bay and having climbed up from Lake Malawi, the M5 descends into the town, skirts a roundabout, and runs alongside the main shopping area before linking with the M1. At this junction, the M1 south is aligned with the M5 but the route north is a right-hand turn.

Much of the town can be explored on foot. Along Orton Chewa Avenue are **petrol stations, banks**, a branch of **Times Bookshops** and a **PTC** store. The **post office** is opposite

the banks. Storm drains and broken kerbs often make it difficult to park at the side of the road or drive into petrol stations. There are times when a four-wheel drive vehicle seems necessary even in the town centre. The PTC is often less well stocked than the **Kandodo** store to say nothing of the condoms prominently displayed at the checkout. The store is situated in what is effectively Mzuzu's commercial hub: the triangle formed by the M1, M5 and Boardman Road. **Bakeries** and the **Tourist Office** are also here. The **bus station** is nearby but the office of the **Shire Lines** bus company is near the **clock-tower** on Orton Chewa Avenue.

Mzuzu's **market** is also located in this triangle. The market, larger than it seems at first sight, is comparable with that in Old Town Lilongwe. It is well worth a visit. Mzuzu's location, on the main route to Tanzania, means that there is often a wider range of goods available than one might expect for the size of the town. As in all Malawi's markets, look out for the stall of the African doctor.

A visit to the Tourist Office can help sort out queries about accommodation and such matters as vehicle hire and the state of roads. It would be easy to be put off by the dilapidated state of the office with its faded and peeling wall posters and lack of brochures. What it lacks in sophistication it makes up for in the friendliness of the staff. If there's a look of astonishment when you walk in, perhaps the fact that they may see only one or two customers a week has something to do with it. The office is almost opposite the Kandodo store.

On the road leading to the Mzuzu Hotel is (left) the local **Courthouse**. The sculptures outside the new building are worth stopping to see. Also worthy of a visit is the **Museum** on M'Mmbelwa Road which is a turning off Orton Chewa Avenue, midway along the dual carriageway section. The building is the last in an arcade of shops. It is open from 07.30 until noon and from 13.00 to 17.00 every day except public holidays. The various domestic items, old weapons and other artefacts trace something of the history of the Northern Region. A lack of funds leaves the museum unfinished. The **Police Headquarters** is on the right, past the museum, while a small **market** is on the other side of the road.

The former Teacher Training College on the road out to Rhumpi opposite the airport is now a much enlarged and smarter **university**.

Like every town in Malawi, there is a quite surprisingly large number of security guards who go on duty around five o'clock in the evening and patrol private and public buildings all night. In Mzuzu they can be seen assembling for their duty parade near the Stansfield Motor Company in the town centre. All are in uniform and the work often reduces the unemployment rate at only a modest cost. There is not an excessive amount of urban crime so the security guard is sometimes more of a status symbol for his employer than he is a necessity.

The Mzuzu Club

In a town not noted for its sights or entertainment centres, the Mzuzu Club might be considered a highlight for any visitor. The club is sited along Kabunduli Road which is an extension of Viphya Drive, just beyond the Mzuzu Hotel. Viphya Drive is a turning at the roundabout which is at the eastern end of the dual carriageway section of Orton Chewa Avenue — the M5.

The original social club was set up for and by expatriate members of trading companies which had become established in Mzuzu after World War II. It moved to its present site in the late 1950s — when Viphya Drive was known as Tea Caddy Lane. Appropriately, additional land allowed a golf course, all of three holes, to be built.

Today the three hole course has grown three-fold, tennis has been added to the amenities and there is a wooden clubhouse. It hardly matters whether or not you play golf, a visit to the club should be on the itinerary of every visitor to the town just for the experience. Temporary membership of the club comes with a stay at the next door Mzuzu Hotel but it is unlikely that entrance would be barred to anyone willing to pay the modest K20 green fees.

Clubs of indifferent quality can be hired from the hotel reception, again for K20. A score of young boys seem to inhabit the course and the sight of a bag of clubs is sufficient to signal a competitive assault on the would-be golfer. The security fence is scaled, crawled under and breached in a frenzied rush to offer service as caddie, flagman or general factotum. They may ask for up to K100 for a round but will reluctantly settle for K20. They will sell you five balls for K50 but not buy them back. Lost balls appear to be unrecoverable — until you are out of sight.

The clubhouse is in something of a time-warp. Handicap charts and honours boards bear, for the most part, English, Scottish and Welsh names but members today are the small number of local business men and their families who retreat to the club at weekends. There is a bar and a restaurant but service is not conspicuous. It has seen grander times but still retains much of the atmosphere of a colonial-days club. The snooker table waits in vain for the after-tiffin frame.

Out on the course the nine holes present their own challenge, not least when you have negotiated the locals who use the open ground as a thoroughfare, and arrived at a green. Now you discover the purpose of a sort of collapsible T-square which has so far

Above: Mzuzu's modern courthouse. Opposite: A magical sunset over Lake Malawi.

nestled in the golf bag along with your clubs. The greens boast not a blade of grass but are stretches of sand around the hole with the appearance of a flattened bunker. It matters little where the ball lands. The caddie will immediately snatch it up, place it at a point roughly the correct distance it landed from the hole but on a path which he has just flattened with the T-square. Leave your handicap at home and accept the challenge: you'll not have to put up with other golfers, the course is usually deserted.

PART THREE: PLACES AND TRAVEL

Above: The tobacco crop arrives from the farms to be sorted before going to auction.
Opposite: The western slopes of the Viphya Plateau with a scattering of small farms and villages.

Central Malawi

Much of central Malawi comprises the massive Central African Plateau which forms the western edge of the Great East African Rift Valley, and Lake Malawi. So gently does it undulate that there is little sense that one is actually at an altitude of some 1200 metres (4000 feet). It might as well be a plain. Only when closer to the lakeshore does one appreciate the cooler, less humid climate of the uplands. Central Malawi extends south-wards by a narrow belt of upland forming a border with Mozambique. This is the **Dedza Highlands**; beyond is the **Shire Valley**. To the north the plateau gives way to the **Chimaliro Hills**.

The plateau is cut by rivers flowing east-north-east to the lake and their valleys, together with the occasional inselberg, form the most prominent landscape features. Inselbergs add another 150 to 300 metres (500 to 1000 feet) to the plateau levels and have a beauty all their own. Around **Dowa**, to the north-east of Lilongwe, is a steep-sided plateau about 300 metres (1000 feet) above the surrounding surface and to the east of the region is Lake Malawi. The plateau's descent to the lake is sometimes dramatically steep and occasionally imperceptible.

One national park and a wildlife reserve, the country's most famous school and just one significant town are in this region, all some-what overshadowed by the importance of the capital city, **Lilongwe**.

Lilongwe's influence on the economy of the region grows as each year passes. Companies, previously content to have their headquarters in **Blantyre**, now open offices in Lilongwe. But it will be a long time before central Malawi will achieve more than ranking as the country's second most important agricultural region. Climate on the plateau gives a range of opportunities for both tropical and sub-tropical crops but maize remains king of the subsistence crops and tobacco dominates the cash crops. Tsetse fly problems have limited cattle rearing but there have been recent successful control programmes. An interesting development has been in horticulture with flowers being grown for export to, of all places, Amsterdam.

Travelling in central Malawi and seeing something of the very simple life of the smallholder farmers, the vast majority of the population, only serves to make the high-rise buildings of Lilongwe's Capital City appear to be implants from another planet. This contrast is made all the more obvious in the dry season when the straw-thatched mud huts of the arid brown plateau are seen in juxtaposition with the concrete and white of the city buildings set in well-watered gardens.

Kasungu

Kasungu is an important market town north of Lilongwe but it does its best to keep out of the limelight. On many maps it appears to stand astride the road to the north, the M1, but in fact it lies just to the east of that route. Many a traveller has driven past on the M1 unaware of the presence of the town.

Getting there

From Lilongwe:	121km/75miles	M1
From Mzuzu:	240km/149miles	M1
From Nkhotakota:	126km/78miles	M18

Lilongwe	To Airport	Mponela	Bua River	To Kasungu National Park	Kasungu
					Turn to Kasungu
	M14	M7	Madisi	M18	
8km	12km	8km	25km	20km	15km	12km	19km	100m	2km

Lilongwe to Kasungu: M1, M18: 121km

Most travellers will approach the town from the south, from Lilongwe, possibly on their way to Mzuzu and the north or en route for the Kasungu National Park. The road, M1, is rather better than adequate for the little traffic it carries and, just north of Lilongwe, there are even some tracks for bullock carts running parallel to the tarmac to ensure the truck or car an easy passage. The M1 runs out of Lilongwe and passes the airport turning (left) after about 20 kilometres (12 miles) from the Old Town. This stretch of the road used to be lit but almost all the lamp standards have been cut off near the base and stolen. For most of its path north there is little to distract the driver. Small farms lie back from

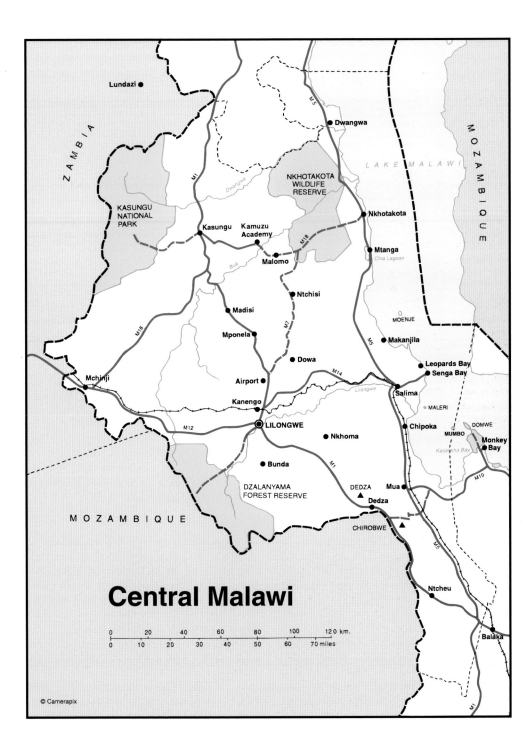

Central Malawi

Lundazi ●

Dwangwa ●

Z A M B I A

M O Z A M B I Q U E

L A K E   M A L A W I

KASUNGU
NATIONAL
PARK

NKHOTAKOTA
WILDLIFE
RESERVE

● Nkhotakota

Kasungu ● Kamuzu
Academy

● Mtanga
Chia Lagoon

● Malomo

Bua

● Ntchisi

● Madisi

MOENJE

Mponela ●

● Makanjila

● Dowa

M14

Mchinji ●

Airport ●

Leopards Bay ●
Senga Bay ●

Lilongwe

Salima ●

Kanengo ●

◎ LILONGWE

MALERI

● Chipoka

DOMWE

● Nkhoma

MUMBO

Monkey
● Bay

● Bunda

Kasankha Bay

DZALANYAMA
FOREST RESERVE

DEDZA
▲

Mua ●

● Dedza

M O Z A M B I Q U E

CHIROBWE ▲

M10

0		20		40		60		80		100		120 km.
0	10	20	30	40	50	60	70 miles					

Ntcheu ●

Balaka ●

© Camerapix

101

Above: A smooth weathered rock stands as one of Malawi's many *inselbergs*.

the road and, for Malawi, this is a thinly populated region. The plateau is largely unrelieved flatness without the usual sprinkling of inselbergs. After 28 kilometres (17 miles) from Lilongwe there is the M7 turn-off (right) to **Ntchisi** and the **Nkhotakota Wildlife Reserve**. Two small towns are passed through: **Mponela** and **Madisi**, both of which have petrol stations; Mponela's is at the southern approach. Anyone going direct to Kasungu National Park might be advised to refill at one of these or at Kasungu because the pump at the park may well be dry. Mponela acts as a market centre and, in the dry season, a turning on the right is an alternative way to get to the Ntchisi Forest Reserve. Madisi and Mponela are important as collecting centres for the region's tobacco crops.

Some 35 kilometres (22 miles) north of Mponela the road crosses the **River Bua**, a major watercourse which drains into Lake Malawi after threading a path through Nkhotakota Wildlife Reserve. When the M1 is 100 kilometres (62 miles) from Lilongwe it is joined by the new section of the M18 which is the link to Mchinji and the Zambian border.

Another 19 kilometres (12 miles) brings the M1 to the southern turn to **Kasungu National Park**. This is the S114. However, it is easier to travel another kilometre to the next left turn, the S117, signposted to the park.

Just beyond the S117 junction another road, the M18, leads off to the east (right), taking the traveller, in two kilometres, into the centre of Kasungu. The small town is signposted and just visible from the M1. Another three kilometres north on the M1 is a further turning (right) into the town. The northern regional capital, Mzuzu, lies another 238 kilometres (148 miles) further north.

Where to stay
Like most similar towns there is a choice of accommodation, mostly low-cost and attracting the backpacker market.

Kasungu Inn
An exception is the Kasungu Inn, formerly a government resthouse but now privately managed. This small, single storey inn offers simple but acceptable accommodation. Service is a little slow and choice in the restaurant is limited but Kasungu Inn makes a good base for a day's visit to Kasungu National Park. To reach the inn if coming from the south, turn off the M1 at the M18 junction by the petrol station and continue past the T-junction leading to the Kamuzu Academy for a few hundred metres. Approaching from the north, take the first signposted turn (left) into the town and Kasungu Inn is some 2 kilometres down this road and on the right.

Sightseeing
Kasungu acts as service and market centre for the tobacco growing area in which it is set. One of its claims to fame is that almost all of its fairly modest rainfall occurs in the five months of wet season (roughly December through to April). For the rest of the year, rain is a very rare occurrence indeed.

The town boasts stores, including a **supermarket**, a **post office**, **banks** and **petrol stations**. There is a **health centre**, a **private clinic** and the **District Hospital** in the town. The open **market** is worth visiting, but perhaps the town's main attraction is that it affords the opportunity to see a very typical Malawian town with a minimum of

Above: Hippo swim alongside Lifupa Lodge.

European influence. It is the sort of place to wander around and absorb the atmosphere. Its function as a service centre for the local region, ensures that there will be lots of activity even if there is little excitement.

Kasungu National Park

Kasungu National Park is 2316 square kilometres (894 square miles) mainly of natural *Brachystegia* woodland and bush with occasional small patches of open grass. It is the second largest park in Malawi. A number of major rivers drain off the upland and it is at the dambos on these streams that the animals will often gather to drink.

The great attraction of Kasungu is not the easy availability of game sighting. It is that, as in other Malawian parks and reserves, one can experience the wild much as it has been for centuries. Tracking is great fun and you never know what you might encounter round the next bend in the path or sheltering behind a mass of undergrowth and trees. This is not the wide open grasslands of some of the East African game parks where there are

convoys of safari trucks and the animals seem to line up as though for a photo-call. The most northerly part of the park is usually inaccessible for game viewing but that still leaves a substantial area. Like most parks, there is always an element of luck in seeing the game.

Getting there

From Lilongwe:	172km/107miles	M1, S114
From Mzuzu:	294km/183miles	M1, S114
From Nkhotakota:		
	181km/112miles	M18, S114
From Kasungu:	55km/34miles	S114

(Note: Distances are to Lifupa Lodge)

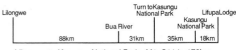

Lilongwe to Kasungu National Park: M1, S114: 172km

Access to the Kasungu National Park is off the M1 on to the signposted road, almost opposite the Oilcom petrol station at the junction to Kasungu town. This is the S117, marked to **Mchinji** and the park. A right turn at the crossroads, after 700 metres, leads on to the S114. If travelling from the south, the

103

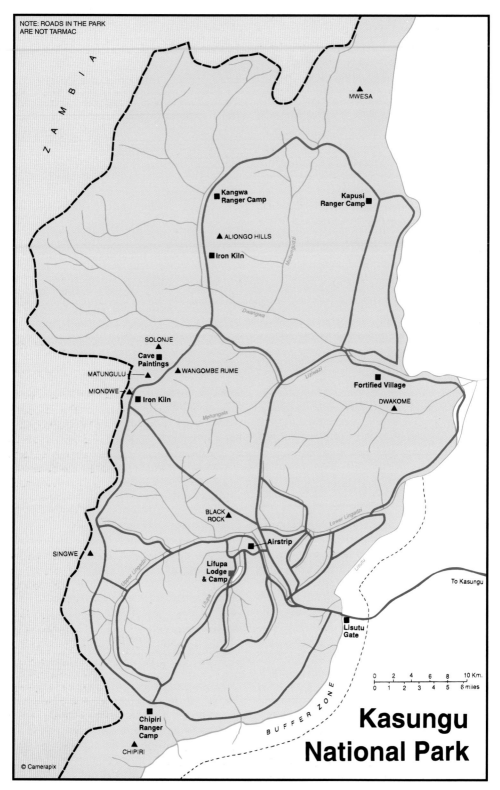

NOTE: ROADS IN THE PARK
ARE NOT TARMAC

Z A M B I A

MWESA ▲

■ Kangwa
Ranger Camp

Kapusi
Ranger Camp ■

▲ ALIONGO HILLS

■ Iron Kiln

Masangadzi

Dwangwa

SOLONJE ▲
Cave ■
Paintings

▲ WANGOMBE RUME

Liziwazi

MATUNGULU ▲

MIONDWE ▲
■ Iron Kiln

Mphangala

Fortified Village ■

DWAKOME ▲

BLACK ▲
ROCK

Lower Lingadzi

SINGWE ▲

Airstrip ■

Lifupa
Lodge ■
& Camp

Upper Lingadzi

Lifupa

Lisulu

To Kasungu

Lisutu
Gate ■

| 0 | 2 | 4 | 6 | 8 | 10 Km. |
| 0 | 1 | 2 | 3 | 4 | 5 | 6 miles |

Chipiri
Ranger
Camp ■

B U F F E R   Z O N E

CHIPIRI ▲

© Camerapix

Kasungu
National Park

signposted turn one kilometre before the S117 is directly on to the S114.

Not so long ago the road to the park presented real difficulties. Now it is a broad, re-graded gravel road which has cut the travel time by half or more. The first short section is actually poor pot-holed tarmac as far as the entrance to one of Dr Banda's many palaces, set on a hillside among the trees. This is **Nguru-ya-Nawambe** but the gates are closed so it has to be viewed from afar. From here the new gravel road takes one through typical smallholder farming areas on an almost imperceptible climb towards the park.

A little way along the road, look back to see a conical inselberg with all the appearances of a volcanic cone.

Much of the farming along the road is tobacco. Long, open-sided drying sheds can be seen and simple brick-built flues contrast with the mud and thatch houses. Fluctuating yields and prices decide the fortunes of the farmers but it is a question of survival and not riches.

With the road little used by traffic, except to the park, children are apt to disregard the dangers. Care must be taken especially now the road encourages moderately fast speeds. Close to the park, tobacco gives way to plantations of trees which form part of the buffer zone between the park and the farmed area.

At about 35 kilometres (22 miles) from the M1, the electric fence of the Kasungu National Park is reached and **Lisitu Gate** is another 600 metres (650 yards). Entrance is US$5 per person per day with US$2 for a vehicle. The gate is closed between sunset and sunrise. In the rainy season (January to March) there may be very limited access with most park tracks being impassable.

The new gravel road continues through the park to **Lifupa Lodge**. The campsite is signposted to the right — down a shady track — after about 18 kilometres (11 miles) but the lodge is a further 300 metres.

When to go
As in all parks, the best time of year to visit is when the water supply is low and the animals tend to keep closer to the dambos and streams which have not dried out. This period is between August and mid-November.

Above: A mating pair of lions in Kasungu National Park.

In the rainy season (January to March) there may be very limited access with most park tracks being impassable. November and December are probably the best months for bird-watching. This is also the best time to see the wild orchids. As to time of day, as always the best viewing is to be had towards sunrise and sunset.

Where to stay
Lifupa Lodge
The only camp in the park is Lifupa Lodge which enjoys a sheltered site overlooking Lifupa Lake and Dam. It has relatively recently been transformed from a very modest set of rondavels and simple camping site into something which now aims to rival the best in other parks of Malawi. Since privatisation, the lodge has had a number of management changes and there have been some significant improvements and developments. The present management is keen to continue up-grade facilities. Game viewing can be arranged for those who do not wish to go it alone. Sundowner cruises have been mooted and it is planned to offer fishing on the lake. There is a pleasant bar and open restaurant with a

Above: Kasungu's buffalo can be dangerous if they feel threatened.

log fire in the evenings above the restaurant, a viewing lounge overlooks the lake.

The lodge comprises 16 chalets including two luxury suites, all with en suite facilities. A stay in one of these can be on a fully inclusive basis with all meals and a range of safaris. The game drives are in open Land Rovers and all safaris are with a guide or scout. However, if you take your own vehicle to Kasungu, you can arrange private safaris at the lodge. Petrol should be available but don't rely on supplies.

A little distance from the lodge is a camping site for visitors providing all their own gear, and a fully equipped camp. There is a separate toilet block with hot water, showers and flush lavatories. You can hire a cook, be self-catering or have meals at the lodge. There is also a bar. Campers can join in any of the safaris from the lodge.

Because of management changes, it is best to check, before arrival, as to whether the camp is functioning.

The new Lifupa will undoubtedly have some teething troubles as it develops but it is a most welcome change in the right direction: to bring up-market facilities to Malawi's attractive game parks.

Sightseeing

It is claimed that Kasungu has the largest **elephant** herds of all the parks. This may have been so in the past but Liwonde, Vwasa and even Nkhotakota are more likely places to see these magnificent creatures. Here they wander through the thicket rather than venture out on to the more open grassland but will be seen in the open when they seek water. Elephants should be treated with caution. Some years ago a lone male took an interest in a car at Lifupa, lifted the back up a metre off the ground and then dropped it. Fortunately, with typical African ingenuity, the mechanic at the park office effected the necessary repairs. Herds on the move will be audible but it is not uncommon to come across a small group unexpectedly and the cautionary signs must be taken seriously.

In recent times rumours have spread that most of Kasungu's wildlife has disappeared, lost to poachers from across the Zambian border, to local people keen to find an easy source of meat or simply relocated to other parks. The thickness of the woodland does suggest that the elephant population has diminished but, although numbers are few, there is still a sufficient variety of animals to make game viewing attractive.

Hippo, **elephant**, **lion**, a large herd of **buffalo**, **zebra**, **oribi**, **puku**, **impala**, **common duiker**, **hartebeest**, **warthog** and **bush hare** — might all be seen over a two-day visit — it's an impressive list and gives lie to the rumour. Also reported have been **jackal**, **hyena** and **sable antelope** but **leopard** and **wild dog** are rarely seen.

The best viewing is where woodland borders open grassland but seeing hippo is guaranteed at the lodge or camp. Their home is the lake alongside Lifupa. At night they often cross the lake to wander round rondavels so the snorting you hear may not just be from the visitor in the next lodge. If viewing the hippo on a walking safari it is essential to keep quiet and out of sight. Easily disturbed they will step into the water from their sand beach and only their eyes and ears will be visible.

Records at Kasungu state that over 350 species of birds have been sighted in the park. The woodland is home to most but they are not easily seen. The best viewing is reputed to be at the dam at the end of the lake outside the lodge.

Some of the park's specialities, which are quite common, include the **Coqui francolin** and **Anchieta's (red and blue) sunbird** in the woodland areas and the **Egyptian goose** and **yellow-billed duck** near water. Of the less common birds which may be seen there are **black storks**, **wattled cranes** and **miombo pied barbets**. Down by the dam **herons**, **saddlebilled storks** and even **osprey** come to drink. In the open grasslands, as at the dam, it is best to find a simple natural hide and exercise a little patience.

The woodland areas are not so easy for birdwatching. A trek through the trees will usually disturb the birds which will then take flight. A good pair of binoculars is essential equipment.

The most unwelcome wildlife which might be experienced in Lifupa are the tsetse fly. Although eradication programmes, previously funded by the EU, are still being carried through with some success, the flies are still a problem. Traps are scattered through the bush. Before the eradication programme started, it was quite common that, driving in the park, you would find, that the back screen of the car was completely obscured by the flies. Now they are far less of a menance. Their vast numbers, in the past made cattle farming impossible and led to the setting up of the park as a forest reserve.

Kasungu National Park also has some **sites of historical interest** but to find them it will certainly be best to have a guide. The most accessible are the cave paintings and an iron kiln sited near the Zambian border north-west of Lifupa. North-east of the lodge close to the eastern limit of the park is a fortified wall, believed to be part of an ancient enclosed village. It is hoped that these sites will be made more accessible in the future.

Practical matters

Driving round Kasungu without a scout is possible although the tracks are not always clear and there will be places where only four-wheel drive makes sense. The new main road makes it especially difficult to drive off on to the tracks. It is probably best to ask for a guide at the lodge and one can usually be arranged at relatively short notice. There is a rangers' camp near the lodge.

If driving without a guide it might be best to enquire at the lodge, to ask about conditions and to let them know your route. The Ministry of Tourism, Parks and Wildlife has a simple but clear map of the drivable tracks. Nothing beats a walking safari and for this, one should hire the services of a game scout. The management of Lifupa Lodge will arrange fully conducted game drives and walking safaris at a modest cost for each drive or walk.

Because of changes in management of the park and some loss of game through relocations to Liwonde National Park, it is as well to check the current situation before making a visit to this park.

Right: Many of Malawi's rivers are reduced to a trickle in the dry season. Cattle and people share what's left.

Kamuzu Academy

The site of the Academy is **Mtunthama** which is a thriving community of some 8-10,000 almost totally dependent upon the school. It has a bank, as well as shops, a market and petrol, and there is a national monument area near the entrance to the Academy. Mtunthama, means "place on the hill" and it was there that Hastings Kamuzu Banda, the country's first President, received his elementary education from Scottish missionaries — under a *kachere* wild-fig tree — or so it is said. The tree as well as a hut and a drum tree are still there, in the national monument area, but education today is in the magnificence of the Kamuzu Academy.

The Academy was the brainchild of Dr Banda. The idea of a school to rival the best in Europe was his and most of the enormous cost of the project was met from his resources. The foundation stones were laid in 1977 and four years later, on 21 November, the Academy was opened by its founder.

The school was intended to provide an education for the most gifted young Malawians (regardless of means) along the lines of the English public school. Even today it is often referred to as the "Eton of Africa". Typically, in the context of Malawian culture, the school has always catered for girls as well as boys.

The aim, to produce well educated Malawians who could go on to university in Europe or America and return to the country as its leaders in the professions, in the public services and in commerce, has been achieved, or partially so. There is a leakage to posts abroad but this can only be expected until Malawi has sufficient high-level jobs to offer.

The Academy has had its critics. It has been condemned for being elitist, for including the Classics in its curriculum, for being too selective and for being political in its selection. On the other hand, there is emerging evidence that the contributions of its alumni are beginning to have a very positive effect on the country's development into the 21st century.

Getting there
From

Lilongwe:	167km/104miles	M7, M18
Lilongwe:	145km/90miles	M1, M18

Mzuzu:	264km/164miles	M1, M18
Nkhotakota:	108km/67miles	M18
Kasungu:	24km/15miles	M18

Kasungu		Bua River		Nkhotakota Wildlife Reserve and M7		Nkhotakota
	To Kamuzu Academy		Malomo		Nkhotakota Wildlife Reserve	
21km	16km	12km	18km	47km		12km

Kasungu to Nkhotakota: M18: 126km

The road to the Academy is the M18 whether you approach from the west or the east. In fact, the road begins at the Zambian border at **Mchinji** and cuts north-east to join the M1 just south of **Kasungu** town. This part of the M18 is relatively new and is of a good standard. It briefly becomes the M1/M18 21 kilometres (13 miles) south of Kasungu.

Most visitors' starting point for a call at the Academy will be Kasungu town and the surface of the M18 is excellent along this section. A couple of poorly signposted T-junctions lead the M18 out of the town. The early part of the route is through an area

Above: Famous as the *Eton of Africa*, the Kamuzu Academy is a notable achievement.

worked by smallholder tobacco farmers whose subsistence crop is the ubiquitous maize. Here and there, coffee rivals tobacco as the most important cash crop. There are one or two villages along this part of the M18 and in many ways it resembles the path of the S114 to Kasungu National Park.

After 21 kilometres (13 miles) from Kasungu town, there is a turning left to Mtunthama village and the Academy.

If approaching the Academy from the east, the starting point will probably be **Nkhotakota village** on the Lake. This time the journey will be very different because the eastern section of the M18 is still really very poor. A four-wheel drive vehicle will be necessary and even then some short stretches will seem almost unmotorable. It is that part of the road nearest Nkhotakota which is the most difficult, as the path climbs up from the Lake. Some of the inclines have all the appearance of dried-up waterfalls. Work has started on the eastern section of the road. Eventually the whole of the M18, from Kasungu to Nkhotakota will be of a high standard.

The road leads through the **Nkhotakota Wildlife Reserve** and provides an opportunity to experience this wilderness and possibly see some game. After 59 kilometres (37 miles), the M18 is joined by the M7, the road between Lilongwe and Nkhotakota Wildlife Reserve via Ntchisi. Much of the route along the M18 is thinly populated but after a sharp turn to the right at about 77 kilometres (48 miles), the small village of **Malamo** is reached. Although small, this is a service village for the area with a post office and a roadside market. Twelve kilometres (seven miles) later, a large bridge carries the road over the important **River Bua** and gradually the small farms increase in number and frequency until the turn-off to the Academy is reached on the right. It is signposted to the PTC in Mtunthama but actually leads to a roundabout where the village lies to the right and the Academy to the left. After about 100 metres there is a sign to the famous *kachere* tree. The Academy is about a one kilometre further on.

When to go

To see the Academy as a working institution it is necessary to go in term time. However, it is essential to check with the authorities if you wish to be shown around the school.

Where to stay

It is possible to stay at the Academy by prior arrangement with the Bursar. Alternatively, a day's visit from Lilongwe is possible and, of course, the Kasungu Inn is only just down the road.

Sightseeing

Before going on to the school, most visitors stop to look at the national monuments: the *kachere* tree and the drum tree. It all started here, where Dr Banda is said to have received his early education. A drum, used to call the children to their lessons, was hung from a tree, today's 'drum tree'. Legend has it that Dr Banda learnt his alphabet under the *kachere* tree and moved on to 'Standard One' in a nearby hut. The original wattle and daub hut is gone but a new structure has been built. It has to be said that sceptics cast doubt on the whole story, as on so much concerning Dr Banda's earliest days. Certainly the trees don't seem to provide the shade that the story claims.

The Academy is like nothing else in Malawi. Some would say it has no parallel in all Africa. In appearance it could easily be mistaken for an English public school or an expensive American college. The magnificent buildings and grounds are in a park-like setting with a lake fringing the main block which itself is dominated by a clock tower. Boarding houses and a chapel are set in the surrounding gardens. The facilities for sports and games are quite outstanding. Games pitches are immaculately maintained and there are squash courts and a large swimming pool. There is even a 9-hole golf course. It is clear that little expense was spared in the building and equipping of the Academy. It should be possible to view the interior as well as to wander through the grounds.

With the fall from power of Dr Banda, the Academy's future looked uncertain. The generous funding was cut back, fees increased and there was even talk of closure. Fortunately the most pessimistic predictions have proved ill-founded and the school flourishes. Malawi's President, Dr Muluzi, has written encouragingly about the Academy.

Changes have occurred in the past few years. What was once a totally ex-patriate staff has now been augmented by well qualified Malawians and is now truly international. There is also a developing international flavour to the pupil numbers. The first young English student arrived to study an Advanced Level course in 1995 and then an American girl joined the school for a period. The Academy has between twelve and fifteen non-Malawian students, mostly from Africa. It aims to become something of an international institution.

There was a fall in the number of pupils when fees were raised after the 1994 change in government but the present complement of over 360 students is an encouraging recovery. There are more girls than boys on roll. About 25 per cent of students are on generous scholarships. The aim is to attract more scholarship funding because the Academy is dependent upon fees and monies raised by some modest economic activities such as the sale of farm produce and the hosting of conferences. Meanwhile the children of the country's better-off, including those of government ministers, pay fees (currently about US$2000 per term) which are modest by European standards but prohibitive for all but rich Malawian families. Pupils take United Kingdom examinations and many go to university. Along with Latin and Greek there are courses in computing, technology and science.

It may seem just a little odd to include a school visit on one's itinerary but this is no ordinary school. It is an experiment in development and no-one who visits the Academy can fail to be impressed.

Nkhotakota Wildlife Reserve

The reserve is the oldest and largest in Malawi. It is also one of the least developed. A total of some 1802 square kilometres (695 square miles) of rugged terrain stretches along the edge of the Great Rift Valley and it is the scenery which is the reserve's particular attraction. Some of Malawi's most important rivers flow through this wilderness on their ways to Lake Malawi. There are countless streams and waterfalls which cascade from the steep edge of the escarpment.

There is little truly open ground. Most of the reserve is *Brachystegia* woodland with patches of tall grass and occasional areas of rainforest and evergreen. This woodland is particularly characteristic of the wetter parts of the plateau. It consists of a great variety of trees which are deciduous but which don't shed their leaves until the new foliage is about to burst forth in a colourful display.

It is the attraction of the wilderness as well as the wildlife that lures visitors to the reserve. A walking trip through the woodland can take one back to the days of David Livingstone: nothing has changed.

Getting there
From

Lilongwe:	114km/71miles	M1, M7
Lilongwe:	188km/117 miles	M1, M18
Salima:	123km/76miles	M5, M18
Kasungu:	67km/42miles	M18
Nkhotakota:	12km/7miles	M18
Mzuzu:	307km/191miles	M1, M18

Looking at a map one would probably conclude that Nkhotakota Wildlife Reserve could be reached very easily along the M18. Unfortunately, that road is very poor as it approaches the reserve from the west or the east and also on its way through the reserve. It is planned that the road shall be reconstructed but, until it is, it is worth considering

alternatives. Anyone wishing to explore the reserve is best advised to use the services of one of the lodges which are along the lakeshore east of the reserve. A safari into the reserve can easily be arranged. For details of these lodges, see the Lake Malawi section of the book

With a good four-wheel drive and determination the M18 route can be used but a more interesting drive from Lilongwe is on the M7. If the **Chipata** campsite is the target

then the problems are reduced if using the M18 from the west or if using the M7. The reason is that, for Chipata, the worst of the M18, nearest to the lake is avoided. The M18 is described as the route to Kamuzu Academy.

Lilongwe		M16 to Dowa		Ntchisi		M18
	Join M7		To Ntchisi Forest Reserve		Nkhotakota Wildlife Reserve	
28km		13km	27km		15km	31km	4km

Lilongwe to Nkhotakota WR: M1, M7: 118km

If travelling from Lilongwe, the shortest route by way of the M7 is perhaps the most interesting. It is also a good drive to test both the car's suspension and the driver's nerve. The road is sandy and corrugated with a pot-holed section of tar in **Ntchisi** town. However, it's worth noting that parts may not be drivable in the wet season without four-wheel drive.

To reach the M7 from Lilongwe, the route is first along the M1 northwards. The M7 is a

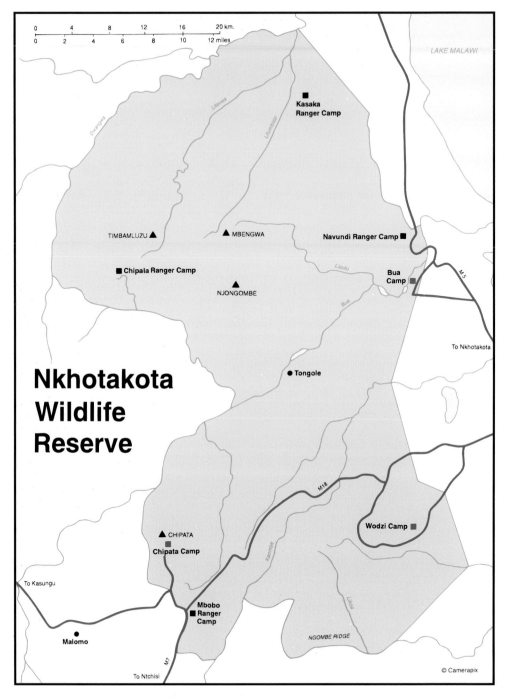

Map labels:

20 km.
12 miles

LAKE MALAWI

Kasaka Ranger Camp

TIMBAMLUZU ▲   ▲ MBENGWA   Navundi Ranger Camp ■

■ Chipala Ranger Camp   Bua Camp ■

▲ NJONGOMBE

M.5

To Nkhotakota

Nkhotakota Wildlife Reserve

● Tongole

M18

Wodzi Camp ■

▲ CHIPATA
■ Chipata Camp

To Kasungu

■ Mbobo Ranger Camp

● Malomo

NGOMBE RIDGE

M7

To Ntchisi

© Camerapix

right turn off the tar about 28 kilometres (17 miles) out of the capital, having passed the airport link road. After a further 13 kilometres (8 miles) there is a right fork on to the M16 towards **Dowa**, an important township on a ridge rising to 1690 metres (5570 feet). The high altitude gives a pleasant cool climate and this, together with well-watered fertile soil, has attracted a high density of population. Beyond Dowa the M16 links with the M14.

Staying with the M7 it is a gentle climb up to Ntchisi. There are some good views but the

114

wooded areas are patchy with little feeling that one is driving through forest. However, about 40 kilometres (25 miles) after leaving the M1, just beyond a small village, where the tree cover thickens, a turning right leads to a resthouse in the extensive **Ntchisi Forest Reserve** where there are views to Lake Malawi. The turning is difficult to identify, especially if coming from the south. Look for a radio mast on a hill just to the north of the turn.

The resthouse, now called the **Ntchisi Forest Lodge**, was built in the 1920s by the District Commissioner for Nkhotakota. The lodge's setting is very beautiful, in one of only two remaining montane forests in the country. The forest is cut through by small streams and punctuated by moss covered boulders. The floor of the forest is decorated by a profusion of wild flowers in the warmer months (September to January) and Himalayan raspberries are there for the picking during October and November.

The accommodation is in four rooms plus a sitting room and a kitchen. This is a self catering lodge but, as usual, a cook is on hand to do the work. Bookings can be made through **Makomo Safaris**.

Ntchisi is 55 kilometres (34 miles) from the M1/M7 turn. Despite its isolated position it is an important centre for the collection of the tobacco crop and provides most services including petrol, shops, a bank agency and, at the northern end, a post office.

Leaving Ntchisi, the descent is mostly along a ridge down to the valley of the **River Kaombe** to the Nkhotakota Wildlife Reserve and the junction with the M18. Just four kilometres before reaching the junction with the M18, the road enters the Nkhotakota Wildlife Reserve. If you don't see the signposts, monkeys and baboons are likely to signal your arrival. To the right of the road is the **Mbobo** rangers' camp. At the T-junction, a turn to the left leads to Kasungu while to the right is to continue through the reserve and on to Nkhotakota.

When to go

Apart from the rainy season, a visit to the reserve could be at any time in the year. However, if walking or climbing, the high temperatures of October to late November, before the rains break, should be avoided.

Where to stay

There are only the most simple of camps in Nkhotakota. Visitors are expected to bring all they need, from bedding and tents to food and drink. Water and firewood are made available but it is necessary to boil water used for cooking and drinking. At the present time it has to be admitted that the reserve is not easy to use by the average traveller.

There is talk of a new camp funded by a Japanese consortium. If this goes ahead, it could transform Nkhotakota.

The most accessible and best of the campsites is **Chipata**. There is a simple rondavel but it is better to take a tent. The camp is signposted off the M18 just west of the junction with the M7. If coming via Ntchisi, turn left at the M18 junction. Both Mount Chipata and the Bua River are accessible from the camp.

Bua and **Wodzi** camps are even less well equipped than Chipata and are not recommended. Bua, in a pleasant riverside clearing, is reached by taking the 533 road from the Lakeshore Road (M5) turning off at Mphonde, 12 kilometres (7 miles) north of Nkhotakota village. There's a nearby scout camp and the site has the potential to be developed. The Wodzi Camp is in the southeast of the park and reached by a signposted track leading off the M18 a little way into the reserve coming from Nkhotakota village.

Attractive alternatives to staying in the reserve itself are lodges on the lakeshore such as the **Ngala Beach Lodge**, **Sani Beach Resort** or **Njobvu Safari Lodge**. All will usually take guests into the reserve. It is also possible to stay at the **Kasasa Club** at the Dwangwa Sugar Estate. These alternative accommodation options are described in the section on Lake Malawi.

Sightseeing

Just how much game inhabits Nkhotakota is difficult to say. There are no roads through the reserve, apart from the M18, and the absence of open ground compounds the problem of game viewing. Even the Ministry of Tourism, Parks and Wildlife admits that this is not a reserve for those intent on seeing large numbers of animals on a single short visit, though they may well be there. Certainly there are large numbers of **elephants**, various species of **antelope**,

Above: The Bua river flows through Nkhotakota Wildlife Reserve. Opposite: The M14 winds its way from Lilongwe to Salima

including **sable**, **eland** and **bushbuck**, as well as **buffalo** and both **lion** and **leopard**. There have been stories of lions attacking mopeds on the road through the reserve, apparently upset by the humming noise of the engines. Smaller mammals such as the **warthog** are common but, because of their size, even less frequently seen. A good guide is essential if one is to see game in this vast area. There is much to see in Nkhotakota but its very wilderness makes trekking and finding game difficult. If luck comes your way there may be sightings of a very wide variety of mammals which could include **kudu**, **hippos** and **Lichtenstein's hartebeest**. **Crocodiles** inhabit the rivers.

Wildlife that can be most readily seen are the birds. The **giant kingfisher** and the **palm nut vulture** are among the 130 recorded species. Two of the **bulbuls**, the yellow-streaked and the **grey-olive** are not found in other Malawi national parks and reserves. The **wood owl**, **freckled nightjar** and **stone-chat** are common sightings.

There is also a reasonable certainty of fish life in the larger rivers, especially the two most important, the **Bua** and the **Dwangwa**. Most notably the Bua is renowned for its *mpasa* or **lake salmon**. In even greater abundance is the smaller *sanjika*, found in many streams.

To get awesome views of the reserve and across to Lake Malawi, **Chipata Mountain** makes a not too difficult climb. The summit is 1638 metres (5374 feet) and the peak is accessible by a path leading up from the main camp of the same name.

It has to be said that the principle attraction of the reserve is the beauty of its vast unspoilt wilderness. Along the banks of the Bua one is following the same path as the slaves of the nineteenth century. The scene is little changed.

Practical matters and activities

A visit to this reserve, which is to be anything more than a drive through on the M18, should be planned well in advance. It is important to have an armed scout as a guide if for no other reason than that a safari in Nkhotakota is going to be on foot, not in a vehicle — there are no roads which can be driven by visitors. A trek will be the ideal way to combine bird

watching with a spot of angling. If staying at one of the nearby lakeshore lodges, it will usually be possible for arrangements to visit the reserve to be made by the lodge owner. This is by far the best way to see this very wild place.

If **fishing** is to be done you will need the equipment and a licence from the Ministry of Tourism, Parks and Wildlife. The season for the enthusiastic angler in search of the *mpasa* is April to June.

Going to the Lake

Lilongwe to Senga Bay:
        119km/74miles   M1, M14, S122

Lilongwe to Senga Bay: M1, M14, S122: 119km

There can be very few visitors to Malawi who don't manage at least one short excursion to the county's famous lake. For those staying in the capital, Lilongwe, it is only a short drive taking less than two hours. The route is along the M14 which was realigned and rebuilt only a decade ago. The road surface is as good as any in the country as far as Salima but it is one of the most trafficked routes in central Malawi. Salima is under an hour and a half's drive from Lilongwe on this route and the lake is about 21 kilometres (13 miles) further on.

An east-west railway line, not seen from the M14, follows a similar path to the road. Malawi's rail network was substantially increased after independence and this line was opened as late as February 1979.

To reach the M14 from Lilongwe, take the M1 eight kilometres (five miles) north out of the Old Town and turn right at the signpost just after the railway crossing. This takes you past Lilongwe's industrial area which includes a massive fertilizer factory and Africa's second largest tobacco auction floor at **Kanengo**. Some 22 kilometres (14 miles) from Lilongwe is the new studio of a **wildlife artist**. The small building to the left of the road is clearly marked. Pencil sketches and paintings are offered for sale.

Because the road has been realigned, especially in the case of the section near Lilongwe, there are quite long stretches which run through open rolling countryside with very little settlement. What would seem to have been a more obvious route, at least on a map, namely the valley of the River Lilongwe, is ignored and higher ground preferred. This allows for impressive views as the road rises to the crests of its many undulations. In the early morning the sun rises directly ahead making photography interesting but difficult.

Here and there, where the new road runs on the path of the old, there are loose agglomerations of mud huts which are the nearest thing to a small Malawian village. Generally speaking, no one will mind a visitor stopping to have a look round provided there is no invasion of their privacy. A few words and some little gift for the children and a welcome is assured. One or two larger villages are encountered, for example, **Chezi**, 39 kilometres (24 miles) from the M1 turning. The road falls gently towards Salima along a winding path through rolling hills. Here and there, wicker furniture is for sale by the roadside.

On the outskirts of Salima the M14 reaches a staggered junction with the north-south Lakeshore Road, the M5. After 89 kilometres (55 miles) is the turning left to the M5-north. In another 6 kilometres (4 miles) a right hand turn takes the M5-south. At this point the road east becomes the S122 and runs through the centre of **Salima** and on to the lake at **Senga Bay**. Both these places are fully described in the Lake Malawi section of the book.

Going West

Lilongwe to Dzalanyama Forest:
        50km/31miles   S124
Lilongwe to Zambian Border:
        119km/74miles   M1, M12

Lilongwe is not far from either the Zambia or Mozambique borders. Mozambique is to the south-west of the capital city while Zambia is due west. It is possible to cross into Zambia but, going south-west from Lilongwe, the barrier of the **Dzalanyama Mountains** bars the way. Instead of the border itself, the attraction is the great and beautiful **Dzalanyama Forest Reserve**.

Lilongwe		Dzalanyama Forest Reserve		Dzalanyama Forest Lodge
	30km		20km	

Lilongwe to Dzalanyama Forest Lodge: S124: 50km

The forest is a protected area to safeguard the water catchment of Lilongwe. To reach the forest gates is to take Sir Glynn Jones road in Old Town Lilongwe and continue along what becomes the S124. To get into the reserve proper, the distance is about 30 kilometres (19 miles).

The extensive highlands are mostly *Brachystegia* woodland. There are also significant areas of evergreen forest and all are cut by rivers (including the **River Lilongwe**) and their tributary streams. Here and there are dambos. Today there is little game although, in the past, the woodlands teemed with large and small mammals — hence the name, **Dzalanyama**, which means "place of meat". Unfortunately the local people and hunters took this to be an invitation. Now there are still some **antelopes**, **monkeys** and **baboons** but the **warthogs**, **leopards** and **hyenas**, which used to be common, are rarely seen.

The forest remains a great place for exploring, trekking, and mountain biking. The birdlife is very good. Look out for a couple of rare species, the **olive-headed weaver** and **Stierling's woodpecker**. The variety of flora is interesting and includes some wonderful ferns.

It is possible to stay in the reserve at the **Dzalanyama Forest Lodge** which is sign-posted and a further 20 kilometres (12 miles) inside the forest gates. The track is rough and it is best to leave about an hour and a half to drive from Lilongwe to the lodge. This former resthouse has been privatised and is now in the hands of **Land and Lake Safaris**. The lodge, which has four double rooms, is self-catering but a cook can be provided. It is a splendid place to stay to soak up the delights of the reserve. Bicycles can be hired and there are natural pools and streams for a quick, cooling dip.

Above: Dried mice for sale. Not to everyone's taste. Following pages: Nkhotakota Wildlife Reserve, a true wilderness unaffected by man. David Livingstone would recognise scenes like this.

To go to the Zambian border makes an interesting day trip out of Lilongwe, with the possibility of crossing into that country if your papers are in order. It is not uncommon for travellers to drive to the Zambian capital using this route rather than to fly. The distance to Lusaka from Lilongwe is 695 kilometres (432 miles) and, in view of the state of the roads on the Zambian side of the border, it constitutes a long day's drive. This route is also the way to **Mfuwe** and Zambia's **South Luangwa National Park**, one of southern Africa's best game reserves. Many tour operators and safari companies offer a stay in South Luangwa as an add-on to a holiday in Malawi.

The road to the border is the M12 and its quality makes for generally easy driving in all seasons. The junction with the M1 is just north of Lilongwe Old Town past the sports stadium which lies back from the road on the left. Coming from Capital City, use Presidential Way, turn left at the round-about on the M1 and take the first major turning right on to the M12.

The route is quite well settled and there is plenty to see of the life of the farming

Lilongwe			Zambian Border
		Mchinji	
	109km		10km

Lilongwe to Zambian Border: M1, M12: 119km

119

communities along the way. It affords an opportunity to appreciate the scale and importance of small agricultural industries: millers, sugar cane processors, timber merchants. Queues of smallholders line up with their sacks of grain or bundles of cane for the middle-man to take his share of the meagre profits. Many of the little street-villages have small shops and all have bottle stores.

Along this route you may come across boys selling dried mice carefully arranged on sticks. If you cannot believe what you are seeing, stop. The boys will run up eager for a sale and you may well feel rather less hungry for the next meal. Some Malawians consider them a delicacy. The whole mouse, unskinned, is prepared by boiling in salt water followed by drying.

As with other near-border roads, there may be police road-blocks. Usually, little interest is paid except to goods-carrying vehicles but it is important to stop, to be carrying a passport (and visa if needed) and not to take photographs. If you cross the border into Zambia a yellow fever vaccination certificate might also be asked for when you return to Malawi.

Just before the border is the important little market centre of **Mchinji** with a good range of services. To the north the **Mchinji Hills** rise to 1750 metres (5740 feet). A large forest reserve cloaks the highlands. For a walk along the ridge, turn right on to the **Mkanda** road (just before the market). This is the S20. After crossing the railway continue until the ridge is reached. Parking is possible here and a track leads up to the radio tower where there are magnificent views across the plateau in Malawi and to the mountains in Zambia.

Although the M12 might be considered to offer little of special interest, the insight it gives into daily life in the countryside and the fact that the road is very good, make it attractive as a drive out from Lilongwe.

It should be noted that there is now a new good tar road from Mchinji to the north-east, meeting the M1 21 kilometres (13 miles) south of **Kasungu** town. It forms part of the new cross-country route linking Zambia to Lake Malawi. The turning for this road is to the right in the village of **Mgawa**, a little before reaching Mchinji.

Dedza

Dedza township lies south of **Dedza Mountain** (2170 metres/7120 feet) on the Central African Plateau which fringes the Great Rift Valley. The settlement's elevation is over 1600 metres (5250 feet) and to the east the plateau drops steeply to Lake Malawi. Although off the modern M1, its site is actually on the former road to Lilongwe.

Dedza is an important centre for a well-farmed and long-settled district. Perhaps because of its attractive moist and cool climate various groups have made the area their home over the centuries. There is a history of conflict as new migrants attempted to oust established tribes. Even in the early twentieth century, problems arose when families from over the nearby border with Mozambique would cross into Dedza in an interesting move for tax evasion.

Getting there

From Lilongwe:	84km/52miles	M1
From Blantyre:	227km/141miles	M1
From M1/M8 Junction:	112km/70miles	M1

Lilongwe			Nathanje		To Nkhoma and Chilenje				Dedza
	To Bunda		To Ngala				To Chongoni		
	10km	4km	9km	12km		41km		8km	

Lilongwe to Dedza: M1: 84km

Dedza township can be reached by the M1 south out of Lilongwe. It can be visited either as a day trip out of a Lilongwe base or en route to Blantyre. The route has some interesting features along it as well as being part of the link between the official capital, Lilongwe, and what remains the commercial capital, Blantyre. The whole journey is on tarred surfaces and driving is without problems even in the wet season. With remarkably little traffic using the road, a good steady driving speed is possible.

The M1 leaves Lilongwe on its way south through the Old Town and soon rises by a gentle gradient on to a higher part of the plateau. The views are excellent: rolling hills, rugged ridges and the occasional inselberg to act like a marker along the path.

Some of these inselbergs offer interesting excursions off the M1 and can either be

Above: The famous Dedza pottery is just off the M1 road south of Lilongwe.

tackled as day trips from Lilongwe or as side-trips on a journey south.

Only a short distance from Lilongwe is **Bunda Mountain**. If you are up to a moderately strenuous walk up a steep gradient path there are very good views to be had across the plateau towards Lake Malawi. To reach the mountain — it is actually one of the countless inselbergs which litter the plateau — look for **Bunda College** signposted to the right of the M1 just 10 kilometres (6 miles) from Lilongwe. Turn here. Now off the tarred road a drivable track leads to **Mitundu School** after about 16 kilometres (10 miles). At the school the turning is left to the college. The route continues past the college and in half a kilometre a turning to the left goes towards the mountain. It is best to continue driving round the inselberg to the far side where there are some houses. Leaving the vehicle, the route to the top is a steep but easy-to-see path.

This trip should be possible even for the average car as long as it is not attempted in the wet season, roughly November to Easter. It can also prove a tiring climb in the hottest weather which comes just before the rains.

Other uplands which, time permitting, are worth a short detour off the M1 are the Nathenje Hills and Ngala, Nkhoma, Chilenje and Chongoni mountains. All provide interesting walks and good views but excursions to most of them mean leaving the tarred M1 for short distances of dirt road.

Fourteen kilometres (a little under nine miles) out of Lilongwe and just before Nathenje village are outcrops of rocks collectively known as the **Nathenje Hills**. The outcrops continue southwards to just beyond the village. There's no need to turn off the road; the interesting rocks and their vegetation, various succulents, can easily be seen. It is worth stopping here and exploring a little.

Driving on south, the turn-off for **Ngala** is reached after about 23 kilometres (14 miles) from Lilongwe. By following the sign to the right of the M1 to **Nathenje** and continuing for another seven kilometres (four miles) the foot of the mountain is reached with paths to the summit.

Nkhoma and **Chilenje** mountains are to the left of the M1 another 12 kilometres (7 miles) beyond the Ngala turn-off. Look out

Above: Women return to their village with water and washing after a visit to the well.

for a sign to a Mission Station. The untarred road is not very good but the views from the tops of these mountains can be excellent. **Chilenje Ridge** makes for pleasant walking but is more distant from the main road. If attempting these excursions it is always helpful to ask local people to point out the best paths to follow.

Two access tracks lead from the M1 to **Chongoni** but the better is the one furthest south. About 76 kilometres (47 miles) out of Lilongwe, to the left, is a sign to a **Forestry College**. Taking this dirt road to the college (six kilometres/four miles) and then turning left, after three kilometres (two miles), will bring one to signs pointing to the **Chencherere** rock shelters, dating from neolithic times. They contain geometric paintings, the work of the **Batwa** people who hunted the then abundant wildlife on the cool slopes of the plateau. There is a wonderful sense of history to be felt standing in the homes of the hunters and food gatherers who inhabited the area two or three thousand years ago.

Most of the route between Lilongwe and Dedza is still settled today. Small villages and groups of farms are scattered across the open plateau below the ridges and hills. Cattle, often with young boy cowherds riding the cows, graze with little restriction. Maize is grown and small vegetable plots fringe some of the watercourses or nestle around the farms. Processions of women and children bring massive head-loads of firewood to the huts and, here and there, stacks of wood are laid out for sale at the side of the road.

The landscape is largely open, cultivated or grassland, trees are few and there is little escape from the sun along the M1. Flat-topped acacias may provide some shelter away from the road but their shade will probably already be occupied by two or three men in earnest conversation or simply resting.

Despite the relatively large number of farms, not a lot of activity is evident. Where water can be gained from shallow wells, knots of women collect their daily supply in heavy metal drums. Clay, put into wooden moulds, is made into bricks for their huts and left to dry in the sun. But mostly the plateau is a silent and open place and not even the cries of children are to be heard — unless you stop. Then, from nowhere, five, ten, twenty bare-footed children will come running to see what you might have for them, or simply to stand and stare.

Some 84 kilometres (52 miles) out of Lilongwe the Dedza turn-off is reached. The town lies off the M1 but is well sign-posted to the left of the main road.

To reach Dedza from the south, perhaps from Blantyre, see the description "Going North" in the South Malawi section. If coming to Dedza from this direction, the entrance to the town is to the right but there is more than one road. Wait until seeing the Dedza Pottery sign (on tiles) before turning off the M1 to the right.

When to go

If visiting the Dedza Pottery, its hours of opening are between 07.00 and 17.30 every day of the week. If climbing Dedza Mountain, then it may be best to avoid the worst of the wet season (December-March) although the orchids and wild flowers are at their most beautiful as the rains start. For the best views one should avoid July to September when smoke from the bush fires is a real problem.

Where to stay

There is a range of budget accommodation and the former government **resthouse** is to be up-graded but most visitors to the town will be en route between Lilongwe and Blantyre and the former is a good base for a day trip to Dedza. There had been talk of opening a forest lodge on the mountain but this seems unlikely at the present time.

Sightseeing

The main road through the town has some traffic calming humps and eventually curves back to rejoin the M1. When Malawi's main north-south road was built it bypassed Dedza. The town had been on the major road but now enjoys a more sheltered existence.

Dedza lies at 1600 metres (5300 feet) and is the highest town in the country. Its main road passses through fringes of forest which stretch up towards the mountains some 600 metres (2000 feet) higher. Wood is much in evidence, not least in its use as a building material.

Dedza offers the usual basic services, including petrol, but it is little more than a village so expectations should not be high.

There is a substantial **hospital** and **market stalls** line much of the road. The simple airstrip rarely sees an aircraft and the nine-hole **golf course** is in a sorry state although attempts have been made to restore it to a playable condition.

It is possible to journey up the **Dedza Mountain** in the forest reserve north of the township but the track is poor and driving difficult even in the dry season. The adventurous should make enquiries at the petrol station if attempting this drive. It should be possible to drive up to the radio mast and then walk the rest of the way to the summit. Given a bright day the effort is worth it because once up on the ridge there are spectacular views to the east. In clear air it is possible to see right across Lake Malawi and into Mozambique. Although a designated forest reserve, there are also patches of grass-land which are home to countless wild flowers including, in the rainy season, **wild orchids**.

Hidden among the pine trees are caves with **Stone Age paintings** and strange markings made by the **Nyau**, a secret society associated with witchcraft (particularly prominent in the 1980s).

Many visitors take the Dedza turn-off simply to visit the township's famous pottery. To reach the **Dedza Pottery** turn off the M1 then immediately left again (sign-posted) along a straight but bumpy road. The workshops are located about one to two kilometres down the road and on the left. There are two small car parks, one for wet weather and one for dry, indicated by a sign in ceramic tiles. The brick buildings, with their smoking chimneys, are quite extensive. The main one houses both shop and craftsmen. It is possible to watch the potters at work and a tour of the workshop can usually be arranged without prior notice.

The pottery is colourful, some with hand-painted designs, but not especially imaginative or unusual. The mugs, dishes, small bells, thimbles and other items would not seem out of place in a pottery in Europe. Should you want something unusual or have a specific design in mind, this can be arranged and the finished work forwarded to you by the pottery.

If the pots don't impress, the cakes in the

garden teashop behind the workshops are well worth investigating. Tables and chairs are arranged in a neatly kept garden and this is a fine place to rest on a journey between Lilongwe and Blantyre.

Going South

Dedza to M1/M8 Junction:
112km/70miles   M1

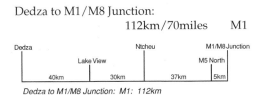

Dedza to M1/M8 Junction: M1: 112km

South from Dedza the M1 runs for almost 70 kilometres (43 miles) along the Mozambique border to Ntcheu. To the east of the road are the **Bembeke Hills**, yet more sugar-loaf inselbergs. Some of the hill slopes have cultivation terraces cut into the red lateritic soils. Further along there are street villages with shops and bottle stores as well as goods laid out on the ground at the side of the road. The left-hand side of the road is Malawi but immediately to the right is Mozambique. At the height of the civil war in Mozambique, refugees slipped across the border and were absorbed into the Malawian population. Most have now gone home but the contrast between the flourishing trade on the Malawi side of the road and the shells of abandoned shops on the Mozambique territory is clear for all to see. There are extensive views west into Mozambique. Some of the villages which can be seen have recently been re-occupied by those returning to a more peaceful land.

The traders in the villages are some of the most persistent in Malawi and to stop is to invite a rush of eager salesmen to surround your car. Most of the goods are vegetables including the area's speciality, potatoes, but one village appears to have cornered the market in cloth.

Proximity to the border means that police patrols and road-blocks may be expected but should cause the traveller only a moment's delay. It is worth noting that driving at night along this section of the M1 is not recommended. About 40 kilometres (25 miles) south of Dedza the road reaches close to the edge of the plateau, affording a view of the southern limits of Lake Malawi. Unsurprisingly this point is called **Lake View** but it may not be easy to locate especially when driving south and having to look back over one's left shoulder to see the distant stretch of water. However, an easily spotted building, on the left of the road if going south, is the **Lakeview Grocery**. There are intermittent viewpoints for about a kilometre. It is worth trying to pick out **Cape Maclear** as a marker to identify other parts of the Lake. It has to be said that haze may well obscure the view except on the clearest of days.

Ntcheu is a large village with a busy market but there is little else of interest to the traveller. The village is 154 kilometres (96 miles) from Lilongwe and, beyond the settlement, the road curves south-eastward away from the Mozambique border. There is a gentle descent towards the great Shire River, off the plateau and into the Rift Valley. The scenery is of a rolling landscape patterned by very large traditional villages. Some of these villages are built on gentle terraced slopes, others in shallow depressions or valleys. All have the appearance of the classic African village and a panorama of village life, round mud huts with conical thatched roofs. Clothes and children are washed, the next meal is prepared, new thatch is bound, dogs bark and babies cry. From the vantage point of the road, often above the level of the village, the extent and intimacy of the views are breathtaking.

After some 37 kilometres (23 miles) from Ntcheu, a major turning, left, is the modern M5 road coming from the lakeshore. About 5 kilometres (3 miles) further the M1 and the M8 join. From here the M1 turns right to head southwards to **Blantyre**, while the M8 runs eastwards to **Balaka** and **Liwonde National Park**. All three places are in South Malawi.

Opposite: A village meeting in Central Malawi.

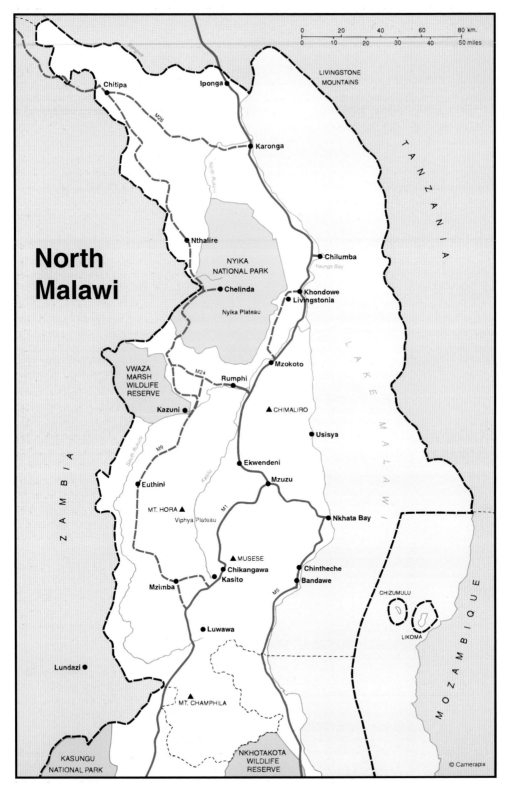

North Malawi

North Malawi

Most countries have a forgotten region. In Malawi it is the north. While the centre and the south blend into one another seamlessly and Lake Malawi has an authority and status all of its own, the north is different.

Immediately leaving central Malawi and entering the north there is a sense that this is the start of a new adventure. Gone are the gentle undulations of the central plateau, here are the **Chimaliro Hills** and the **Viphya Highlands**. True, the landscape often has a rolling character, but the scale has changed. Where altitudes of 900 to 1200 metres (3000 to 4000 feet) were commonplace in central Malawi, now much of the land is above 1500 metres (5000 feet).

North Malawi, dominated by the great Viphya Highlands, is home to the regional capital, **Mzuzu**, and the unique **Nyika Plateau**. The undulating plateau of the Viphya stands at 1500-1800 metres (5000-6000 feet) with inselbergs adding a further 300 metres (1000 feet). North-west is Nyika, the highest plateau in Central Africa, reaching skywards to an impressive 2500 metres (8000 feet). Comprising a central

granitic core, the edges of Nyika are scarp-like and in the north-east the plateau forms the wall of the Great Rift Valley. Rivers have carved deep valleys into weaker rocks and one meaning of the name *Nyika* is "where the water comes from".

Not all the north is quite so high as Viphya or Nyika. The **Mzimba Plains** which lie to the west of the Viphya Highlands and south of Nyika are at a modest 900-1350 metres (3000-4500 feet). These "plains" are drained by the **South Rukuru River** which flows through the **Njakwa Gorge**, is joined by the **Kasitu River** and eventually tumbles dramatically into Lake Malawi. It is these two rivers which separate the great plateaux of Viphya and Nyika.

Towards the border with Tanzania, at the northern extremities of this region, the **Lufira Plateau** is at a similar altitude to the Mzimba Plains but there the great **Malingu Mountain** range spills over from Zambia in the west to reach almost 2200 metres (7200 feet). Again, tucked away in the far north, are the **Misuku Hills** (2000 metres or 6500 feet).

Yes, north Malawi is a region where hills are really mountains. Only Lake Malawi offers a lowland fringe along its shore, but, quite often, steep cliffs drop almost sheer into the lake.

The generally high altitudes of the north compensate for its more equatorial position and temperatures are relatively low compared with much of the rest of the country. Rainfall is variable, from some of the highest of Malawi's figures on the mountains exposed to easterly airflows to some of the lowest in areas west of Viphya and south of Nyika.

North Malawi is the least well-populated area of the country. The terrain and relatively poor soils see to that. River valleys, especially the Kasitu and the Lower South Rukuru, attract the greatest concentrations of villages but much of the area is only thinly settled. Although there are some important forest reserves there is little beyond subsistence farming, with maize as the prime crop.

Left: *Inselbergs* ('island mountains') rise majestically, often adding a further 300 metres (1000 feet) to the high plateau.

Viphya Plateau

Viphya is a great, dissected plateau aligned parallel to the Great Rift Valley which contains Lake Malawi. The highest peaks rise to over 1800 metres (6000 feet) and inselbergs attain even greater altitudes. **Nkalapia**, for example, reaches 2121 metres (6960 feet). Perhaps the most spectacular of the 'island mountains' is **Elephant Rock**.

The mountains comprise two blocks, separated by a lower lying area, a saddle, in which stands the regional capital of **Mzuzu**. This dips some 600 metres (2000 feet) below the main plateau.

The Viphya Highlands rise relatively gently from their western margins where the great **South Rukuru River** flows in a north-easterly direction before turning towards the Lake. The eastern flank, however, is steeper and, in the north, where it meets the Lake, drops so abruptly into the waters as to

Above: The intensely wild and unspoilt Viphya is criss-crossed by small valleys.
Opposite: The Luwawa Falls, one of many water-falls which punctuate the rivers flowing off the Viphya towards Lake Malawi.

leave no space for lowlands at the shore. Indeed, there isn't even space for a continuous road along this part of the Lake's edge (despite what is shown in a well-known guide-book and on a popular tourist map of the country). The steep drop continues beyond the shore-line as the mountain mass plunges a further 700 metres (2300 feet) to the floor of the lake. This is the deepest part of the whole of Lake Malawi.

The watershed of the plateau separates the steep gradient rivers flowing eastward, directly into the Lake, from the rivers with slower and longer courses to the west. Other rivers like the **Luwawa**, cut valleys through the heart of the plateau.

The plateau receives heavy rainfalls on the eastern side but forms a rainshadow on the west where the South Rukuru Valley has some of the lowest rain figures in the country. In both cases, most of the rains occur in the short wet season.

This is a true, exciting wilderness. It is an area easily overlooked as visitors to Malawi make their way up the M1 or the M5 roads ignorant of the nearby attractions of the mountains.

Getting there
Lilongwe to Mzuzu: 360km/224miles   M1

Kasungu			To Luwawa	To Kasito		Mzuzu
	Join M1		M9 to Mzimba		Elephant Rock	
2km		124km	8km	27km	30km	49km

Kasungu to Mzuzu: M1: 240km

There is no one route into the Viphya, but the main north-south road, the M1, runs through the heart of the plateau. The winding road gradually climbs up the plateau from the south and is in a generally sound state of repair. In places, where the M1 runs close to steeply falling valley sides, there are safety barriers, a rarity in Malawi. From the road it is possible to see something of the beauty of the region but it's really necessary to explore the tracks and paths across the highlands properly to appreciate their magnificence.

To reach the accommodation at **Luwawa Forest Lodge**, take the M1 north out of Kasungu town. After 111 kilometres (69 miles) there will be the first sign to Luwawa. This should be ignored and in a further eight kilometres (5 miles), a second sign (to the

Above: Afternoon tea in the tranquil setting of Luwawa Forest Lodge.

right), marked Luwawa D73: Luwawa Forest Lodge, will be seen. This access can be used. Its eight kilometre (five mile) road is suitable for ordinary cars except in the worst of the rains. However, rather further north, is another signed entrance, by the Coca-Cola sign, and this is the one recommended by the lodge. If coming from Mzuzu, then again the M1 is the road to use and the entrance (left) is about 114 kilometres (71 miles) from Mzuzu.

Kasito Lodge is off the M1 just south of Chikangawa forestry village. Look for the sign on the left of the M1 if heading north.

When to go
Rainfalls can be quite heavy in the months of December to April. The rest of the year is pleasant with warm days and cool nights.

Where to stay
Luwawa Forest Lodge
This is another success story for privatisation. The lodge was the property of the Forestry Department and had been used to accommodate the engineers who built the north-south road, the M1. It has been transformed.

It is reached along a quite good dirt road, through forest, leading from the M1 (see above). The lodge stands on open ground in where gardens and shrubs have replaced forest and the view is to a lake. A watchtower, a short drive from the lodge, not only gives excellent views but it is a wonderful place to be to see the sun set. The sense of wilderness is ever present and the silence is broken only by birdsong. There is a sort of magic about the place. The bungalow-like buildings consist of a dining room, bar and lounge with a *khonde* (verandah) together with a detached block of four double en suite chalets. There is also hostel/dormitory accommodation and a campsite away from the main buildings.

This is a very eco-friendly place to stay. The electricity is derived from solar or wind power, the water comes from a nearby deep well and the vegetables are grown in the lodge's "permaculture-oriented garden". This is also an ideal place for family holidays. It is safe, malaria free and there are plenty of activities.

Kasito Lodge
There are two lodges at roughly the same

point on the M1 a very short distance south of Chikangawa village. If travelling from the north, the lodge to the left is called **Resthouse No.2**. Signposted and to the right, down a one kilometre path, is Kasito Lodge (formerly Resthouse No.1). It is Kasito that can be recommended.

Kasito has a total of fourteen beds in five rooms. Each room has a washbasin but there is a shared bath and shower room. There is a large lounge with an open fireplace and while short on luxury the lodge has a certain charm, as do the staff. There is a dam nearby but not visible from the lodge. However, the views are pleasant.

Food should be brought but a cook is available. This is a simple but inexpensive stop-over.

Sightseeing

To visit the Viphya is to experience the wild. The vast area of the plateau is a place to wander and to commune with nature. In the forest plantations there is a sense of peace and tranquillity as one walks through the dense, sweet-smelling pines

The birdlife is famously varied. Luwawa Forest Lodge has adopted the **lesser double collared sunbird** as its logo and there are **osprey**, **eagles**, **buzzards**, **herons** and **egrets** to be seen. **Bearded vultures** have also been reported.

Much of the Viphya Highlands' attraction is, paradoxically, because so much is uninhabited. The vast areas of primary montane forest and plantations of high standing pine, patches of *Brachystegia* woodland and riverine forest — these are home to wildlife but not to man. While the birdlife is widely spread, mammals tend to be seen more easily near the dambos and along the stream courses. **Bushbuck, duiker, monkeys** and **baboons** are common and sightings of **leopard**, **civet**, **porcupine** and **mongoose** are likely. **Hyenas** are more often heard than seen.

A drive along the M1 can itself be rewarding. There are some exceptionally fine views from the road south of Mzuzu where gaps in the hilly terrain allow panoramic vistas towards the broad plains of the **Kasitu River**. Little clusters of mud and thatch huts look like some model in a museum's display.

There is a series of granite *kopjes*, or inselbergs, to be seen from the road south of Mzuzu but the most famous is **Elephant Rock**. This massive outcrop rises to over 1800 metres (6000 feet) and is practically clear of vegetation. Its fractured crystalline surface is a landmark for miles around. The giant grey rock, with its partly domed structure, is aptly compared in appearance with the shape of a trunkless elephant. The M1 road passes close to it about 50 kilometres (30 miles) south of Mzuzu. It is to the east of the road.

Apart from Mzuzu, the only other settlement within the Viphya, which might be classed as a town, is **Mzimba** on the western slopes. This little town has lost some of the importance it enjoyed when it was on the former main north-south road. Today it remains the centre of one of the few areas where Turkish tobacco is grown. There are limited services in the town but there is a bank, a store and petrol is available. To access Mzimba is quite easy from the M1. Two routes are possible. Coming from Mzuzu and south of Chikangawa village, the M1 descends towards the valley of the Mzimba River and a road (M22) leads off to the right towards the town. However, a tarmacked and shorter road to Mzimba is the M9 which, again to the right going south, has a junction with the M1 about five kilometres (three miles) after bridging the river.

The important village of **Chikangawa** itself lies on the M1 just beyond Elephant Rock when travelling south. Near to the village is the timber works of Raiply (formerly Viply) which exploits the products of the Viphya pine forests. The warm moist climate of the Viphya Mountains is ideal for pine and rates of growth are often five to ten times those found in temperate climates. All the same, these great plantations have not been the economic success that had been hoped for. The Viphya Forest is said to be the largest plantation in Africa.

Practical matters and activities

Short treks into the forest can be done with safety especially around Luwawa Forest Lodge where there are marked trails. For longer treks, a guide from one of the lodges should be used. It is very easy to get lost if away from the marked tracks.

Above: The views towards Lake Malawi across the Viphya Plateau invite a trek to the lakeshore.
Below: One way to reach the Lake from Luwawa Forest lodge is to hire a bicycle

Most of the activities are organised by the Luwawa Forest Lodge although anyone can wander in the forests. The lodge has a supply of maps with the paths marked. Two special **wilderness trails** are available from the lodge: one walking and the other by mountain bike. Both trails lead down to Lake Malawi and to **Chinteche Inn**, a beautiful lodge on the lakeshore. The guided walk is over four days with three overnight camps. The bike ride follows a different and longer trail. Whether walking or cycling, these trails provide an unrivalled opportunity to see the fauna and flora of the Viphya. Porters and guides are provided on both trails.

Back at the Luwawa Lodge there are numerous activities from squash to angling and from abseiling and rock climbing to sailing on the lake and orienteering. There are plans to have 4x4 driving instruction and even an assault course. The owner of the lodge, George Wardlow, is an enthusiastic instructor for the Duke of Edinburgh Award. For the less active, Luwawa Forest Lodge can be a place simply to sit and enjoy the views and watch the birds. As to the future, there are plans for further developments. There's talk

Above: Giant tree trunks are hollowed to make the fishermen's traditional canoes.

of an airstrip and even a golf course but the owner is determined not to lose anything of the character of this wonderfully natural place.

Going to the Lake

Mzuzu to Nkhata Bay:
47km/29miles   M5, local road

Mzuzu   Nkhata Bay

M5 Lakeshore Road
42km   5km

Mzuzu to Nkhata Bay: M5: 47km

The easiest access to Lake Malawi from the Viphya Highlands is to take the M5 from Mzuzu to Nkhata Bay. The M5 is actually the Lakeshore Road but this stretch comes west, away from the lake, to approach Mzuzu. Although not completed until the 1950s the engineering and condition of the road are neither as new nor as good as the modern M5 south of Nkhata Bay. Potholes are common and large.

After rising out of the shallow basin which is Mzuzu's site, the road gradually makes the descent from the Viphya Mountains to the lake. Although the fall is through some 700 metres (2300 feet) there are no difficult hairpins athough there are a few steep gradients. The road twists and turns through a hilly landscape cloaked with lush vegetation. It's evident that this is a path downwards from the escarpment at the edge of the Great Rift Valley. Near Nkhata Bay there are some really steep slopes. Lake Malawi is hidden from sight and the best scenic views are to be had by looking west and to either side of the road. There are often brilliant sunsets as the disc disappears behind the Viphya Mountains.

The route is through a mix of small-scale farming and plantations of pine and rubber. Some land is intensively cultivated and well-ordered plots are devoted to the usual cash and subsistence crops. Vegetables produced here supply the needs of Mzuzu and Nkhata Bay but some of the output goes further afield. For example, the banana crop has a wide market partly because, unlike the pathetically small fruit one sees through most of Malawi, the quality and size is good. One or two crops are less common. Cassava is grown and attempts have been made at developing citrus groves. There is even a little

industry in the form of boat building. Giant tree trunks are patiently fashioned into dugout canoes so commonly seen on Lake Malawi. Unfortunately, if you stop to watch and photograph the work, tools are downed and the whole village assembles and poses for a group photograph sitting on and obscuring the canoes. Another photo stop can be the bottle store with the intriguing title of *Pub with No Name*.

After 42 kilometres (26 miles), and before reaching the village port of **Nkhata Bay**, the M5 turns right at a T-junction and becomes the Lakeshore Road. To reach Nkhata Bay, is to continue straight on for a further five kilometres (three miles) along a local road.

Nyika National Park

Nyika is at once Malawi's largest park and one of the most unusual in the whole of Africa. It extends for about 3134 square kilometres (1210 square miles). Composed essentially of granite together with other crystalline rocks, this great plateau tilts gently from 2500 metres (8000 feet) in the west down to 2100 metres (7000 feet) in the east. The dome-like massif is cut by numerous rivers with dambos and these reach Lake Malawi often by way of waterfalls off the eastern edge of the mountains. As has been said, one meaning of the name Nyika is "where the water comes from" and this is one of Malawi's most important water catchment areas. The eastern border of the plateau forms the wall of the Great Rift Valley.

Partly because of the height of the plateau, it is almost uninhabited except around its outer margins. There is little history of permanent settlement over recent centuries but in the mid-1800s local people took refuge on the plateau from the Ngoni tribes who had spread up into Malawi from the south. The fear was that the Ngoni were involved in slave trading but this was not the case although they did take into domestic slavery those who opposed them.

Since 1965, when Nyika was designated Malawi's first national park, it has been protected. In 1978 the area was expanded to take in some of the steep slopes at its rim.

The climate is greatly modified by altitude and on a cloud-free night it can be distinctly cool with the possibility of ground frosts in the dry season. It is wetter in the east than the west but the usual seasonal variations apply. The relatively low temperatures of the plateau make it largely free of tsetse fly and mosquitoes.

The scenery is reckoned to be some of the best in central Africa and to say that it is spectacularly beautiful is not to resort to hyperbole. These great domes of whaleback-like hills have gentle slopes despite their massive scale. It is as though the landscape had been sculptured by a giant. Everything around is dwarfed by the setting.

Nyika is largely montane grassland with patches of evergreen forest, chiefly to the east. Below about 1800 metres (6000 feet) savanna woodland begins to dominate. It is thought that the whole plateau was once forest that was destroyed by fire and that the grassland is a secondary cover. Be that as it may, the general absence of trees on the higher parts allows splendid views in every direction. In parts it looks like English downland — enlarged by a factor of ten. Small pockets of woodland occupy the sheltered hollows.

To visit Malawi and not see Nyika is much like visiting Egypt and neglecting the Pyramids.

Getting there
From

Mzuzu:	129km/80miles	M1, M24, M9
Lilongwe:	486km/304miles	M1, M1, M24, M9
Nkhata Bay:	174km/109miles	M5, M1, M24, M9
Karonga:	225km/141miles	M1, M24, M9
Rumphi turn off:		
	65km/40miles	M24, M9

(*Note:* Distances are to Thazima Gate. Chelinda Camp is a further 60km/37miles)

Opposite: The journey between Rumphi and Nyika is though open country without a town or major village.

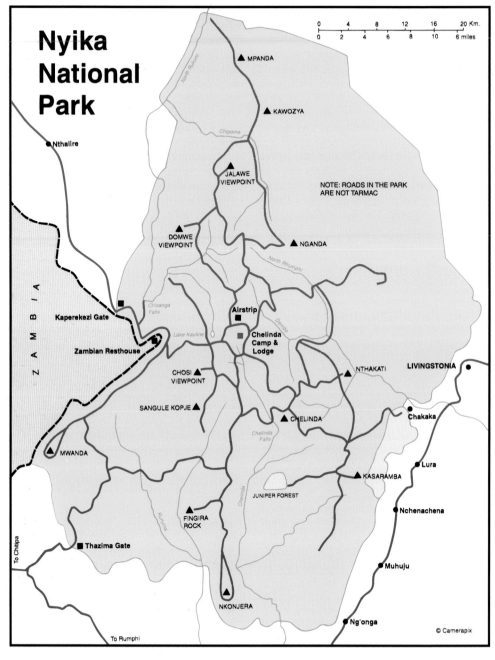

Nyika National Park

NOTE: ROADS IN THE PARK ARE NOT TARMAC

Nthalire

MPANDA

KAWOZYA

Chipome

North Rukuru

JALAWE VIEWPOINT

DOMWE VIEWPOINT

NGANDA

North Rhumphi

ZAMBIA

Chisanga Falls

Kaperekezi Gate

Airstrip

Lake Kauline

Dembo

Chelinda Camp & Lodge

Zambian Resthouse

CHOSI VIEWPOINT

NTHAKATI

LIVINGSTONIA

SANGULE KOPJE

CHELINDA

Chakaka

MWANDA

Chelinda Falls

Chelinda

Lura

KASARAMBA

JUNIPER FOREST

Nchenachena

Runyina

To Chitpa

FINGIRA ROCK

Thazima Gate

Muhuju

NKONJERA

Ng'onga

© Camerapix

To Rumphi

Mzuzu		Rumphi Turn Off	Rumphi	South Rukuru River	To Vwaza WR	Thazima Gate		Chelinda
	64km		3km	2km	10km	50km		60km

Mzuzu to Chelinda: M1, M24, M9, minor road: 189km

To reach Nyika from Mzuzu is to follow the northern section of Malawi's north-south Highway, the M1. The first part of the route leads not only to Nyika but also to the Vwaza Marsh Wildlife Reserve and to the Livingstonia Mission. The surface of this road is tarred and generally in a reasonable condition.

As the road leaves Mzuzu it passes the town's airport (right) and the university buildings (left), climbs gently and passes through the large village of Ekwendeni.

Above: Rumphi is a busy market town and bus terminal. Following pages: The rolling, whaleback hills of Nyika National Park rise to an impressive 2500 metres (8000 feet). There is nowhere else in Africa quite like it.

Thirty years or so ago, **Ekwendeni** was a bigger service centre than Mzuzu. From here the path follows the important **Kasitu River** which runs along the edge of the Vipyha Plateau. The scenery is very fine and the heavily eroded uplands make a wonderful backdrop to the river lowlands. Farming here is largely with cattle which, in places, have been allowed to overgraze the land. Elsewhere the valley is well wooded giving colour to the scene even in the dry season.

At what is known as the **Rumphi turn-off**, a left turn is taken on to the M24. The junction is a great place for local people to pick up lifts and the traders on the side of the road do good business as villagers wait patiently for a bus. The M24 strikes a direct path towards the Njakwa Hills which rise steeply from the plains. In just three kilometres (two miles) it reaches the hills and cuts through a very pretty gorge as it bridges the **South Rukuru River**. Two kilometres further on is the little town of Rumphi.

Rumphi is a market centre for the agricultural lands to the west. Its bustling activity reminds one of Old Town Lilongwe. There is a purposeful feel about the place.

No sitting around here; everyone is busily engaged: buying, selling, catching and loading buses. Rumphi is the place to re-fill the car fuel tank before setting off for Nyika or Vwaza. The petrol station at the centre of the town stays open after 18.00 for those returning from the parks.

The little town seems prosperous enough but the area has had mixed fortunes. The main cash crop is coffee and fluctuations in world prices have often seen the menfolk forced to seek work in the gold mines of South Africa. Today the large number of buses and the extensive bus station suggest that there is still reliance on nearby Mzuzu for employment as well as services.

West of Rumphi the M24 is untarred and of indifferent quality. In the dry season, any vehicle leaves a wake of dust but in the wet season the road can be quite difficult.

The next stretch of the M24 runs through well-farmed land with isolated homesteads and a few villages. There's much toing and froing between the clusters of huts and people walking on the road pay scant attention to what little traffic shares it with them. It is always best to give pedestrians a wide berth.

137

Here and there people gather at a local mill, their bags of grain forming a queue to the door of the shed while the women seek shade and gossip. The fortunate will have the use of a bullock cart but most will have to walk with heavy headloads back to their houses.

After 10 kilometres (6 miles) there is the turn, on the left, to Vwaza, the S49 road. For Nyika the route continues along the M24 to join the M9 with a turn to the right. The M9 will be found to be little more than a rough track, totally untarred but drivable by car in the dry season. Road improvements are planned but, meantime, a four-wheel drive vehicle with good ground clearance is very strongly advised because the roads in the park are particularly difficult. In the wet season four-wheel drive is essential.

As the M9 approaches the park, small farms alongside the route begin to thin only to be replaced by more woodland and forest as the path winds steadily upwards towards the Thazima Gate to the park at 1646 metres (5400 feet). The scenery is pleasant enough but does not quite compensate for the necessarily slow progress that will be made over the final part of the journ ey. If in a hurry, this may well be a frustratingly slow pace.

Entry to the park is through **Thazima Gate** which closes at 18.00 both for entrance and exit. Because driving after dark is strictly forbidden, for those staying overnight it will be better to arrive by 16.00 to allow time to drive to the camp. Accommodation should, of course, have been reserved. As with all Malawian parks and reserves, the entrance fee is a very modest US$5. The road continues by the side of the Zambian border, passing a track (left) to the Zambian Resthouse (for some time closed) shortly before turning off (signposted to the right) to Chelinda Camp. As usual, the main camp is the best starting point for exploring. The total distance from Mzuzu to Chelinda is 189 kilometres (117 miles).

The road from the gate to the camp gives only a glimpse of the glorious scenery that awaits but the rather wretched state of the tracks is a warning. Speed in the park is limited to 40 kilometres per hour (25 miles per hour) but conditions often make this seem outrageously excessive.

Flying into Nyika by small aircraft is possible and preferable. There is a one kilometre grass landing strip serving Chelinda just north of the lodge. Proflight Air Services have charter flights into Chelinda.

When to go
To see the orchids, the wet season (January to March) is the time to go. For the rest of the year, conditions for activities such as riding, trekking and cycling are ideal. For wildflowers, September and October are good months.

Where to stay
Chelinda Lodge and Camp
Chelinda offers a range of accommodation. Tucked away in a forested area, to the right of the entry road and before the stables, is a **campsite** where tents can be hired and there is an ablutions block. Cooking can be done in permanent shelters on the site. This is a very roomy and atttractive place to camp.

To the left of the main road into the main Chelinda Camp is a **youth hostel** but this is generally only used by local groups.

About two kilometres further on is the old **Chelinda Camp** comprising buildings which were originally the Parks Department Camp before privatisation. Now greatly improved, the camp has six en suite twin rooms and four cottages. The cottages, which sleep four people each, have two bedrooms, a living room, kitchen and bathroom. If you bring your own food, a cook will be provided for your cottage. The cottages are built across the hillside but the double rooms are in a block near the main reception area.

For couples and single visitors, the rooms may be preferable to the cottages. Numbers five and six are the best rooms.

In cooler weather (frosts are not unknown) log fires are lit in the rooms and cottages at night. The reception block consists of a small bar, lounge, dining room and small shop. The outlook of the camp is over one of three trout lakes formed by small dams.

Two cautionary notes: the electricity is switched off at 22.00 and supplies of vehicle fuel from Chelinda's tank cannot be guaranteed.

The final accommodation option is **Chelinda Lodge**. Opened in 2000, this is a

Above: Village women queue with their maize at a small mill along the road towards Nyika.

luxury complex of eight log cabins each of which has en suite facilities and a galleried section. It is sited about one kilometre from the camp, set on a slope with a backdrop of tall trees and magnificent views to the front across the rolling hills. Everything is well designed and the interiors are beautifully furnished. There is a central restaurant with balcony, bar and shop. The lodge is linked to the airstrip by a five kilometre (three mile) road.

All the accommodation and the activities are managed by the **Nyika Safari Company**.

The Zambian Resthouse
About one kilometre across the border, into Zambia, before reaching Chelinda, is the old Zambian Resthouse. It is no longer in use although restoration is mooted.

Sightseeing
The attraction of Nyika is the whole environment: scenery, flora and fauna, rather than just game viewing. Indeed, the openness of the high plateau means that game will quickly take fright and a close view may be impossible. This is a park where

binoculars may well be needed although many of the animals can be approached on foot more easily than in a vehicle.

The montane vegetation attracts a wide variety of antelope. Commonly seen are **eland**, **bushbuck**, **grey duiker**, **kudu**, **roan** and **reedbuck**. Most of these are essentially browsers so the best places to view are on the borders of the woodland areas. Reedbuck, the most common species, rarely go far from their watering place so they may be easiest of all to track down. In contrast the diminutive duiker is easily hidden in low scrub and can go without water for considerable periods. The reedbuck are especially tame and herds of over three hundred eland have been seen.

Very easy to see are the **Burchell's zebra** which graze the grasslands, sometimes in small groups of two or three and occasionally in larger herds. They are not especially timid and it is often possible to have good sightings of them. For those who take the opportunity to ride over the plateau on horseback, the zebra, often joined by antelope, will run alongside the horses.

Leopards are the predators of both zebra

Above: Chelinda Camp in Nyika National Park has attractive cottages.

and antelope and, although they are nocturnal by habit, the lack of competitors in Nyika means that a sighting is a real possibility. The park is reputed to have the highest density of leopard in the whole of central Africa. Good viewing can be had in the forested areas around Chelinda or where reedbuck, their favourite prey, are plentiful. **Spotted hyena** are also present and have been known to lurk around the camp at night.

Smaller mammals are in abundance. **Warthogs** and **bushpigs** live in the woodland areas and also feed off the grasslands. The former are largely nocturnal but the latter will be seen during the day. To mistake one species for the other could be regretted for while warthogs will scamper away, tails raised, bushpigs may attack if they feel threatened. Just inside Thazima Gate, the woodland is a favourite habitat for **baboons**.

Two large mammals, the **elephant** and the **buffalo** are in the park but mostly confined to the north or the lower slopes out of sight of visitors using Nyika's primitive road network. However, early in 2001 quite large numbers of elephants, including young, were seen close to Chelinda. This is the first time

that elephants had been so close to the lodge and camp that anyone could recall.

Nyika is a paradise for birdwatchers. Over four hundred species are recorded, many on their migration paths. Rare **Denham's** (or **Stanley's**) **bustard** and **wattled crane** both have homes in the park. The wattled crane comes close to Chelinda to find food in the nearby dambos. Three or four sub-species of bird are unique to Nyika. One, the red-winged francolin is often to be seen running along the park's roads near to the Thazima Gate. The evergreen forest near Chelinda attracts the colourful **bar-tailed trogon**, the shy **cinnamon dove** and the orange fronted **starred robin**.

Nyika's flora has its own interest. Here is the richest variety of **orchids** in the whole of this part of Africa. Not only have over 200 types been recorded but a dozen or so are unique, found nowhere else in the world. Terrestrial orchids, rooted in the ground, are best sought near the peaty dambos, while the trunks of trees in the evergreen forests support the epiphytic varieties. The grassland areas are rich in **wildflowers**, especially after any dry season fires. Rising like a very colourful

Above: Horse riding is popular on Nyika, especially a canter through Lake Kauline.

phoenix from the ashes, great carpets of small flowers quickly clothe the rolling hills.

Towards the south-east corner of the park is an evergreen forest of **juniper**. It has been protected since 1948 and some of the oldest trees reach to a magnificent height of about 50 metres (160 feet). The presence of small stands of juniper outside the forest suggest the cover was once much larger and has probably been destroyed by fire 2-300 years ago. This is the most southerly juniper forest in Africa. There is a clear path for walkers through the forest.

Around the park

One of the attractions of Nyika is that the park lends itself both to walks and drives and a scout is not strictly necessary although one is advised and can be obtained by asking at Chelinda. There are many specific features which should be on most itineraries.

In the main part of the park and not too far from Chelinda are three circular drives. These used to be more popular before Chelinda came under private management and when there was less opportunity to join an organised safari. Despite their reduced attraction, they are described below because it should still be possible to get a scout to show you round although a map should be available at Chelinda Camp. In any case the drives take in many of the features that will be seen on an organised safari.

Drive No.1 is the North Circular Route. Three tracks off this route take you to viewpoints. **Domwe**, to the west, gives views into Zambia but **Jalwe**, north off the circular route, is more interesting.

Jalwe is a rocky hill which can give good views of game. The point is reached by a motorable path off the drive. Elephant, antelope and buffalo can usually be seen but binoculars will be needed because the animals seek the shelter of **Chipone Valley** in the northern quarter of the park. If the game move out of the valley on to the neighbouring **Kawozya-Mponda Ridge**, sightings will be easier.

A third track leading to a viewpoint off the drive goes to **Nganda Hill** (recognisable by the aerial at its summit) which, at 2600 metres (8500 feet), is the park's highest point, and the second highest in Malawi. From the motorable rise near the summit an estimated

Above: Nyika Plateau is a beautiful and uninhabited wilderness spreading over 3000 square kilometres.

seventy-five per cent of the whole park can be seen. Although this is the most difficult to get to of the three viewpoints, no visit to Nyika should omit this best of all lookouts in the park.

Drive No.2 is the South-east Circular Route. This drive takes in five attractions: Kasaramba, the Chelinda Falls, the Nchenachena Falls, the remnants of what was once a large juniper forest and Fingira Rock. **Kasaramba** is a viewpoint which, in good weather, allows one to see over the forested edge of the plateau to Lake Malawi. It is said that the Livingstonia Mission can be picked out from Kasaramba but it might be best to have your binoculars ready and hope the weather is exceptionally clear. There is a short walk from the motorable track to get to this viewpoint.

Very close to Kasaramba, in fact about 100 metres (330 feet) before you reach the viewpoint, is a track to the left which leads down to the **Nchenachena Falls**. It is best to walk because the track is usually in a poor condition. After three kilometres, the falls come into view as they drop 30 metres (100 feet) at the escarpment's edge.

Continuing on the same park track westwards beyond Kasaramba leads to the **Juniper Forest**. This is partly a relic of a larger cover and partly the result of modern planting in the 1950s and 1960s. Game viewing is good here.

Returning to the drive, a little way beyond the turn-off to Kasaramba, are the **Chelinda Falls**. These are easy to find because the drive crosses the river Chelinda and the path to the falls goes downstream from the bridge. A walk of about one-and-a-half kilometres (one mile) is needed to reach the falls and although they drop only 10 metres (33 feet) it is a very pretty place: a popular spot for picnics.

Another quite poor, but just about motorable track leads off the drive to **Fingira Rock**, a prominent granite dome in which there is a cave halfway up the eastern side. This was used as shelter in neolithic times and, apart from numerous artifacts, a human skeleton has been found along with scores of bones. Iron Age rock paintings have also been found there in the form of geometric patterns.

Drive No.3, the South-west Circular Route, is closest to Chelinda and the shortest of the drives. Its only special attraction is **Chosi**

Hill where leopards and hyenas have their haunts.

Not on the Circular Drives but certainly worth visiting are the **Chisanga Falls**. To get to the falls from Chelinda, return along the main entrance road to the M9 which runs through the park. Instead of turning left to Thazima Gate, go right on the M9 towards the Kaperekezi (Zambia) Gate. After about 18 kilometres (11 miles) from Chelinda there is a short two kilometre footpath (right) down to the falls. The triple falls of Chisanga go over the edge of the Nyika Plateau and are part of the North Rukuru River. Not only are the falls a splendid sight but the area is noted for its birdlife and red duiker antelopes.

Finally, close to the road leading to Chelinda Camp from the M9 (to the left, just before reaching the evergreen forest) is **Lake Kauline**, without inlet or outlet. It is often referred to as the *magic lake* with healing powers attributed to its waters. It is said always to be at the same level irrespective of season and that a serpent lives in its waters. Its true origin is uncertain but is probably the result of a landslip blocking the natural drainage.

Above: The second largest of the antelopes, a roan, takes an interest in the photographer.

Practical matters and activities

Most visitors to Nyika will be staying at Chelinda using Nyika Safaris' accommodation. The company will arrange activities including game viewing and sightseeing. However, it is possible to make your own, independent, arrangements. In that case, although not compulsory to use a guide for walking or driving in the park, it is wise to do so and often saves time. Tracks are none too clear and are poorly signposted. The office at Chelinda Camp should be able to provide a scout. The charge should be per party or per car and not per person. A four-wheel drive vehicle with good ground clearance is needed and driving at night is forbidden.

There are three planned circular routes out and back from Chelinda but there are other tracks to more distant parts of the park which branch off these circuits. If driving without a scout check the state of the river bridges with the camp office — and do not forget your binoculars.

The Nyika Safari Company, which runs Chelinda, is famous for its **horse safaris**. A well managed stables near the camp has some twenty or so mounts suitable for beginners to advanced riders although children are only accepted if they are competent riders. Rides can be as short as two hours or as long as an eleven-day safari (riding about 4-7 hours a day). The horse safaris provide an experience of a lifetime. Antelope and zebra run alongside the horses and nights are spent in tented camps on the plateau under the stars. For a safari it is best to bring suitable clothing as there is only a limited supply for loan. Jodphurs, half chaps, suitable shoes and a hard hat are advised. Tack is western McClellan.

An obvious but more strenuous alternative to riding is a **walking** safari, carrying light equipment for rough camping around the park. A scout will be happy to accompany you and share the burden. There are some specific trails for which the Chelinda Camp office will provide details. A five-day trek would be enough to see examples of the varied terrain and wildlife. Regular treks to Livingstonia and the Lake are arranged.

Angling is possible on the lakes trapped behind the three dams around Chelinda.

Only fly fishing is permitted but rainbow trout can be caught in all three lakes. A licence must be purchased at Chelinda Camp office and a boat, on the lake nearest the camp, can be hired. Although it is possible to hire rods and to purchase flies, it is far wiser to bring your own. Best opportunities for fishing are between November and January. The season is 1 September to 30 April. A programme of re-stocking is in progress so some restrictions may be in force.

Mountain biking is available from Chelinda Camp. Bikes can be hired and a guide is advised for anything but the shortest ride. As with treks, it is possible to journey down to the Lake.

A final reminder: it can be cold on Nyika when the sun goes down. A sweater, or two, should be taken if staying on the plateau.

Vwaza Marsh Wildlife Reserve

The reserve's full name, Vwaza Marsh Wildlife Reserve, recognises that for much of its extent of 986 square kilometres (380 square miles) it is a flat and ill-drained alluvial plain, at about 100 metres (3300 feet). A few rocky outcrops of hills break the general flatness of the landscape.

The reserve is cut by numerous tributaries of the **River Luwewe** which flows largely north to south. This dominant channel joins the **South Rukuru River** at **Zaro Pool** in the south-west corner of the reserve and then flows west to east to run along the border with Zambia.

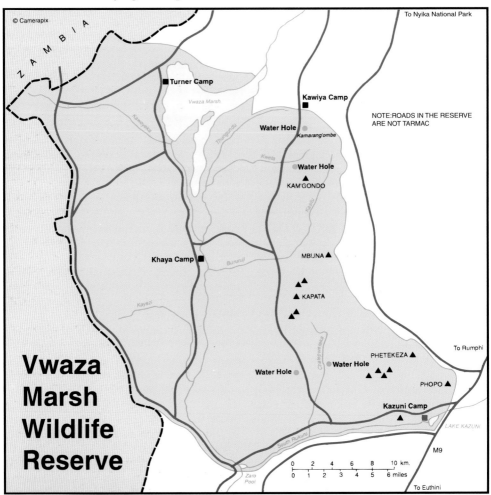

Above: A typical rural scene along the road between Rumphi and Vwaza Marsh Wildlife Reserve.

There is a wonderful mix of vegetation in Vwaza: forest and grassland, thin woodland and marsh. It is this rich variation in habitat that attracts such a splendid range of birdlife. Here and there are scattered stands of deciduous *mopane* woodlands found in Malawi only in Vwaza and the Shire lowlands of the south. The leaves of the *mopane* have the frustrating habit of turning edgeways to the sun and so provide very little shade for those on a walking safari.

Getting there

From

Mzuzu:	98km/61miles	M1,M24, S49
Lilongwe:	458km/285miles	M1, M1, M24, S49
Nkhata Bay:	145km/90miles	M5, M1, M24, S49
Karonga:	196km/122miles	M1, M24, S49
Rumphi turn off:	34km/21miles	M24, S49

(*Note:* distances are to the Lake Kazuni entrance)

Mzuzu to Vwasa Marsh WR: M1, M24, S49: 98km

Vwaza Marsh Wildlife Reserve is on the Zambian border to the north-west of Mzuzu. Access from Mzuzu is the same as for Nyika up to the point, some 10 kilometres (6 miles) from Rumphi, where the M24 meets the minor road, the S49. Turning left on to this road is to find oneself on a track which is even more rutted than the M24. It is best to try to maintain a steady but modest speed if driving this corrugated track; any high speed is likely to end in disaster. The path is across plains which, except in the few months of the rainy season, have an almost desert-like dryness. Vegetation is sparse although trees survive by sending their roots down to the water table.

Unfortunately the desert character of the landscape literally spills over on to the road. To add to the trials of the motorist, vast patches of sand can be encountered and unless the vehicle is kept moving slowly over these you may need the help of local people to push you on your way.

Small groups of huts, mango trees and low bushes are scattered across the lowland which has as its backdrop low hills encircling the plains. This is in fact the valley of the **South Rukuru River**, almost invisible from

Above: Vwaza Marsh Wildlife Reserve is noted for its elephant herds. They are regular visitors to the river near Kazuni Safari Camp.

the road. Close to the park, river and road converge and 19 kilometres (12 miles) from the M24 junction, the **Lake Kazuni** entrance to Vwaza Marsh Wildlife Reserve is reached as the main road turns to bridge the river.

Because of the poor state of the roads west of Rumphi, they should not be attempted in the wet season (December-April) except in a four-wheel drive vehicle.

If approaching Vwaza's Lake Kazuni Gate from Nyika, take the second marked turning (NOT the first) to the right of the road towards Rumphi. This is a quite interesting road through open country and smallholders' tobacco farms.

The entrance fee to the reserve is, as usual, US$5.

An airstrip is planned in the reserve but it will be some time before flying into Vwaza will be possible.

When to go

Because of its relatively low altitude, the reserve can be rather hot and humid in the period just before the rains (September to November). The roads are practically unusable in the wet season (December to April) but Kazuni Camp is open to visitors all year.

Where to stay
Kazuni Safari Camp and Kazuni Camp

The accommodation at Vwaza has been transformed since its management came into the hands of the Nyika Safari Company, which also runs Nyika National Park. The old camp had become so run-down that hardly anyone stayed in the reserve.

Now Nyika Safaris have built a delightful new reed and thatch camp comprising four en suite double chalets and a manager's chalet which is occasionally let to visitors. This is the Safari Camp. It has a dining area, open to the sides but roofed. The outlook is over **Kazuni Lake**, home to hippos and birdlife and a watering place for all manner of game animals.

The old tented camp has now been upgraded and is simple called Kazuni Camp. It has an improved central ablution block and meals can be provided if ordered in advance. If visitors bring their own food, there is a cook available.

Above: There are herds of hippo in Lake Kazuni alongside the Safari Camp.

A full range of walking and driving safaris is available whether visitors are in the new or the old camp.

Sightseeing

Vwaza is noted for its rich birdlife, including a variety of water and riverine species. Of the larger mammals, **buffalo, elephant, hippopotamus** and species of **antelope** should be seen even on a short visit.

Records show sitings of some 270 species of birds. Included in the list are **stork, heron** and the **white-faced tree duck**. Various types of **eagle** and **falcon** also find their prey here. Two birds, **Swainson's francolin** and a rare **white-winged starling** are to be found in Malawi only at Vwaza. The best viewing is along the water courses and near the pools and marsh. There is no particular season when viewing is best. A visit any time during the year is rewarding.

Close to Lake Kazuni Gate, where the South Rukuru River flows out of the reserve, is as good a place as any to see **elephant**. Herds of upwards of thirty or forty make frequent excursions out of the bush to use the river for drinking and bathing. The reserve's guides, who are well aware of their patterns of behaviour and movement, should be able to point out the best places to view in safety. One such is the road bridge over the river just outside the reserve. When the water level is low, elephants make holes in the sandy river bed with their trunks until water filters through the silt.

Although generally presenting no real threat it has to be appreciated that it is not very wise to position a vehicle in the path of a six ton male elephant. Forward facing ears is not an encouraging sign. Because of the elephants' destructive nature and voracious appetites, local people who farm just outside the reserve have mixed feelings about the animals. Occasional breakouts from the reserve can wreak havoc to crops, there being no protective buffer zone. This conflict of interest is difficult to resolve and more may need to be done so that local communities can benefit from the potential rewards of this and other reserves. Already a start has been made with the local people being given permission to fish in Lake Kazuni.

Buffalo are attracted to the river and to Lake Kazuni. However, their less predictable

Above: Vwaza Marsh Wildlife Reserve has much to commend it. Not least is its genuine wilderness.

roaming habits when water is plentiful, make them harder to track than the elephants and viewing on a short visit to the reserve cannot be guaranteed. Generally speaking, buffalo are more frightened than frightening but solitary males might attack and those of Vwaza have been known to do so.

Hippos are best looked for around the larger pools and lakes. Again Lake Kazuni is a favourite spot. They graze underwater as well as on land and spend little time during the day out of water especially when it is hot. Occasionally large numbers can be seen basking on mud banks in Lake Kazuni and they can be approached quite closely when water separates them from the observers. In most circumstances hippos are not especially dangerous in the sense that they will attack a human. The real problem is that they do not take kindly to anyone blocking their paths and will simply carry on running — quite fast — regardless of what is in the way. Since they can weigh 2500 kilograms (5500 pounds) it is better to avoid such a situation.

Smaller mammals such as the **warthog** are common in Vwaza but the big cats, **lion** and **leopard** are less likely to be viewed. Three of

the largest antelopes, the **eland**, the **kudu** and the **roan**, have been viewed recently in Vwaza but their preference for shelter makes sighting difficult. The more likely places to view are where some of the wooded hilly areas of the reserve border grasslands. At the other end of the size scale, **common duiker** are also around the reserve. **Impala** are everywhere. Across the western border of the reserve is Zambia, a quite wild region extending from that country's North Luangwa National Park. Poaching in this part of Zambia has been prevalent for decades. Provided the activity does not spill into Malawi there is a favourable consequence as some animals, especially lion and leopard, are believed to have started to seek sanctuary in the Vwaza reserve.

Although so much can be seen just inside the reserve around Lake Kazuni, a greater appreciation of its wealth of wildlife can be had by driving the track along the South Rukuru River to Zaro Pool and then going north towards the marshlands and the Khaya campsite. Stopping for a walking safari along these routes will add to the delight of a visit to Vwaza. It is quite likely that no other human beings will be seen no matter how far you drive. The reserve has yet to be discovered.

Practical matters and activities

The reserve's furrowed tracks are in a poor state and it is often difficult to tell exactly what is track and what is a patch of grassland or a path recently trodden down by a herd of elephants. For this reason, if for none other, it is not very practical to attempt to see Vwaza without the help of expert guides. In any case a scout from the reserve's staff camp (to the right as you enter the reserve) would be necessary.

Fortunately, Nyika Safaris, who run the camp will provide all that is necessary for a game drive or a walking safari. Whether staying at the tented Kazuni Camp or the new Kazuni Safari Camp, the services of Nyika Safaris will be available.

If spending time in Vwaza, some protection from tsetse fly, in the form of clothing and repellents, is advisable.

Livingstonia Mission

Livingstonia is an outstanding example of the work of the Scottish missionaries in Malawi, following in the tradition established in the 1870s. The site of the mission is a case of third time lucky. The original Livingstonia site chosen by **Dr Robert Laws**, a disciple of **David Livingstone**, was at Cape Maclear. However, the mosquito and malaria drove Laws to move northwards up Lake Malawi to Bandawe. Again, this proved an unhealthy place for his community and family. With great reluctance, he moved again, in 1894, to this place of incredible beauty high above Lake Malawi at almost 900 metres (3000 feet). Its original name was **Khondowe** but was renamed Livingstonia in honour of Law's mentor.

The new home for the mission was decidedly healthier and it provided opportunities for farming and a ready supply of timber. The main drawback was isolation. Laws designed the road link to the lake, a quite astonishing piece of engineering for one trained in medicine.

The mission established a school, a technical training centre and a hospital. Livinstonia has made an immeasurable contribution to education in Malawi. As the community grew a church was built and, using waterpower, electricity came to Livingstonia as early as 1905. The Stone House, which still survives, was the Laws' second family house at Livingstonia, built in 1903.

After half a century of work in Africa, Robert Laws returned to the United Kingdom. Despite the difficulties and ill-health he had experienced in Malawi, he was in his eighty-fifth year when he died in 1935.

Getting there

From

Mzuzu:	125km/77miles	M1, T306, T305
Mzuzu:	142km/88miles	M1, Gorode Rd
Karonga:	114km/71miles	M1, Gorode Rd
Rhumpi turn off:		
	61km/38miles	M1, T306, T305
Rhumpi turn off:		
	78km/48miles	M1, Gorode Rd

One of two different routes can be used. Access is from the M1 but the approach can be direct from the shore of Lake Malawi or by using a minor road from the south-west. The latter, through the beautiful Henga Valley, is the recommended route if approaching from Mzuzu because the climb up directly from the lake is exceptionally difficult and, facing away from the lake, the wonderful views it affords cannot be appreciated. Driving down this road is a different matter. Both routes are described. One attractive option is to use the Henga Valley route to reach Livingstonia and to make the return journey by the M1. If taking this circular route, the total distance for the round trip Mzuzu-Livingstonia-Mzuzu is about 250 kilometres (155 miles).

If approaching from Karonga, there is really only the option of a direct approach from the M1 as it runs along the base of the plateau.

Mzuzu to Livingstonia: M1, Gorode: 143km

The M1 from Mzuzu is a good fast road shared with the routes to both Nyika and Vwaza. After passing the **Rumphi turn-off** the M1 continues to run parallel to the **Kasitu**

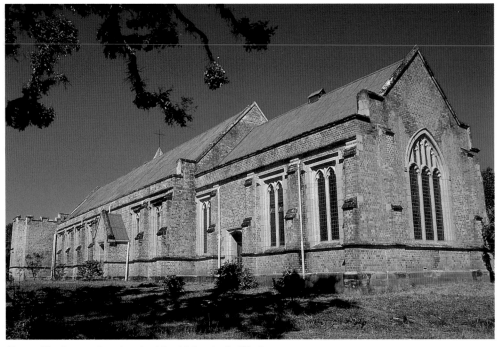

Above: The impressive church at the Livingstonia Mission.

River, soon to join the **South Rukuru River**. In 25 kilometres (16 miles) is the house of a certain **Mr S S Ng'oma**. Various notices on this quite extraordinary structure proclaim: *S S Ng'oma: Grocery, God is Love* and *Ng'oma House built 1970*. Constructed variously of stone, wood and corrugated iron, this is the house of Malawi's No.1 eccentric. Now in his eighties, Mr Ng'oma is well prepared for life — and for death. His grave is already dug in the garden and is protected by stone pillars supporting an iron roof. Even the headstone is prepared: painted a gaudy red it reads *S S Ng'oma B 1913 Died ..... .* The interior of the house is like a Heath Robinson creation only more extraordinary. The rooms are full of all manner of useful and, apparently, useless knick-knacks collected over his long life. His coffin stands handily near his bedroom. Sanitation has not been neglected. A lavatory pipe leads out of an upstairs window and on to the ground below.

If Mr Ng'oma is not at home, his daughter is usually very happy to show any unannounced visitor round the house. It is customary to leave a gratuity.

Shortly after this monument to eccentricity

and just beyond **Mzokoto** village a decision has to be made as to whether to continue with the M1 or to take the Henga Valley, 'back' route. For the Henga Valley route, look out for a left turn on to the T306 at a crossroads. This is at about 100-150 metres after passing the Phwezi Secondary School. This route is described later.

Continuing with the M1, its path is just above the South Rukuru before bridging the river by the **Fufu Falls** (strictly, rapids) before it rises over a spur. Now it winds up to a splendid viewpoint from which, at about 1000 metres (3000 feet) one can see over Lake Malawi.

From here the M1 follows a curving path down to the lakeshore plains as it passes (left) an important coalmine near the Lura turning. Again, there are good views of the lake and its sandy bays. Inland, lush valleys are etched into the flank of the plateau. The lake here is very pretty with near-white sands filling shallow bays and access to the shore is possible. There are a number of small lakeshore lodges of very modest standards along this part of the lake. Near to these lodges is the point where *mv Viphya* sank in

Above: The views of Lake Malawi from Livingstonia are unsurpassed.

1946. (The story of this disaster is in the section on the lake).

Now the M1 soon comes to **Chitimba** to meet the **Gorode Road** up the plateau's steep face to the Livingstonia Mission. The turning, left, is signposted and for about one kilometre the road is flat, running across the plain. Then the 'interesting' section begins. This is the tortuous climb up Dr Law's Gorode Road, a winding track with twenty hairpin bends. Some of the bends are so sharp that vehicles occasionally have to backtrack as they gingerly hug the very edge of the Rift Valley. This is not the sort of drive enjoyed by anyone with a modicum of vertigo.

The road was originally designed by the mission in 1905 and, although improvement work has been done on the lower hairpins, the money ran out and the road is in a poor condition, especially during and after the rains. The great attraction of this road is that it gives unsurpassed views of the lake including the sweeping curves of the **Chitimba Bay** and **Young's Bay**. For anyone with a camera there is the temptation to stop every hundred metres to take yet another shot.

Having reached the top of the plateau the road levels out. Now, with one's back to the lake, the scene changes. Trees now line the road and in a short distance there are the **Manchewe Falls**, signposted to the right. There is just enough space to leave a vehicle and a path leads off through the trees to a point where the falls can be viewed in all their magnificence. Waters from Nyika Plateau crash down almost 300 metres (1000 feet) on their way to Lake Malawi and it was their power which was hasnessed to provide the mission's electricity in the days of Dr Laws. A short walk back towards the falls gives a very good view of the rapids at their head.

After another one-and-a-half kilometres along the road there is the entrance to the Livinstonia Mission on the left.

The alternative **Henga Valley** route to Livingstonia is found by taking the turning off the M1, as described above, just 100-150 metres after passing the Phwezi School on to the T306.

The T306 turns back on itself to cross the South Rukuru River between two sections of the **Pwezi Rapids** which characterise the river at this point. The road then turns eastwards again to meet the T305 at a T-junction

Above: The Livingstonia Mission was established in 1894 and is now a thriving community.

about seven kilometres (four and a half miles) from the M1. This road leads directly to Livingstonia.

Although parts of the road surface are poor, rutted and potholed, it is just about drivable in a car in the dry season. In the wet season a four-wheel drive with good clearance is essential. The path of the road begins in the broad, generally well-cultivated valley of the South Rukuru which separates Nyika from Viphya. To the north-west the Nyika Plateau rises to awesome heights. Gradually the road winds upwards through the Henga Valley passing no villages but countless smallholdings whose neatly laid out fields of vegetables contrast with the long grasses of the uncultivated land. In some places the slopes have been terraced and the red lateritic soil gives the appearance of a rather grand broad staircase. Each little thatched hut farm has its banana trees close by. Only here and there does one see primitive irrigation from mountain streams used to cultivate rice.

This is rather a special road with a magic all its own. Even in a country as unspoilt as Malawi this small region traversed by the

T305 is somehow a very private place. There is a feeling that one is an intruder yet not unwelcome.

The signposted turning off (right) to the Livingstonia Mission comes quite suddenly as the road begins to level out having climbed steadily up the back of the **Khondowe Plateau**.

When to go
Any time in the year is suitable although rains can be heavy in the wet season (from December to April).

Where to stay
Livingstonia Old Stone House and Resthouse
Both offer very simple accommodation but food should be brought. Someone at the mission will do the cooking for you. Booking ahead is advisable, if you can make the connection. Don't expect luxury. The Stone House is somewhat more attractive and atmospheric than the resthouse that is at the other side of the small town. One day someone will realise the potential of the Stone House and its site and a renovated and refurbished lodge will emerge.

Above: The Old Stone House was Dr Robert Laws' home at the Livingstonia Mission.

Sightseeing

Much of what Laws achieved at Livingstonia still survives today. The **church** is in a poor state of repair but has a beautiful stained glass window over the main entrance, which shows David Livingstone at Lake Malawi meeting the Chiefs. This was a 1952 gift of Dr J C Roach in memory of her father. The bell tower roof was in a state of collapse and unsafe but some work has been effected on this. Climbing up the tower offers some views through the slatted windows but a locked trapdoor bars access to the final section.

The red brick walls of the church need repointing and the whole structure is in a sorry state. It would seem that what Laws achieved, nature and man's indifference is intent upon destroying.

Much the same can be said about the **Old Stone House**. It now serves as a resthouse but, again, is in urgent need of a coat of paint and a thorough clean. The balcony from which Dr and Mrs Laws could view Lake Malawi is most often festooned with the drying washing of the backpackers who use the accommodation. Until the buildings and its surroundings are put in order it cannot be recommended as a place to stay except perhaps for overnight accommodation.

One end of the Old Stone House has been converted into a small **museum**. Unfortunately it is in a sad state of decay and neglect. Surely there must be funds to put such a treasure in order. Some of the exhibits are priceless. There are glass photographic slides, old photographic prints, wall displays, furniture and equipment — dating from the earliest times of the establishment of the mission. There's even an old wash basin used by the Laws' family. Original letters dating from 1854, gifts received by Dr Laws, his Moderator's hat, all are here but all need to be properly preserved. The tropical climate and neglect will soon see their destruction. Fascinating are the minutes of meetings held in the early days of the mission in the 1870s. Many original documents are not made available for viewing and their condition remains unknown.

The entry fee for the museum is K10 (assuming you can find someone to take your money and to open the door). Officially, the museum is open from 07.30 to 17.00 and after 13.30 on Sundays.

Away from the Old Stone House and the church is a sprawling collection of red brick buildings including a shop. The community seems to be thriving and still leads a near self-sufficient existence. It is something of a scandal that the historic buildings and their surroundings have been left to decay for the want of what would be a modest sum for restoration work.

The great beauty of Livingstonia is no longer the buildings and their crumbling fabric but the site itself. Just in front of the Old Stone House is the very edge of the Great Rift Valley. The views across Lake Malawi into Tanzania rival those from the Zomba Plateau in south Malawi. To see the sun rise across the lake is a sight never to be forgotten. A feeling of being on-top-of-the-world is unavoidable. This is a great place to sit and soak up the views.

Going North

Mzuzu to Tanzania Border:
275km/171miles   M1
Chitimba to Tanzania Border:
148km/92miles   M1

Chitimba to Tanzania Border: M1: 148km

There is a small but significant number of travellers who enter Malawi from Tanzania or who move on to that country from Malawi. The route through the north into Tanzania is the M1. Out of Mzuzu this is also the route to Nyika and Vwaza, as far as Rhumpi, and one of the routes to the Livingstonia Mission as far as **Chitimba** at the foot of the Livingstonia escarpment. From the Mission turning, the M1 pulls back from the lakeshore, skirts around **Chitimba Bay** and **Young's Bay** and passes through one of Malawi's major rice growing areas. It is unique in that nowhere else in the country can the crop be grown without irrigation. The rainfall here is adequate.

As the road runs behind Young's Bay a minor road, S102, leads off right to **Chilumba**. The lake steamer *Ilala* calls at the jetty in

Chilumba and this can be a departure point for a visit to **Likoma Island**.

Taking a path close to the lakeshore the M1 continues northwards with exceptional views to the Livingstone Mountains across the lake in Tanzania. At 226 kilometres (140 miles) from the starting point in Mzuzu, the small but important town of **Karonga** is reached.

Karonga may now seem a rather sad, run-down sort of place but it has a most interesting history. In the late 1880s the town was the headquarters of the notorious Arab slave trader **Mlozi**. With the support of his own 'army', Mlozi exercised real power over a wide area, trading in goods as well as people. Eventually he was captured and put to death in 1895. Trade of the non-human kind then came under the sole control of the powerful **African Lakes Company** (later, Corporation) which had previously enjoyed an uneasy relationship with Mlozi. The two lakes which feature in the company's name are Lake Malawi and Lake Tanganyika and its trading empire stretched to the east coast of Africa.

Karonga's other place in the history books arises from an attempt by forces from German East Africa (later Tanganyika, then Tanzania) to capture the town in 1914 during World War I. They were repulsed, first by a local militia and then by reinforcements from the **King's African Rifles**. There was considerable loss of life although the exact numbers killed and wounded are not known. Some graves can still be seen in the town cemetery which is by the Council Offices. Outside the post office is the site of an artillery emplacement in a hollow baobab tree. Disaster struck the town in 1979 when, after exceptionally heavy rains, the level of the lake rose and flooding occurred. Some form of flood protection is still under discussion.

There are some useful services in the town. As well as the post office, there is a petrol station, and a PTC. It may be convenient to break a journey in Karonga but accommodation is limited. Best is the **Karonga Club Marina**. Situated almost on the beach in Karonga town, this is a relatively new establishment. It provides simple but adequate accommodation and food. There are a dozen chalets with en suite facilities, and the atmosphere in the club is notably friendly. Best of all are the views across the lake. In the very unlikely event that the club is full, there is a small resthouse in the town centre, by the roundabout. There are only four rooms and one bathroom. No food is provided so it is best to eat at the club.

At Karonga, the M26 leads to **Chitipa**, a large village in the extreme north-west of Malawi. This is a poor road with little to attract the traveller into attempting the 202 kilometre (125 mile) round trip. Historically it was the African Lakes Company's route to Lake Tanganyika: the two-lakes link. Known as the Stevenson Road, it was never quite completed. There are always plans to rebuild the road but. . .

On the M1 there is another 49 kilometres (30 miles) to the border with Tanzania, just beyond the village of **Iponga**. This road dates from the 1880s when it was used for trade between Karonga and the north. It was also the route for the slave trading of Mlozi's empire. The border is at the bridging of the **Songwe River**. Travellers with the correct papers can cross into Tanzania taking the route north to **Tukuyu** and on to **Dar es Salaam**.

Bottom: Deserted sandy beaches fringe Lake Malawi. Below: Like children everywhere, young Malawians enjoy a beach holiday.

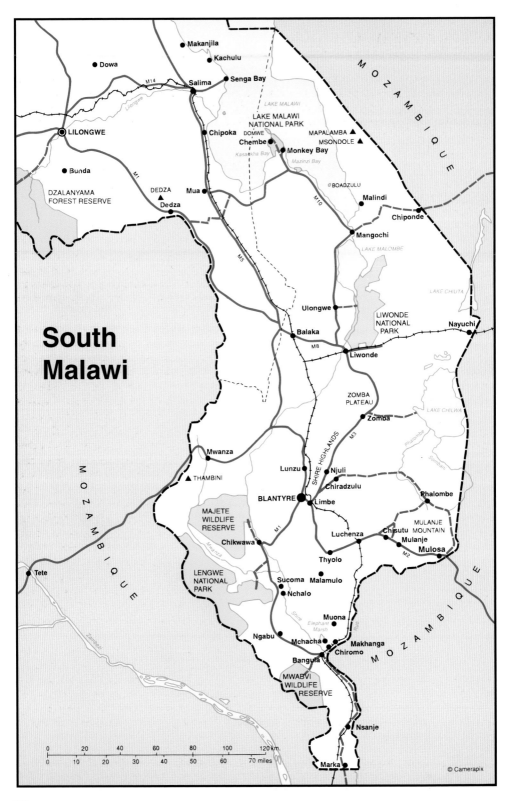

South Malawi

LAKE MALAWI
NATIONAL PARK

Makanjila

Kachulu

Dowa

Senga Bay

Salima

M14

Chipoka

LILONGWE

Chembe

DOMWE

MAPALAMBA ▲

MSONDOLE ▲

Monkey Bay

Mazinzi Bay

Kasankha Bay

Bunda

M1

DEDZA

DZALANYAMA
FOREST RESERVE

Mua

Dedza

BOADZULU

Malindi

Chiponde

Mangochi

LAKE MALOMBE

M10

M5

LAKE CHIUTA

Ulongwe

LIWONDE
NATIONAL
PARK

Nayuchi

Balaka

M8

Liwonde

ZOMBA
PLATEAU

LAKE CHILWA

Zomba

M3

Mwanza

THAMBINI ▲

Lunzu

Njuli

Chiradzulu

SHIRE HIGHLANDS

BLANTYRE

Limbe

Phalombe

MAJETE
WILDLIFE
RESERVE

Luchenza

Chisutu

MULANJE
MOUNTAIN

Mulanje

Chikwawa

M1

Thyolo

M2

Mulosa

MOZAMBIQUE

Tete

LENGWE
NATIONAL
PARK

Sucoma

Malamulo

Nchalo

Muona

Elephant
Marsh

Ngabu

Mchacha

Makhanga

Bangula

Chiromo

MWABVI
WILDLIFE
RESERVE

Nsanje

Zambezi

| 0 | 20 | 40 | 60 | 80 | 100 | 120 km. |
| 0 | 10 | 20 | 30 | 40 | 50 | 60 | 70 miles |

Marka

© Camerapix

158

South Malawi

The southern third of the country is the most populated, the most developed and the most low-lying of all Malawi's regions. Economically dominated by Blantyre and physically by the great Shire Valley and Mulanje Mountain, there is diversity and contrast in south Malawi which is unknown in the rest of the country.

Snaking through the region, the **Shire River** drains Lake Malawi. (The former spelling of the river's name: Shiray, is a good approximation of its pronunciation.) The river follows the same rift or trough that is occupied by the lake but here it is a valley of varying width and only the northern section, just south of the Shire's exit from Lake Malawi, is drowned to form a lake: **Lake Malombe**. Malombe's surface is only two metres below that of Lake Malawi but by the time the Shire flows out to Mozambique in the extreme south of the country it will have fallen through 437 metres (1435 feet). At just 36 metres (124 feet) above sea level, this is the lowest point in the country.

The south also has Malawi's highest peak, the great **Mount Mulanje** (also Mlanje) which towers to over 3000 metres (9850 feet). This is the highest mountain in the whole of central Africa. Malawi's highest and lowest points are less than 110 kilometres (68 miles) apart.

To the west of the Shire Valley is the continuation of the **Dedza Highlands** and to the east is the high ridge of the **Shire Highlands**, a large plateau-like upland around 1000 metres (3280 feet). The **Blantyre** and **Limbe** conurbation is sited on this ridge but is surrounded by isolated peaks rising to over 1600 metres (5250 feet). Two other notable landscape features lie in south Malawi: the **Zomba Plateau**, north-east of Blantyre, and **Lake Chilwa** on the eastern border with Mozambique.

Zomba is a table-like mountain rising to over 2080 metres (6800 feet) with sheer scarp-like edges dropping to the Shire Valley in the west and to the **Phalombe Plain** in the east. Lying on this plain is the shallow Lake Chilwa.

The heaviest concentrations of population, outside of the urban areas of Blantyre-Limbe and Zomba, are in the Shire Valley and on the Shire Highlands. Particularly popular areas are south of Zomba, in the most southerly parts of the Shire Valley and in the plantation districts between Blantyre and Mulanje.

Alongside the traditional subsistence crops such as maize and the equally traditional smallholder economy, south Malawi has the bulk of the country's large scale estate or plantation farming. Vast areas are devoted to the monoculture of sugar and cotton, as in the Shire Valley, or tea and coffee in the Mulanje and **Thyolo** area (the old name, and the pronunciation, is Cholo). Tobacco, too, is a major estate and smallholding crop.

The region has no less than four game parks or reserves one of which, **Liwonde**, is arguably the best in Malawi and **Lengwe** is attractive. However, the two wildlife reserves, **Majete** and **Mwavbi**, are either too isolated or devoid of game to be worth visiting on a short visit.

The climate of south Malawi is greatly influenced by the presence of the high plateaux and mountainous areas. The traveller in this part of the country will be aware of the contrasts between the lowest parts of the Shire Valley, where temperatures and humidity will be high much of the year, and the relative coolness of the Shire Highlands, the Zomba Plateau and the Mulanje Massif.

There are quite remarkable variations in weather conditions over short distances in the south. It can be sunny in Blantyre when, a few kilometres away in Limbe it is pouring with rain. However, the basic seasonal variations, which apply to the rest of the country, are also effective here.

Despite the greater development of south Malawi it should not be assumed that, outside the towns, services and facilities needed by travellers are in any greater supply. Likewise, the quality of road surfaces is certainly no better and, because of the rather greater use, is often worse.

Following pages: The Mulanje Massif is Central Africa's highest mountain, rising to over 3000 metres, nearly 10,000 feet.

Zomba Plateau

To travel to Malawi yet not to visit the Zomba Plateau would be unthinkable. Zomba is a magnificent table-top mountain that overshadows the town. Actually there are two plateaux, Zomba and **Malosa**, neatly dissected by the **Domasi River**. But it is the southern section, Zomba, close to the town, that draws the traveller.

The top of Zomba Plateau stands at 1800 metres (5900 feet) with some peaks rising to over 2080 metres (6800 feet). On three sides, the massif has scarp-like edges. Towards the town and to the south it presents a face of over 750 metres (2500 feet) while to the west the fall is even greater. Here it forms the faulted edge of the Great Rift Valley and Shire lowlands and the height from plateau top to valley floor is all of 1200 metres (4000 feet). Zomba Plateau has a slight depression in the centre with the higher ground and the peaks forming an outer rim. Streams run radially through the forests over small waterfalls and rapids until they join to form the **Mulunguzi** that drains towards the south-east.

Getting there
From

Blantyre:	79km/49miles	M3, Local Road
Lilongwe:	297km/185miles	M1, M8, M3, Local Road
Mangochi:	134km/83miles	M3, Local Road
Zomba:	13km/8miles	Local Road

(Note: Distances are to Le Méridien Ku Chawe at the top of the plateau)

Blantyre to Zomba Plateau: M3, minor road: 79km

To reach Zomba from Blantyre, the route is the M3. The surface of this road is generally kept in good repair. To join the M3 from central Blantyre take the Glyn Jones Road downhill to the roundabout and new clock tower and continue on the broad Masauko Chipembere (previously Kamuzu) Highway. Just after the **Chichiri Stadium** (left) the road becomes a dual carriageway and passes under the **Independence Arch**. At the next major junction, keep left and continue on

the road towards Zomba going through the northern outskirts of Limbe. The M3 is joined from Limbe by continuing along Churchill Road past the **Tobacco Auction Floors**.

Shortly after leaving the main built-up area of Blantyre-Limbe, a minor road, S146, leads off (right) to **Mount Mulanje**. To the right of the M3 the peak of **Chiradzulu** (1773 metres/5817 feet) can be seen and, on a clear day and in the same direction, there are views of Mulanje itself. Chiradzulu is worth a visit from a Blantyre base. The turn off to Chiradzulu is the same S146 as for Mulanje. What remains of the evergreen forest reserve is very attractive for its birdlife, monkeys and antelopes.

The road up to Zomba town runs along the ridge of the **Shire Highlands**. At first there

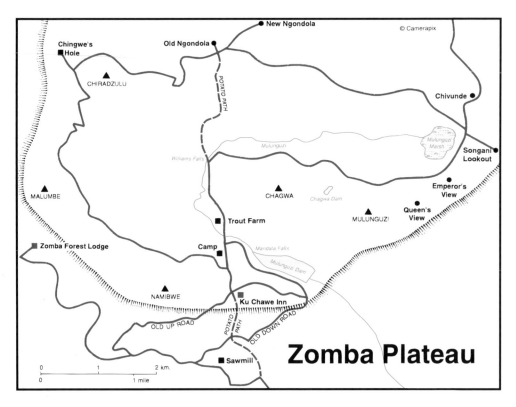

Zomba Plateau

are numerous markets along the roadside. Small villages, some near the road and others on the slopes of the nearby peaks, are closely spaced. Gradually the settlement thins, only to increase again near Zomba.

Njuli village, about 16 kilometres (10 miles) out of Blantyre, has a market. Many of the village markets are interesting to visit. Most of them are primarily vegetable markets but there will also be firewood, cloth, brightly coloured plastic bowls and, of more interest to the curio hunter, locally made pottery. If you wander through these markets you may be met by curious stares but your smile will always be returned with genuine warmth. The largest of the villages is **Namadzi**, 24 kilometres (15 miles) from Njuli. Here there are shops, petrol and the 'Sharp-Sharp' nightclub. These village night-clubs are the equivalent of the English pub.

Perhaps the best place to stop on this road is six kilometres (four miles) south of Namadzi. Here there is one of the Museums of Malawi: the postal museum. It is to the left of the road in a fenced off area. Its proper name is the **Mtenga-tenga Postal Hut** and it is an old resthouse. This is a philatelist's delight. There are not just fine collections of stamps but a whole host of exhibits showing the development of postal services in Malawi from colonial times. There are photographs and even old post boxes. The resthouse was one used by the mail runners (*tenga-tenga*). Roughly half way between Zomba and Blantyre, probably the most important of all the mail runs, it gave the runners thirty kilometres, or a day's travel before an overnight rest.

The final stretch into Zomba town is through pleasantly wooded countryside. After passing the barracks (left) in Zomba, look for the sign marked **Le Méridien Ku Chawe** and turn up left there to get to the plateau top.

If coming from Lilongwe, Liwonde or Mangochi, the route is described (in reverse), in the Getting There section for Liwonde National Park. From these directions, the turn up to the plateau top in Zomba town is the same but will be to the right of the M3.

From the turn off the M3, at the sign marked **Le Méridien Ku Chawe**, the road runs past the **Gymkhana Club** and the entrance to **State House**.

Above: Timber production is important to Zomba's economy. Top: Early, morning and the summit of Zomba Plateau is above the clouds.

Above: The primitive beauty of Zomba is one of its great attractions.

Since 1968 there had been two roads to the top: one for up traffic, one for down. Prior to that time a single road was open alternate half-hours for traffic up and down. Now there's been another change. With the enlargement of the **Mulunguzi Dam** the old Down Road has been widened to take traffic in both directions. The junction of the Up and Down roads is at about three kilometres (two miles) after leaving the M3. The old Up Road goes to the left and, what now should be called the 'Up and Down Road', goes to the right. With the improvements, the road no longer presents any difficulties and it allows for wonderful views. The town of Zomba can be seen as well as the surrounding plains and mountains. The road passes the new and extended **Mulunguzi Dam** and **Mandala Falls** and continues to the campsite still on the improved surface.

To go down from the plateau from the Ku Chawe Inn, turn right at the exit from the hotel and go past the stables. Bear left to come out on the old Down Road where a right turn begins the descent.

In addition to the road up to the top, there are a number of tracks which can be walked.

The **potato path**, which is signposted off the road at the bottom of the plateau, goes more or less straight up the mountain face and comes out near the Ku Chawe Inn. From there it leads across the top, through a village, **Ngondola**, and down the other side into the valley of the **Domasi**. Although it is the potato path that is best known, there are actually a number of similar tracks. The name comes from the use made of these paths to carry down vegetables from the plateau into the markets of Zomba town. Quite apart from the energy required to climb these steep paths, walkers are advised not to use the tracks if alone.

When to go

There are heavy rains during the months of December to April. The vegetation is at its most lush in May and June. The coolest months are July and August. The flowers for which the plateau is famous are best seen in late November and December.

Where to stay

For the backpacker there is a good **campsite**, close to the Ku Chawe Inn, with running

Above: The terrace at the Ku Chawe on Zomba Plateau affords splendid views of the plains below.

water and communal ablutions. It attracts relatively large numbers but it will always have space for an extra tent. There are one or two **private cottages** on the plateau which occasionally take guests or are let out to visitors.

Le Méridien Ku Chawe

The Ku Chawe, built on the very edge of the plateau, always claimed to have the best site of any hotel in Malawi. Now its boast can be extended to it being simply one of the best in all respects. It is difficult to compare the Ku Chawe with town or lakeside properties but it is certainly a very attractive place to stay.

The old hotel was a mix of what had the appearance of being ex-army huts plus a rather awful modern accommodation block over-hanging the edge of the plateau. In 1992 rebuilding started only to be halted by a fire and then restarted on new lines. At New Year in 2001, the Inn was again badly damaged by fire. Rebuilding went ahead with futher improvements. Only the public areas were affected; the accommodation remained untouched.

The architect of the first rebuilding seems to have had a passion for bricks and arches but the effect is of open space and elegance. The main building is in red brick each one hand-made and polished by Malawian craftsmen. The restaurant has a towering central chimney place and the main bar, with its own gallery, is well stocked. Public rooms and circulation areas are well-furnished but service is just a little slow. Why are two waiters needed to open a bottle of wine?

The views out from the hotel, looking over a small terraced garden are stunning and almost the equal of the named viewpoints on the plateau. These are best appreciated from the terrace just outside the restaurant, where breakfast is served.

There is an outdoor chessboard with giant, carved African figures. A small shop is alongside the reception area.

Accommodation is in comfortable, airy rooms along a terrace. The ground floor rooms have verandas leading on to little areas of garden. On request, a wood fire will be provided in the rooms in the evening and it may well be needed at this altitude.

Above: Waterfalls and crystal clear pools can be encountered not far from the plains below.
Top: The first tree planted when Zomba plateau's afforestation began.

This is a wonderful hotel in an unforgettable setting. It should be on every visitor's itinerary. One may wake up in cloud and watch it disappear as the sun rises to reveal the plains and small hills of another world 750 metres (2500 feet) below. It is the nearest most of us get to the experience of an astronaut looking down on planet earth.

Zomba Forest Lodge
This is another example of successful privatisation. The lodge is now run by **Land and Lake Safaris** rather than by the Forestry Department as a resthouse. The original building was the home of a Colonial Officer who served on the famous HMS *Gwendolen* which was involved in World War I's first naval battle — on Lake Malawi. The lodge is sited about half way up the plateau. To reach the lodge it is necessary to branch off on to the old Up Road and then take a short, signed path for some six kilometres (four miles). The road is not easy in an ordinary saloon car.

There are just five double rooms, each with en suite toilet and shower. Guests have sitting and dining rooms and the use of a kitchen. It is self-catering but a cook (noted for his curries) is available. Lighting is by candles and lanterns. There is a generator if fuel is supplied.

Views from near the lodge are excellent. The glistening Shire River can be seen as it meanders across the valley below. The lodge is a less expensive alternative to Ku Chawe and it has a special atmosphere of its own. It will be additionally attractive when mountain bikes are added to the activities on offer.

Sightseeing
Much of the plateau is forested, indeed it is one of Malawi's Forest Reserves. Three forestry villages are sited on the slopes of the mountain and foresters will be seen walking enormous distances across the plateau while groups of women carry headloads of firewood to their houses. Afforestation has taken place for a hundred years and there are now great stands of **cypress**, **Mexican pine** and the slower growing but magnificent **Mulanje cedar**. A nursery plantation is located close to the Ku Chawe Inn.

In the ravines and on other steeper slopes, where commercial forestry cannot take

Above: There are some wonderful picnic spots on Zomba Plateau.

place, there is an incredible variety of natural vegetation from jungle-like creepers to **wild flowers**, from **ferns** and **thornbushes** to **orchids** and **lichen**. The really wild areas are best seen by walking along the edges of the streams and by the waterfalls. It is here too that large **butterflies** flutter, hover and milk the nectar of the flowering plants. Among the less welcome wildlife are outsize ants which cling to shoes and have to be dislodged with a stick. On the lower slopes are plenty of **monkeys** and **baboons**. **Leopard** and **hyena** are also in the forest but most unlikely to be seen.

Birdlife is varied and prolific. A visitor's first sighting will probably be the large **white-necked ravens** which live near the hotel. Less in evidence but present on the plateau are **long-crested eagles** and **augur buzzards**.

The best way to see as much of the plateau as possible in a short time is to drive around it. Unfortunately the roads suffer damage from the giant logging trucks so it is best to enquire about their current state. The main route is called the **Outer Circular Road**.

The Outer Circular Road (about 25 kilometres/16 miles) takes about half a day if stopping and making short walks to view-points. The route is marked, but not everywhere are the signposts clear. Some of the junctions are numbered and although one cannot always count on this, these numbers are referred to below. The Outer Circular Road is best driven in an anti-clockwise direction simply because the last section west of Ku Chawe Inn is exceptionally rocky and quite steep. It is much easier to negotiate this descending rather than attempting to drive up it. If in any doubt about which track to follow, use the one that keeps closest to the edge of the plateau.

Near to Ku Chawe Inn, the sound of a car may bring boys running to offer to act as guides. They will expect a modest tip and may help with route-finding. It is probably sufficient simply to ask for directions if you need and not to take them in the car. However, it is common practice to offer lifts to local people who might otherwise have to tramp many miles across the plateau.

From the Ku Chawe Inn, turn left and then right past the curio sellers whose wares are spread out along the roadside. There are often more sellers than there are guests at the hotel. Pieces of crystal are on offer — usually

Above: The great Zomba Plateau rises to 1800 metres, almost 6000 feet.

from small boys — but perhaps the best buys are not the curios but the locally picked wild berries, including raspberries. Very young children often chase after cars attempting to sell posies of wildflowers.

The first junction should be ignored but bear left and the next turning right takes one on the start of the Outer Circular Road. To the right is the camping site. The road descends to cross the **Mulunguzi River**, passes the **Trout Farm** and then rises. After about one and a half kilometres, to the left, is an opening in the forest with space to park a car. It is there that the Mulunguzi spills over a series of shallow rock steps then plunges over a sheer drop to form **Williams Falls**. It is a pretty spot, best photographed in the early morning light. The more energetic can walk the **Mulunguzi Trail**, a riverside path between the falls and the trout farm. It makes a very pleasant diversion.

From the falls, the road turns eastward. In about three kilometres (two miles) there is a junction (7) to the right which seems at first to cut back in the same direction one has come. Taking this road leads to the **Chagwa Dam**. Chagwa is a relatively shallow reservoir and although its purpose is to

store water for Zomba town, it has all the appearances of a natural lake. There is a conveniently placed bench and a hut on its bank and it is a great place for a picnic. On a hot day it may be tempting to strip off and take a cooling bathe but this is strictly forbidden because of the lake's function. The silence is broken only by the croaking of frogs.

Continuing on the road past the dam, the path leads to another, unnumbered junction. Taking the right fork (somewhat obscured) leads to two of the main viewpoints on the plateau: **Queen's View** and, a little further along, **Emperor's View**. The first was named after a visit, in 1957, by England's Queen Mother and the second takes its name from Emperor Haile Selassie of Ethiopia. This point was once said to provide the "best view in the whole of the British Empire".

Of course, at 1800 metres (6000 feet) any view is especially dependent on the weather but spread out below are the vast **Phalombe Plains** to the south of Zomba, peppered with inselbergs. The town too can be seen laid out like some architect's model. Look for the Great Hall of the **university**. Beyond, on a clear day, **Lake Chilwa** and even **Mount**

Above: The Zomba Plateau looks down into the Domasi River valley.

Mulanje (70 kilometres/43 miles away) can be seen. There is plenty of space to park on the grassy edge of the plateau and it is quite likely that there will be no other visitors to spoil the quietness of this truly beauteous place.

The road leading away from these viewpoints rejoins the main Outer Circular Road. In a short distance, there is a turning right (9) in the form of a rough track for some 500 metres to **Chivunde Peak** and the **Songani Lookout**. This rocky viewpoint stands at 1808 metres (5932 feet) giving views across the plains and to Lake Chilwa. Again, this is a wonderfully quiet place to sit and soak up the beauty of it all. The small outcrops of rock are partly vegetated with mixed ferns, low bushes, wild flowers and the occasional tree.

Leaving behind the Songani Lookout, the road passes a turning off to one of the forestry villages (right) in the **Chivunde Valley**. Bathing in the Chivunde River, reached by a short drive or walk towards the village, is permitted and the crystal-clear water is bilharzia-free. The road continues along the northern edge of the plateau where the slopes down are distinctly less steep. There are still very good views to the

north across deep valleys and forested hills towards **Malosa**. From Songani, the road at first cuts a dead straight path through the forest then, passing another link track, to a forestry village, **Ngondalo**, winds along a low ridge. It then skirts the **Chiradzulu Peak** (2030 metres/6660 feet), to the left and arrives at junction 12 to one of the plateau's strangest features. A short track, descending gently, leads to **Chingwe's Hole** on the edge of the north-west corner of the plateau.

Here there is a deep, tree-filled cleft in the side of the sheer plateau wall with the deep well-like feature known as Chingwe's Hole. Its depth is at least 20 metres (65 feet) and it culminates in a cave. The popular story associated with the Hole is that it was a place of burial where bodies were lowered into the hole by rope (*chingwe*). Whether this is true or not is difficult to say. Apparently nothing has been found in the cave.

There may be curio sellers at the Hole but they do not worry visitors and seem almost resigned to the fact that a sale is unlikely at this remote corner of the plateau.

Returning to junction 12, the Outer Circular Road rounds the western borders of the

Above: Nursery trees to replace those felled on Zomba Plateau.

plateau. Some three kilometres (two miles) from the junction and after some of the most winding tracks on the plateau, a road leads off to the right towards an easily seen radio signal station. Although this path is motorable and does give views to the west of Zomba it is not usable for the whole length because turning is restricted with access to the radio signal station being barred. The last turning place is marked.

The Outer Circular Road now continues through forest back towards the Ku Chawe Inn and it is this section which may prove the most difficult for ordinary saloon cars. Its steep rocky track should be driven slowly.

A shorter alternative to the Outer Circular Road is a drive down to Mulunguzi Dam. The dam will have been passed on the drive up to the plateau top but it is still worth a visit even if only to get a better look at the Mandala Falls. Leaving from the Ku Chawe Inn, go past the curio sellers and bear right at the first turn. A little way along is the entrance to the campsite. Towards the bottom of the slope bear right and then pull off the road to the left to get to the **Mandala Falls**. The falls should be audible as well as visible.

With the enlargement of the Mulungazi Dam, the falls may seem less impressive but the area around remains a quite exceptionally charming place. It is possible to walk or clamber along the edge of the stream by the falls. Sunlit glades puncture the forest canopy and the mix of vegetation is a delight. Trees with lianes tempt you to swing, Tarzan-like, across the stream. A walk upstream will lead to the Trout Farm, and continuing along what is called the Mulunguzi Trail takes one to the Williams Falls.

Returning to the road from the Mandala Falls, its path now descends to the Mulunguzi Dam, just to the left of the road and down a steep slope. This is another of Zomba's reservoirs with a footway across the dam. It has been greatly enlarged since 1999 and the area still has an untidy, building-site appearance. No doubt it will look more attractive when the vegetation recovers. Using the footway over the dam it is possible to explore a little of the forest.

The **Trout Farm**, a little way along the Outer Circular Road from Ku Chawe, makes for an interesting visit combined with a picnic on the banks of the Mulunguzi River.

Practical matters and activities

Near to the Ku Chawe Inn is a scale model of the plateau housed in a small exhibition hut. It is worth examining this before setting out on a drive or walk. There are very many roads and tracks, perhaps up to 80 kilometres (50 miles) but it is definitely best to keep to the two routes shown on the map (above). Even these paths are quite awful in places and a vehicle without good clearance may well have some difficulty. However, most cars, driven slowly and with care, should accomplish the circuit. The roads are used by large trucks from the forestry department and it is these and the rains of December to April that inflict much of the damage.

Where timber has recently been felled it is important to look out for branches littering the road. To prevent damage to the car's exhaust system it is better to remove these rather than attempt to drive over them. It may also be necessary to roll aside any small boulders falling on to the track when trees are being cut down.

Look out for signs warning against leaving valuables in your car and "No Camping". This may be the only clear indication that this is a parking place at a beauty spot.

Walking the plateau is an obvious alternative to driving round it or it may be combined with a drive. There are plenty of paths to choose from but it is essential to use a map and guide book. It is also very important not to be caught out on the plateau after sunset. Disorientation in a forest is not only frightening, it can be dangerous. The hotel usually has a supply of *Zomba Mountain: A Walkers' Guide* by H and K Cundy. This is an excellent little book although the maps may be difficult to read. The less ambitious can find plenty of short walks through the forest close to Ku Chawe Inn or simple short excursions from a drive round the plateau.

Angling is popular. Fly fishing for rainbow trout is possible from September to April on the Mulunguzi River and lakes above the dams. Rods should be brought as should a supply of flies. The fly-tying workshop which used to be in Zomba town is, sadly, no longer there. It had an international reputation for excellence. The workshop now makes footballs. Enquiries regarding fishing can be made at the trout farm. Licences to fish the

Above: There's no shortage of fuel wood on Zomba.

streams are just K10 for up to eight fish. The farm has been privatised and is much improved. There's a charge to vist the farm (K100 per vehicle, K30 per person). Accommodation is planned there. The un-skilled angler can obtain lessons from the Plateau Stables.

Riding is on offer at the Plateau Stables run by one of Malawi's true characters, Brian Burgess. Colonel Burgess's stables are just a short distance from Ku Chawe Inn. Take the road to the immediate right out of the hotel entrance and the stables will be found to the left of the road with the Burgess's residence a little further on. After many years with the Colonial Service, Colonel Burgess has established a dressage school from the stables he set up in 1977. His pupils have come from all over the world and he provides accommodation in two well-appointed and wonderfully sited cottages near his house. Since the enlargement of the Mulunguzi Dam, the dressage school has not functioned but its revival is being considered. However, the horses are still there and experienced riders can, by prior arrangement, hire horses to go on accompanied rides on the plateau.

Above: On a drive round Zomba Plateau one can expect to meet giant lumber trucks which have the right of way. Below: Among the hundreds of bird species of Malawi's wetlands few are more common than the hamerkop.

In addition to running the stables, Brian Burgess gives lessons to budding flute-players and tuition to those wishing to take up fly-fishing. All this culture and high life at 1700 metres (5500 feet) in the middle of central Africa.

Lake Chilwa

Lake Chilwa is Malawi's second biggest lake. But in times of drought, or even at the end of the dry season, it shrinks perceptibly. In the past it has been even bigger than today.

According to **David Livingstone**, Lake Chilwa (Shirwa) in 1859 reached almost to the foothills of Mount Mulanje, perhaps some 30 kilometres (19 miles) further south than today. This observation is probably broadly accurate for the lake lies in a natural depression which runs northwards from Mulanje and into Mozambique. In the past Lakes Chilwa and Chiuta were contiguous. In Livingstone's day the lake was also much deeper, maybe even four times its present

maximum depth of about three metres. Vast tracts of lake-bed sands or swamps now occupy areas previously under water.

There are inhabited islands in the lake. **Chisi** and **Thongwe** islands must be some of the most remote communities in all Malawi. Thongwe is towards the northern limits of Lake Chilwa and its people live in much the same way as did their forebears a hundred years ago. Unfortunately, diseases such as cholera and the islands' remoteness mean that visitors to Malawi are unlikely to witness these rather special places.

The lake is forever changing size and depth in rapid response to fluctuations in rainfall. Recent years of drought have left it shallow and shrinking but it is still close to 2500 square kilometres (950 square miles). Very high evaporation rates take their toll on the volume of the lake and give it a high salinity. Beyond the swamps, rapidly growing *napini* woodlands have colonised the sandflats.

Whatever its size, it remains a wonderful area of wetland and lake, comparable in many ways with Elephant Marsh. It is all too rarely visited but rewarding to those who venture east of Zomba.

Above: Fishermen rely on Lake Chilwa for their livelihood. Top: Lake Chilwa, one of Malawi's great wetlands.

Above: Malawians have a sweet tooth. Sugarcane is for sale along the roadsides.

Getting there

From

Blantyre:	93km/58miles	M3, minor road
Mangochi:	148km/92miles	M3, minor road
Lilongwe:	311km/193miles	M1, M8, M3,
		minor road
Zomba:	27km/17miles	minor road

The starting point for a visit to the lake will be Zomba. To reach Lake Chilwa there is just one motorable road linking the lake to Zomba. A little north of the town is the turn-off (east) to the village of **Kachulu** on the lakeshore. The turn is signposted to Mikuyu. The road is almost totally untarred but is quite adequate for a car and there is hardly any traffic to speak of. After about five kilometres (three miles), and on the right, is an airfield, largely used for military purposes. A right turn here leads to Jali and, eventually, to Phalombe and Mount Mulanje. The road to Chilwa ignores this turn and carries straight on. In another three kilometres is the sign-posted turn to **Mikuyu Jail** (see Zomba Town).

The rest of the route runs through open countryside with small farms close to the road. It is interesting for the insight it gives to life away from the major roads and towns. People living hereabouts will hardly ever see anyone who is not a near neighbour so you can expect some curiosity at your presence. The land is well cultivated with the usual crops but some prominence given to banana and cassava. Some of the small hills which rise above the generally flat plain are being reafforested.

Near the lake boat-building rivals farming and simple shallow-draught boats are constructed in the quiet shade of the trees.

Suddenly there is a cluster of buildings which make up the lake village of **Kachulu**. Drive through the village and the lake comes into view.

When to go

The lake will be at its largest size and, there-fore, most impressive at the end of the rainy season in April. By August it will have shrunk and before the next rains, from December, it can seem to have disappeared completely when you are at Kachulu.

Where to stay

There is no accommodation at the lake but

Above: Boats and dugout canoes line the shore of Lake Chilwa.

this is a destination which is easily accessible from a base in Zomba, or even Blantyre.

Sightseeing
The lake makes an interesting side-trip from Zomba or Blantyre. Much of the lake is reed-filled, so much so that if it were not for the scores of boats pulled up alongside the earth causeway, one would be forgiven for thinking this was not a lake at all. Boats vary from small dugout canoes to moderately sized craft complete with motors and a canopy to shield passengers from the sun.

The objective of all these boats and their owners is to fish the lake. Even in the driest years there is some sort of catch to be had. A simple scales weighs-in the largest specimens while smaller fry are carried away in baskets.

For a very small, negotiable sum one of the fishermen will agree to take you through the reeds and on to the lake. For the really adventurous it will be a dugout canoe but for the more timid there are more substantial vessels. The rewards of such a trip are an experience of the calm silence of this very large lake and an opportunity to see the wealth of birdlife whose home this is.

Pelican, flamingo and innumerable **hamerkop, heron, egrets** and **ducks** — all inhabit these wetlands.

For an unforgettable day on the lake, take a picnic. Lake Chilwa is off the track of most travellers but it is worth the effort and time needed to reach it.

Practical matters
In an environment such as Lake Chilwa there will be plenty of biting insects so it's best to be well protected from them and from the sun. If going out in a boat, it is wise to be absolutely clear about the price you are to pay and you should make it clear you want to be back well before sundown when the insects will be at their worst.

Liwonde National Park

Although one of the smaller national parks (548 square kilometres/211 square miles), Liwonde is especially attractive for a number of reasons. It is equally accessible from Lilongwe, Blantyre and the southern lake-shore and it has the **Shire River** running

Above: Elephants are very tactile animals. The river in Liwonde National Park is a magnet for large herds.

through it, allowing for game viewing by water. The range and number of game animals is better than in any other park and the accommodation is excellent.

The park's western boundary is just one kilometre from the Shire River. The park stretches up to 17 kilometres (11 miles) east from the river and its north to south limits are over 50 kilometres (30 miles). In the dry season the roads allow access to much of this vast area except the far north.

The terrain is largely part of the flood plain of the Shire River. Close to the river and along its tributaries are areas of swamp but the greater part of the park is typically *mopane* woodland, deciduous trees with open glades of grassland. Distribution of grassland and woodland is largely controlled by soil and this mix is ideal for game and game viewing. Along the Shire River, palm trees add to the variety and provide the photographer with classic tropical backgrounds. The park's vegetation is renowned for its powers of regeneration, greatly aiding its game carrying capacity.

Much of the park's activity was formerly associated with the camps in the south but Mvuu Lodge and Camp, on the Shire, occupy a more central position and their facilities are top class. A new game lodge is being developed in the south of the park.

Getting there

1. To Mvuu Lodge and Camp river crossing:
From

Blantyre:	159km/98miles	M3, minor road
Zomba:	93km/58miles	M3, minor road
Lilongwe:	269km/167miles	M1, M8, M3, minor road
Mangochi:	60km/37miles	M3, minor road
Liwonde township:	43km/27miles	M3, minor road

2. To the southern gate (leading to Chinguni Game Lodge)
From

Blantyre:	122km/76miles	M3, minor road
Zomba:	56km/35miles	M3, minor road
Lilongwe:	240km/149miles	M1, M8, M3, minor road
Mangochi:	77km/48miles	M3, minor road
Liwonde township:	6km/4miles	minor road

Above: Mosques are common along the odd slave trading routes.

If coming to Liwonde from Blantyre, the first part of the route, on the M3, is as for Zomba town and Zomba Plateau (see above).

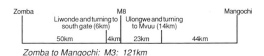

Zomba to Mangochi: M3: 121km

Beyond Zomba, the M3 slips gently down to lower ground as it runs round the north-east face of the **Malosa Massif**, Zomba Plateau's twin upland on the other side of the **Domasi Depression**. This is a good road. As it descends into the valley of the Shire it is possible to look down on to villages from a commanding position. The landscape is hilly and really quite beautiful even though there are no individually outstanding features.

Farming along this section of the M3, towards the Shire River, varies from sugar on the wetter lands to terracing for vegetable crops on the hillsides. In places the iron-rich soil is quite red. Sugar cane is for sale at the side of the road and partly chewed strands litter the roadway. The sellers may be amused if you stop to buy some but there's no knowing if you will acquire the taste which all Malawians seem to have for raw cane.

Rather splendid mosques contrast with simple Christian churches usually standing a little back from the road. The mosques remind one that this was the route used by the Arab slave traders.

Also along the road, there are for sale **wooden chairs** and **toys** for children. The little chairs are well made but the toys look somewhat fragile. Model trucks, made from coloured paper, wire and wood, with a handle to steer them by, seem to be very popular with Malawian children, as do toy helicopters. Other roadside villages sell all manner raffia- and basket-ware as well as cane furniture.

Some 35 kilometres (22 miles) from Zomba is a long row of huts where there are **chiefs' chairs** for sale. These chairs, which dismantle into two easily transportable pieces, are favourite buys for many visitors to Malawi. They vary in quality but the best are beautifully carved and the prices are only a fraction of what is charged in African curio shops in Europe and America. Other villages close to here also make the chairs so it's worth looking around.

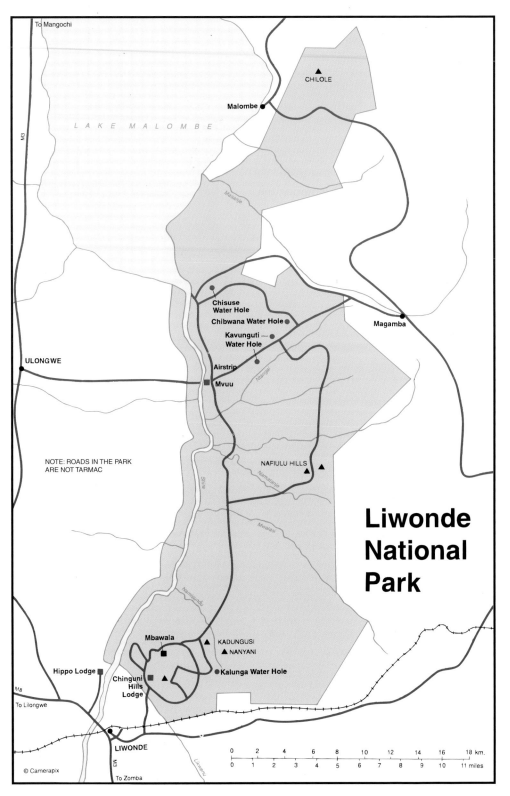

To Mangochi

L A K E   M A L O M B E

M3

CHILOLE

Malombe

Masanje

Chisuse
Water Hole

Chibwana Water Hole

Kavunguti
Water Hole

Magamba

ULONGWE

Airstrip

Mvuu

Maroqi

NOTE: ROADS IN THE PARK
ARE NOT TARMAC

NAFIULU HILLS

Namatanje

Shire

Mwalasi

Liwonde
National
Park

Namasonbu

Mbawala

KADUNGUSI

NANYANI

Hippo Lodge

M8

To Lilongwe

Chinguni
Hills
Lodge

Kalunga Water Hole

LIWONDE

M3

© Camerapix

To Zomba

Liwonqu

| 0 | 2 | 4 | 6 | 8 | 10 | 12 | 14 | 16 | 18 km. |
| 0 | 1 | 2 | 3 | 4 | 5 | 6 | 7 | 8 | 9 | 10 | 11 miles |

On the final 15 kilometre (9 miles) approach to the **Shire River**, there are fine views of the valley. Just before the river is reached, there is a turning into **Liwonde** township. If going into Liwonde National Park by the south gate, turn into the town and look for the signpost to turn left to the gate. If going to **Chinguni Game Lodge**, it is just five kilometres (three miles) into the park from the gate. To get to **Mvuu Lodge and Camp** through the park is a long drive from this gate and the road is unusable in the wet season. To reach Mvuu, it is better to continue on the M3. Ignoring the turn into Liwonde town, the road goes under a railway bridge. This is the main north-south line to Mozambique. The M3 then crosses the river by way of the **Kamuzu Barrage**. The barrage controls the flow of water down into the Lower Shire Valley and helps to maintain the level of Lake Malawi. At the northern side of the barrage is what amounts to an extension of Liwonde town — a market strung along the road. Traders here all seem to have been educated in a school for tenacious selling. Arms are thrust through the open windows of any car which stops and there is a reluctance to take "no" for an answer. Wooden bowls are much in evidence but fruit, fish and other foodstuffs are also on offer. The inter-city buses stop here and trays of food are held up to passengers leaning out of the windows. In the middle of this 'village' is a signposted rough track to **Hippo Lodge** (formerly Kudya Discovery Lodge). This is also the turn to take if going to Liwonde National Park by boat. This is also the place where **Waterline Boat Safaris** start and where those travelling to Mvuu Lodge by boat embark, if they have made the necessary prior arrangements. Travel by boat is the only way to avoid the near impassable park roads in the wet season.

If going direct to **Mvuu Lodge and Camp**, the route is to continue along the M3. In a few kilometres from Liwonde town there is the junction with the M8 which leads to **Balaka**. This is a slightly confusing junction. In the first place the M3 turns right there while it is the M8 which seems to be the road to follow. Secondly, there's an old signpost at the turning with the old numbering showing the M8 to be the M1.

From this turn, the M3 is poorly surfaced

Above: A walking safari in Liwonde. Top: A hippo family in Liwonde National Park ventures into the waters of the Shire River.

Above: Fish are laid out to dry near the shore of Lake Malombe.

with frequent potholing restricting driving speed. The road has now risen above the valley floor but the scene changes little. Small tributaries of the Shire are crossed. In the dry season there is hardly a trickle of water but what still runs is used for washing clothes and children.

Much of the interest is in the scenes of daily life: water wells which have an unending stream of visitors, roadside sales of locally grown sugar cane, shy yet curious children who are certain to gather if you stop.

At **Ulongwe**, 27 kilometres (17 miles) from the Kamuzu Barrage, there is a turning right to the Mvuu Lodge and Camp. A signpost points the way to Mvuu along a small road leading eastwards from the village but note that the sign is on the opposite side of the M3 to this road.

This 14 kilometre (9 mile) minor road is interesting; some would say challenging. It is signposted but in case an alternative track has to be taken, the best plan is to telephone the **Mvuu Camp Office (Central African Wilderness Safaris)** in Lilongwe before setting out and ask for a situation report. If a bridge is down it may be necessary to cross

some shallow water courses by driving down and back up the other side. Whatever route you are given you can be assured a car will make it. If you get stuck, there are plenty of people about to push.

Tracks cross open grasslands and then woodland where there are a few villages to pass through before reaching the Mvuu gate just two kilometres from the Shire River.

Once inside the gate (open from sunrise to sunset), and after making payment of US$5 per person at the office, a two kilometre track leads to a small clearly marked car park. Leaving the car, go to the river's edge and there will be a man there to raise a red flag to signal your need for a boat. (In fact, the flag is no longer the effective signal. A radio has been found to be more reliable but the flag remains a nice touch.) In no time, a boat will come across from the camp to carry you and your luggage to the other side of the broad river. As with the road up from the southern gate, this minor road access may be impassable at times in the wet season.

If coming to Liwonde National Park from Mangochi, perhaps from one of the southern lakeshore resorts, the route is the M3 south.

Above: In full flight, a fish eagle in Liwonde National Park. Following pages: A sundowner cruise on the Shire River rounds off a day's safari.

The road quickly leaves Mangochi and begins to run along the western shore of **Lake Malombe**. This substantial lake, lying in a natural depression, was probably once part of Lake Malawi. It is very shallow and, in the dry season, evaporation sees it shrink to expose fertile land which is used for maize and sugar. This area is well settled by families whose time is divided between fishing and farming. Set up along the lake's beach are large drying tables covered with little silver fish. Unfortunately, the lake is being dangerously over-fished. There are good views (left) of the lake and the fishing activities.

As the road leaves the shoreline of Malombe, it continues southward and quite soon the village of **Ulongwe** and the turning (left) to **Mvuu Camp and Lodge** are reached. The rest of the journey to Mvuu is as described. If going to the southern gate and **Chinguni Hills Lodge**, stay on the M3 through Ulongwe and follow the same road down to Liwonde town. The route to the south gate of the park has already been described.

M1/M5 Junction to Liwonde: M8, M3: 43km

To reach Liwonde National Park from **Lilongwe**, the route is, at first, the M1 (described in the Central Region as 'To the South') as far as its junction with the M8. Then, instead of continuing on to Blantyre by staying with the M1, it is the M8 whose path is followed. This is a short but important west-east road which links the country's north to south road systems. Although potholed, the road is not difficult and it takes one through the important little town of **Balaka**.

Lying in a depression, Balaka is at almost exactly one-quarter of the way along the M8. It is a town with an interesting history. It owes its origin and growth to the building of the railway prior to World War II. It is this line which runs south into Mozambique. The township grew up around the point where the road and railway crossed. It rapidly developed in importance as a trading and

Above: Waterbuck find Liwonde's environment an ideal habitat.

administrative centre. There have been times when there was a real danger of the population growth outstripping the water supply. The M8 loops round the town which actually lies on the S55 to the north (left) of the main road. All the usual services are available and there is a large central market, cut by the railway. There is a fine modern Catholic church on the M8 (right) just as the road reaches the town.

The M8 continues beyond Balaka on a shallow down gradient to run almost directly into the M3. To turn south (right) is to take the M3 to Liwonde town and to the southern gate of the national park. It is also the way towards Zomba and Blantyre. The north bound M3 leads off to the left at this junction with the M8 where there is a small village. This is the road to Ulongwe and **Mvuu Camp and Lodge** as described.

Finally, the easiest, but relatively expensive, alternative to reach the park is to use a light aircraft from Lilongwe or Chileka (Blantyre) airports to a landing strip near to Mvuu Camp. Enquiries for this service should be made with **Central African Wilderness Safaris** or **Proflight Air Services** in Lilongwe.

Air links to the lakeshore and the South Luangwa Valley in Zambia can be arranged.

When to go
The park looks at its best in April and May, just after the rains, but game viewing is best in October and November when the vegetation has died back and the game is seeking water. The rainy months of late December through to March see Liwonde at its most lush but apart from birding, this is probably a time to avoid. June to September is cooler.

Where to stay
Mvuu Camp and Lodge
The Mvuu Camp was taken over from the government by a commercial company (Central African Wilderness Safaris—CAWS) in 1994, since when it has provided the best game park accommodation in Malawi and the equal of some of the best in Africa. Access has been described but it is worth repeating the advice to telephone CAWS before arrival to check on the road situation.

Mvuu provides two different sorts of accommodation. The **camp** consists of a site for those with their own tents and a permanent

Above: Mvuu Camp restaurant in Liwonde National Park is sited on the bank of the Shire River.

camp of twin-bedded safari tents and four chalets. Only two of the chalets are always available for hire. There is a large open restaurant but for those wishing to self-cater, good facilities are provided and a cook is available.

In mid-2001 eight accommodation units in the camp were upgraded to be en suite. Hot and cold showers are available, standards are high and everything is run very efficiently.

Grass has been sown not only to improve the appearance but also to give a cooler surface. A new fence has been built around the camp to keep out wandering hippos at night. A wide range of safari trips is available with preference being given to those on full board.

Alternative accommodation is provided at the **lodge**. This is a luxury complex some way from the camp but still enjoying a riverside setting. Accommodation at the lodge is inclusive of all safaris, only the drinks come as extras. Visitors use just four twin-bedded tents or a new honeymoon suite, all with en suite facilities and solar-powered electricity.

Everything is provided and with a maximum of ten people there at any one time it is the nearest to a private safari as one can

expect. Each tent has been carefully placed so that others cannot be seen. A small balcony area at the end of each tent overlooks a lagoon where animals come to drink at all times of the day. Hippos will be heard grunting just a few metres away during the night. (*Mvuu* means hippo.) The "honeymoon tent" is more discreetly sited and luxuriously furnished than the rest. There's even a double bath which gives views over the lagoon.

Meals are served in a large, raised, game-viewing rondavel which overlooks both the broad river and the lagoon and where there is a well-stocked bar. On some evenings, dinner may be outside in a *boma* (enclosure) and one is surrounded by the noises of the bush. There is a rock plunge pool and even a "loo with a view". The lodge is run independently from the camp; there are no shared facilities or safaris and even the landing stage at the river is exclusive.

Boating, walking or four-wheel drive safaris are available on demand. This is a truly luxurious way to see Liwonde with the added advantage of knowledgeable guides on hand at any time. Visitors are made at home and one soon feels more like a friend than a client.

Mvuu is undoubtedly one of the best sited camps in south or central Africa. Whether staying at the lodge or the main camp, a visit will be a highlight of a tour of Malawi.

Chinguni Hills Lodge

This new lodge became operational in 2000. Using as its nucleus the former park wardens' accommodation, the lodge is a product of Malawi's move towards privatisation. It is still in a development stage.

It occupies a splendid site in a saddle in the Chinguni Hills just five kilometres (three miles) into the park from the main gate near Liwonde town. The elevated position of the lodge allows for spectacular views over the Chikalogwe Plains and the southern part of Liwonde is good for game sightings.

There are currently just four en suite double rooms, plus dormitory accommodation, and there is a campsite 300 metres from the lodge. For those on the campsite and using the dormitory self-catering is possible but there is a restaurant and bar.

Chinguni offers well-managed and reasonably priced accommodation for a stay in the park and has the attraction of being quickly reached from the main road. The road from the park gate to the lodge is usually open all year.

Hippo Lodge

Just outside Liwonde National Park is Hippo Lodge, until recently called Kudya Discovery Lodge. It is located alongside the Shire River near the southern limits of the park. Approaching from Blantyre on the M3, the lodge is signposted (right) in the village just to the north of the crossing of the railway and river. Access is via a rough road with drifts. The lodge is an option to consider if visiting Liwonde. It is moderately priced but, being outside the park, cannot quite compete with Mvuu or Chinguni. A new management took over in late 2001 and changes can be expected. It had become somewhat run down.

Sightseeing

Liwonde offers the best game viewing in Malawi. Since the early 1990s improved conservation practice has been complemented by relocations of animals into the park from other parks and reserves in the country and from outside the borders, especially from South Africa.

One of the strengths and attractions of Liwonde is its range of habitats and ever changing environments. The **Shire River** runs right through the western edges of the park and there are dambos and marshlands away from the river. Elsewhere there are open grasslands and *mopane* woodlands to add to the contrasts.

A large **sanctuary** (an enclosure of some 30 square kilometres/11 square miles) has been constructed within the park to encourage breeding in a safe environment. One outstanding success has been with the rare **black rhino**. A pair was introduced from Kruger National Park in South Africa with funding from the British firm of J & B Whisky. The pair produced their first offspring in July 1997. Since then, with introductions, the herd has risen to eight.

Lions have recently returned to the park from across the Mozambique border. **Buffalo, wildebeest** and a range of **antelope** have been added to the game stock and the 'big five' will have a more permanent presence if the pride of lions takes up residence. Burchell's zebra and hartebeest have already been on the shopping list.

The Shire River is home to large numbers of **hippo, crocodile** and **mud turtles**. With some twenty-five hippos per kilometre of river, this is possibly the highest density in the world. The crocodile population is equally impressive and a recent survey identified some especially large specimens.

The river also attracts other mammals to drink at its edge or to take a dip in its waters. **Elephants** will frequently be seen plunging into the river and even crossing it. The antelopes include **bushbuck, waterbuck, reedbuck, oribi**, beautiful **kudu**, the diminutive **klipspringer** and the magnificent **sable**. There are large numbers of impala which have become remarkably unaffected by man's presence.

Leopards and **hyena** are present but rarely seen. On the other hand, there are regular sightings of **genet** and **civet** and occasionally of **serval**. There are **warthogs** and **bushpigs** and the usual troops of **vervet monkeys** are often seen near Mvuu and Chinguni. Other

Above: The palms along the banks of the Shire River are home to great colonies of cormorants.

mammals very likely to be seen include the mongoose.

The birdlife of Liwonde is famously rich with over 400 species recorded. Attracted by the river and the variety of habitat, the numbers are as impressive as their range. **Fish eagles** and **cormorants** are seen by the Shire as are **herons** and **hamerkops**. The grasslands attract a range of **bee-eaters** while the woodland areas are the best places to see resident **sunbirds** and the migratory **European swallow**.

Practical matters and activities
Both Mvuu and Chinguni will arrange for **game drives**, **walking safaris** or **boat trips** to see the wildlife. The uncrowded nature of the park is appreciated whichever way you view it. It is very rare indeed to come across other visitors no matter which way you decide to travel. At the Mvuu Lodge, guests are encouraged to try all three methods and there is no doubt that the walking safaris and the trips along the river in a boat are very special experiences. To take a sundowner boat trip, watching the birds go to roost and seeing the crocodiles and hippos at very close quarters while you sip your pre-selected glass of wine or Malawi gin and tonic, is often the highlight of a visit to Liwonde.

Particularly because of the proximity of the Shire River and the riverine marshlands, it is especially important to take malaria prophylactics. For night drives it is wise to have something warm to wear particularly in the months of July and August.

From Mvuu Camp and Lodge, overnight stays in a **local village** can be arranged. Guests cycle to the village where they sleep in mud huts, eat local food and meet the villagers. A comfortable mattress and a mosquito net are the only concessions to 'luxury' living. This fascinating experience also benefits the villagers who receive almost US$50 per guest.

A variety of trips up the river to view game can be had from **Waterline River Safaris**. Their boats have a jetty near Hippo Lodge. These boat safaris are an attractive alternative to game drives in the park.

Above: Chawani Bungalow, a good base from which to explore Thyolo and Mulanje.

Thyolo

Thyolo (pronounced, and previously spelt, Cholo) may conjure up different pictures in different minds. Some will think of the great escarpment overlooking the Lower Shire Valley. For others it will be a forest reserve. But, for most, it will be a picture of neat tea plantations.

The first tea grown in Africa was in Malawi when the plant was introduced by the African Lakes Company in 1888. Initially it competed with coffee but rapidly overtook it. Tea came to Thyolo in 1908 and is now the dominant crop over large areas of the district. The climate is conducive to relatively good yields and, although it is grown in northern Malawi, this is the only area where it is strictly economically viable. Vast areas of softly contoured land are given over to tea, the plantations or estates being owned largely by international companies. Tea is Malawi's second most important cash crop, after tobacco, and contributes about twelve per cent of its export earnings.

Getting there

From

Blantyre:	39km/24miles	M2
Mulanje town:	42km/26miles	M2

Blantyre   Thyolo
                  Bvumbwe
         16km   23km

Blantyre to Thyolo: M2: 39km

Thyolo is almost equidistant from central Blantyre and Mulanje town. In each direction the road is the M2. Following rebuilding at the turn of the century, this road is now one of the best in Malawi. The reconstruction was not simply a matter of re-surfacing. The opportunity was taken for some realignments and for widening.

To reach the M2 road from Blantyre, take the main highway to Limbe and continue through the town on Livingstone Avenue. After passing the Limbe Club (left) there is a turning left to the M2. This is the Thyolo Road. To the right is forest and as that clears one is into **Bvumbwe**. Here are the **Gangecraft** workshops where carved curios and other items are made. The workshop is worth a visit and items are for sale. It may be best to

Above: Tea is one of Malawi's most important crops with Thyolo the main centre. Top: Thyolo's shops serve the needs of those working on the tea plantations.

Above: Jacaranda in flower: a colour contrast with the tea garden. Opposite: Stands of bamboo, a grass, are grown in amongst Thyolo's tea estates.

telephone to check that it is open to visitors on any particular day.

After passing through pleasant rolling countryside with a mix of agriculture and forestry, the massive **Thyolo Tea Estates** begin to dominate the scene and Thyolo town is reached.

When to go
There is no time when a visit cannot be made although, as usual, it may be best to avoid the wet season. The forest reserve and the views into the Lower Shire Valley are at their best just after the rains, May to June. For the tea estates, October to April is best.

Where to stay
Many visit Thyolo while staying in Blantyre. It is a short drive to the town and the road is very good.

Chawani Bungalow
This is a splendid place to stay if exploring the forest or the escarpment. Alternatively it is the ideal retreat if seeking a quiet couple of days to enjoy the glorious scenery. The bungalow is on the **Satemwa Tea Estates**, on the mountain slope, and has views across the verdant green tea gardens towards Mount Mulanje. The building, well into the estate and beyond the tea factory, was once the home of the tea plantation manager. Accommodation is in four double rooms. Although the bungalow is self-catering, a cook can be hired. Reservations can be made through most of the safari tour companies in Lilongwe or Blantyre. Booking ahead is important. It is often full at weekends.

There are two other cottages on the estate which are let out to visitors.

Sightseeing
Thyolo is one of the oldest of Malawi's towns, something of a contemporary of Blantyre. It is now a service centre for the estate region, bigger than a village but somehow not quite a town. Most of it lies to the south of the M2 and not seen from that road. All the usual facilities are there, a supermarket, bank and petrol. On the Blantyre side of town is the **Thyolo Club** (signposted) where one can get refreshments including locally produced tea.

It is a pleasant little place with a sense of order and neatness.

Towards the Mulanje end of the settlement, it becomes a street village with a string of small stores and an extraordinary number of tailors in rundown premises. The famous **Chiperoni blanket factory** is on the edge of town.

Mostly dependent upon the time available, the **tea** growing area around Thyolo can either be driven through or a visit can be made to one of the estates.

Unlike the tea estates in South Asia, almost all of the plucking is done by men. Incidentally, tea is plucked not picked. The men will be seen walking between the lines of bushes, their distinctive coloured clothing giving a splash of yellow or red to the otherwise green landscape. The young, brighter green leaves are dropped into baskets carried on their backs and their pay is related to the weight of the leaves they take to the weighing huts. Teams of ten to twenty work together and march single file on the road as they make their way to and from the plantations. Their living conditions in squalid 'workers' lines' may shock but most of the estates have a paternalistic approach to their employees and their families and there are benefits to be gained from this system.

The orderliness and scale of the tea and coffee estates contrasts strongly with the smallholdings that make up most of Malawi's agriculture. Tea is naturally a tree but in order to facilitate plucking, the trees are carefully pruned to bush size. They are defiantly green even in the dry season.

The estates are quite pleasant places to picnic. There are shade trees, there is an attractive calm about the scene and the drink has, of course, to be Thyolo tea.

Thyolo Forest Reserve is a great place for **walkers** and **birdwatchers**. The forest clothes part of the **Thyolo Mountain** which rises to over 1400 metres (4600 feet). Although there has been illegal felling, the forest is still covers a significant area criss-crossed by paths. It contains some valuable hardwoods but many will explore the forest for its birdlife. One rarity which might be seen is the **green-headed oriole**. The bird's green head and wings contrast with its bright yellow underparts. The **Cholo alethe** is said to sing before the rains, thus providing a warning against a soaking. Less common, indeed quite rare, are **Natal thrushes** and **bronze-naped pigeons**.

There are **monkeys** and other **small mammals** in the forest but sightings cannot be guaranteed. However, you'll certainly hear the noisy **samango monkeys**.

From Thyolo town, the S151 road leads to Elephant Marsh and, in the past, was a recommended route. Unfortunately, the condition of the road is such that, without local knowledge, it is not one which should be attempted. With a guide it might be possible to reach the edge of the **Thyolo Escarpment** but to continue to Elephant Marsh is not a realistic aim. If going to the escarpment edge, two small settlements, **Muona** and **Mchacha** will be on the route but there's little else.

To reach the **Zoa** and **Nchenachena Falls** to the south of Thyolo is very difficult and shouldn't be attempted without a guide. The falls are in the **Ruo Gorge** which is to the east of the Thyolo Escarpment. A viewing platform is being constructed. However, the only alternative to a difficult drive and trek is to use the railway, travelling by the Presidential Train or a specially adapted maintenance coach. The conversion of the Presidential Train to tourist use has not proved a great success and there can be no guarantee that a train is running at any time. At best there are irregular trips.

Practical matters and activities
Anyone wishing to arrange a visit to a tea estate should get in touch with one of the company offices. The easiest way to contact them is to look in the telephone directory under Thyolo or Mulanje and try to make an appointment. It may be necessary to telephone three or four before you strike lucky.

Short tours of the estates are possible at any time of the year on weekdays but much of the activity is during the main plucking season: October to April.

Some care should be exercised if trekking through the **forest reserve**. Paths are not always clear and it is possible to get lost. It may be possible to take a local guide from the Forestry Department Office.

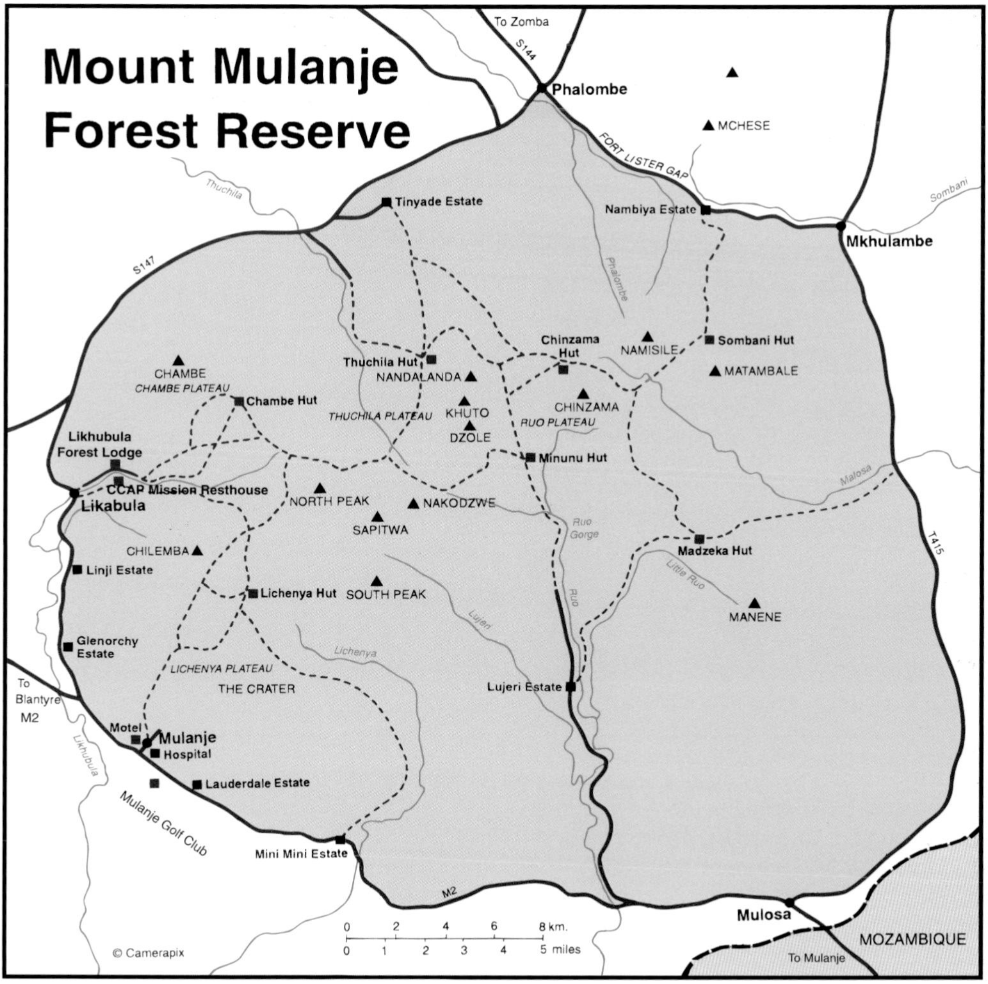
Mount Mulanje
Forest Reserve
To Zomba
S144
Phalombe
MCHESE
FORT LISTER GAP
Thuchila
Tinyade Estate
Nambiya Estate
Sombani
Mkhulambe
S147
Phalombe
Chinzama Hut
NAMISILE
Sombani Hut
MATAMBALE
CHAMBE
CHAMBE PLATEAU
Thuchila Hut
NANDALANDA
Chambe Hut
KHUTO
CHINZAMA
THUCHILA PLATEAU
RUO PLATEAU
DZOLE
Likhubula Forest Lodge
Minunu Hut
CCAP Mission Resthouse
Likabula
NORTH PEAK
NAKODZWE
Malosa
SAPITWA
Ruo Gorge
CHILEMBA
Madzeka Hut
T415
Linji Estate
Little Ruo
Lichenya Hut
SOUTH PEAK
Ruo
Lujeri
MANENE
Glenorchy Estate
Lichenya
LICHENYA PLATEAU
To Blantyre
M2
THE CRATER
Lujeri Estate
Motel
Mulanje
Hospital
Likhubula
Lauderdale Estate
Mulanje Golf Club
Mini Mini Estate
M2
Mulosa
MOZAMBIQUE
To Mulanje
© Camerapix
0 2 4 6 8 km.
0 1 2 3 4 5 miles

If a trip on the railway to the falls is attractive, enquiries should be made at the **Tourist Office** in Blantyre. There can be no guarantee that a train will be running even during the period of a lengthy visit.

Mount Mulanje and Mulanje Town

The Mulanje Massif rises to over 3000 metres (9850 feet) and is the highest mountain in Central Africa. It is a truly spectacular sight not least because of its bare rock flanks which tower over 2100 metres (7000 feet) above the surrounding plains. This plateau with peaks is about 600 square kilometres (230 square miles) in area. The highest peak is **Sapitwa** and the great block of mountain is split in two by the **Fort Lister Gap**, a broad pass eroded by the **Phalombe** and **Sombani Rivers**.

The massif is largely syenite and granite, igneous rocks with large crystals. The effects of weathering can be seen in the giant slabs of rock which peel from the surface. Erosion by rivers running along lines of weakness or cracks (joints) in the rock has resulted in deep clefts striking back into the heart of the mountain. Where they meet, cauldron-like hollows have developed and this led early explorers into thinking this was a volcanic mountain.

The height of the Mulanje Massif is such that it creates its own climate. Wettest areas face south where annual rainfalls may exceed 2500 mm (100 inches). The mountains can

Above: An open-air clothing market operates near Luchenza.

also trigger the *chiperoni* during the otherwise dry season. This moist wind brings mists and light rain to nearby Blantyre and the Phalombe plains as the air is forced to rise over Mulanje. Apart from the *chiperoni*, most rain falls on Mulanje between December and February although the highest parts of the plateau can get heavy bursts of rain in almost any season. Temperatures, affected by the altitude, can drop close to 0°C at night on the higher slopes and there is likely to be a difference of about 10-12 C° (28-34 F°) between the temperature of the plains and those of the mountains.

Getting there
From
Blantyre to Phalombe:
    85km/53miles   M3, S146, S145, S144
Blantyre to Mulanje:
    66km/41miles   M4, M2
Mulanje to Phalombe:
    35km/22miles   S147
Phalombe to Muloza:
    45km/28miles   T415, minor road
Blantyre to Mulanje:
    81km/50miles   M2

Mulanje to Muloza:
    28km/17miles   M2

A number of different access routes are possible. The best route is the M2. This is now an excellent road even if it is not the shortest. There is an interesting back way via **Chiradzulu** and there is the short route on the M4 but this road is poor.

Blantyre to Mulanje: M2: 81km

If using the M2, the road goes via Thyolo and the early part has been described. Its whole length is newly upgraded and re-engineered to a high standard. Beyond Thyolo the tea estates continue, some with large stands of timber, others with areas of coffee. There are also some very good examples of bamboo to the left of the road. Almost hidden among the trees to the right of the road is a fine, modern Dutch Catholic church. Look for the sign: **Addolorata Catholic Parish**. The brick church, built by local labour and using local materials, has

Above: Mount Mulanje, a great massif of syenite and granite, rises to over 3000 metres, almost 10,000 feet.

some fine murals and is usually open. The whole mission station is modern and well-kept. Those associated with it are justly proud of what has been achieved.

As the tea estates are left behind, coffee continues but in turn that is soon replaced by the ubiquitous maize as lower ground is reached. The main railway line is crossed just before the small town of **Luchenza**. This is a busy settlement with a range of shops and services including petrol. As one passes the town's limits at the eastern side, the important **Thuchila River** is crossed and there is often a big clothing market. The Thuchila flows south from here before it runs into the great **Ruo River**, itself a tributary of the Shire.

Local clays are used for brick making, as is evident from the number of small kilns near the road, and also for pottery. Pottery can be purchased — look for the sign to the left of the road. Along this section of the M2 there are opportunities to buy sugar cane, bananas and vegetables, laid out at the side of the road.

Twelve kilometres (seven miles) beyond Luchenza, the junction (left) with the M4 is reached.

From the M4-M2 junction, the combined road is the M2 and it is just a short way into Mulanje town. In under three kilometres, with the **Mulanje Massif** continuing to form a quite magnificent backdrop to the view north-east, there is a small village, **Chisitu**. Just six kilometres (four miles) further and after a petrol station (right) there is a turning to the left which leads to **Phalombe**. There's the amusingly named 'Las Vegas Bottle Store' at the turning. This minor road also accesses **Likabula** (also **Likhubula**), the starting point for walks and climbs in the mountains. To reach Likabula, follow the road for just over nine kilometres (five miles) when there is a turning (right) towards the village and forestry station.

At the Likabula turn is the village of **Chitakali** which, in two more kilometres, becomes **Mulanje** town without any noticeable break.

Blantyre to Mulanje: M4, M2: 66km

As has been said, the M4 is an alternative route to Mulanje from Blantyre. Coming out

197

Above: Mulanje Mountain; the trek to the top begins.

For those with plenty of time and a wish to explore, there is yet another option if travelling to Mulanje from Blantyre. This time the route starts on the M3 and then follows minor roads. Apart from the chance to view some of the more remote rural areas of this part of Malawi, this route enables the traveller to see the famous **Chiradzulu Peak** 1773 metres (5817 feet). Plenty of time should be allotted to this journey because almost all will be on indifferent dirt roads.

To reach Chiradzulu from Blantyre take the Zomba road: M3 and turn off (right) on to the S146 signposted Chiradzulu. The first part of this road, as far as Chiradzulu, is tarred but then deteriorates into a dirt road as it descends towards the foot of the mountain. **Chiradzulu Peak** has a marked cleft at the summit. It is one of the main peaks rising from the **Shire Highlands**, the edge of the Great Rift Valley.

At Chiradzulu take the right fork to continue on the S146 gradually descending to the Phalombe Plains. A number of small streams are crossed by bridges which consist of planks of wood nailed to two supporting beams. It is as well to inspect the bridge before crossing because frequently the nails have worked loose and stand proud of the surface. Getting a puncture in this isolated area is no way to start a journey to Mulanje.

The landscape is mostly that of a broad plain. Small patches of sunflowers brighten the view and little clusters of mud huts may offer the traveller refreshment in the form of a "tea room". One such establishment has a man and a woman painted on the wall either side of the doorway. Curiously the man seems to be wearing a military uniform and the woman appears to be pregnant.

The **River Phalombe** is crossed by a substantial concrete slab bridge. In the dry season the river's bed may be dry and local people dig down to the water table to create pools for washing clothes. Parts of the bed, where the soil remains moist, are used to grow vegetables.

Just after crossing the river the road divides and, without the help of signposts, it is difficult to tell exactly which path to take. The road down to Phalombe village is the turn right almost immediately after crossing the bridge but if in doubt someone will be

from Blantye the main road to Limbe is followed. In Limbe the route runs through the centre of the town via Livingstone Road (the lower of the two roads through town) and continues to become the M4. This means ignoring the marked turn off to Thyolo (M2).

Although the M4 route is shorter by some 15 kilometres (9 miles) it has the disadvantage of a wretchedly poor surface except for the first 15 kilometres (9 miles) out of Blantyre. There is some industry near to Limbe but the rest of the journey is through smallholdings. Ten kilometres (six miles) after passing through **Thuchila** there is a short cut to **Phalombe**, the S147. Just before reaching the junction with the M2, the road becomes especially dusty in the dry seaon and something of a skid-pan when it's wet. The only compensation is a view of simple thatch-roofed houses against a background of quaint conical inselbergs rising from the plains. It is here that the M4 meets the M2. The turn is left then through Chisitu, Chitakali and into Mulanje town.

around to ask. Simply mention Phalombe and a direction will be pointed out.

After a short winding course, the road (S144) takes a generally straight path heading for the Mulanje Massif. The mountains become more and more impressive as one gets closer and provide an excellent background to any photography along the road. There is something almost unreal about the view as Mulanje emerges from the haze, completely dwarfing the road and villages as it rises sheer from the flat plains.

Smallholder farmers cultivate these plains. People on bikes, or more likely walking, share the road with the very few vehicles which use it. Drivers should be cautious. Children use the road to roll their hoops or play with a stuffed bag which takes the place of a football. The few water pumps along this road attract knots of women who stop to gossip before returning to their homes with impossibly heavy buckets on their heads.

Approaching Phalombe village the landscape, even in the dry season, becomes greener as the tree cover increases. Arriving at a T-junction, the Mulanje Massif now completely overshadowing the scene, turn right to enter **Phalombe** village.

To reach Mulanje town from here one can take the short route by continuing through the village or the longer path by backtracking from the village and following the road all the way around the eastern side of the mountain — a long journey. These routes are described in 'Sightseeing' and allow a complete circuit of Mount Mulanje.

When to go
The rainy season is certainly a time to avoid. Between April and December there will be little rain but the *chiperoni* mists can be a problem at almost any time although least likely from September to December. It can be cold as one climbs the mountain and frosts are common in the winter months.

Where to stay
The need to find accommodation in Mulanje town is not pressing. If making a short visit, perhaps to drive around the mountain, this can be done in a day from a base in Blantyre. If walks on the mountain are planned, then it's probably best to use Likabula Forest Lodge or the mountain huts referred to below. However, if staying in the town, for whatever reason, there's not a large choice.

The best on offer is the **Mulanje View Motel** to the left of the road if travelling east. The hotel has simple and very inexpensive accommodation in single or double rooms, some of which have en suite facilities. There is a restaurant and a campsite. Despite the name, the views are disappointing. This is not the place to see the mountains in all their glory. Next door is the slightly cheaper **Mulanje Motel**.

Camping is to be had at the **Mulanje Golf Club**. The club is on the right of the road if travelling east and almost out of town. It is possible to use the facilities of the club, including its restaurant.

If an exploration of the mountains is planned then there is little reason to stay in the town

At **Likabula** there is a Forestry Station where the mountain huts can be booked and paid for. There is also some accommodation in a **mission (CCAP) resthouse**. For a modest price self-catering is available with a cook to prepare the food you have brought. There is usually no problem with finding a bed. Stalls selling carvings are nearby and a vehicle can be parked at a cost of K100.

Slightly more sophisticated accommodation is at the **Likhubula Forest Lodge** just a short drive up a mountain track. To reach the lodge, turn off left before the Forestry Station. This lodge was the Forestry Resthouse until it was privatised in 1999. It is well kept, clean and beautifully sited. There are five rooms in various combinations, singles, doubles and a triple. Only one is en suite but an annexe also provides en suite accommodation. There is a lounge and kitchen, with a cook available if you bring your own food. A room costs about K1000 and the whole lodge can be hired for K8000 per day. A nice touch is the fact that a copy of Frank Eastwood's *Guide to the Mulanje Massif* is in every bedroom.

There are seven huts up in the mountain for those walking or climbing Mulanje. Six are run by the Forestry Department with the Mountain Club of Malawi. The other is owned by the mission and does have some cooking pots and pans. Currently, they provide very simple accommodation although there are

Above: Likhubula Forest Lodge is a base from which to explore Mount Mulanje.

plans to up-grade them and to build more huts. Apart from seats and tables, there is no furniture although some do have what passes for wooden bunks. Visitors need to bring all they will need. The exception is fuel for cooking fires. This is provided, as is water, by an employee of the Forestry Department (the *mlonda*). It is he who will collect the receipt for the fee paid at the Forest Station when the hut was booked. If he doesn't appear, the guide or porter will stand in. Strictly, wild-camping on the mountains is forbidden although not unknown

Sightseeing

The little town Mulanje has an enviable setting with the Mulanje Massif on one side and neat tea estates on the other. There are strictly two settlements there: the busy market centre of **Chitakali**, on the west and the older part of the town, Mulanje proper, a little further along the road.

There are all the usual services and the Mulanje District Hospital stands in land-scaped gardens. At the eastern end of the town is the **Mulanje Golf Club** with its sandy greens and notoriously slow service

in the restaurant. Beyond the town, towards the Mozambique border, there are more tea estates, with their own factories.

But, of course, for most visitors to Mulanje, it is the mountain that is the attraction, not the town.

Like most mountains, Mulanje has its moods. It can be very wet. It can be shrouded in cloud. It can be washed in the light of a full moon when the face of **Chambe Peak** is like a floodlit wall. It can be hot in the day and remarkably cold at night. But, whatever its mood, it is an enchanting and exciting place to be.

Narrow gullies have been cut by fast flowing streams. There are amphitheatres of rock, giant basins. The mountain offers a variety of challenges. It can be a test of mountaineering skills or it can simply be a fairly strenuous trek to the magnificent viewpoints which are Mulanje's rewards to those who accept the challenge. The advice must be: check with your guide, adopt a pace and route to suit you and enjoy Malawi's great mountain.

The Mulanje Massif is clothed in an assortment of vegetation which reflects its range of altitude and its changing aspect. Perhaps the best-known species of forest tree is the cedar which takes its name from these mountains. The massif stands at the northern limits of its natural habitat but this does not prevent the **Mulanje cedar** rising to over 30 metres (100 feet). This majestic tree stands straight and proud, its two metre diameter trunk protected by a thick fibrous bark. The best place to see these trees is in the ravines at altitudes above 1400 metres (4600 feet). Fires in the past have destroyed large sections of forest but the Department of Forestry has largely eliminated this hazard.

The wettest ravines, on the south facing side of Mulanje, also harbour dense tropical rainforest which includes the **podocarpus**, almost as tall as the Mulanje cedar. Many of the plants of the plateau are semi-temperate in character: **heather** and **heathland** and a variety of grasses. There are spectacular carpets of **flowers** especially after the rains. **Whyte's sunflower** grows in rocky shelters, the **venus fly-trap** catches and consumes its prey and **red hot pokers** add their colour to the scene. In the wooded areas there are varieties of **fern**. Elsewhere, only **lichen** attempts to conceal the nakedness of the bare rock peaks.

The animal life of Mulanje is less varied than the vegetation. Although **monkeys** (**vervet** and, more rarely, **blue**) will be seen or heard, the most common mammal to be encountered is likely to be the **klipspringer**. This little antelope, appearing to stand on tiptoe in order to get a better view, will be found in forested parts of Mulanje. Its green-tinged hair makes it difficult to spot until it takes fright and runs. Small mammals such as **hares** and **voles** are present in large numbers. **Snakes** are fairly common but present no real danger. Most are small and quite harmless but on the lower slopes, among the trees, the **forest cobra** has been recorded. This grows to up to two metres in length but the chances of meeting one are very small indeed. For most people the large numbers of **butterflies** on the massif will be a greater attraction.

Birds are encouraged by the variety of habitat. **Buzzards** and the **black eagle** are present as are the more widespread **white-necked ravens**. The black eagle, at 84 centimetres (33 inches), is one of the largest birds in southern Africa. It often flies at low altitude where its size is especially impressive. The birds favouring grasslands are, of course, more likely to be seen when on the move than those in the forested parts of the mountain.

Flora and fauna apart, the attraction of the mountain is in the incredible wilderness of this unique landscape. It is, after all, the highest mountain in Central Africa. Little wonder that the views are unsurpassed. As one climbs up Mulanje, one leaves the tropics behind and enters a temperate environment. This may not be Kilimanjaro but it's not a bad substitute.

One way to see a lot of the massif is to drive around it. Missing, of course, will be the views from the mountains and there will be none the intimacy with Mulanje that a climb will afford. But a drive is not without merit.

Driving round the base of Mulanje, from a start in the town is to take the M2 back towards Blantyre and then to turn off on to a minor road (right) at the 'Las Vegas' bottle store at the western edge of the town. This road leads past tea gardens, some edged with palm trees. After just over nine kilometres (five miles) there is the turn (right) into the forest towards **Likabula** which will be the starting point for those wishing to walk in the mountains.

Carrying on along the road takes one round the northern side of the Mulanje Massif. Close to the road after passing through **Chambe** market is the peak of the same name whose smooth bare summit reaches 2557 metres (8389 feet). Nearing Phalombe village, there are a number of small settlements strung out along the road.

Phalombe is very much a service village with market, stores, bank and petrol. There is a magnificent red brick Catholic church set back from the road (right). It enjoys a wonderful setting, surrounded by trees and with the Mulanje Massif towering behind it.

On the northern side of Phalombe village a right turn leads into the Fort Lister Gap at the south-eastern end of which is the village of **Mkhulambe** and the T415 road. Turning right on to this road takes one to the Mozambique border and the village of Muloza.

This section of the circular path round the massif is a trouble-free way of seeing all

Above: The Catholic Church at Phalombe has a backdrop of Mount Mulanje.

aspects of this great mountain. On entering the **Fort Lister Gap** there is a rise over a low col which separates the main massif from a smaller, yet still impressive mountain, **Mchesa** (2289 metres/7510 feet). The views are splendid, as is the quiet peacefulness of this little-used road. On the left hand side are the remains of the fort which gives its name to the gap.

Fort Lister was built in 1893 to intercept the slave traffic which was using the pass. Ten years later, no longer needed, the fort was abandoned to the elements. One of two graves at the perimeter of the fort is that of a cousin of the writer **Robert Louis Stevenson**.

Descending from the col and driving along the T415, Mozambique is just a stone's throw away to the left. A number of streams have to be crossed. In the dry season the water courses may be empty and, alongside the bridge, paths are often cut so that there is the option of driving across the bed of the stream. After inspecting the bridge this may well be the majority of drivers' choice.

Close to **Muloza** there is no alternative: the only crossing of a river is by driving over a widened dam as the waters lap around the vehicle's wheels.

Muloza is the border village before entry to Mozambique. It was here that large camps for Mozambican refugees were set up during the civil war in that country. From Muloza village a turn right on to the M2 takes one back into Mulanje.

For some, a drive round Mulanje will prove challenge enough but many will be lured by its mysterious beauty to explore further.

Practical matters and activities
There are one or two warnings which should be heeded if visiting Mulanje. When driving round the base of the mountain one must not expect tarred roads. The M2 is good but the remaining roads have rather poor surfaces, are narrow and, to the north, are used by local people unused to traffic. Speeds should be modest.

Mulanje, like any other high mountain, has to be treated with respect. Walking any distance up in the mountains without a guide is foolish. Some of the slopes and rock faces are for serious climbers only. Thick mists from the *chiperoni* can be a hazard and a sudden rainstorm may turn a mountain stream into a raging torrent in a matter of minutes. If a rainstorm occurs, it is best to seek shelter on higher ground away from the streams. In dry periods, pools along the streams' courses can be used for bathing; none is better than the **Likabula** Pool.

A final caution: there is talk of large scale quarrying on Mulanje in the future. It must be hoped that, if this does come to be, the environmental issues will be sympathetically addressed.

Those with little time or unable to tackle serious **walking** will find that there are numerous paths leading off the circular route which can be investigated without even losing sight of the road. On rising slopes and often with only low vegetation, visibility back to the road is generally unrestricted. If leaving a vehicle unattended it is best to put any potentially attractive items into the boot.

Anyone looking for more serious walking or **climbing** will probably set out from

Likabula village. Access to the village from Mulanje town has been described. As soon as a visitor turns in towards the village he is likely to encounter a rush of eager boys offering to act as a guide into the mountains. It is best politely to ignore all these offers of help until a reliable guide can be organised. There are said to be seventy registered guides and another twenty "who know the way". Guides cost K350 to lead up the mountain (and another K350 to bring you down). There is an overnight charge of K200 and one is expected to pay for the guide's food. Porters can be hired at the same fees.

A new guiding operation is being developed. It is called **Mountain High Rangers**. The aim is to offer professional guiding by trained personnel who operate from Likabula Lodge. Anything from a short walk to a full-scale climb will be catered for.

From the lodge it is just an hour-and-a half's walk to a pretty waterfall. In a four-wheel drive vehicle it is possible to drive to the waterfall along a rough track. The drive takes about half an hour.

To walk or climb up the mountain a guide will be needed. Many visitors spend two or three days exploring, using the seven huts that are sited up the slopes. The guides will recommend routes and Frank Eastwood's book, *Guide to the Mulanje Massif*, is a mine of information for walkers and climbers.

Organised **rock climbing** has taken place on the Mulanje Massif for decades. But it is not recommended for the visitor without local knowledge or assistance. Anyone wishing to climb on Mulanje is advised to contact the **Mountain Club of Malawi** or the Mountain High Rangers, preferably before arriving in Malawi. The club, which maintains the mountain huts in conjunction with the Forestry Department, will be happy to advise and provide assistance.

Fly-fishing for trout is possible in the **Lichenya River** which drains off the south-west of the massif. A licence is needed and can be had from the Forestry Department.

Lengwe National Park

Lengwe is a relatively small park of 890 square kilometres (344 square miles). It was upgraded from the status of reserve in the early 1970s and has been developed only in its most easterly parts, near the entrance gate. Very few visitors seem to use the park and this is one of its advantages. However, the animals tend to take fright easily.

The vegetation is thicket, with some deciduous woodland and more dense tree growth along the stream courses. The eastern area is quite flat, allowing for a good and well marked network of driveable tracks. To the west there are only two tracks neither of which is recommended. It is to the west that the level rises and low hills, outcrops of sandstone, break the skyline. Further hills rise in the southern extremity of Lengwe in the **Panga** area.

Lengwe is separated from the Majete Wildlife Reserve by the valley of the **River Mwanza**.

Getting there
From

Blantyre:	74km/46miles M1,	minor road
Sucoma:	17km/11miles M1,	minor road

Blantyre to Lengwe NP: M1, minor road: 74km

Lengwe National Park is easily reached from Blantyre or Sucoma by taking the M1 and then using a short minor road to the park.

The M1 is the only major road into Malawi's most southerly territory. To join the road from Blantyre's central triangle take Victoria Avenue down from the Mount Soche Hotel. After passing the Blantyre Sports Club (right) and crossing the River Mudi take the second right turn into Joachim Chissano Road. This is signposted to Chikwawa. Gradually the outskirts of Blantyre are left behind and one is into more open country.

The M1 is quite good tarmac as far as the crossing of the Shire River near Chikwawa. The continuation southwards is gradually being rebuilt. Work started back in 1997, the reconstruction consists of raising and widening the road largely by overlying the old tarmac with a new gravel surface. At its best it can be a fast trouble-free route but there

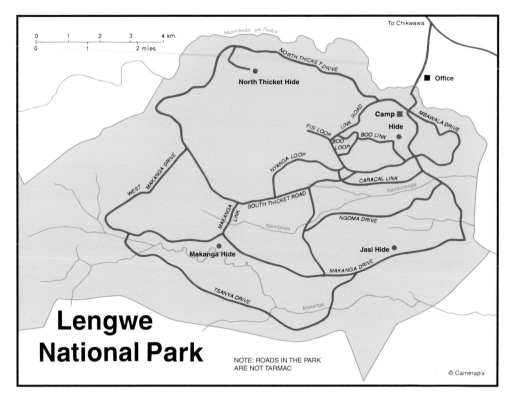

Lengwe National Park

NOTE: ROADS IN THE PARK ARE NOT TARMAC

© Camerapix

is still much work to be done and currently the potholed tarmac reappears south of Sucoma.

Perhaps the most attractive part of this route is as far as the Shire crossing. Not only is the road surface good but the views it affords are stunning. The general impression as one leaves Blantyre is how remarkably green everything looks even in the dry season. Then, as the road begins to wind its way down towards the edge of the Shire Valley, every bend reveals another scene of extraordinary beauty. At first the views are mostly north-westwards across rolling hills but soon the great valley of the Shire is seen with the river a serpentine thread of shimmering silver across the landscape.

To the right of the road the land drops steeply and clusters of farms are seen as a patchwork of thatched roofs. Narrow foot-paths lead up to the road from the huts and the villagers bring firewood and charcoal to the roadside for sale to passers-by. Although the farms seem deserted, as soon as you stop someone will come running up the slope anxious to make a sale.

At one point, clearly seen to the left of the M1, there is a ledge where one can drive off the road, park the vehicle and enjoy the view at leisure without distraction. As the edge of the **Thyolo Escarpment** is reached the breadth of the scene increases until it seems as though the whole valley is visible. These are almost aerial views.

Perhaps the best time of day to drive this section of the M1 is in the early morning when the mists, which fill the valley bottom, are beginning to thin. There is a certain magical quality to the view. The M1's steep descent ends dramatically as the flat valley floor is reached.

The exceptionally broad Shire comes close to the escarpment's edge as the M1 crosses the river by the **Kamuzu Bridge**, 45 kilometres (28 miles) out from Blantyre. The west side is a steep river cliff but, opposite, the low bank is intensively cultivated. Even some midstream islands are planted with vegetables in the dry season. Further down river, hippos and crocodiles can often be seen at the river's edge. Early in 2001 and again in 2002, the crocodiles had become such a nuisance that culls were allowed.

Above: The Lower Shire River is broad and placid but can be subject to menacing floods in the rainy season.

On the western side of the bridge the road briefly rises away from the river and there is usually a police post. Although the police will most often signal cars to proceed without stopping it is worth noting that they do not like either the bridge or the check-point to be photographed.

A short distance from the bridge the road curves to run parallel to the river above its western bank. On the bend a few hundred metres up from the bridge is the turn-off to **Chikwawa** and the **Majete Wildlife Reserve**.

As the roads into Lengwe National Park are approached, the vast plain of the Shire opens out. There is an uncanny flatness, almost as though it were man-made.

There are two turnings (right) for Lengwe, the first eight kilometres (five miles) and the second 19 kilometres (12 miles) after crossing the Shire from Blantyre. The second, clearly signposted, is the one to be taken. This quite straight road runs through the sugar cane estates which dominate this area of Malawi. The road is dirt and exceptional care should be taken if irrigation sprays are on when it may become no better than a skid pan. If you do slip into a ditch, estate workers will soon

have you on the road again.

After five kilometres (three miles) is a village and three kilometres further is a turning left (signposted) to the park. Follow the signs to the outer gate, which may well be unmanned, and proceed through to the reception hut at the inner gate.

If approaching Lengwe from Sucoma it will, of course, be the first left turn from the M1, marked to the park, which should be taken.

Entrance costs are US$5 per person and the gates are open from dawn until dusk.

When to go
Tracks in the park are unsuitable for driving in the wet season and the park, because of its low altitude, is oppressively hot in October-November. May to August is a good time to visit although the best time for game viewing will be towards the end of the dry season when the animals will be looking for water at the holes.

Where to stay
Lengwe Main Gate Camp
There are four chalets, each accommodating four people, near the main gate by the scout

205

Above: The M1 bridges the Shire River near Chikwawa.

Although the park has predators such as **leopard**, and large numbers of **buffalo**, sightings will be much a matter of chance because of their preference for the inaccessible western areas of the park. What will be seen will be plenty of **antelope** including what is rare for Malawi, the very beautiful **striped-backed nyala**. Nowhere else in southern Africa is it seen so far north. Magnificent **kudu** also roam the park as do **common duiker**, the small **Livingstone's suni** and **bushbuck**. **Impala** are almost certain to be seen but there are no elephants.

The advantages of the hides, many of which are in thick bush, is that one may see a mix of wildlife together at the water-hole. **Baboons** and **warthogs**, **antelopes** and **bushpigs** will all drink together. For **buffalo**, try the **Jasi hide** which is at the south-east corner of the tracked area. **Blue monkeys**, uncommon in other parks in Malawi, are regularly sighted in Lengwe.

In the dry season, the fairly open thicket allows the larger mammals to be seen quite clearly and in the eastern parts where, more used to vehicles, they will be unfrightened by a stationary car although any sign of movement may disturb them.

The **birdlife** of Lengwe is attractive with about 300 or so species recorded. These include some fairly rare birds, some seen nowhere else in Malawi. Particular birds to look for include the **black and white flycatcher** and the **gorgeous bush-shrike**. In the case of the shrike, it is the male which is gorgeous with its scarlet throat and black gorget and tail. The **crested guineafowl**, apparently wearing a black plumed hat, and the **barred cukoo**, with its elegant long tail, are just two other species generally not to be seen elsewhere in the country. A delight to the eye is the richly coloured **Böhm's bee-eater**.

Practical matters and activities

With few facilities but easy access from Blantyre and the fact that the hides and drives are fairly close to the gate, Lengwe is most suited to a day's visit, or even combined with Majete Wildlife Reserve.

If arriving early in the day or paying a visit in the late afternoon, the hides and water-holes should be especially rewarding. One such waterhole is quite close to the main gate

camp. There are kitchens and an ablution block but nothing is provided except running water and, if you are fortunate, electricity. There will probably be someone to do the cooking but make sure all water is thoroughly boiled. There is a viewing platform nearby overlooking a bird pool. There is also a **campsite**.

The camp is little used but there is talk of up-grading. Alternative accommodation is not too far away at Sucoma and many visitors to Lengwe go to the park as a day's excursion from Blantyre. In the future, it is planned to develop bush camps in the park. If this comes to pass, Lengwe will enjoy the popularity it deserves.

Sightseeing

Lengwe is especially arid outside the rainy season and many of the water courses become dry sandy channels. This aids game viewing because it forces the animals to use the few pools that are permanent supplies of water. There are four hides and man-made pools in the eastern area of the park just a short distance from the main gate.

Above: Lengwe National Park has southern Africa's most northerly herds of the beautiful nyala antelope, seen here at a waterhole.

and is signposted as the Lengwe hide. Cars can be left a little way from the hole and a short walk will bring you to a raised platform overlooking the pool. (Don't mistake the nearby water tower for the viewing platform.)

Three other waterholes with adjacent hides are also within easy reach of the circuit of tracks in the eastern part of the park. These are Jasi (south-east of the circuit) Makanga (south-west) and North Thicket (north-west).

Absolute silence is the rule in a hide. Even a noisy camera shutter can disturb the animals. If viewing from a vehicle, the best plan is to stop and switch off the engine.

One of Lengwe's strengths is that signposting makes it relatively simple to find your way about. A self-driving safari is feasible and may be rewarding. This is really the only park or reserve in Malawi where this is so. The mixture of thicket and open ground gives variety and, potentially, good viewing.

However, if staying in the park, it would be profitable to hire a scout from the Camp Office and take a walking safari. On a drive through the park, ask to be taken into the

western area where there are some natural waterholes along the Nkombedzi wa Fodya River. Across this more remote area is the old telegraph link between Cape Town and Cairo.

Majete Wildlife Reserve

Majete, at 691 square kilometres (267 square miles), is third in size of Malawi's reserves and is certainly not the best for game viewing. Its attractions are largely scenic and the **Shire River** must be most visitors' favourite. The area is cut by a large number of east flowing rivers which rise on the western edge of the Great Rift Valley. These join the Shire or its tributaries, the **Mwanza**, in the south, and the **Mkurumadzi** which runs through the north-east corner of the reserve. In the dry season the stream channels may be empty.

The vegetation is mixed woodland, *Brachystegia* in the west and *Combretum/Terminalia* in the east. There is open grassland away from the river courses. To the western

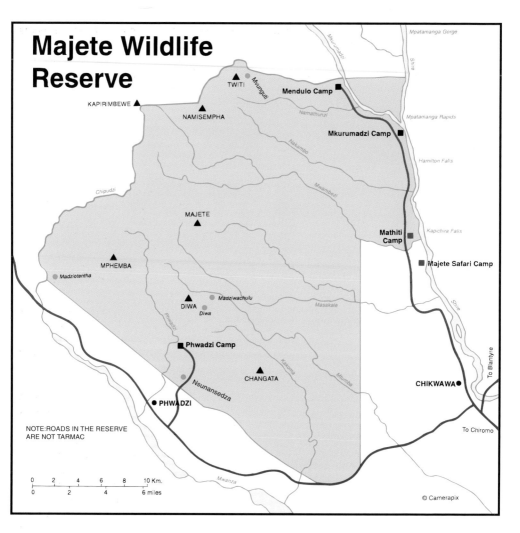

Majete Wildlife Reserve

KAPIRIMBEWE
TWITI
Mvurgui
Mendulo Camp
NAMISEMPHA
Namathunzi
Mpatamanga Rapids
Nakambo
Mkurumadzi Camp
Hamilton Falls
Chipudzi
Mwambezi
MAJETE
Mathiti Camp
Kapichira Falls
MPHEMBA
Majete Safari Camp
Madziotentha
Madziwachulu
DIWA
Diwa
Masakale
Phiwadzi
Phwadzi Camp
Shire
CHANGATA
Kakoma
Nsunansedza
Mumba
CHIKWAWA
To Blantyre
PHWADZI
NOTE: ROADS IN THE RESERVE ARE NOT TARMAC
To Chiromo

| 0 | 2 | 4 | 6 | 8 | 10 Km. |
| 0 | 2 | | 4 | | 6 miles |

Mwanza

© Camerapix

side of the reserve a line of hills breaks the slope up to the Rift Valley's edge.

Although one sometimes sees claims of a wide range of animals inhabiting the reserve, sightings will be largely a matter of luck. It is the series of falls and rapids on the Shire River which have been the objective of most visits to the reserve. These are the **Murchison Cataracts**, the lowest being **Kapichira Falls**, which in 1859 forced **David Livingstone** temporarily to abandon his voyage up the Shire River towards Lake Malawi (Nyasa). Sixteen years later the Livingstonia missionaries took their craft to pieces and, man-handling it beyond the cataracts, resumed their journey by water up the Shire.

Today, the falls are seeing changes Livingstone would never have imagined. A large hydro-electric installation has transformed the scene. This is progress at a price.

Getting there
From

| Blantyre: | 65km/40miles | M1, T416 |
| Sucoma: | 45km/28miles | M1, T416 |

Blantyre | Turn to Chikwawa and Majete WR | Majete Wildlife Reserve
River Shire | Majete Safari Camp
45km | 1km | 18km | 1km

Blantyre to Majete Wildlife Reserve: M1,T416: 65km

Getting to Majete is quite easy from Blantyre. The route is the same as for Lengwe National Park as far as the crossing of the Shire. At a bend on the M1, just a few hundred metres after the river is crossed, look for a turning right. This road, the T416 (also sometimes called the D135 or the E19) leads to Chikwawa. If coming from Sucoma to Majete, the bend in the M1 is reached after 26 kilometres (16 miles) and the bridge is in view. Much or the T416 has been improved in order to take vehicles going to the power station being constructed on the Shire.

Chikwawa is a busy little village and, beyond the settlement, the road takes a sign-posted sharp left turn to go past smallholder farms and give good views of the lush flood-plain. The turning to the **Majete Safari Camp** (right) is 18 kilometres (11 miles) from the M1 and in 500 metres a minor road (left and signposted) leads to the wildlife reserve gate. To continue straight on leads to the bridge which carries traffic for the power station.

When to go
With little game to view, the attraction is the falls and they are at their best during and just after the rainy season. Unfortunately, the reserve is closed from December to late March or early April and the tracks remain difficult for some weeks afterwards. From September to November it will be hot but those intent on fishing should visit in October or November.

Where to stay
The old camps in the reserve are not to be recommended. The one near the **Mathiti gate** is now only for rangers although camping is permitted there. A very attractive alternative is to use the nearby safari camp.

Although bush camps are planned for Majete Wildlife Reserve, the lack of game is the real handicap to development.

Majete Safari Camp
The camp is sited just 2 kilometres off the T416 and not far from the reserve gate. After an uncertain start the camp was closed in 1997 and then re-opened under new management. Refurbishment took place to give attractive accommodation in just four separate brick and thatch lodges with en suite facilities and verandahs. There is an open restaurant and bar and, wonderful surprise, the small **Livingstone chapel**. Appropriately, this is near the spot at which David Livingstone had difficulties in navigating up the Shire.

Most recently, the Safari Camp has again experienced management problems. It seems impossible to make a reservation but one can just arrive and book in. The upkeep of the lodges has been somewhat neglected.

The setting of Majete Safari Camp could hardly be improved. A terraced garden leads down to the river and its cataracts and a more charming place couldn't be imagined.

Sightseeing
The variety of terrain and vegetation should attract large numbers of animals. Un-fortunately, hunting reduced their number in the past and restocking has not taken place.

Most prolific are antelope, from the large **kudu** to smaller **bushbuck**. Typically, they may be seen on the edges of the woodland where it gives way to grass. **Baboons** inhabit the deep ravine areas but larger mammals such as elephant and buffalo are no longer in the reserve. **Leopards** used to be quite numerous but their nocturnal habits, their preference for the higher ground to the west and the general lack of prey, makes a sighting unlikely.

Fish, notably **tiger fish**, are plentiful in the Shire River but **birdlife** is not one of Majete's particular attractions. The number of recorded species is a lowly (for Malawi) 140 or so. One particular bird, the **rock pratincole**, rare elsewhere in Malawi, is attracted to the rock strewn Shire River.

Few visitors to Majete now go to view game or the birdlife. The attraction is largely the accessibility of the **Shire River** and it **cataracts**.

As has been said, two major falls on the Shire River are reason enough for an excursion to Majete. Just inside the main gate, a short and treacherous track (right) leads down to the **Kapichira Falls**. There is parking by a large baobab tree and it is possible to scramble down to the falls or take the view from high up on the bank. Here the foaming white waters of the Shire crash through a rocky gorge over a series of steps. Many visitors get no further than this point, enthralled by the beauty of the scene. They take a picnic here and return to Blantyre or Sucoma. It is still unclear what the effect will be when the new dam and power station is complete. The works across the river already rather spoil the view.

The second accessible cataract is the **Hamilton Falls** which are five kilometres (three miles) north of Kapichira at a point where the reserve road is close to the river. Again, this is a favourite picnic place for visitors

Practical matters and activities

Entry to the reserve is US$5 per person and US$2 for a vehicle. Very few people visit Majete so you are likely to have the reserve to yourself. Ten vehicles a month (in the high season) is considered busy.

There are two main tracks in the reserve. One leads to the Phwadzi staff camp in the south-west while the longer road runs close to the north-eastern edge of the reserve. It should be noted that there is no link to the Mpatamanga Gorge. Anyone determined enough to drive any distance into the reserve should use a four-wheel drive vehicle with high clearance.

The lack of tracks limits the reserve's potential for game viewing and the only alternative is to hike with the aid of a guide. If

Above: Majete Wildlife Reserve is a true wilderness of undisturbed woodlands. Top: The delightful Livingstone Chapel ovelooks the Shire River at Majete.

contemplating this, it's advisable to contact the Ministry of Tourism, Parks and Wildlife in advance. It should be possible to hire a scout from the staff camp just inside the Mathiti gate.

For anglers, tiger fish is the quarry below the Kapichira Falls. The best time of year is September — October. No licence is required but no tackle is available for hire.

If for no other reason, the lack of good accommodation in the reserve suggests a day's visit out from Blantyre rather than a longer stay.

Above: David Livingstone's travels up the Shire River foundered here at the Kapichira Falls.

Sucoma

SUCOMA stands for SUgar COrporation of MAlawi but, written as Sucoma, has become the place name of the vast sugar estate which straddles the M1. Compared with tea, sugar is a modern cash crop in Malawi although the cane was grown on a small scale near Zomba in the 1880s. The international conglomerate Lonrho set up the estate in 1964 and it is now massive by any yardstick. Sugar cane seems to stretch as far as the eye can see. An expansion programme was carried out in 1993, including new factories and improved irrigation systems.

Nchalo is the service village for the estate. The settlement spreads untidily along the road and there is a petrol station and a supermarket.

Getting there
From Blantyre: 73km/45miles   M1

Blantyre to Sucoma: M1: 73km

The M1 goes directly from Blantyre to Sucoma. The route has been described above as far as the turning into Lengwe National Park. The entrance to Sucoma is just eight kilometres (five miles) further on. The road is straight and wide but beware of mud on the road creating a skid pan after rain. The landscape is now man-made. Broad borders planted with flowering shrubs only partly hide the irrigated fields of sugar cane. Here

and there is the solitary baobab tree or stands of deciduous trees. On reaching **Nchalo** village, turn left to get to the heart of the estate and the club. The entrance is very clearly signposted.

When to go
As elsewhere in the Lower Shire Valley, the hot season from October to December is to be avoided. In the rainy season flooding may occur.

Where to stay
Sucoma Sports Club
The Sucoma Sports Club can be used for accommodation when visiting areas of interest in the Lower Shire Valley, or simply as a place to stop off for refreshment. To find the club, follow the main road leading into the estate from the entrance and then look for the signs to Sucoma Sports Club. The distance to the club is about seven kilometres (four miles).

Strictly, the club serves the managers of the estate and their families but there seems to be no objection to casual visitors using it

Above: Sucoma's sugarcane contrasts with flowering bushes along the roadsides.

for a meal or a drink. The club building is unpretentious and the service has to be requested rather than being offered. All the same, the food is passable and the cool bar is quite well stocked. Outside, at the back, there is a small swimming pool alongside the Shire River which runs past the club gardens. Air-conditioned chalets provide modest but acceptable accommodation.

Sightseeing
Although the main reason for a visit to Sucoma is often to use the facilities of the club, the impressive features of the estate itself can be seen by driving on the estate roads. These form a regular grid network of wide and well maintained paths used by workers walking to and from the fields and also by the heavy machinery which works the plantation. Towering cane casts a shadow across the roads. Everything is very neat and the M1 itself is lined by flowering bushes which create an almost garden-like scene. Through the estate there is the noticeable sweet smell of molasses. All stages of cultivation can be seen, from nursery plots to vast fields of tall mature cane.

The estate has a small wildlife sanctuary where it may be possible to see the only giraffe in Malawi. There are no records of giraffes ever being resident in the country although this is debatable given a habitat which would be suitable.

Practical matters and activities
The Sports Club has tennis and squash courts, a snooker table in the clubhouse and a boat on the river. The boat, called the *Poop Deck*, has been accurately likened to *The African Queen*. It is available for hire and sightings of hippo and crocodile are almost certain even on a short trip up or down the river. It has to be said that the state of the boat and the near certainty of crocodiles have made many a visitor decide to forego the pleasure of a river cruise. A quiet drink in the shade of the tree-lined riverbank may be preferable.

Care should be taken if driving round the estate. Irrigation water causes the dirt roads to be very slippery and the large trucks with trailers have right of way.

If asking the way to the Sports Club, don't just ask for "the Club" — there are two — emphasise *Sports* Club.

Elephant Marsh

This is a destination which most travellers may find too difficult to reach. Floods in recent years have played havoc with the roads and only the most determined will attempt to get to the marsh until reconstruction has taken place.

Elephant Marsh is part of the flood plain of the **Shire River**. Because the marsh is difficult to define, its area is variously quoted as being from 400 square kilometres (150 square miles) to 1200 square kilometres (450 square miles). The uncertainty arises from the fact that its area varies from season to season and year to year. At its northern margins it is best classified as semi-permanent marshland. To the south it becomes a small lake and islands of salt are home to palms while the marsh supports a floating mat of vegetation (sudd) which grows so thick in places that boats are unable to penetrate it. In particularly wet seasons, when rainfall figures are high, the whole area may be under water, threatening the villages like **Chiromo** and **Makhanga** which mark its southern limit. It is there that the **River Ruo** joins the Shire. The Ruo forms the border between Mozambique and Malawi and twice in the 1950s (1952 and 1956) and again in 2001, the Ruo overflowed into the marsh and caused serious flooding problems. In fact, so great was the volume of the Ruo that its waters actually started to flow upstream in the Shire's channel.

The name Elephant Marsh was given to these swamplands by David Livingstone who reported 800 elephant in a single sighting. Half a century later most of the great herds had been hunted to destruction and today the largest surviving mammals are crocodiles and hippos.

Getting there

From

Blantyre: 145km/90miles	M1, S151, minor road	
Sucoma: 72km/45miles	M1, S151, minor road	

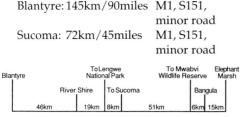

Blantyre to Elephant Marsh: M1, S151, minor road: 145km

There are three possible road routes to Elephant Marsh if approaching from Blantyre. The best road is the M1 passing Sucoma and continuing on to Bangula (130 kilometres/81miles from Blantyre). The road as far as Sucoma has already been described. From Sucoma and the village of Nchalo, the road is of indifferent quality as the estate is left behind. Now there is the vast open plain of the Shire, of no great scenic merit. There is only one settlement of note before Bangula is reached, the village of **N'gabu** where there is a range of services including a bank, petrol and a small resthouse. Shortly before reaching **Bangula** the turn-off to the **Mwabvi Wildlife Reserve**, is passed on the right. On reaching the little town of Bangula, the road has rejoined the path of the **Shire River**. The town is an important communications node.

It is here that problems may begin because of serious flood damage to roads and bridges in recent years, including 2001. Until such time as reconstruction work is completed it has to be admitted that Elephant Marsh is likely to be off limits for all but the most intrepid traveller.

When the damage is repaired, to reach Elephant Marsh from Bangula is to turn off left (S151) and continue through **Makhanga** village towards another smaller village, **Muona**. A signpost before you reach the village will direct you to **Mchacha** where **James' Landing** is the point from which to explore the marsh.

Ignoring Elephant Marsh, only the most adventurous will want to travel south from Bangula. Those who do will find that, the M1, as it crosses the railway and continues southwards, becomes a rather poor dirt road which again is almost impassable in the rainy season. There have been years when the Shire, here swelled by the waters of the River Ruo, has overflowed and severe flooding has occurred.

The path of the M1 to **Nsanje** is sandwiched between the Shire (which forms the border with Mozambique) and the railway line. Just before the border town the road crosses the railway.

The little town is the most southerly of any size in Malawi. Beyond Nsanje, the M1 crosses the **Ndinde Marsh** before linking with a minor Mozambican road.

Even the most curious visitor to Malawi,

who explores the M1 south of Nsanje, will find that there is very little of interest in the last 20 kilometres (12 miles) of Malawi's north to south highway.

As has been said earlier, it used to be possible to combine a visit to Thyolo and the tea estates with one to the marsh. This was by taking the the S151 south out of Thyolo leading down to Bangula. However, current road conditions make for more difficulties than the traveller is likely to wish to encounter.

More interesting, but only to be attempted in the dry season, was the compromise route taking the M1 out of Blantyre but turning off (left) to the S150 as the floor of the Shire valley is reached and before the river crossing. The S150 runs along the foot of the great Thyolo escarpment which forms a wall-like edge to the Shire valley. Yet again, this route can't be recommended at present because of very poor road conditions.

An interesting alternative is to take a train from **Limbe** to **Makhanga**. This will be a fascinating journey but the service is unreliable and irregular. It is essential to check the situation with the Tourist Office in Blantyre well in advance.

When to go

The wet season, and for a couple of months after the rains, is to be avoided. This part of the Shire Valley frequently suffers severe floods. There was tragic loss of life in 2001. The M1 is likely to be the only road open in the wet season. June to October is probably the best time to visit but it will be increasingly hot and humid in late October.

Where to stay

The remoteness of the marsh is a problem. It is really quite difficult to get there and back in a day out from Blantyre or Thyolo yet there is only the most simple accommodation in the area. Perhaps the best arrangement is to stay at the Sports Club at Sucoma and to travel south from there. This will involve a round trip of only some 125 kilometres (78 miles).

Sightseeing

Navigating the marsh's network of channels, this wilderness is reminiscent of Lake Chilwa. Anyone interested in birdlife will be in for a treat. **Fish eagles, storks, kingfishers, herons** and countless other species will be seen even on a short visit. The best time for viewing is the early morning as at that time of day one will avoid the worst of the heat and humidity.

Crocodiles inhabit the Marsh and are generally not a nuisance. However, in recent years their numbers have increased and culls were permitted in 2001 and 2002 when they began to prey on the local villagers. The large numbers of **hippo**, which once were common in the marshlands and lake, have been reduced by hunting, but **otters** may be seen. It is often easier to hear the wildlife than to see it among the reed grasses. In more open areas where **water hyacinth** and **lilies** cover the surface, movements are more easily detected.

A visit to Malawi without experiencing either Lake Chilwa or Elephant Marsh would be an opportunity lost, but, it has to be said, Chilwa is the more accessible. These are wetlands at their most wild and natural. It is likely, with the population pressure that is characteristic of Malawi, that one day Elephant Marsh will be drained and brought into agricultural production. Its fertile alluvial soils are potentially very rich.

Practical matters and activities

It is important to check on the current situation before going on a trip to Elephant Marsh. This is a remote area. It is subject to flooding and roads and bridges are easily washed away. The most reliable information may come from the Sports Club at Sucoma. If travelling from Blantyre, one can enquire at the Tourist Office but it is unlikely that anyone there will have recently been so far south.

The best — the only — way to see the marsh is by boat. By going to James' Landing it should be easy to find a willing boatman

Opposite: Terraced slopes on the Thyolo Escarpment.

who will take you out for about K70 an hour. There are dugout canoes and one or two rowing boats. It is wise to take a careful look at the craft before embarking. Many are in a poor state of repair. Insect repellent and protection from the sun are essential.

Such is the nature of the Elephant Marsh that it is advisable to go there with a guide who knows the area rather than attempt it on your own. Enquiries can be made in Blantyre.

Mwabvi Wildlife Reserve

Mwabvi, at 135 square kilometres (52 square miles) is the smallest of Malawi's reserves and parks except for the Lake Malawi National Park. It is an exceptionally beautiful area where rivers cut through narrow gorges and there is a variety of vegetation from grass to woodland and even some quite dense forest.

Because of its location and poor roads, the reserve receives very few visitors. How well stocked it is with game is uncertain. There are tales of black rhino and lion but authentic sightings are rare. One wonders whether the difficulties of access allow free rein to the imagination of the few visitors who do go there.

There are moves afoot to improve visitor access and accommodation with some simple camping gear being available at the gate but the remoteness of the reserve is a real handicap. When the proposed bush camps have been established, Mwabvi may again be worth a visit.

Getting there
From
Blantyre: 138km/86miles M1, minor road
Sucoma: 65km/40miles M1, minor road

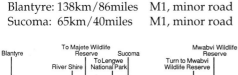

Blantyre to Mwabvi WR: M1, minor road: 138km

Access to Mwabvi from Blantyre or Sucoma is by the M1 as already described. The minor road leading into Mwabvi is virtually impassable in the wet season and a high clearance vehicle is needed in any season.

The turning off the M1 is rather less than five kilometres (three miles) after crossing the **River Thangadzi** just after a village named **Sorgin**. With an absence of signposts it is wise to ask directions. The minor road (right) cuts back to recross the river. Before reaching the little village of **Dande**, take a right turn (asking, if the road is unclear) and this leads to the reserve's entrance. If you find yourself in Dande, someone will put you right.

When to go
The best months are those which avoid the hot and wet seasons. This leaves the period June to September.

Where to stay
Mwabvi Camp
The setting of the camp is most attractive, near to the Mwabvi Gorge and some nine kilometres (six miles) from the gate. The track to the camp is the right fork in the path after entering the reserve.

The camp itself, two rondavels of corrugated steel, will attract very few. The rondavels are none too clean, and exceptionally hot except when the sun has been down some hours. Nothing is provided but there is a scout camp nearby. A better plan is to take one's own camping gear but this is not always a practical possibility.

Sightseeing
Undoubtedly, the biggest attraction of the reserve is the **Mwabvi Gorge** where the river plunges through outcrops of sandstone close to the Mozambique border. There, at pools alongside the river, animals come to drink. As has been said, the wealth of the reserve in terms of the mammal population is really something of a mystery but sightings of antelope, particularly **kudu** and **sable**, are likely. Small mammals, such as the **rock dassie** or **hyrax** are common, as are **warthogs**.

Most certain of all sightings will be of the great variety of birdlife. Some 200 species have been recorded, one of which is rare in Malawi's other parks and reserves. This is the **double-banded sand grouse**. The banding refers to the fine black bands on its underparts. The birds come to drink at pools as the sun sets and this may be a chance to see them. Another uncommon species is the

black tailed grey waxbill, also seen in Nkhotakota Wildlife Reserve. These birds keep to the woodland but a glimpse of red above the black tail may help to identify it.

Practical matters

This reserve is really not for the casual visitor. If considering Mwabvi it is probably best to ask at the Wildlife Society of Malawi's office at the Heritage Centre in Blantyre in order to find out what is the current situation in the reserve. If determined to go, hire a Land Rover or similar vehicle. Only in the dry season should a visit be contemplated and all camping equipment and food will need to be taken.

There is quite a lot of water in the reserve and this, together with high temperatures, means that insects can be a nuisance. Protective measures should be taken.

Going North

Blantyre to M1/M8 Junction:
                    115km/71miles   M1

Blantyre		River Shire		M1/M8 Junction
To Chileka Airport and Mpatamanga Gorge		M6		
8km	50km	1km	56km	

Blantyre to M1/M8 Junction: M1: 115km

This part of the M1 is a modern road, completed only in the late 1980s. It is part of the shortest route between Blantyre and Lilongwe (311 kilometres/193 miles). To join the M1 from central Blantyre, drive down Glyn Jones Road from the direction of the Mount Soche Hotel. At the bottom of the hill is a roundabout with a Kandodo store and two petrol stations. Turn left at the roundabout and this road forms the M1.

The road runs north through the suburbs of Blantyre and (right) the district of **Mussa**. Small houses are scattered across the hillsides in a patchwork of vegetable plots.

The first section of the M1, up to the S127 (left) road to **Chileka Airport** is almost an extension of Blantyre. The S127 not only leads to the airport but eventually links with the S137 (left at a Y-junction) which leads to the **Mpatamanga Gorge**. When the **Shire River** is reached a short walk down river will bring you to the gorge. Here the river

funnels through a 10 metre (33 feet) gap. This extraordinary sight is worth the 60 kilometres (37 miles) journey from Blantyre. The minor roads are motorable although difficult in the wet season. The site is a favourite place for picnics.

Beyond the S127 junction, the scene along the M1 becomes rural rather than suburban. The route is through hilly country with plenty of baobab trees in evidence, through the large village of **Lunza** and then descending slowly towards the Shire Valley. Avoiding a direct route, the road begins to swing south before it crosses the Shire. The river is broad and impressive. The low banks are tree-lined and there are plenty of hippo and crocodile in its waters. This does not seem to deter local women who bring their washing down to the stream's edge.

Soon after bridging the river, there is a major junction. Turning left here is on to the M6, the road to the townships of **Mwanza** (104 kilometres/65 miles from Blantyre) and the Mozambique border (116 kilometres/72 miles from Blantyre). The M1, however, turns right at this junction and follows a splendidly engineered section northwards.

Surprisingly little traffic uses this road and there is little to distract one's attention from the wild rolling landscape. Plains alternate with lines of hills and isolated inselbergs. Clusters of mud and thatch huts, some with perhaps a hundred or more homes, lie back from the road but if you stop, children will come running to investigate. You may be offered dried mice which the boys sell from sticks.

The route continues along a rather flat watershed between the **Mulunguzi** and **Lilongwe Rivers** until the junction with the M8 to **Balaka** (right) is reached. Beyond Balaka, this road links with the M3 on the way to Liwonde National Park. Going north (left) along the M1 leads to Lilongwe but a turning right just beyond the M1/M8 junction takes one on to the M5 — the Lakeshore Road which goes, initially, to the Mua Mission.

Lake Malawi

Malawi is one of Africa's smaller countries with one-fifth of its surface being water. Accounting for all but a small fraction of that is Lake Malawi (formerly Nyasa, which means lake). In Africa, only Lakes Victoria and Tanganyika are larger.

Lying in part of the Great East African Rift Valley system, Lake Malawi's size is impressive: 585 kilometres north to south and 80 kilometres east to west. Converted to imperial measure this gives rough dimensions of 365 miles by 52 miles, hence the sobriquet: the **Calendar Lake**. It drains an area of more than 126,500 square kilometres (48,840 square miles) which is a little larger than the country itself. Almost all the larger rivers flowing into the lake come from the west and, remarkably, only one river, the **Shire**, flows out. The waters eventually spill into the Indian Ocean via the Zambezi.

The level of the lake's surface, at about 470 metres (1540 feet) above sea level, is actually subject to significant variations, not just because of the vagaries of Malawi's rainfall but also because of immensely high rates of evaporation. For decades there have been plans to raise the level of the lake by building a barrage but the shore is so well settled that this would not be a popular move.

The lake is generally more shallow towards the south but off **Usisyia**, in the north, it reaches a depth of more than 700

Above: Children play in the surf at Senga Bay. Top: 'You've been warned'.

metres (2300 feet), making the floor well below sea level. The width of the lake's shorelands vary from nothing to over 25 kilometres (16 miles), the edge of the Rift Valley rising steeply in places and more gently in others.

Lake Malawi plays an important role in the country's economy. Although only a relatively small proportion of the shorelands attracts crop growing, the land is generally well settled. The reason is clear to see in numerous fishing villages which line the lake's edge. In the south, where the shallower, fish-rich waters are, the fish caught are part of a cash economy with surpluses sold for consumption in the towns around the country. In the more northerly parts of the lake, fishing is largely part of the general subsistence economy.

The lake must also be recognised as one of the country's leading tourist attractions — perhaps the most important asset in Malawi's huge potential for an expanding tourist industry. Visitors marvel at the beautiful golden sand beaches and appreciate all that this freshwater, tideless, inland sea has to offer. Many, seeing the lake for the first time, cannot believe that this is not the Indian Ocean.

The lake has so much to offer the visitor that it must surely be only a matter of time before it becomes one of the great attractions for travellers to this part of Africa. Whether it be water sports, its own national park, enticing off-shore islands or simply the abiding beauty of the lakeside, there is something for all tastes. Only the relative shortage of first class accommodation holds back its development. With the relatively recent improvements to communications effected by the building of the M5, the so-called Lakeshore Road, a start has been made. The lake is Malawi's seaside, without the problem of tides. The few days in the year when winds whip up the surface to storm conditions do nothing to lessen the attraction of this vast inland sea.

NOTE: *The most accessible and popular sections of the lakeshore are the south and central strips. The northern section has rather less to offer the traveller but has been dealt with in the section on North Malawi. It is that region which provides the only easy access to the north of the lake.*

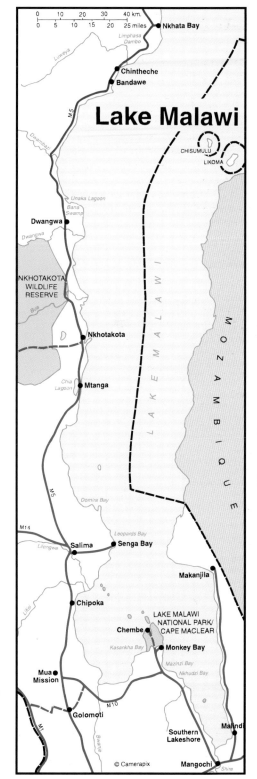

Mangochi

Mangochi isn't on Lake Malawi but, if approaching from the south, it is the last settlement of any size before reaching the lake. The town is a useful service centre for those staying in resorts along the southern shore and for those visiting Cape Maclear.

Mangochi is sited between Lake Malawi and **Lake Malombe** on the western bank of the **Shire River** which here links the two lakes. Although lying mostly to the east of the main roads, by the junction of the M3 and M10, and having only simple accommodation, it is worth making an excursion into the town. It has an interesting history.

Before Malawi achieved independence, the town was called **Fort Johnston**. To control and limit the slave traffic passing north-wards to Zanzibar, a fort was built in 1891 on the east bank of the Shire River, just a few kilometres out of the present town. It was named after Nyasaland's first Consul General, **Sir Harry Johnston**. The site of the fort was ill-chosen and, in 1897, it was moved to the position now occupied by the town.

Fort Johnston's importance was initially as a garrison town and as the headquarters of Lake Malawi's diminutive naval force. Gradually it grew as a major service point for the southern shoreland of Lake Malawi. In the 1930s it was to become a railway port but a change in plans saw the line re-routed through Balaka and Fort Johnston has to be content with its connections by road.

The town may now look a little run-down but its broad streets hint at a rather more grand past. In fact, Mangochi claims to be the first example of town planning in Central Africa — the work of the surveyor **Alfred Sharpe**.

A new bridge has been built which crosses the Shire River here. Japanese funding was used for this work and it interrupted the passage of boats along the river.

Getting there
From

Lilongwe:	297km/185miles	M1, M8, M3
Lilongwe:	263km/163miles	M14, M5, M10
Blantyre:	187km/116miles	M3
Salima:	171km/106miles	M5, M10
Liwonde township:		
	71km/44miles	M3

The town lies on the M3, making it easily accessible from all Malawi's larger settlements. It is close enough to Zomba (121 kilometres/ 75 miles) and the southern lakeshore resorts (11 to 28 kilometres/7 to 17 miles) for a day's visit to be quite easily accomplished. The roads shown above are of variable quality. If approaching from the north, the route is the M10 which meets the M3 at Mangochi. This road is described later. The M3 from Zomba has been described in the section devoted to Liwonde Natioinal Park in South Malawi.

When to go
As with all of Lake Malawi's attractions, there is no special time to visit but, if dry weather is wanted, choose May to November. Anywhere near the lake is unlikely to be excessively hot even in November.

Where to stay
Most international travellers will prefer to stay at one of the range of hotels on the southern lakeshore. In Mangochi there are some very simple resthouses and the **Holiday Motel** which has some en suite rooms and a restaurant. To find the motel, go down the main street (the M3) towards the bridge. At the roundabout, turn left and then take the second right turn.

Sightseeing
Much of what is worth seeing in Mangochi has some historical significance.

Near to the bridge over the Shire at the eastern side of the town is a simple **clocktower**, erected in 1903 (not 1901 as the notice on it claims) as a memorial to Queen Victoria. Close by should be a rather sad looking piece of artillery, a **Hotchkiss gun**. This six-pounder

---

Opposite: Mangochi's Queen Victoria clocktower stands close to the Shire River.

DEPARTMENT OF ANTIQUITIES

NATIONAL MONUMENTS
QUEEN VICTORIA MEMORIAL TOWER
IN MEMORY OF QUEEN VICTORIA
1837 – 1901
ERECTED 1901

M V VIPYA MEMORIAL
IN MEMORY OF THE 145 PASSENGERS
AND CREW WHO LOST THEIR LIVES
WHEN THE VIPYA SANK
30ᵗʰ JULY, 1946

Sponsored by Helen Grey
Managed by Tourism International
AGRICULTURE

was taken from the Lake Patrol Gunboat *Gwendolen*. While the new bridge construction was taking place, the gun was relocated to the museum but it is due to be returned to its former place. The story behind the boat is one of the semi-comic episodes which seem to occur in even the most tragic of wars.

Before the start of World War I, the *Gwendolen* shared the waters of Lake Malawi with a similar German boat which was stationed along the northern shore of the lake in what was then German East Africa. At the outbreak of war, the *Gwendolen's* captain was ordered to set sail and destroy the German boat. As it happened, the German crew had not been told that hostilities had commenced so they were totally unprepared when the *Gwendolen* opened fire. In fact, their boat was still on the slipway. The German boat was put out of action and its captain and crew became very surprised prisoners of war. Remarkably, this was the first recorded naval action of the Great War.

Also alongside the Victoria Clock Tower is a large stone memorial to those who drowned when the motor vessel *Viphya* sank in a storm in 1946. A small plaque on the memorial states simply: "In memory of all those who lost their lives in the sinking of the *Viphya*, 30 July 1946. RIP." In fact, 145 perished in what was the lake's most tragic disaster.

As a legacy of the slave trade, many of the town's population are Muslims, as were their former Arab slave-masters. However, the Christian community is well represented and the modern **Catholic Cathedral**, with its slender bell tower is worth visiting. There is also a Catholic Seminary just north of the town.

There is a small **museum** off the main street to the right. After years of renovations and restorations, it was partly reopened in late 1999 while work continued. The museum tells the story of the history of Lake Malawi, including the slave trade. The eclectic exhibits include stuffed animals and a fascinating set of nineteenth century medical instruments.

When, in 1971, Fort Johnston became Mangochi there was a spate of building. A new local government building, a post office and banks were added. The **banks** and **post office** will be found to the left of the main road linking the M3 with the bridge over the Shire. There are both **PTC** and **Kandodo** stores in Mangochi. The former is on the M3 and the latter in the core of the old part of the town near the river. There is a **tourist office** on the right of the main street a little way beyond the post office. There are also a number of petrol stations.

For many years the town has been singled out as the site of a new lakeshore airport. The day when it will be built may not be so far away.

There are plenty of trees in the town and they afford welcome shade during the heat of the day. There are good examples of the "sausage tree" (*kigelia africana*). The outsize fruit of the sausage tree has recently been used to provide the basis of a cream which, it is claimed, will cure some forms of skin cancer. In fact, the raw fruit has been used for years by local people to treat burns and skin ailments.

Practical matters and activities

Whether approaching Mangochi from the north or the south, it should be noted that the town lies off what will be seen as the main road. The M10 from the north runs seamlessly into the M3 at a T-junction. It is the M3 which turns into the town.

Anyone wishing to explore the eastern side of the lake can do so from Mangochi. The M3 crosses the **Shire River** by the new bridge on the eastern side of Mangochi town. Beyond the bridge, the standard of the road deteriorates and there is little to entice the traveller. Eventually the M3 reaches the **Mozambique border** at **Chiponde**, 55 kilometres (34 miles) from Mangochi.

An even worse road, the S129 branches off the M3 eight kilometres (five miles) after the Shire crossing. This leads to **Malindi**, on the lakeshore, and on to **Makanjila** the most northerly settlement on the Malawian eastern side of the lake. Apart from giving good views west across the lake, with opportunities for excellent sunset photographs, it has nothing to commend it. Malindi's only rather questionable claim to fame is as the site of Malawi's first ever aeroplane crash in 1916.

DEPARTMENT OF ANTIQUITIES
NATIONAL MONUMENTS
6 PR HOTCHKISS GUN FROM
GUENDOLEN PATROL GUN BOAT
LAKE MALAWI
1889-1940

Sponsored by Vizara Vinds
Managed by Tourism International
A BETT COMPANY

IN MEMORY OF
ALL THOSE WHO
LOST THEIR LIVES
IN SINKING OF
M.V. VIPYA,
30 JULY, 1946.
R.I.P.

Above: Memorial to the worst ever shipping disaster on the lake. Top: The Hotchkiss gun in Mangochi is a memorial to World War I's first naval battle — on Lake Malawi.

The Southern Lakeshore

The greatest concentration of resort hotels and campsites on Lake Malawi lies to the north of Mangochi on the western shore of the lake's southernmost reach. Here the lake is at its shallowest and most fish-rich. The shores are also relatively storm free and its waters provide excellent opportunities for swimming and other water sports.

There are a number of resorts to choose from, each providing comfortable accommodation, largely en suite, and with its own beach. Each has its own special character and choice is largely a matter of taste although prices also vary. The resorts cater for those who wish to do more than relax and sunbathe. Often in conjunction with specialist operators, a variety of activities, mostly involving the lake, is available. The larger resorts are occasionally used for conferences. The term "resort" may be misleading but it is the one most generally used here. It simply refers to individual hotels and lodges, none of which is especially large.

Despite horror tales of bilharzia, where the hotels have carried out clearance programmes, the shore can be considered safe.

Getting there
From Mangochi to

Palm Beach:	11km/7miles	M10
Nkopola Lodge:	22km/13.5miles	M10
Club Makokola:	23km/14miles	M10
Sun 'n' Sand:	27.5km/17miles	M10
Boadzulu:	28km/17.5miles	M10

From Mua to

Palm Beach:	96km/60miles	M5, M10
Nkopola Lodge:	85km/52.5miles	M5, M10
Club Makokola:	84km/52miles	M5, M10
Sun 'n' Sand:	88.5km/55miles	M5, M10
Boadzulu:	79km/49miles	M5, M10

(Note: Distances are to the turn-offs from the M10)

Mangochi			Club Makokola				M10/S128 Junction
		Mulangeni	Nkopola Lodge	Boadzulu Sun 'n' Sand		Koma Crocodile Farm	
	Palm Beach						
11km	7km	4km	1km	4.5km	500m	19km	3km

Mangochi to M10/S128 Junction: M10: 50km

Approaching the Southern Lakeshore from the north has been a problem because of the poor state of the M10 west of the Monkey Bay junction. Roadworks have now been effected to restore accessibility.

From the south there are no problems. The drive up to Mangochi has already been described and from there the M10 is a good road up to the Monkey Bay turn-off. Just outside Mangochi is a new **Roman Catholic Seminary**.

The road is flat and straight and it is possible to appreciate that one is driving on what was once the bed of the lake. The sandy flats and palm trees are not seen elsewhere along the lake. The lake cannot usually be seen from the road. The fishing villages, the hotels and the lakeshore homes of rich Malawians lie about a kilometre or so to the east of the M10's path. After 47 kilometres (29 miles), the **Koma Crocodile Farm** is to the right of the road.

The road divides after 50 kilometres (31 miles), the turning to the left is the continuation of the M10 to the Mua Mission while to carry

Above: Cruising on Lake Malawi is becoming more and more popular.

almost straight on is to take the road to Monkey Bay and the Lake Malawi National Park. This is the S128.

When to go
This is one of the driest parts of the lakeshore and what little rain occurs is usually in an afternoon and short-lived downpour. The lake provides cooling breezes in the hottest months. It hardly matters, therefore, what is the time of the year, this will be an attractive destination. For short, unbooked stays, it might be noted that accommodation is especially in demand at weekends.

Where to stay
There are over a dozen lodges, hotels and camping places along this part of the lake. All are reached by signposted turnings on to dirt roads off the M10, east towards the lake. They vary from the truly luxurious to the very simple. Some are sophisticated, some brash and some family-friendly. Prices vary and are generally a good guide as to what to expect. One, **Nanchengwa Lodge** is the favourite camping place for backpackers and over-landers. It is about 25 kilometres (15 miles)

south of Monkey Bay. A relatively new property is the **Baobab Beach Resort**. It is reasonably priced but its strange brick architecture and lack of a proper beach mean it is not to everyone's taste. The views, especially from its *Noah's Ark bar*, built out into the lake are good.

Mulangeni has great potential but there were management problems following the death of the owner and the present position is unclear. The resort is just 18 kilometres (11 miles) north of Mangochi. Inexpensive but adequate accommodation is also available at the **OK Motel** (signposted at about 24 kilometres/15 miles north of Mangochi) and at **Martin's Beach Hotel**, near Nkopola Lodge. **The K Lodge**, is a converted lake-shore house in Nkhudzi, at the more northerly extremity of the southern lakeshore. It offers simple, friendly accommodation in seven rooms.

Palm Beach Resort
This is the most southerly of the more up-market resorts on this part of the lake. Just off the M10, it is signposted to the right of the road if travelling from Mangochi.

Above: Palm Beach Resort has chalets in its gardens bordering the lakeshore.

There is a variety of chalets of different sizes, all en suite, and rather more expensive 'owner's' cottages. There are also two camping grounds with ablution facilities. There is an air of informality about the place with the management keen to meet guests' individual needs. There is no swimming pool but the beach is good and water sports can be arranged.

Sunbird Nkopola Lodge

The turning to Nkopola Lodge is 22 kilometres (13.5 miles) north of Mangochi on the M10. A short dirt road links the lodge to the M10.

Managed by Le Méridien Hotels, Nkopola Lodge is a favourite for many who holiday on the lake. It has a high proportion of return visitors and has rather more character than its competitors. In fact, it is really two or three resorts in one, offering a variety of accommodation.

The oldest section, now referred to as the hillside rooms, is a simple hotel built into the rocky cliff face only a stone's throw from the beach. This block also houses reception areas, a couple of small shops and the restaurant and bar. There is also a beach bar. It is beginning to show its age but the rooms

have good views over the lake even if the monkeys jumping up and down on the roof may provide an extra early morning alarm.

Set in well-kept gardens are beach-front chalets with their own patios. The accommodation is superior to the hillside rooms and quieter. There are also family-sized rondavels. A little apart from the rest of the resort is the **Nkopola Beach Club**. This is a cheaper alternative with simple accommodation including family-sized tents with a thatch-over roof and space for tents and caravans. Those staying at the Beach Club can use the main resort's facilities.

The hotel restaurant is adequate if unexciting but the so-called 'speciality-nights' when restaurant meals are replaced by a barbecue buffet on the beach can be somewhat chaotic. Whether the entertainment (largely Malawian 'traditional' dancing) compensates for the cold, sand covered food eaten in the dark is a matter of opinion.

The proximity of a village, whose residents may be seen driving cattle into the lake a few hundred metres south of the lodge should not deter. The diminutive beach at Nkopola is safe and generally bilharzia-free. There is

Above: Nkopola Lodge has a beautiful beach used for a variety of water sports.

secure and partly shaded parking as well as a petrol pump at the hotel. Despite its size, booking ahead is essential, especially at weekends.

Club Makokola

Just a kilometre further north on the M10 from Nkopola is what everyone simply calls 'Club Mak'. Despite being near neighbours, the two resorts have very different atmospheres. While Nkopola somehow never lets you forget you are in Malawi, Club Mak has an air of international sophistication. However, its beautiful carvings and furnishings are strong African credentials. One of its greatest attractions is a splendid 600 metre beach of golden sands.

On a site of 263 hectares (650 acres) it is more spaciously laid out than Nkopola and is particularly neatly kept. The garden areas always look as though they have just been tended. The reception was redesigned and resited just a few years ago and there is a 44 metre (145 foot) swimming pool with a beach bar. Club Mak is particularly proud of its 9 hole, par 3 golf course on which a PGA tournament is played each year.

Currently there are rondavels along the beach front and further air-conditioned accommodation in a double-storey block. This new wing provides four family rooms and four twin rooms.

All the accommodation has been up-graded. The rondavels along the beach have been splendidly rebuilt and refurbished. What were two separate en suite rooms are now suites with large-sized sitting rooms and bedrooms. The bathrooms are especially well appointed with both shower and bath and a separate wc. The furnishings are all locally made and there are impressive carvings from the Mua Mission. There is a honeymoon suite with its own plunge pool and the reception block has been completely rebuilt.

Alongside Club Mak is a landing strip sometimes rather grandly known as the Lakeshore Airport. It is a simple affair but allows both Air Malawi and Proflight Air Services to fly in their passengers to within walking distance of the hotel reception. Currently, Air Malawi has scheduled domestic services two or three times a week to and from Blantyre and Lilongwe, but nothing should be assumed and an enquiry close to

Above: The beach at Club Makokola is a full 600 metres of golden sand.

the time of travel is vital if using these services. It is relatively easy to arrange to be picked up from Club Makokola if travelling on to one of the other resorts. The final destination resort will see that a car is available.

A significant proportion of Club Mak's international holidaymakers, using the convenience of the airstrip, never set foot on Malawian soil outside the resort and the airports. An increasing number, however, more aware of the charms of the rest of the country, spend a week at the lake and the rest of their time exploring Malawi's many other attractions. The company which owns Club Mak also runs Mfuwe Lodge in the Luangwa game park in Zambia and can now offer two-destination packages.

Sun 'n' Sand
Further north along the lakeshore is Sun 'n' Sand just 4.5 kilometres (3 miles) north of Club Makokola on the M10. Signposted to the right of the main road, a minor road leads into the resort.

Sun 'n' Sand, which opened in 1995, is the most recently built of the larger lakeshore resorts. Arguably Sun 'n' Sand has taken some

time to settle down and establish a reputation but it is now a popular resort especially with residents of Blantyre and Limbe. It is also the venue of a number of conferences during the year. However, its large and crowded site will make it almost impossible to have quite the style and character of Nkopola or Makokola. The beach is disappointing.

There is an especially wide range of accommodation including one bedroom rondavels with en suite shower, three bedroom chalets with self-catering facilities, and twenty air-conditioned executive chalets. A large swimming pool (40 x 20 metres/130 x 65 feet) has been built together with a children's pool. There is a central restaurant and several bars, some on the beach. Tennis, squash and TV and video lounges provide alternatives to the usual lakeside activities.

While some of the accommodation stretches along the shore, a large section of the resort complex stands back in an arc around the pool.

The somewhat embryonic state of Sun 'n' Sand makes it important to obtain up-to-date information before booking. There are even plans for an airstrip. The hotel is especially popular with Blantyre's Asian community.

Above: Cormorants have colonised Boadzulu Island in Lake Malawi.

Boadzulu Lakeshore Resort

Next door to Sun 'n' Sand is the small resort of Boadzulu. The en suite chalets are set in a garden stretching down to the beach. There are five executive suites. A bar and restaurant overlook the lake. Boat trips to the famous bird island, from which the resort takes its name, are free to residents.

This is a simple and inexpensive alternative worth considering among the wide choice of resorts along this southern lakeshore.

Sightseeing

The raison d'être for a visit to the Southern Lakeshore is usually to enjoy the lake and to engage in some of the activities it offers. However, there is much to do other than water-sports or lying on the sun-drenched beaches.

Off shore is **Boadzulu Island**. Most of the hotels can arrange a boat trip to see the vast colony of **white-breasted cormorants** which breed there. The smell of the guano may be off-putting but the number of birds is impressive. There are also large **monitor lizards** on the island that quickly consume any small bird or egg which falls from the twig nests.

Different habitats along the shore attract a range of birds. The **collared palm thrush** and the **palm swift** are attracted to the stands of palm trees while the **mottled spinetail** can be seen around the baobab trees.

The bird which most interests visitors is the magnificent **fish eagle**, Malawi's national bird. There are larger concentrations of these eagles here than anywhere else in the world. Although they might be seen anywhere along the lake's shore, a guaranteed sighting is at Nkopola Lodge. Each evening a waiter goes to the lake's edge and, after a few blasts on a whistle, a fish eagle appears from the trees to dive for the fish he throws into the water. All rather artificial perhaps but an easy and sure way to get some good photographs and this is no tame eagle. Apart from the eagle and the ever-present **monkeys**, Nkopola's other permanent residents are the **rock hyraxes** or **dassies**. These small creatures, looking like giant well-fed hamsters, are, incredibly, evolutionarily related to the elephant. They live in the rocky promontory that marks the northern limit of the resort.

There are some very large **baobabs** along the M10. The "upside-down" tree (so called because for much of the year it is leafless and its thick branches look like roots) look somewhat absurd and provide no shade. In contrast, along the road and particularly near the turning to Monkey Bay, there are graceful acacias whose branches spread widely from slender trunks, forming a canopy.

Some 47 kilometres (29 miles) north of Mangochi, signposted to the right of the road, is the **Koma Crocodile Farm**. Its opening times seem to vary according to demand but 16.30 is the official closing time. However, visitors are so few that so long as someone is still present with the keys, the farm will be opened up at almost any time. Entry is charged at K40 with children half price.

It claims to be the only crocodile farm in Malawi but this isn't so. The eggs come from the Majete Wildlife Reserve and there are monsters of four metres in length down to recently hatched youngsters. The number of crocodiles on the farm varies from time to time but large numbers, up to the age of six years, are usually on view. The skins and meat are sold commercially but the skulls can be purchased at the farm. To see the animals fed will be a matter of luck because they may have a month or so between meals.

Bottom: The extent of Nkopola Lodge's beach can be appreciated from the air. Below: Most lodges provide spectacular views of the lake.

Above: Crocodiles bask in the sun at the Koma crocodile farm.

On the lake side of the crocodile farm is a fishing village. To reach the village simply continue along the track, beyond the farm. From the village, boats set out with lights to fish the lake at night. Massive nets ensure a good catch.

Close to the **Monkey Bay** and **Cape Maclear** junction, there are **curio sellers** in the shade of simple thatch stalls. It is a good place to bargain and, in many cases, prices are reasonable although the quality is not always very high. The best time to browse will be when a minibus full of tourists has arrived and the stallholders are busy.

Other places to buy **carvings** and curios are along the entrance drives into Club Mak and Nkopola Lodge. Close to Nkopola is the village where much of the carving takes place. The carvers are keen to show you around but you will be expected to buy something.

There is occasionally fruit for sale along the road and this will be a better buy than the wares of the 'tyre doctors' whose near-bald offerings are best ignored.

Practical matters and activities

There is a great range of **water sports** on offer from the hotels. **Swimming** is possible along any of the hotel beaches as well as in the hotels' pools. Bilharzia should not be a problem here. The hotel managements are very sensitive to this issue, but use of beaches away from the resorts may be unwise. Generally, the beaches are safe for children who enjoy the uncrowded golden sands.

Most of the hotels have **boats** and **water-skiing**, **scuba diving**, **parasailing** and **snorkelling** are available with expert tuition. Club Mak has a 22 metre lake cruiser, the *mv Sunbird*. This has recently had a complete re-fit and will take up to eight passengers on overnight **cruises** along the lake and as far as Liwonde National Park along the Shire River. Interestingly, lake cruising is become more and more popular with new boats operated by other companies.

Yachting has a notable place on the lake. The famous Lake Malawi Sailing Marathon is the longest freshwater race in the world. Visitors wishing to sail should make enquiries in advance of a stay at a lakeshore hotel.

There is **tennis** (2 courts) and **squash** at Club Mak although the squash court is not at

Above: Sailing is one of the many water sports for which Lake Malawi is well-known.

Nkopola and **beach volleyball** is at most of the resorts. Only Club Mak has a **golf course**. The beautiful Mlambe nine-hole course was laid out at great expense and in 2000 had the first of its now annual PGA Pro-Am Tournaments.

Most of the hotels do not charge for activities that don't involve boats or expensive equipment. The managements are always adding to their activities so the examples given above are only an indication of what is offered.

The waters of Lake Malawi are always warm enough for swimming and the fact that there are no tides and that the water is fresh make a lakeshore holiday especially attractive.

A word of caution if driving along the M10 on this Southern Lakeshore. By Malawi standards there is quite a lot of traffic as well as the usual animal and human users. The road is straight and without gradient and this invites speeding. Care should be exercised.

Following pages: Lake Malawi is often called 'the lake of stars' as its surface shimmers in the sunlight. The mountains in the background are the eastern shore.

Monkey Bay

Monkey Bay provides a sheltered harbour behind the **Cape Maclear** headland which splits the southern extremity of Lake Malawi into two. There is evidence that this area was home to Stone Age man between ten and five thousand years ago. The inhabitants were the *Nachikufan*, a distinct racial type, neither Bushman nor Bantu, whose descendants today form some of the non-Bantu tribes of this part of Africa.

The shelter of the bay has continued to be an attraction and the town's modern development owes much to the fact that it was deemed to be the only place on the lake which was deep and sheltered enough for a floating repair dock. In fact the waters of the bay can be quite rough when winds, blowing north or south the full length of the lake, whip up a *seiche*, an oscillating wave which derives from a tilt in the lake surface.

Monkey Bay became the headquarters of the quaintly named **Malawi Army Naval Unit** as well as that of the **Malawian Lake Service**.

Getting there

From

Lilongwe:	225km/140miles	M14, M5, M10, S128
Blantyre:	249km/155miles	M3, M10, S128
Mangochi:	62km/38miles	M10, S128
Salima:	133km/83miles	M5, M10, S128

```
                              M10/S128
                              Junction        Monkey Bay
Mangochi
                      Koma Crocodile    To Cape
                           Farm         Maclear
              47km              3km   6km    6km
```

Mangochi to Monkey Bay: M10, S128: 62km

The M10 west of Monkey Bay had been allowed to deteriorate but repairs have since been effected.

The final access road to Monkey Bay town is the S128 which leads off the M10 a distance of 12 kilometres (7 miles) on a tarred surface into the town. After six kilometres (four miles) the road to Cape Maclear branches off to the left. The road on to Monkey Bay is a dead end. It is the natural extension of the M10 coming up from Mangochi and, until quite recently, carried the same route number.

When to go

There is no special time to visit Monkey Bay; the conditions are the same as on the Southern Lakeshore.

Where to stay

There really is neither any point in staying in the town nor is there any accommodation really suitable for the international traveller. Monkey Bay is so close to Cape Maclear and to the string of hotels on the Southern Lakeshore that most visitors simply make a half-day trip into the town.

Sightseeing

Although the name, Monkey Bay, has a sort of allure, the small town is something of a disappointment. Little of the bay can be seen because much of the area around it is protected land and belongs to the state. From the restrictions, one might get the impression that this is a major nuclear submarine naval base (African style of course) instead of a rather tired-looking service centre.

Monkey Bay has the offices of Malawi Lake Services, who run the Lake Malawi passenger vessel, the *mv Ilala*. They operate from the jetty and this is the terminus for the lake boats. A trip along the lake on the *Ilala* is an altogether different and worthwhile experience — if you can spare the time. It has to be said that the service is not a hundred per cent reliable as far as sticking to its schedule is concerned.

Right: Beautiful acacias are common in Lake Malawi National Park. Below top: There are more fish eagles along the southern lakeshore than anywhere else in the world. Below bottom: The rock dassie or hyrax, is an inquisitive creature distantly related to the elephant.

There are some new developments in the fishing industry taking place in Monkey Bay. The aim is to increase the scale of operations and make them a more commercially viable operation.

There is not a great deal to attract the casual visitor but the town has a range of services including **petrol,** and **shops**.

Practical matters and activities

If driving near the harbour in Monkey Bay, look out for some dangerously large traffic-calming humps in the road. Because of the number of state activities in the town, it is important to take heed of various restriction notices.

239

Cape Maclear and Lake Malawi National Park

The **Nankumba Peninsula** is composed largely of granite which solidified below the surface only to be exposed as uplift occurred and erosion took its toll. Outcrops of this resistant rock form the rounded hills characteristic of the Lake Malawi National Park and its dozen or so off-shore islands. Cape Maclear is the main headland and its name has become synonymous with the whole peninsula.

As with Monkey Bay there is a long history of settlement of this part of the lakeshore and when the Scottish missionaries arrived in the mid-nineteenth century they were taken by the site's beauty and established a mission on the headland.

David and **Charles Livingstone**, after a visit in 1861, named the cape in honour of **Sir Thomas Maclear**, at that time Astronomer Royal at the Cape of Good Hope and a friend of the Livingstones. A mission, established in 1875, had mixed fortunes. Called the **Livingstonia Mission**, the little settlement on the western side of the cape flourished at first under the direction of **Robert Laws**. In an area still rich in wildlife, crops were grown and buildings erected. Drawn by the security of the mission and by the education and medical services it offered, the site began to attract migrants from the surrounding areas. However, the mosquito and the tsetse fly began to affect the health of the European settlers and, by 1881, Dr Laws decided to seek a new site on the lake but further north, at Bandawe. In 1896 the original mission settlement at Cape Maclear was finally abandoned.

In the early 1930s, much of the peninsula was declared a protected forest reserve and in 1946, close to the original mission site, a small hotel was built. This was the first tourist hotel in Malawi. For a while it thrived, gaining from trade which came when, in 1949, BOAC (the forerunner of British Airways) began to use Cape Maclear as a stopping point for its flying boat service

between the United Kingdom and South Africa. Alas, the service was shortlived. Like the mission before it, as business withered, the hotel was closed in 1951. The building was taken down.

In 1980 much of the peninsula, the off-shore islands and the lake waters up to 100 metres off-shore were declared a national park. This was the first national park in the world to have as a primary aim the

conservation of fresh water fish. It is a UNESCO World Heritage Site.

There is a substantial and rather untidy village, **Chembe**, on the north-facing coast which merges with the park. It is home to a fishing community but many earn a better living through their involvement, often freelance, with the tourist trade. It is one of the largest fishing villages on the whole of the lake.

Getting there

From

Lilongwe:	238km/148miles	M14, M5, M10, S128, minor road
Blantyre:	262km/163miles	M3, M10, S128, minor road
Mangochi:	75km/47miles	M10, S128, minor road
Salima:	146km/91miles	M5, M10, S128, minor road

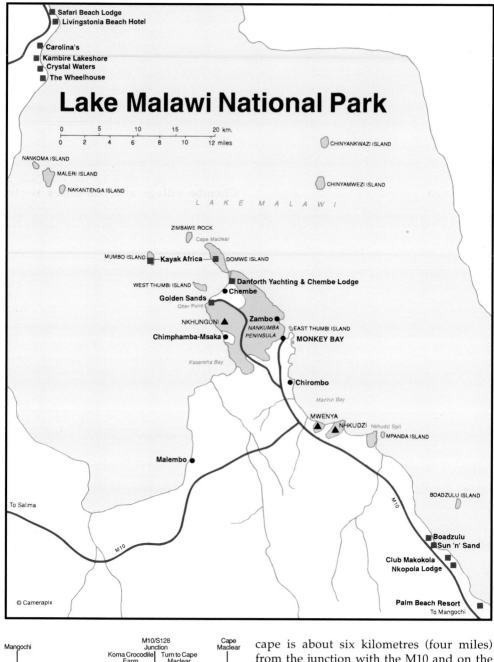

Lake Malawi National Park

Safari Beach Lodge
Livingstonia Beach Hotel

Carolina's
Kambire Lakeshore
Crystal Waters
The Wheelhouse

CHINYANKWAZI ISLAND

NANKOMA ISLAND

MALERI ISLAND

NAKANTENGA ISLAND

CHINYAMWEZI ISLAND

L A K E   M A L A W I

ZIMBAWE ROCK
Cape Maclear

MUMBO ISLAND — Kayak Africa — DOMWE ISLAND

WEST THUMBI ISLAND — Danforth Yachting & Chembe Lodge
Chembe

Golden Sands
Otter Point

NKHUNGUNI ▲

Chimphamba-Msaka

Zambo
NANKUMBA
PENINSULA

EAST THUMBI ISLAND

MONKEY BAY

Kasankha Bay

Chirombo

Mazinzi Bay

MWENYA

▲ NHKUDZI   Nkhudzi Spit

MPANDA ISLAND

Malembo

To Salima

BOADZULU ISLAND

M10

Boadzulu
Sun 'n' Sand

Club Makokola
Nkopola Lodge

© Camerapix

Palm Beach Resort
To Mangochi

M10

Mangochi		M10/S128 Junction	Cape Maclear
	Koma Crocodile Farm	Turn to Cape Maclear	
47km	3km	6km	19km

Mangochi to Cape Maclear: M10, S128, minor road: 75km

The main roads to Cape Maclear are identical to those for Monkey Bay and the same note of caution regarding the M10, to the west, applies. Travelling towards the bay on the tarmacked S128 the turn-off for the cape is about six kilometres (four miles) from the junction with the M10 and on the left. It is signposted. Though the focus of the national park is at Cape Maclear, the protected area is actually entered shortly after this turning. There is no gate.

This final, minor road has been repaired and significantly improved and there are even some short tarmac sections. However, it is mostly a dirt road, corrugated and dusty and, no doubt, will soon revert to its former poor state unless a programme of repairs continues. For the present it should cause few difficulties but it is not a road to hurry on.

But who would want to speed through some of the finest scenery in Malawi. Dome-shaped hills, undulating valleys, boulder strewn slopes, trees aplenty and in great variety — the road winds its way to Cape Maclear as though an intruder in this world of extraordinary silence and serene beauty.

When to go
The best time of year to visit is probably May to September. There will be plenty of fish in those months and temperatures are moderate. November can be very hot and from mid-December through to April there may be squally rain showers.

Where to stay
For many years there have been plans to build an international-class hotel at Cape Maclear. Despite the very obvious potential for the success of such a venture, so far nothing has come of what have been mainly paper exercises. Now it really does seem that within a few years development will take place, sympathetic to and in harmony with the cape's natural beauty. This could make the cape one of Malawi's premier tourist resorts.

In the meantime, Cape Maclear has become somewhat of a mecca for backpackers and the accommodation, with a few significant exceptions, reflects their tastes and needs. Some backpackers now see Nkhata Bay as offering more than Cape Maclear.

Among the cheaper accommodation options are **Stevens Resthouse**, well-known to the backpacker fraternity, **The Ritz**, a divers' haunt and **Fat Monkey**, a campsite used by overlanders. All are to be found by taking a right turn on the road just before the park's gate.

Golden Sands
Despite the fact that it occupies one of the best sites along the shore, near Otter Point, and despite its rather pretentious full name, Golden Sands Holiday Resort is something of a disappointment. It is owned by the Ministry of Tourism, Parks and Wildlife and consists of a collection of run-down chalets

just inside the park gate and close to the beach. The accommodation is en suite but rudimentary. The chalets sleep two or three persons on a self-catering basis and there is a shady area for camping. The merits are largely in the site's quieter setting than the lodges further along the shore near Chembe village and in the security offered.

Chembe Lodge
The lodge has some of the best accommodation in the park. It is sited on the east side of Chembe village and comprises twelve permanent tents under the shade of straw canopies. Two of the tents are en suite. The lodge has an eight-metre (twenty-six foot) sailing catamaran which can be used for sailing safaris on the lake.

This well-run establishment is under a new innovative management determined to maintain its reputation and add to what it can offer its guests.

Nswala Safari Lodge
The lodge is not as well-known as those in or alongside Chembe village. To reach Nswala, turn off (left) when you come to the small filling station on the road through the park. The lodge is in an area called **Kasankha Bay**, six kilometres (four miles) after leaving the main Monkey Bay road. There are four stone and thatch chalets on the beach, one of which is family size, and three reed and thatch chalets on the hillside. None of the chalets is en suite but there are plans to up-grade.

There is a restaurant, lounge and beach bar. This is a very pleasant spot with excellent views of the lake and of its famous sunsets. Camping is allowed and there is parking space for camper vans.

The current situation should be checked because of ownership and management changes.

Kayak Africa
If a deserted island paradise sounds attractive then there can be little better than to use Kayak Africa for a stay at Cape Maclear. This company has camps on two unpopulated and mosquito-free islands, **Domwe** and **Mumbo**, off-shore from the cape and about 10 kilometres (6 miles) apart. The accommodation, up-graded in 2001 to a very high standard, is in a small, tented camps on each

Above: Chembe village is surrounded by Lake Malawi National Park.

of the islands. To reach the islands, guests can kayak themselves out across the lake (it takes about two hours to Mumbo and about half that time to Domwe). Alternatively a boat can be arranged.

On the islands there's plenty to occupy the time. The diving is excellent and instruction is available. A leisurely paddle around or between the islands, soaking up the sun in a hammock, pottering around over the rocks and discovering caves — then enjoying the meals, including freshly baked bread: this is the stuff of dreams. If it all seems too self-indulgent then remember that some of the profits go to help the local community.

A stay with Kayak Africa will be a wonderful experience to be remembered for ever.

Danforth Yachting and Guest House

A welcome new venture at Cape Maclear is Danforth Yachting. The company has a really beautiful guesthouse with four en suite, air conditioned, double rooms. But the main attraction is a luxury catamaran yacht, the *Mufasa*, which sleeps eight guests and can be used for cruising on the lake. Cruises can be from one day to eight days. On the longer

cruises, the yacht can sail as far as Likoma Island. The cruises are effectively lake safaris with stops at various lodges round the shoreline. This is a very exciting addition to the lake's many attractions.

Sightseeing

Apart from troops of **baboon**, something of a nuisance in the park, the most visible fauna of Lake Malawi National Park are the hundred or so species of birds and the *mbuna*, the colourful tropical freshwater fish in the lake.

The focus of most visitors' attention is the crystal-clear lake water which laps the sandy shore. Teeming shoals of small fish provide a kaleidoscopic display of brilliant colour. Use of a snorkel or glass-bottomed boat isn't necessary. The fish, never much below the surface, will feed out of your hand as you trail it over the side of a boat. There is no need to be an expert on aquatic life to find observing the fish a fascinating experience. The finest sightings will be around **Otter Point**, a beautiful rocky headland at the northern tip of the cape.

Lake Malawi boasts the largest number of

Above: Kayaking has become one of the most popular activities on the lake. Below: Mwala wa Mphini, a granite boulder in Lake Malawi National Park. The markings are a naturally occuring phenomenon.

fish species of any lake in the world. Lake Tanganyika disputes this but the count must be a near draw. Of the species in Lake Malawi, an extraordinary number are endemic to the lake. The majority of species are of the *Cichlidae* family. It is these cichlids which include the brightly coloured *mbuna*. This is a Tonga word for these tiny fish. Twelve centimetres (five inches) is a big fish as far as *mbuna* are concerned.

Of the birds, three species are most commonly seen: **white-breasted cormorants**, which have colonised some of the islands, **fish eagles** and the **hamerkop**. The cries of the large raptors, the fish eagles, will be heard everywhere and their size ensures that they will be seen. Another diver for fish is the **pied kingfisher**. In the reed beds there are **weavers**, especially the **lesser-masked** and the **yellow weaver**.

Although there are **crocodiles** and **hippos** in the park, little will be seen of them. Away from the shore there are **rock hyraxes** and varieties of antelope such as the **kudu** and **grey duiker** but, again, they will need seeking out.

The flora should not be overlooked. The forested areas away from the lake contain interesting **baobabs** and **acacia** woodlands although the park is essentially *Brachystegia* woodland.

Close by the gate is a small museum and aquariums. The latter need much more work on the presentation and are not very attractive. The little museum (strictly an environmental centre) is worth visiting.

There is more to the park than the lakeshore

Above: Lake Malawi boasts the largest number of fish species of any lake in the world.

and the multi-coloured fish. Away from the lakeside the park is a place of great beauty and calm. Some have called it another Eden. Certainly it is a wonderful place to walk, climb and explore. Some of the hills give excellent views of the lake.

Close to the gate are the graves of some of the early missionaries who perished there in the late 1870s. For the most part the memorials are just simple crosses but that of **Dr William Black** is a plaque attached to a large boulder. The plaque is original but the crosses are modern replacements.

Along the main road through the park and about a kilometre or so from the official gate, there is a signposted track (to the right if travelling into the park but most easily spotted on the return). This leads just a short distance to **Mwala wa Mphini**. This large granite rock face is a protected natural monument and at one time the regular striations which mark its surface were thought to be man-made and to have some ritualistic significance. In fact they are natural and caused by differential weathering of crystalline rock. They are nonetheless remarkable.

Practical matters and activities

There have been recent improvements in accommodation in the park and day visits are quite easily made from the resorts between Mangochi and Monkey Bay or from Senga Bay

Although the park covers much of the peninsula, the official gate at which payment is made (US$5 per person) is near to the shore. The little museum is also a good place to park a car in relative safety. There's a small filling station just a little way from the Monkey Bay road into the park, where the track leads off to Nswala Lodge. In fact the lodge and the filling station are under the same ownership.

Cape Maclear is rightly famous for its water sports. There are plenty of opportunities to hire equipment for the day for **snorkelling, sail boarding, scuba diving** and **boating**. The novice can obtain instruction at a modest price and many go to Cape Maclear in order to master the art of scuba diving. Signs indicating availability of equipment for hire and of instruction will be found near the Golden Sands camp and in Chembe village. A number of companies specialise in providing water sports and instruction.

Above: There are plenty of opportunities for diving in the warm waters of the lake.

Kayak Africa doesn't only offer **kayaking**. There are excellent facilities on the islands for **snorkelling** and **diving**, including instructions to advanced levels. And, of course the waters around the islands are bilharzia free. Likewise, Danforth Yachting provides a unique **sailing** experience and also for scuba diving.

Every visitor to the cape is likely to be pestered by boys and young men offering boat trips to view the fish. Bargaining is expected and the asking price will quickly reduce by a factor of three. Ask to be taken to Otter Point. In the village, to the right of the park gate, curios are on sale and it is possible to buy small, and dead, fish to throw into the lake. If you are lucky, a fish eagle will swoop to get an easy meal. If going out in a boat to view the *mbuna*, take a few biscuits. Fish will soon be eating out of your hand as you dip it into the water.

One should not be put off by the rather untidy appearance of the cape around the village and by the Golden Sands camp. Instead, enjoy the natural beauty of what is a stunningly attractive place.

The one activity that is strictly forbidden is fishing.

Four warnings should be heeded if visiting Cape Maclear. In their own quite different ways, mosquitoes, monkeys and baboons can be a nuisance.

More seriously, care should be exercised if engaging in watersports or swimming. There are real risks of contracting bilharzia. This does NOT apply to the waters off Domwe and Mumbo Islands nor if using a boat well off shore. It is particularly important to take precautions and to avoid areas where there are reeds.

It is very likely that drugs will be offered to anyone who is clearly a tourist. Most especially there will be boys wanting to sell marijuana. In Malawi this is called chamba (not to be confused with chambo which is the lake's best known fish) or Malawi Gold. Transactions are illegal, as is possession.

Finally, as in any area which attracts large numbers of backpackers and other tourists, it is a sad fact of life that robberies do take place. It is important to be cautious and not to wander alone after dark.

Mua Mission

The mission, the first established in Malawi by the Roman Catholic Church, is just over one hundred years old, its foundation being in 1899. The Mua parish, run by the White Fathers, dates from 1903 and stretches from the escarpment, bordering the Great Rift Valley, down to the plains by Lake Malawi. A village has grown up round the nucleus of the parish buildings and now occupies the hillside down to the nearby **KuNgoni Waterfalls**.

The modern development of the mission owes mush to a Canadian White Father, **Claude Boucher**, who founded the **KuNgoni Art and Craft Centre** in 1976. The aim was to harness the skills of local craftsmen and exploit the richness of Malawian culture. A museum has been established and the mission now acts as a school for wood carvers who will later make their own living from their handiwork throughout Malawi and beyond. The work is not limited to wood carving; pottery, paintings and batiks are also produced.

Getting there
From

Lilongwe:	156km/97miles	M14, M5
Salima:	64km/40miles	M5
Blantyre:	204km/127miles	M1, M5
Blantyre:	298km/185miles	M3, M10
Mangochi:	111km/69miles	M10
M1/M8 Junction:	89km/55miles	M5

Mua Mission can be approached from the east, Monkey Bay and Cape Maclear, from the south, Blantyre via the M1/M8 junction, or from the north, Salima. The route from the north will be dealt with under Salima and Senga Bay.

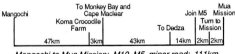

Mangochi to Mua Mission: M10, M5, minor road: 111km

The M10 from the Monkey Bay junction to Mua is different from the section up from Mangochi. The surface is more variable and there are drifts (signed by what looks like and upside-down hump) which may be flooded in the wet season and should be driven with care in any season. However, there have been major works on this road and it is much improved.

The vegetation alongside the road is thick scrub with some areas of maize cultivation. Contrasting with the Mangochi to Monkey Bay section, there is very little traffic and much of the route seems to travel through

an unpopulated wilderness. The only hint of human habitation may be a bus stop in the middle of nowhere.

After travelling 43 kilometres (27 miles) from the Monkey Bay junction, there is a turning off the M10 (left) to a minor road, the S127. After crossing the M5 at Golomoti, this road becomes a short cut to the M1 south of Dedza. The quality of this minor road is poor.

The M10 continues westwards in its approach to Mua. Now there are the distractions of some small villages but looking due west there is some truly magnificent mountain scenery. Rising abruptly from the flat lakeshore plains is the escarpment which forms the edge of the Great Rift Valley. These are the Dedza-Kirk Mountains, at their most majestic in early morning light.

The M10 meets the M5 some 107 kilometres (66 miles) from the starting point of Mangochi. Here the turn is right. Mua village is to the left of the M5 some two kilometres north of its junction with the M10. The road to the mission climbs a further two kilometres past the **hospital** and bears right past the **church** into the visitors' section of the settlement: the **KuNgoni Arts and Craft Centre**.

Above: Young men work on the carvings for which the Mua Mission is renowned.

M1/M8 Junction		M5/M1 Junction			S127 East	M10 To Dedza		Mua Mission Turn to Mission	
5km			64km		1km	15km		2km	2km

M1/M8 Junction to Mua Mission: M1, M5, minor road: 89km

The road up to Mua from the south is the M5 which leads off the M1. It is the M5 which is called the Lakeshore Road.

A lakeshore road is said to have been one of Dr Banda's "dreams" when he was interned in Rhodesia (Zimbabwe) from 1959-60. Ironically, when the road was finally completed in the mid-1990s Banda had fallen from power and had exchanged Gwelo prison for house arrest in Blantyre.

The road, partly along entirely new paths and partly reconstructed from pre-existing roads, has made an important difference to north-south communications in Malawi. Its surface is generally good to very good and it is well engineered although it is subject to flood damage as many of the country's biggest rivers cross its path as they flow towards the lake. Despite the good quality of the road it is remarkably quiet with little traffic.

Although called the Lakeshore Road, the M5 is rarely in sight of Lake Malawi and, in its southern section from near Balaka almost to Mua, it is nearer to Malawi's western border with Mozambique than it is to the lake. All the same, it is one continuous road running roughly parallel to the western shore, linking the scattered settlements at the water's edge.

The M5 does not start in any village or town but begins life from where it branches north from the M1. This is five kilometres (three miles) north of the M1/M8 junction. The M8 leads east to Liwonde National Park and the M1 south to Blantyre. The nearest settlement to that junction is Balaka on the M8.

Leaving the M1, the M5 runs with the **Dedza-Kirk Mountains** rising to the west and broken uplands, leading down to the Shire Valley and the lake, to the east. The road allows for easy driving, following the same line as the country's main railway, occasionally to be seen to the right. The route crosses a number of rivers, mostly tributaries of the **Bwanje** which flows into Lake Malawi to the west of the Cape Maclear peninsula. In places, damage has been caused to the road when rivers rise in the wet season.

After 64 kilometres (40 miles) there is the junction (right) with the **Golomoti Road**, S127, which is a minor road link with the M10. A kilometre further on, after crossing a river, a turning to the left is the continuation of the S127. This is an interesting short cut to Dedza over the mountains but the road is dirt and is very difficult when wet.

Continuing on the M5, after 80 kilometres (50 miles) from the M1, the junction with the M10 is reached and in a couple of kilometres there is the road (left) up to Mua Mission.

When to go
Any time of the year is suitable but avoid Sunday mornings and religious holidays.

Where to stay
There is no accommodation at the mission. A day's visit from Salima, Senga Bay or the Southern Lakeshore is quite easy.

Sightseeing
Visitors can see the woodcarvers, some as young as ten or eleven years old, at work in large open-sided rondavels with heavy thatched roofs providing shade. The pillars supporting the roofs have been carved with scenes portraying the history of Malawi.

Most of the work done by these quite extraordinarily skilled craftsmen finds a home in churches around Malawi and overseas but there is a small shop (shut for an hour at noon) which sells smaller and largely secular carvings to visitors. For ridiculously low prices, by western standards, one can come away with a piece of real artistic merit. As you leave the shop, each craftsman looks up interestedly from his work to see if what you have bought might be the product of his labours. It is worth noting that there are more goods, including large carvings, on show and for sale in the buildings alongside the museum.

A special building, opened in late 1997, houses the **Chamare Museum**. Here are exhibitions detailing the three ethnic groups of Central Malawi: the Yao, Ngoni and Chewa. Its exhibits are unique and well worth a visit. Properly to appreciate the museum one needs a guide and about an hour to spare.

The outer walls of the building are painted with murals telling the history of Malawi. Inside, the museum is in three rooms. The entrance room displays various exhibits telling

Above: The M10 road from Monkey Bay leads towards the Dedza-Kirk Mountains, the edge of the Rift Valley. Top: A carving from the Mua Mission.

Above: The Chamare Museum is part of the Mua Mission. Below: Fascinating murals decorate the exterior of the Chamare Museum. Opposite: A view towards the escarpment from Mua Mission's gardens.

the story of the mission. This room is used for talks when groups visit. The next two rooms are celebrations of the **Chewa** tribe, in the

second room, and the **Yao** and **Ngoni** tribes, in the final room.

As well as calling into the museum, visitors are encouraged to stop off at the **church**. The brick building is not especially attractive and its impressively large interior has about as much architectural merit as a sports hall. What are of fascinating interest are the carvings which demonstrate the skills of Mua's craftsmen at their best. The Mua Mission is a gem. To drive past on a journey to, say, the lake or Blantyre without calling in would be to miss a rare treat.

Practical matters and activities
Although there are opening and closing times for the shop and museum, it will usually be possible to find someone to open up for you. A donation towards the mission is appropriate, especially if not buying anything. A fee of US$5 is charged for a guided tour of the museum.

After viewing the museum and visiting the shop, it is possible to look around the gardens set on the hillside or to visit the mission's animal sanctuary.

Salima and Senga Bay

Salima's limits are difficult to define. It straddles the M14/M5 junction and then makes an untidy foray down the S122 towards Senga Bay. Its importance derives from its function as a communications and service centre. Salima's fortunes took a turn for the better when, in the late 1930s, it became a railhead on Malawi's main international route.

An earthquake and flooding in 1989 wrought serious damage to the town, severely testing its inhabitants' ability to recover from the disaster. That they did is greatly to their credit. The road improvements of the 1990s have given it an enhanced status, making it perhaps the most important settlement close to Lake Malawi.

Senga Bay, one of the most beautiful along the western shore of the lake, is situated at one of the narrowest points on the lake where the eastern shore is clearly visible and where, traditionally, cross-lake traffic is landed.

Getting there

From Lilongwe:	98km/61miles	M14
From Blantyre:	264km/164miles	M1, M5
From Mzuzu:	338km/210miles	M5
From Mangochi:	171km/106miles	M10, M5

Add 21 kilometres (13 miles) via S122 (see below) for Senga Bay.

The route to Salima from Lilongwe, the M14, has been described in the Central Region section of the book: Going to the Lake. The road from the north, the M5, is described in the next section.

To reach Salima from the south is to use the M5 up from Mua.

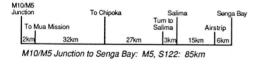

M10/M5 Junction to Senga Bay: M5, S122: 85km

From Mua the road begins to cross the lakeside plains. At 32 kilometres (20 miles) north of Mua there is a turning (right) to **Chipoka**. This little town was to have become a major lake port for the railway. A small jetty was built but little trading ever took place. It is a port of call for the *mv Ilala*. The rich dambo soils of this area have been important for the production of cotton but ideas of large scale development in the early days have never been realised.

In a further two kilometres, the M5 crosses the **Lifise River**, a favourite place with local

women to do the family washing. In the dry season, clothes are laid out to dry on the exposed sandbanks in the middle of the river.

At 59 kilometres (37 miles) north of Mua the M5 turns left while to the right is the road to Salima and Senga Bay. To stay on the M5 is to run through what are effectively suburbs of Salima until, after six kilometres (four miles), the M5 turns sharply right, to the north, while the road continuing west is the M14 to Lilongwe.

However, taking the turn into Salima town, the road is the S122 and this is Salima's main street. As the town comes to an uncertain end,

the S122 continues eastwards as Senga Bay's main access. The route is across flat and marshy terrain of little intrinsic interest but home to large numbers of birds. The road has recently been up-graded — not before time.

About halfway along the S122 is the large **Mpatsanjoka dambo**, and nearby is Salima's civil and military **airport**. Motorists may be disconcerted by notices: "Caution: beware of parachute drops". Charter aircraft land there by arrangement and customs and immigration officials will meet international flights. There are no scheduled flights.

Before the lake is reached a number of

signposted turnings to the right lead towards the bay and Kambiri Point where there is a range of accommodation options. Continuing on the S122 the road approaches **Senga Bay** and a turn off to the left leads to the Safari Beach Lodge. Finally there is a gated entrance to the Livingstonia Beach Hotel.

When to go
The best times to visit are the months of May to November although the latter couple of months in this period may be quite hot.

Where to stay
There is little reason to stay in Salima town. Only the most simple accommodation is available. International visitors inevitably make for Senga Bay where there's a wealth of choice. Two of the best, on the northern headland of the bay, are the Livingstonia Beach Hotel, one of the best known in Malawi, and the Safari Beach Lodge. In the bay and around the southern headland, **Kambiri Point**, is a cluster of lodges and hotels providing a range of accommodation at a variety of prices. Among them is **Crystal Waters** which has chalets and camping. A particular favourite with campers is **The Wheelhouse**. The **Red Zebra Lodge** has accommodation alongside the fish farm.

All the lodges and hotels are well signposted off the S122 but in the maze of roads around the bay it may be necessary to enquire.

Le Méridien Livingstonia Beach Hotel
This hotel is often described as "Malawi's best" although this would no doubt be disputed. Undoubtedly it is one of the most attractive. Its history is interesting. One of the first hotels on the lakeshore, and then called the Grand Beach Hotel, it has had numerous ownership and management changes. Most important was the influence of the van Osch family who took command in the 1990s and transformed the hotel into the international standard property it has become. Most recently, the Le Méridien group acquired the management in 2000. It is often known, simply, as LBH.

The hotel is set in immaculate gardens and faces directly on to a splendid golden sand, private beach. It is a mix of colonial style and more modern-looking rondavels. What was previously the owner's house has been converted into luxury suites. The rondavels enjoy a high level of privacy, set slightly away from the main buildings.

The dining room is on the first floor of the hotel, reached by a wooden stairway on the outside of the building and enjoying good views of the lake. Meals are also served outside on the terrace where there is a second bar. Postcards, on sale in the hotel's small shop, confirm that the outside appearance of the hotel is much as it was before World War II. There is a sympathetic blend of the essentially colonial and the more modern developments.

There is a swimming pool in the gardens and a tennis court.

Alongside the hotel is what has justifiably been claimed to be the lakeshore's best camping site, Steps. The site is invisible from the hotel, has its own stretch of beach and is run quite separately. Most of the hotel's guests are unaware of its existence.

Safari Beach Lodge
The lodge is just a stone's throw from Livingstonia Beach Hotel but is in a forest reserve and separated by a headland. It occupies a rocky site above the beach which is reached by steps though a garden. Originally a forest resthouse, it is now in private hands and still being developed. Acommodation is in three en suite rooms in the lodge or in new permanent en suite tents which are wonderfully sited on rocky platforms overlooking the lake. The tents are so placed that they afford maximum privacy. All the accommodation is attractively priced and excellent value.

The beach, though small, is exclusive and has a mix of yellow and black sands. The black sands contain titanium oxide. The lake here, as at LBH, is bilharzia free. A boat is available and water sports are possible including water skiing.

The dining room menu is distinctly German, reflecting the owner's origin. Visitors are probably most surprised by the presence of a house-trained duiker. Guests can watch as other antelope, baboons and even small predators come to feed on scraps left out at the bottom of the lodge. The owner's dog has adopted a small monkey which rides on its back.

Safari Beach Lodge has a lot to commend it.

Above: Safari Beach Lodge delightfully situated on Lake Malawi and in a forest reserve.

Kambiri Lakeshore Hotel

The is probably the best of the hotels and lodges at the southern part of the bay. It is set in gardens and the accommodation is in nineteen en suite rooms. Despite its name, the hotel is about 100 metres back from the shore and the lake is almost invisible from the bedrooms. All this same, this is a comfortable, well-run hotel. At the time of writing it is up for sale.

Carolina's Lakeshore Resort

Carolina's has everything from dormitories to chalets. Most of the rooms, not en suite, are in four houses each with five rooms. The A-frame chalets are en suite and there is a very extensive beach with lots of activities, This is a well run resort which is reasonably priced.

Sightseeing

The lasting impression of Salima will be of a town which is busy and purposeful. There are **banks**, **petrol stations**, a **post office**, a large **bus station** and countless stores including **supermarkets**. There is a lively **market** to the south of the main road through the town.

Salima is as well served as one can reasonably expect.

In some respects it is thoroughly urban. Bars with unforgettable names like the "Come Again Booze Centre" or the "Hangover Clinic Bottle Store" line the main street. On the other hand the inhabitants of Salima have not quite come to terms with the idea of traffic using the roads. Pedestrians, goats and chickens pay scant regard to the trucks, buses and cars which compete for space on what are quite heavily used roads. On the outskirts of the town, vast quantities of straw are prepared for Malawi's traditional thatched roofs.

It is worth spending just a little time walking around Salima to observe and enjoy its character.

Rocky headlands enclose the **Senga Bay** and round the northern one, **Namikombe Point**, is a second bay, **Leopard's**. Just a couple of kilometres off-shore is **Namalenje Island**, opposite the Livingstonia Beach Hotel. Colonised by birds, including **cormorants** and **fish eagles**, the island and its trees are stained white with guano. **Monitor lizards** share the island with the birds.

Above: Namalenje Island is a boat trip away from Senga Bay. Below (left): The sun is seen rising over Lake Malawi.

There are two places where hippos may be seen. The unambiguously named **Hippo Pools** are a short walk away from LBH over the **Senga Hills**, north of the hotel. There is another small lake, covered with water hyacinth, where the hippo duck below the vegetation only to emerge again apparently festooned by flowers. This lake is difficult to find so it's best to get a guide and point out that it is the pool beyond the **Military Academy**.

The **Red Zebra Café**, on the right of the main Salima-Senga Bay road a little before reaching LBH, is not only a good place to eat, but its owners also have an interesting **fish farm** at Kambiri Point, beyond the Academy. Fish from here are exported to large and small aquariums around the world. There is accommodation there in the **Red Zebra Lodge** and the owners organise trips on the lake.

To the north of Senga Bay the land rises sharply to 375 metres (1230 feet). From the summit of **Nankhumba Hill** there are wonderful views of the two bays, the lake and the eastern shore.

In Leopard's Bay, the next bay going north, there is a fishing village and the community there and in Senga happily share the golden sand beaches with tourists. However, access to the beach in Senga Bay for the casual visitor is becoming increasingly difficult.

Because of the popularity of Senga Bay, there is a line of **craft stalls** along the main road to the bay where the signs to the Kambiri Point hotels are located. There can be over 100 metre stretches of stalls on both sides of the road. The best bargains are usually the

Above: Livingstonia Beach Hotel, with its colonial style, is a lakeshore gem. Below: The hotel has attractive rondavel chalets in its gardens.

carvings and if you want something personal, the boys will carve your name on a key tag in the shape of a fish.

Practical matters and activities

The hotels and lodges should be able to arrange a variety of water sports and trips to **Namalenje** and other islands. There is a choice of **boats** for these trips but excitement is guaranteed. If a dugout canoe is chosen there will be the quite unjustified feeling that one is in imminent danger of being tipped into the lake. On the other hand, if the choice is a motorboat you can be assured that its driver will demonstrate that he can keep it airborne for much of the journey.

Nearly all the hotels and lodges will be able to cater for **divers** and those interested in **snorkelling** and some offer **water-skiing**. The better hotels have the best equipment and the greatest range of activities but it is often possible for non-residents to hire on a daily basis and also to pay for instruction.

Walks to **Leopard's Bay village** or a climb up **Nankhumba Hill** make interesting diversions but there's a great temptation to

stay on the beach, sit in a deck chair under a thatched parasol and soak up the beauty of the bay.

There have been recent reports of some of the craft sellers along the road being something of a nuisance to tourists.

Central Lakeshore Villages: Nkhotakota, Dwangwa, Chintheche

These villages are the largest and most interesting of the scattered settlements which line the central lakeshore. The lake continues to be fringed by idyllic sandy beaches and small coves. Only where a major river empties into the lake or a lagoon stands behind the shoreline is there an interruption to the scene.

There are many small fishing villages along the edge of the lake but there are also long stretches that are totally deserted. Everywhere along this section of the lake, the Rift Valley's edge stands a respectful distance back from the lake's shore.

Nkhotakota, the largest of the three villages, is more interesting for its history than its present day attractions. In the late-nineteenth century the collection of villages known as **Kota Kota** was notorious as a major centre for the slave trade. As Portuguese and Arab slave masters began to develop their activities in Malawi, Kota Kota (Nkhotakota) was one of the points on the western lakeshore for trans-shipment of slaves. Traffic, starting in the early part of the century, was at its height in the 1870s when between 10,000 and 20,000 slaves passed through the port each year.

Attempts were made to stop the slave traffic, the best known being that of **David Livingstone** in 1863. The local slave master, a half-caste Arab by the name of **Jumbe**, had little power in his own right but represented the Sultan of Zanzibar and had the support of the Yao people. In a famous meeting, under a fig tree, Jumbe and Livingstone tried to resolve the matter but Livingstone's powers of persuasion proved inadequate.

Only when the Commissioner, **Harry Johnston**, came to Kota Kota in 1891 was the slave trade ended in a deal with Jumbe which guaranteed his safety and well-being. As a reminder of those times and the Arab slave masters, the village is stongly Muslim. The conversions to Islam have not been lost.

As an important village **Dwangwa** is relatively modern, its significance derived from sugar. The great **Dwangwa River** rises near the western border of the country in Kasungu National Park and then flows practically the full width of Malawi's land surface before discharging into the lake. Mostly sandwiched between the lake and the M5 Lakeshore Road are the massive

Bana Swamplands, a mixture of lagoons and sandspits. The lakeshore plains have been overwhelmed by accumulations of sand washed in by the lake, driven by the prevailing south-east winds. Over time the lakeshore plain has been extended eastward as the lagoons fill and the sandspits are colonised by reeds.

It is in this well-watered area that the **Kasasa Sugar Estate** has grown up exploiting the favourable conditions of water supply, high temperatures, one of the highest rainfalls on the lakeshore and, not least, a plentiful supply of workers for this labour-intensive form of agriculture.

The most northerly of the villages, **Chintheche**, was traditionally a major landing point for the dugout canoes which crossed Lake Malawi, despite the fact that this is the widest part of the lake. The area gained in importance from the traffic but also became notorious for fierce battles in the mid-nineteenth century between the raiding Ngoni tribe and the Tongas.

Getting there

From Lilongwe to Nkhotakota:
196km/121miles   M14, M5
From Salima to Nkhotakota:
111km/69miles   M5
From Kasungu to Nkhotakota:
126km/78miles   M18
From Mzuzu to Chintheche:
78km/48miles   M5
From Nkhata Bay to Chintheche:
41km/25miles   M5
From Nkhotakota to Dwangwa:
56km/35miles   M5
From Dwangwa to Chintheche:
93km/58miles   M5

Salima	Turn to M5 north		Nkhotakota	Dwangwa			Chintheche	Nkhata Bay	
	M5 south	Chia Lagoon	Bua River				Bandawe	Turn to Nkhata Bay	
3km	6km	86km	16km	20km	36km		83km	10km	36km	5km

Salima to Nkhata Bay: M5, minor road: 301km

All three villages lie on the excellent Lakeshore Road (M5). Access from Lilongwe is best via the M14. The M18 is in a poor state at its eastern end.

Driving up from the south, the M5 leaves **Salima** heading west and, six kilometres (four miles) further on, an unsignposted turn right takes the M5 north. At this junction is the M14 to Lilongwe. Continuing northwards the road runs well west of the lakeshore through an area of scattered settlements and smallholder farming. Although Lake Malawi cannot be seen, it is hinted at by the relatively flat landscape and the numerous rivers making their way to spill into the lake.

About 86 kilometres (53 miles) north of M14, a large stretch of water can be seen to the west of the road. This is **Chia Lagoon**.

Northwards, the M5 keeps close to Lake Malawi's shore until **Nkhotakota** is reached 16 kilometres (10 miles) beyond Chia Lagoon. Here is a turn off on to the notoriously poor M18 into **Nkhotakota Wildlife Reserve**. In fact, the M5 north of Nkhotakota village twists and turns on an undulating path then clips the edge of the reserve just beyond the village of **Mphonde**.

The **River Bua** is crossed by a magnificent bridge, 20 kilometres (12 miles) north of Nkhotakota and the M5 runs through **Dwangwa** in a further 36 kilometres (22 miles) north of Nkhotakota. The road keeps fairly

close to the lakeshore but, even so, sightings of Lake Malawi remain few and far between. The road is flat and quite straight. Twenty kilometres (12 miles) north of Dwangwa the M5 crosses a number of narrow bridges. In the next 64 kilometres (40 miles), no less than thirteen such bridges will be encountered on the M5. At least there should be thirteen but, in the rains of 1999, the bridge over the **Dwambazi** (also: **Dwambadzi**) River was washed away and was replaced by a stone causeway. Until the bridge is rebuilt, it is best to make local enquiries regarding the safety of the causeway.

At 83 kilometres (52 miles) north of Dwangwa is **Bandawe**. Ten kilometres (6 miles) further brings the road to **Chintheche**. Here and there are those fascinating glimpses of Malawian rural life. Look out for the **Mpingo wa Baptist Chapel** (a roughly thatched roof perched on wooden pillars) and for brick-making from pits dug in the laterite soils.

When to go

The wet season, December to April, is probably a time to avoid. This part of Lake Malawi's shore experiences some of the highest rainfalls in the country with increasing amounts as one goes further north. If visiting Nkhotakota Wildlife Reserve, the greatest chance to see game will occur in October-November but this will also be the hottest time.

Where to stay

It is not surprising that this long stretch of attractive lakeshore has spawned a relatively large number of lodges. They vary in the quality of accommodation they offer from luxury to very simple. However, none is of any great size but, at the last count, the total was over fifteen lodges. The choice is worth investigating. Just south of Chintheche village the traveller's needs are especially well served with **Kande Beach**, famous among overlanders and for its dive school. Horse riding may soon be offered. **Flame Tree Lodge** is well liked by families while **Sabani Lodge**, noted for its white sand beach, has en suite chalets and a campsite. **Nkhwazi Lodge**, a campsite about one kilometre south of Chintheche Inn, is constructing ensuite

Above: A simple lookout and hide for birdwatchers at Njobvu Safari Lodge.

chalets. Ten kilometres (six miles) south of Nkhotakota, **Sani Beach** is a sensibly priced lodge. **Nkhotakota Pottery** has accommodation in en suite beach chalets and all meals are provided by the coffee shop. The accommodation is essentially for guests on pottery courses but not exclusively so.

Njobvu Safari Lodge

This lodge is on the lake side of the M5, 11 kilometres (7 miles) north of the Chia Lagoon and 13 kilometres (8 miles) south of Nkhotakota. The turn is marked and a rough track leads to the lodge four kilometres (two-and-a-half miles) from the main road. The lodge, comprising good sized, thatched rondavels, a bar and a dining room, is set close to its own beach under mahogany and fig trees. The accommodation is en suite and there is a family-sized rondavel. The area around the rondavels is a little untidy but the welcome makes up for that. Njobvu offers a very wide range of activities including birdwatching, trips on the lake (the lodge has its own six metre (twenty foot) boat, and walks to nearby villages. Safaris into Nkhotakota Wildlife Reserve are a speciality of Njobvu.

Kasasa Club

This is the club of the sugar estate at Dwangwa. Although it is primarily for the use of the estate's management, it does provide accommodation for visitors by prior arrangement. There are chalets for hire which are self-contained and include a reception room, two bedrooms, with a small kitchen and a bathroom. Self-catering is possible or visitors can use the restaurant in the clubhouse. Temporary membership of the club is easily arranged and the sports facilities then come free. There is a swimming pool as well as a 9-hole golf course, tennis and squash courts. There is no access to the estate's lake beaches.

The club lies inside the estate about three kilometres (two miles) off the M5. It is signposted (west of the M5) at the southern end of the town. Because of changes in the arrangements of the management of the estate, the club is often fully booked.

Ngala Beach Lodge

This lodge was formerly called Heidi's Hideout and the locals still know it by this name. It is located off the east side of the M5, about

Above: Ngala Beach Lodge provides very attractive accommodation

18 kilometres (11 miles) north of Dwangwa village. Accommodation is in seven double chalets and a family apartment, all en suite. Ngala also has a campsite. There's a restaurant and bar but a new beach bar, with a site on a small rocky outcrop in the lake, is under construction as is a new swimming pool. A large number of activities are offered to guests. Excursions up into the Viphya Mountains are organised as are trips into the Nkhotakota Wildlife Reserve. Mountain biking is offered and guests can use the Dwangwa golf club. Most attractive are trips to the Chiwi Hot Springs on a small peninsula five kilometres (three miles) north of the lodge. Guests are ferried out to the peninsula and can camp overnight on land owned by the lodge. It's a beautiful spot.

Recent improvements have transformed Ngala into a charming and very comfortable lodge.

Makuzi Beach

Makuzi has the reputation of having the most beautiful beach along this part of the lake. It has recently been taken over by other members of the family who had been the

previous owners. There are eight good quality en suite chalets, constructed in stone, and each individually decorated and furnished. There is also some further accommodation in four rooms with shared facilities and opportunites to camp. The main bar and dining room are raised on rocks above the beach. Solar power is used throughout. The prices are attractive and this must be one of the real gems of the region. Its location is some 10 kilometres (6 miles) south of Chintheche village. Its entrance, off the M5, is shared by the old Bandawe Church.

Chintheche Inn

Formerly a state-run resthouse, Chintheche Inn has been transformed since it was taken over by Central African Wilderness Safaris in mid-1997. The accommodation is the most luxurious along the whole of this section of lakeshore. There are just ten double rooms, each opening out directly on to the very pretty beach. The public areas are alongside and include a shop and an excellent restaurant. The camping site, away from the inn, is very attractive. There is a swimming pool overlooking the lake and a tennis court. Chintheche

Above: Chintheche Inn has one of the best beaches on the lake.

Inn organises a number of activities and one of its strengths is the personal service, reminiscent of a good safari park lodge.

There is a nearby airstrip and Wilderness Safaris will organise air or road transfers. Chintheche Inn is well signposted on the east side of the M5 about 160 kilometres (99 miles) north of Nkhotakota but only 45 kilometres (28 miles) from Nkhata Bay. The inn is along a good short dirt road from the M5.

Sightseeing

Chia Lagoon is 86 kilometres (53 miles) north of the Salima turn on the M5 but only 16 kilometres (10 miles) south of Nkhotakota. In common with some of the swamplands characteristic of this part of the lakeshore, it is caused by a minor rift to the west of a small ridge which runs along the edge of the lake. While swamps occupy much of this ill-drained depression, Chia is a substantial lake or, more strictly, a lagoon, for it has broken through the ridge to link with Lake Malawi itself.

The lagoon is interesting because it has attracted large numbers of fishermen who can be seen navigating their dugout canoes along the channel linking the two lakes. Close to the road, fish are laid out on drying tables and, if you stop, be prepared for a rush of boys with trays of fish eager to make a sale. Winding down a car window is an invitation to thrusting hands with plate loads of fish. Just after crossing the channel linking the lakes is the busy village of **Mtanga**. Strictly, fishing is not allowed in the lagoon for it is a breeding ground for the famous *chambo* fish. In recent years, the *chambo* has been over-fished with the use of fine nets known as 'mozzie nets'.

Two kilometres north of Chia is a **pottery** run by the same company, Paragon Ceramics, which runs the more famous Dedza Pottery. This is a quite new enterprise and still developing. The pottery is about four kilometres (two and a half miles) along a track leading to the lake. It is very similar to that at Dedza (see Central Malawi) but there is accommodation in beach chalets and pottery courses are offered for beginners or experienced potters. It must be the only place in the world where you can combine a pottery course with a beach holiday and safaris into game parks. This is a well-run operation.

Right: Ready for anything. A fisherman carries a bow and arrows as well as a fish trap. Below: The waters of Chia Lagoon attract large numbers of fishermen.

To the north of the entrance to Njobvu Safari Lodge, but on the other side of the M5, are two **hot springs**. The most easily reached is the first if travelling from the south. Frankly, there is little to see.

Perhaps the most interesting of all places to stop on the journey along the M5 is **Nkhotakota**. Although sometimes described as "the largest traditional village in Central Africa", Nkhotakota is really a collection of villages, which made up Kota Kota and now form a single settlement spreading from the lakeside to the M5/M18 junction. The area, which straddles the M5, includes a **supermarket** and **petrol station** at either side of the junction. The more interesting and older part of the village is reached by taking the marked turning to the eastern side of the M5 down to the lakeshore.

This road passes the **St Anne's Mission** in whose grounds is the famous **Livingstone fig tree** under which the explorer attempted to negotiate an end to the slave trade in 1861. It is a chilling thought that this is the same path trodden by tens of thousands of slaves just over a hundred years ago. Inside the mission's grounds on the opposite side of the

square which contains the tree, is the large **All Saints Church** with its baptisimal bath. The roofing iron for the church was shipped out from Scotland. The road outside the mission's grounds leads to the jetty where the lake passenger vessels tie up. The *mv Ilala* can be boarded there for Likoma Island. In case of difficulty in finding the mission, ask for the **Anglican Hospital** which shares the mission's gated entrance.

There is another historical connection. A central open space, now called **Freedom Square**, is where Dr Banda held his first political rally after his release from prison in 1960.

Two **markets**, one to the eastern side of the M5 and to the north of the village and the other on the main road to the lake, have little to commend them to the average visitor.

The **Nkhotakota Wildlife Reserve** is to the west of the village and is accessible from the M5. It has been described in the Central Malawi section.

Dwangwa village is very much a company settlement run by the **sugar estate**. Plantation workers fill the streets and the sweet smell of molasses fills the air. The **Dwangwa River** is dammed with lock gates

Above: The silver harvest of Lake Malawi. There is real danger that the lake is being over-fished. Top: Fish are dried or smoked. Much of the catch is sold away from the lake. Left: Stop along the lakeshore road and you'll soon be surrounded by boys asking you to buy their fish.

Above: All the hotels and lodges on the shore of Lake Malawi offer a variety of activities on the lake.

holding back water for irrigation. Cane is processed in the town and by-products such as ethanol are extracted. Most of the sugar is exported, bringing in much needed foreign exchange, in addition to providing employment for a large number of local people. There are also small **teak plantations**. The town's services, unsophisticated and limited, are there to satisfy the needs of the local population not the passing traveller. However, **petrol** is available and there are enough small stores and street traders to supply most requirements.

Visits to the estate can be arranged by telephoning the Kasasa Club (see Where to stay page 265) in advance.

The village has not a lot to offer but there are two attractions unassociated with the estate. A **crocodile farm** offers guided tours and has both conservation and commercial significance but lacks the well ordered layout characteristic of such farms in other parts of Africa. The establishment is not easy to locate and it will probably be best to ask for directions at the petrol station near the southern limit of the town.

The lakeshore, reached by taking any one of the roads leading off the M5 to the east, is certainly worth a visit. The lake here is important for fishing and one can see much of the traditional activity. If you have the nerve for it, it should be possible to arrange a trip on to the lake in a fisherman's dugout boat.

North of Dwangwa and accessible from Ngala Beach Lodge are the **Chiwi Hot Springs**, another reminder of the fact that this part of the lake is volcanic. There's a delightful little deserted beach by the springs which is owned by Ngala. It's a great place for a picnic or a night's camping.

South of Chintheche village is **Bandawe**. In fact there are two Bandawes about two kilometres apart. The most southerly is the **old mission station** and, beyond that, the new. The early mission was set up in 1881 by **Dr Robert Laws**, after he left Cape Maclear. This was, therefore, the second Livingstonia mission. The old mission station with church and graveyard is on a small headland to the east of the road. Unfortunately, the church is in a poor condition although its design is interesting with banked seating and a laterally sited pulpit. There is a robe and chair that belonged to Dr Laws but, like the relics in the Livingstonia Mission museum, decay is evident. The old missionaries' graves, too, are left untended. Also the grave of 'Mama Jane' — **Jane Jackson** — is here. She was the original owner of the Makuzi Beach lodge who was killed in an accident in Zimbabwe in 1998.

Laws stayed just three years at Bandawe and in that time acted as peace-maker between the raiding Ngoni tribe and the Tonga people. However, malaria again took its deadly toll and Laws moved north once more to set up the Livingstonia mission which still exists on the edge of the Khondowe Plateau. A **new Bandawe mission**, two kilometres further north of the old, was set up in the 1920s

Chintheche village services one of Lake Malawi's beautiful stretches of beach. There are **stores, petrol** and a **post office** housed in one of the many old buildings scattered through the settlement. The lake is scarcely visible from the village but the beaches, one or two kilometres away, are easily reached by using roads leading east off the M5.

The lakeshore has great potential not always realised. Parts of the shore could be cleaner and a more vigorous programme of reed clearance is necessary to eradicate the risk of bilharzia. At their best, the beaches of golden sands, with small headlands of wave-washed rocks, are close to a tropical paradise. The well-wooded shore is home to birds and **vervet monkeys**.

A particular attraction of this part of the lake is the near certainty of seeing local fishermen in their **dugout canoes**. They make wonderful subjects for photographers, especially in the light of a low sun.

Practical matters and activities

Many visitors tend to underestimate the time it will take to drive the whole length of this section of the M5 from Salima to Chintheche. Since one bridge has been replaced by a causeway, allow time to make sightseeing worthwhile.

All the usual watersport activities are available with Chintheche Inn being particularly well equipped for **snorkelling** and **diving**. Even some smaller lodges, offer a PADI dive school. Many have **boats** and will arrange lake trips. Njobvu, for example,

Above: The crystal clear waters of Lake Malawi are ideal for snorkelling.

takes guests south and into the Chia Lagoon. Other boat trips go out to islands in the lake.

Lodges near to Nkhotakota will usually arrange **safaris** into the wildlife reserve. Njobvu and Ngala are especially well placed for this. Njobvu Safari Lodge arranges **elephant tracking** and **walking safaris**. The owner of Njobvu is always keen to ensure his guests see as much as possible of the reserve's game.

Proximity of the lake, lagoons and wetlands to the woodlands, means that **birdwatching** can be very rewarding. Some lodges arrange for birdwatching by boat.

Golf can be had at Kasasa Club's nine-hole course on the Dwangwa Sugar Estate and there is **tennis** there and at Chintheche Inn.

North of Chintheche village is a quite large **rubber plantation** and Chintheche Inn will arrange visits for their guests. The inn also arranges **biking** and **walking** safaris into the nearby Viphya Mountains. A number of the lakeshore lodges will take visitors on **village** walks.

Right: Nkhata Bay is the location of a busy little town and a popular holiday destination.

Nkhata Bay

Nkhata village spreads across a number of spurs which separate narrow valleys leading down to Nkhata Bay; one of the most impressive settings of all the lakeshore villages.

The bay marks the most northerly point reached by **David Livingstone** when he sailed up Lake Malawi in 1861. Disembarking at Nkhata, he believed he had got to the lake's northern extremity. He had had a pretty wretched voyage so perhaps there was a little bit of wishful thinking. Worse was to come because his small expedition lost its way as it set off into the uplands towards the Viphya Mountains. Fortunately tragedy was averted.

Nkhata Bay's small sheltered harbour has long been a focus for fishing and new jetties built in 1958 and 1962, as well as its function as a port of call for passenger boats, have given the village-cum-town a special significance.

Despite its importance as a lakeshore village, the road linking it with the nearest town, Mzuzu, was not built until 1958. That was despite the fact that a natural low-lying saddle in the land provides a relatively simple route between the two settlements.

There haven't been many highlights in Nkhata's history, indeed it might be said that it is best known for three very different but, in their own ways, tragic events. Two are connected with Malawi's road to political independence. In 1953 the village became involved in violent protests against the federation of the two Rhodesias (now Zimbabwe and Zambia) and Nyasaland (Malawi). Then, on 3 March 1959, as a State of Emergency was being declared following further anti-federation disturbances, some twenty protesting villagers were killed by police in their attempt to quell the rioting. Their deaths are commemorated each 3rd March, Martyrs' Day.

The other event for which the village has a place in history occurred in the same decade but was natural, not man-made. On 11 January

Right: Nkhata Bay is the location of a busy little town and a popular holiday destination.

1957, in a storm which spread from the lake, a total of no less than 153 millimetres (six inches) of rain fell in just fifty minutes. In an hour and a half the single storm had produced 191 millimetres (7.5 inches). It was only a little short of the highest ever intensity of rainfall ever recorded in southern Africa. Only the rapid run-off of water on the steep hills on which the village is built prevented total disaster. Even so considerable damage was done.

A more lasting problem with which Nkhata Bay has had to deal has been the exodus of many of its menfolk to work outside Malawi, mostly in South Africa and Zimbabwe. This has deprived the villages of a significant proportion of its able-bodied labour force for many years.

Getting there

From

Mzuzu:	47km/29miles	M5
Nkhotakota:	190km/118miles	M5
Salima:	301km/187miles	M5
Lilongwe:	381km/237miles	M5, M14

The nearest large town to Nkhata Bay is Mzuzu with a moderate quality road, the M5, linking the two settlements. This road has been described in *Going to the Lake* in the North Malawi section.

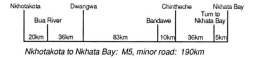

Nkhotakota to Nkhata Bay: M5, minor road: 190km

The M5 also gives easy access to other parts of the central and southern lakeshore. To travel up to Nkhata Bay from Lilongwe would be a quite long drive and from Blantyre would be a very tiring journey. From Chintheche it is just a short drive as the road runs through rubber plantations which have a strange eerie atmosphere, dark, almost menacing. As it descends along the edge of the **Limphasa Dambo**, vast tracts of swampland can be seen to the left of the road. To the right, here and there, are glimpses of the lake especially just after leaving Chintheche.

The road climbs again before the turning (right) to Nkhata Bay at 49 kilometres (30 miles) north of Chintheche. The M5 continues (left) on to Mzuzu but the minor road descends steeply into the village from the edge of the **Kaning'ina Hills**.

Above: Chikale Bay a beautiful secluded beach near Nkhata Bay.

When to go

Of almost all places in Malawi, this is the one to avoid in the rainy season. In the four months December to April, the total rainfall averages 1312 millimetres (51 inches). If that is not off-putting enough, it should be noted that much of this rain occurs as very heavy downpours. In contrast, the average for October is just 1.4 millimetres. Temperatures in the hottest months, November and December, reach the lower 30° Celsius (mid-80° Farenheit).

Where to stay

The popularity of Nkhata Bay with backpackers means that there is no shortage of small, simple and cheap lodges. Everywhere you turn, there seems to be a sign directing you to a three or four dollar a night place to rest your head. There are only two lodges which have the sort of accommodation that usually attracts the international non-backpacker traveller. Both are some distance beyond the centre of town and to the south. Both also enjoy one of the best beaches around these parts: Chikale Beach.

Chikale Beach Resort

This lodge has over twenty brick chalets with thatched roofs. All are en suite and there is a bar-restaurant. Camping is also available. This is a quieter lodge than most in Nkhata Bay and, although the accommodation is simple, it is realistically priced. It it suitable for families who appreciate the beautiful beach setting.

Njaya Lodge

The setting of Njaya is on a hillside overlooking the beach. The views are fine but you have to be prepared to climb a lot of steps to get around the site. There is a mix of accommodation available from a few en suite rooms at the top of the hill to bamboo and thatch huts on the beach. The latter are really very picturesque and are favourites with young couples. The lodge is a lively and popular place to stay, with greater security than some of the lodges in town.

Sightseeing

Nkhata Bay is nothing if not resilient and has survived its various set-backs to become today's lively and interesting lakeshore

Above: Admiring the view across the lake from Nkhata Bay.

village. Some describe Nkhata Bay as 'pretty'. That may be a little fanciful although, when the flame lily and bougainvillea give a splash of colour to the surroundings, it is a pleasant enough place to view. The real attractions, however, lie in the rather extraordinary site and in the activity by the shore.

As the minor road from the M5 junction winds its way down to the lake, the hillsides are dotted with traditional huts seemingly scattered at random. There is no order to the place and that is part of its charm. Straw-thatched homes cling precariously to the site of the deeply dissected hills and only the banana trees appear to be well rooted. There is a constant stream of people, usually heavily laden, making their way up and down the steep and winding road to the shore.

Once close to the lake, the road affords excellent views of the village set around its two bays. The narrow peninsula separating Nkhata's bays has the main jetty on its northern side. It is this jetty which is the calling point for the lake's motor vessels. The busiest part of the village is around the market, at the landward end of the peninsula.

All the usual services are in this part of the village including a **bank** and a PTC **supermarket**. Clothes and vegetables vie for dominance in the **market** but fish provide the lasting memories and the malodour. There is plenty of activity to be seen in the bays for this is an active fishing village. One of the most prized and abundant of the large number of species available is the *sanjika*. South of Nkhata Bay the same fish is caught in the **Luweya** below the waterfalls which mark the river's passage over the edge of the Great Rift Valley.

Just over three kilometres (two miles) south of Nkhata Bay is **Chikale Beach**. To reach the beach, excellent and ideal for children, simply continue along the road which skirts the shoreline of each bay.

Practical matters and activities
It has to be said that Nkhata Bay is a place to be wary. It is better not to wander around after dark if not in a group. Some lodges will supply escorts. During the day, especially in the market area, watch out for bag snatchers. It is unwise to accept unsolicited offers of guided tours.

Many visitors go to Nkhata Bay to dive and there are a number of operations the best known being **Aqua Africa**, on the edge of the southern bay. They will provide instruction at all levels. Equipment is provided. Another water sport, **kayaking**, is available at Njaya Lodge.

Few venture far from the beach or the town but Njaya Lodge, will arrange excursions inland for the more adventurous.

Likoma Island

Off the eastern shore of Lake Malawi, almost opposite Chintheche village, are two islands **Chizumulu** and **Likoma**. Chizumulu is a diminutive two square kilometres (three-quarter square miles) while Likoma is twelve times as big. Both, remarkably, lie within Mozambican territorial waters. Because of their historical connections with Malawi, they were allowed to retain that allegiance when Britain and Portugal came to divide the lake after World War II.

In the 1880s, Christian missionaries, who ministered to the lakeshore people by boat, chose Likoma as a base. The island provided sanctuary from attacks by local tribesmen of the Ngoni and Yao peoples. A very successful mission station was set up to provide education and medical facilities. Established as the headquarters of the **Universities Mission to Central Africa**, work began in 1903 on a quite extraordinarily ambitious project: the building of a cathedral the size of that in Winchester in England.

The mission was fortunate to have **Frank George**, a trained architect, on its staff. Using local labour and materials, the vast granite building gradually took shape and the first service was held in 1905. The arches and cloisters used bricks made on the island and, it is said, mud from anthills replaced conventional mortar.

Getting there
The relevant section of the *mv Ilala* schedule is:

Departure		Arrival	
Nkhotakota:	Sat 08.30	Likoma:	Sat 14.30
Likoma:	Sat 17.30	Nkhata Bay:	Sat 23.30
Nkhata Bay:	Wed 00.00	Likoma:	Wed 06.45
Likoma:	Wed 10.45	Nkhotakota:	Wed 14.00

To reach Likoma Island it is cheapest to use the lake motor vessel, the *Ilala*, which links the lake ports. The service does not always keep to schedule so an enquiry of Ulendo Safaris is advised a day or so before embarking. Other ports can, of course, be used. The smaller island, Chizumulu is called at by the *Ilala*. Currently the Ilala's sister vessel, the *mv Mtendere*, is also being used between Likomoa and Nkhata Bay. How long this service will continue is uncertain.

It may be possible to charter a motor boat from Kaya Mawa, on Likoma, or from Chintheche Inn on the lakeshore. The quickest way to get to the island is to fly from Mzuzu airport using an air charter company.

When to go
Almost any time of the year is suitable for a visit to Likoma Island.

Where to stay
There are plans to erect a hotel on Likoma but, like most such plans, it is unlikely that such a project will see the light of day for some time. Meanwhile, there are a couple of simple camping sites, catering especially for divers, and a guesthouse. And there's Kaya Mawa.

Kaya Mawa
This is a no-expense-spared lodge which was a long time in construction but finally opened in 2000. There are seven cottages cut out of a rocky headland. The honeymoon suite is on its own tiny island. The materials used in construction are all local although the four-poster beds may not be especially Malawian. All the cottages have sunken stone baths and the lavatories have a view to the lake. The restaurant has a 360-degree view and there are locally caught fish and home-grown vegetables on the menu. This is an extra-ordinary lodge in every way.

Sightseeing
Apart from enjoying the views and the beautiful beaches, there is really only one site to visit on the island, the **cathedral**. Its gleaming white roof is more than just a monument to the endeavours of the early missionaries. Set amongst trees it is of real architectural and cultural interest. Especially

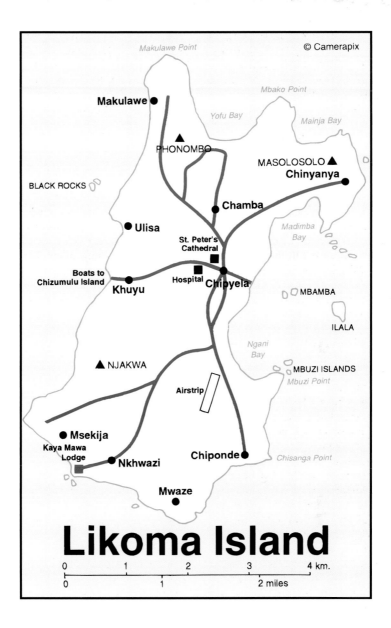

© Camerapix

Makulawe Point

Mbako Point

Makulawe ●

Yofu Bay

Mainja Bay

PHONOMBO ▲

MASOLOSOLO ▲
Chinyanya ●

BLACK ROCKS

Chamba ●

● Ulisa

Madimba
Bay

St. Peter's
Cathedral

Boats to
Chizumulu Island

Hospital Chipyela

Khuyu ●

□ MBAMBA

ILALA

▲ NJAKWA

Ngani
Bay

MBUZI ISLANDS
Mbuzi Point

Airstrip

● Msekija

Kaya Mawa
Lodge

● Nkhwazi

Chiponde ●

Chisanga Point

Mwaze ●

Likoma Island

| 0 | 1 | 2 | 3 | 4 km. |

| 0 | | 1 | | 2 miles |

attractive are the choir stalls carved in soapstone and the crucifix over the pulpit. The latter is carved from wood taken from the *myonga* tree below which the heart of **David Livingstone** was buried in a tin box. This is all the more remarkable because the site of the tree is in north-west Zambia. The cathedral, dedicated to Saint Peter, has some fine stained glass and is in a reasonable state of repair. Before the early 1970s, the building had become somewhat dilapidated but, using money donated by Malawi's then president, Dr Banda, the next decade saw much needed restoration take place.

Practical matters and activities

There are opportunities to engage in almost any form of water sport from Likoma's beaches. **Snorkelling**, **scuba diving**, **sailing**, **windsurfing**, **water-skiing** and, of course, **swimming**: all are available on the island.

Kaya Mawa organises **boat excursions** to neighbouring islands and even across the narrow strait to **Mozambique**

PART FOUR: SPECIAL FEATURES

Above: Malawi's attractions include nine game parks. This is one of many waterholes at Lengwe National Park. Opposite: Fishermen on Lake Malawi silhouetted by the setting sun.
Following page: *Brachystegia* woodland is one of Malawi's most widespread vegetation types.

Malawi's National Parks and Wildlife Reserves

Game viewing is somewhat different in Malawi from many other African countries. While animal sightings may be fewer overall, national parks here are much more about experience than tick lists. Landscape and wilderness are the attractions, offering viewing and exploration at a more fundamental level. No great convoys of minibuses queue to see the animals in contrived conditions. Instead, small groups travel through the bush unknowing of what lies behind the next patch of vegetation.

The variety and beauty of Malawi's diverse landscapes provide a perfect backdrop to game viewing. Laws protect the animals and also the environment, which remains as close to its natural state as possible. There are very few artificial waterholes and the parks are relatively undeveloped at present. This means large areas of near wilderness unexplored by all but a few. There is also the unique attraction of the Lake Malawi National Park — a protected area of Malawi's beautiful inland sea where thousands of brightly coloured fish can be hand fed just below the surface of the crystal clear waters. This was the world's first freshwater national park and is a UNESCO World Heritage Site.

The 1920s saw the first gazetting of protected areas which has culminated in nine national parks and wildlife reserves. The first true national park was Nyika, proclaimed as Malawi National Park as recently as 1965. The current statuses of all nine areas were settled by the beginning of the 1980s.

Locations were not always chosen solely for their natural beauty or existing wildlife populations. Kasungu was gazetted to evacuate people from where tsetse fly had caused a sleeping sickness epidemic whilst Liwonde was established to rescue that area from a century of hunting. However, most of the national parks and wildlife reserves are strategically located as important rain catchment areas. This is particularly so for those on Malawi's watershed western border. The maintenance of natural vegetation prevents the rainwater washing away too rapidly across cleared soils and causing further erosion.

The protected areas are spread across the whole country: Nyika National Park and Vwaza Marsh Wildlife Reserve are in north Malawi; Kasungu National Park and Nkhotakota Wildlife Reserve are in central Malawi; south Malawi has Liwonde and Lengwe National Parks, Majete and Mwabvi Wildlife Reserves, and the unique Lake Malawi National Park. As a rule, the wildlife reserves have less protection, fewer management resources and more limited infrastructure for visitors than the national parks.

The next stage in the history of these protected areas is currently underway, with the handing over of the accommodation and safari operations within them to private companies.

Malawi also has a number of forest reserves. These have limited wildlife protection but do provide welcome escapes and plenty of opportunity for walks in the wild.

Getting there

While reaching some of the the nine national parks and wildlife reserves can be time-consuming, none is really remote. All are accessed by a final stretch of earth road but can be reached by car in the dry season, if not always in the wet. Kasungu, Liwonde and Nyika also have airstrips. Entry by aircraft is rare, but it is certainly possible and is increasingly being offered by private operators.

All parks and reserves should be open from dawn until dusk and charges are currently US$5 per person for non-Malawians.

When to go

Parks and reserves are generally open all year but access to some can be difficult in the wet season (November to March). Peak time for game viewing is August to October when vegetation is low and limited water forces animals to gather at the few remaining sources. It is also the best time for viewing

Above: The vast rolling plateau of Nyika is ideal for riding safaris.

the *mbuna* fish in Lake Malawi. The high heath and grasslands of Nyika Plateau, however, attract animals through the rains, having spent the dry season on the lower slopes. Unfortunately, access can be difficult at this time. For birdwatching, generally the best time is November to December.

Where to stay

Just a few years ago, basic, government run camps offered the only places to stay. By 1997, private companies had taken over the accommodation in four of the nine parks and reserves, upgrading facilities to a much higher standard.

Sightseeing

Malawi is not especially well stocked with wildlife. Animal populations have suffered at the hand of man since trophy hunting began during colonial days. Though protective legislation has helped, finances and resources are insufficient to eradicate such losses completely. Poaching by local people for food and to protect their land, lives and crops occurs mostly at the fringes of the protected areas. Malawi's high population density

creates intense pressure on, and competition for, such land. Poaching for financial gain through the illegal sale of ivory is often blamed on Zambians and Mozambicans. As well as protection, education of local people is required to enable continued and effective management and development of the parks and reserves.

Big cats are only occasionally seen. Lions occur in four of the protected areas but there have been no sightings of cheetahs for a number of years. The leopard is found across almost the entire country but its elusive lifestyle makes sighting difficult. Of the smaller cats, civet is the most widespread though genet, serval and wild cat may also be seen.

Hyena are the most common of the other major predators and can be spotted in all the protected land areas. Jackal and wild dog also have populations in Malawi but are less frequently seen.

The only black rhino now in Malawi have been re-introduced from South Africa and are in an accessible sanctuary in Liwonde.

There are good elephant populations in all the protected land areas except the low lying Lengwe and Mwabvi. Hippos are numerous

Above: A walking safari is an opportunity to get down to detail with an expert guide.

in Malawi and are commonly seen the Shire River, where they number in the thousands. Crocodiles are common in the Shire.

Malawi's buffalo have a reputation for being particularly aggressive and are common except in Majete and at Lake Malawi. Zebra are best seen in Nyika, Kasungu and Liwonde with smaller numbers in some of the reserves.

Of the antelopes, bushbuck, grey duiker, kudu, grysbok, klipspringer and reedbuck are found in most of the protected areas. Roan and eland can also be seen, particularly in Nyika, while Liwonde and Kasungu are the most likely places to spot sable and waterbuck. The rarest species, Livingstone's suni and the beautiful nyala, have good populations in Lengwe. This is the furthest north of all nyala habitats in southern Africa.

Other mammals in the country are monkeys and baboons, bushpig, warthog and porcupine. There are no giraffe populations.

Malawi has a fantastic variety of birds with around 650 recorded species spread across the different landscapes. They are primarily woodland or grassland varieties including Livingstone's flycatcher, red-winged francolin and the endemic Lillian's lovebird. However, the lake, rivers and dams also attract waterbirds such as hamerkop, fish eagle, kingfishers, egret and pelican. Raptors, like the African marsh harrier, black-breasted snake eagle and peregrine falcon, give further variety.

The majority of the estimated 500 fish species in Lake Malawi are cichlids, mostly endemic to Malawi. The small brightly coloured *mbuna* are easily seen in the protected waters of Lake Malawi National Park. The Shire River through Liwonde and Majete also supports good fish populations including **sungwa** and tiger fish, while the Bua in Nkhotakota has *mpasa* (lake salmon), popular with anglers. For more detailed information on animals found in Malawi, see Wildlife and Birdlife and Bird Habitats.

For flower lovers, there is great diversity, including 400 orchid species. These are found at all altitudes around the country. There are also numerous everlasting flowers, proteas, aloes and gladioli with reedbeds and water-lilies in the Lower Shire lagoons.

Above: The impala's markings are unmistakably from the rear.

one park or reserve can be booked through safari tour companies, or direct with the accommodation providers in the park. The new privately run accommodation is of a high standard and organised safaris are offered to guests. Government-run accommodation is simple self catering and safaris are at the individual's discretion, though it is wise to hire a scout. A scout's skilled knowledge ensures that the most is made of a visit and prevents the visitor getting lost.

Finally, day trips are possible, self driven or with a tour operator. However, time is limited for safaris and the best parts of the day for viewing (early and late) are usually missed. Apart from the difficulties of travelling to and from the park in the dark, visitors must leave before the gate is shut for the night.

Types of safari

Any safari is best taken in early morning or late afternoon when the greatest heat is avoided and the animals are most active.

Walking safaris potentially offer the most intense experience, giving a much greater sense of involvement than in a vehicle. Though most animals will sense people first, there is plenty of opportunity for close encounters. Even if there aren't large mammals around every corner, there is a fascinating amount to see and interpret. When walking, it is important to act as instructed. Groups walk in single file and must be quiet and still whenever an animal is encountered. It may also be necessary to crouch or move downwind to avoid detection. Wearing earthy coloured clothing is vital for this type of safari and it is important to be accompanied by a guide. Where organised walking safaris (by private operators) are not available, department scouts can be hired by independent visitors. It can also be possible to arrange to spend a few days walking and camping within a park or reserve.

Driving covers a much greater area than walking, increases the chances of sightings and is a necessity in the more open areas. With self-drive, only clearly motorable tracks are accessible, but there are reasonable networks of marked drives in some parks. Standards vary, though, and some may be impassable, especially in the wet season. Vehicles draw the animals' attention but,

Practical matters

There is a hub to each park where the park office and accommodation found. With private companies now increasingly in control of the accommodation and safari operations, a more organised service is provided and most visitors simply join a safari. If reliant only upon a scout from the Ministry of Tourism, Parks and Wildlife, there is no guarantee that one will be available when you arrive and though booking ahead is possible, the system is not especially reliable. Guide fees should be between US$2 and US$10 and it is worth checking the charge before setting off.

Park visits

These can range from a fully organised, all-inclusive, multi-destination expedition to a simple self-driven day trip.

Safari companies offer the first type: small groups travel from park to park, taking in drives, walks and boat trips. All food and accommodation is provided or arranged by the company in question. There are scheduled tours of varying lengths but trips can also be tailor-made.

Alternatively, a stay of a few nights in

Above: Open safari trucks and a good guide improve the chances of successful sightings.

unless advancing towards them, will not necessarily scare them off. It is important to have the engine turned off when taking photographs from a vehicle as vibrations will cause camera shake, particularly noticeable when using telephoto lenses. However, for close encounters with the larger mammals, it may be necessary to keep the engine running in case a rapid retreat is required. Guides are not required for self-drive safaris, but are still an advantage. Natural coloured clothing is advisable even when driving and if travelling in an open-topped vehicle, movements should be slow when animals are encountered. For self-driven cars without guides, passengers should not get out of the vehicle. Drives in open vehicles in the early morning or at dusk can be cold and blankets may be needed.

Boat safaris can provide excellent viewing opportunities. As well as the crocodiles, hippos and riverine birds in or on the water, animals attracted to the bank to drink are less wary of anything on the water. A sundowner cruise is the ultimate — the boat launches late in the day when the animals are active and the hippos are beginning to

leave the water. After initial viewing, the boat drifts and the occupants sip their personal tipple as the sun sets. Finally, a spotlight illuminates the night activity in the water and on the banks. In Liwonde, the Shire is excellent for a boat safari. In Lake Malawi National Park, young men will offer to take visitors out from Cape Maclear in their small rowing boats to view the fish.

Safaris on horesback are uniquely available in Nyika National Park. As well as being a wonderful experience, riding around the dramatic plateau wilderness, the fact of being on a horse aids animal viewing. Antelope and zebra will not view a horse, even with a rider, as a threat and so allow much closer encounters.

For more sedate viewing, hides allow very close sightings of animals completely unaware of a human presence. Observers of the comings and goings around a waterhole should remain silent or whisper. Lengwe is really the only park where there is a network of accessible hides. In the other parks, guides will be able to show where a patient wait (near a water source) should result in good viewing.

Wildlife

Malawi's wildlife is of interest as much for its setting as for its diversity and numbers. The country is small and, for Africa, quite densely populated. For its area, it has extensive borderlands. These facts have conspired to reduce the wildlife to levels which have seriously threatened many species and forced the country to reconsider its conservation policies.

Much of the population, some ninety per cent, are farmers, the majority eking a poor living from their smallholdings, scattered across the plateaux but concentrated in the valleys and on the plains. Farming and wildlife conservation are not happy bedfellows. The formerly game-rich areas of central and southern Malawi have been particular victims of the conflict which arises when man and beast are in competition for a limited resource: land.

The length of Malawi's borderlands, especially with its neighbour Zambia, has made poaching easy. Even when the poachers have come from the local community rather than from across the frontier it has been easy to blame the neighbours. Penalties for poaching have not been such as seriously to act as deterrents.

These threats to Malawi's wildlife have been real and still play a part in the picture of a country that has embraced conservation rather late in the day.

All this may seem somewhat depressing, but Malawi can still lay claim to an interesting variety of mammals and, most of all, to parks and reserves where they can be seen in unspoilt habitats. While the great game parks of Africa may boast larger numbers and bigger ranges, Malawi claims some of the most natural parks and reserves. No tarred roads or lines of four-wheel drive vehicles are to be seen. Instead, the game can be seen in a near wilderness setting just as they might have been viewed a hundred years ago.

Conservation, relocations, habitat management are all on the agenda. The costs of improvements have been largely met by European and South African donors and much of the parks' day-to-day management is a co-operation between the Ministry of Tourism, Parks and Wildlife and a variety of private sector organisations.

As far as the wildlife is concerned, the distinction between the national parks (Nyika, Kasungu, Lake Malawi, Liwonde and Lengwe) and the wildlife reserves (Vwaza, Nkhotakota, Majete and Mwabvi) is inconsequential. It should also be remembered that Malawi has vast unprotected areas, of varying degrees of wilderness, still rich in the fauna they support.

Large Mammals

Elephants
When David Livingstone arrived in Malawi he reported seeing vast herds of elephant in the marshlands of the southern Lower Shire Valley. Today, only the name Elephant Marsh survives. Fortunately other areas fared better.

With male elephants growing to a height of 3.5 metres (11 feet) or more and weighing on average 6500 kilograms (6.5 tons), their claim to the status of the largest land mammal is undisputed. Their tusks (the most dense organic material on earth) vary in length; over 3.3 metres (11 feet) has been recorded. The tusks commonly weigh 25-40 kilograms (60-90 pounds). Cows are generally smaller than bulls with shoulder heights perhaps half a metre (twenty inches) lower and average weights only rather more than half that of the male. If the male sex organ cannot be seen, the females can be recognised by their somewhat square shaped heads.

Elephants spend most of the day feeding, browsing and grazing. Their destructive feeding habits are well known and it's often possible to locate a herd by following lines of trampled undergrowth and broken trees and branches left as they made their way through

Opposite: Close encounters with an elephant are one of the thrills of a safari in Malawi's national parks.

285

the bush. Using their incredibly sensitive trunks they will feed from high branches as they stand on their hind legs to gain even greater height.

Watching elephants eat is to see them employ not only their trunks — used almost as a hand — but also their tusks and feet. Grass is often thrashed to soften it before being put in the mouth. Few elephants have tusks of equal length because they will use one more than the other. If the tusks were not to be used they would grow even longer. As it is, they are simply worn down and sometimes broken.

The elephant's digestive system is notoriously inefficient. They regularly consume up to 300 kilograms (660 pounds) in a day but so little is digested that it is almost a case of what goes in, comes out, as an examination of their dung will quickly testify. Food is usually the bark and leaves of the mopane but they will also eat grass and seek wild fruits and roots. They seem especially fond of marula fruits.

Elephants also require vast quantities of water and it is estimated that about 150 litres (49 gallons) are drunk in a day. In the dry season, they can often be seen making holes with their trunks in dry stream beds in order to reach the watertable. In Liwonde they have the luxury of the Shire River.

Most elephants live in fairly small, matriarchal groups. Older males will often be on their own. The young are especially delightful to watch, particularly in or near water. Occasionally, and especially when water is short, family groups will be seen moving together in quite large herds. It is possible to get close to elephants as long as one is quiet and down-wind. Elephants have a keen sense of smell and very good hearing. However, they have very poor eyesight and it is believed that they cannot distinguish anything more than a vague shape at 10 metres (30 feet). A sudden break in the profile of a group of watchers may still be detected. Elephants can be dangerous if they feel threatened and especially if the group contains young. Lone males can sometimes be bad tempered.

Sightings are probably easiest at Liwonde where the Shire River acts as something of a magnet. Very large herds have been reported in Nkhotakota but viewing is less easy. Vwaza has quite predictable movements

of elephant and Nyika also sees small herds although only rarely towards the top of the plateau. Kasungu used to boast the largest number and most ferocious of Malawi's elephants but, like other game in this park, their numbers have been greatly reduced.

Rhinoceros
The rhino is undoubtedly one of the most endangered species of all African game animals. Needless killings for the sake of their horns are a well-known tragedy. Malawi used to have quite large numbers of rhino, especially in the south, until modern times. Now only Liwonde supports a relocated breeding herd of the rare black rhino (also called the hooked-lipped rhino from its prehensile upper jaw). The larger, white (or square-lipped) rhino is not present in Malawi.

Rhinos are big animals and faster movers than their bulk might suggest. Bull rhinos can be very dangerous if with females and their short tempers and surprising agility will sometimes see them attack a vehicle if it gets too close. The black rhino can weigh in excess of 1000 kilograms (1 ton) and it is over one and a half metres (five feet) at the shoulder.

The animals feed off twigs and shoots, selecting the more succulent green material. In the same way, they tend to eat grass only when it is well watered. The bulls mark their territory by kicking their dung around where it has been dropped.

The small number of black rhino in Liwonde National Park started with a breeding pair being relocated from South Africa, a gift from J & B Rare Whisky. They produced a calf and there have since been further relocations and breeding successes. The rhino are in a sanctuary in the park but this is accessible to visitors to Liwonde although sightings cannot be guaranteed. The rhino is quite solitary except in the breeding periods but small groups may be seen in Liwonde.

Hippopotamus
Malawi has some of the largest concentrations of hippo in Africa. The Shire River and the lakes are ideal for this great, semi-aquatic animal. Only when they leave the water is their great size exposed. They are almost as tall as the black rhino and can be twice as heavy. Even the small cows weigh up to 1700

Above: Hippos spend much of the day in water or muddy pools.

kilograms (3750 pounds).

Hippos spend most of the hotter part of the day partly submerged, dipping down under the water for up to six minutes at a time before their nostrils and ears emerge. At night, and occasionally during the day, the hippo will come out to eat. In the cooler parts of the day they lie on the edge of the river or lake where they find a sandy bank. The hippo is a grazer and, in the dry season, it may travel 25 kilometres (15 miles) or more to find food.

Hippos are easy to locate because of their habitat and because they are quite noisy creatures. In water they will let out great roars from their cavernous mouths and, at night, they are a likely cause of disturbance as they snort and grunt, like a snoring man, as they hunt for food. In safari camps such as Mvuu (the word means hippo) in Liwonde or Lifupa in Kasungu, the hippos will often forage around the tents and rondavels during the night causing loss of sleep — and possibly some anxiety — among the occupants.

The hippo will usually be seen in groups, or schools, but will quickly slip back into the water if disturbed while basking. They can be very dangerous where there are calves or if encountered singly. It is also unwise to get in the path of a hippo returning to water. They can move remarkably quickly and make no attempt to avoid anything in their path.

Hippos are found in all the national parks and reserves with the exceptions of Lengwe and Mwabvi. The easiest sightings will be in Liwonde, Kasungu and Vwaza. The hippo population in the Shire River in Liwonde is believed to be the most dense in Africa. Hippo are also seen outside the parks in Lake Malawi, in various stretches of the Shire River and in the innumerable lakes and ponds across the country.

Buffalo

Buffalo, like antelope, are even-toed ungulates but are more like cattle. They are heavy animals with cows weighing over 500 kilograms (1100 pounds) and bulls being some 200 kilograms (440 pounds) heavier. Their wonderfully curved horns are singularly impressive and the bull's boss is sometimes likened to a judge's wig.

There are significant herds in all the parks and reserves except Lake Malawi and Majete, but sightings are most likely in

Above: Baboons are common in Malawi. This big male is looking very pensive.

Colour of hair is variable through a range of browns and greys. Males and females both have naked buttocks.

Man has been the enemy of both baboons and monkeys in Malawi and their numbers are well below what one might expect. However, sightings of the chacma baboon are reported in all parks and reserves as well as in many of the forests and highlands of the country. The baboon lives in large troops of forty or so although, in some cases, the troop size may be more than double that number. It is omnivorous and spends much of the day finding food. A rocky habitat or a well forested area is preferred.

Yellow baboon
Very similar to the chacma baboon, this subspecies is likely to be seen only in Nyika although there have been sightings on the Viphya Plateau. Its distinguishing characteristic is its yellowish-brown colour. It is somewhat smaller than the chacma baboon.

Vervet monkey
This is also known as the green monkey. It has a black face but its long hair is grey and coarse. A rim of white hair surrounds its face. The male has a bright blue scrotum. Vervet monkeys live in troops of about twenty or more and favour woodlands along water courses. Their habit of raiding places inhabited by man has been their undoing. They can be a real nuisance along the shores of Lake Malawi around the lodges.

Vervet monkeys are largely vegetarian but not strictly so. They are by no means confined to the parks and reserves, all of which report sightings.

Samango monkey
Generally less common than the vervet monkey, the samango (also known as the blue monkey) is regularly seen only in Lengwe National Park. Here, unusually, it can be seen together with vervet monkeys and baboons. It is slightly larger than the vervet monkey and darker in colour but its behaviour is similar. Samango monkeys are less attracted to human habitation and tend to favour thicker forest. In addition to Lengwe, there may also be occasional sightings in Nkhotakota and in Nyika.

Vwaza, Kasungu, Nkhotakota and Lengwe. The buffalo population in Liwonde is increasing.

With a strong herding instinct, the animals are usually easy to spot and they will simply stand and stare at anyone who comes across them. They are not usually aggressive unless agitated or provoked. However, as so often, single animals, usually males, can be a problem.

The buffalo is usually a grazer but in poorly grassed areas it will also browse. Movement, and much of the feeding, takes place as the day cools into night. During the heat of the day they will usually be found in places that offer shade.

Primates

Chacma baboon
This is the largest primate in southern Africa, apart from man, with an average weight of around 35 kilograms (77 pounds). The baboon is sometimes mistaken for a monkey but the distinguishing characteristics are the baboon's dog-like muzzle and the way the tail humps upward near the rump.

Above: Lions have returned to Liwonde National Park. They are many visitors' favourite sighting.

Large Carnivores

Lion

The "king of the jungle" is not especially well represented in Malawi and only Nkhotakota claims regular sightings. From time to time, lions are seen near Lifupa Lodge in Kasungu but it is only rarely that lions are reported in Vwaza and Nyika. None of the other parks or reserves currently report sightings but the introduction of a pride into Liwonde is planned.

The largest of the cats, the male may weigh perhaps 200 kilograms (440 pounds), with the females some 50 kilograms (110 pounds) lighter. It is remarkably inactive, especially during the day. As the sun goes down and during the night, they may go looking for prey, usually antelopes. The females do most of the hunting but the male will usually eat first. A pride may consist of several adult males and females as well as younger cats. The full grown male is distinguished by its magnificent mane, although this does not grow until the animal is really mature. There have been very rare cases reported of a female with a mane.

Because they are so inactive for long periods in the day, sightings may simply be by chance and it is possible to pass lions just a few metres away, as they lie in the undergrowth, without being aware of their presence. They are most easily located when they are with a kill. The attendance of vultures and hyenas often reveals their location.

Although lions can be man-eaters, their general indolence allows quite close encounters. It is always best to take special care when there are young or in situations where the lion could believe itself to be cornered or threatened.

Leopard

If lions are somewhat rare in Malawi, leopards are more numerous and, in Nyika National Park, they could even be said to be common. In the past they were much more widespread and many upland regions such as Zomba, the Viphya and Mount Mulanje were said to have significant numbers. Even the Shire Highlands around Blantyre had a leopard population. Today, all the parks and reserves still have some leopards but sightings are few.

Above: Caught in the spotlight on a night safari. Leopards are present in most of the game parks and reserves as well as in some of the forested uplands.

Leopards are not as large or as heavy as lions but they are immensely powerful. A fully grown leopard will be less than half the weight of a lion. Its spots (rosettes) are less solid than those of the cheetah for which it is often mistaken. Apart from its greater size and its spots, the leopard can be identified as different from the cheetah by the absence of 'tear marks', the black lines running down the cheetah's face from the inner corners of the eyes to the mouth.

Leopards are not easily seen because they lie in the undergrowth or in the fork of tree branches during the day. Only at night do they hunt. Prey is extraordinarily varied, from insects to moderately sized antelopes. The leopard hunts by stealth, aiming to get as close to its prey without detection before it pounces. They can move, seemingly, without making any noise but, once they decide to go for the kill, the prey is swiftly dealt with. Because they are solitary animals, they may be satiated before they have eaten all of their kill. If this is so, they will generally drag the carcass to somewhere of safety, often pulling it up into a tree. To see a leopard taking an antelope up

into a tree is one of the highlights of a game watching experience.

Leopards are often harried by hyena when they have made a kill. If the hyena pack is large enough, it may force the leopard to abandon its meal. Unlike the cheetah, it will eat putrid meat so a carcass may be returned to over a period of time.

Unless one is blessed by good fortune and sights a leopard in a tree during the day, it is necessary to seek out the leopard when it is out hunting at night. Remarkably, they do not seem to be upset if game viewing torches are employed judiciously after a kill has been made.

Cheetah

Up to about ten years ago cheetah were resident in Kasungu National Park. Before then, Nyika and Vwaza had also reported sightings. It is now very unlikely that cheetah are in any of the parks or reserves although there is always the chance that they may occasionally cross the border from Zambia's Luangwa parks. Perhaps, one day, this most beautiful of cats, which can run at 70

Above: The spotted hyena can be seen in all the parks and reserves and in other remote areas. They are immensely powerful and will eat almost anything.

kilometres per hour (45 miles per hour), will be relocated into the country. Unfortunately the cheetah is not an animal which is in surplus anywhere.

Spotted hyena

The hyena is reported in all of the country's parks and reserves and also on some of the more remote parts of the plateaux and mountains. However, only in Nyika is it commonly seen. It has some of the appearance of a large dog but its shoulders (at 85 centimetres / 33 inches) stand higher than its rump so that it has a clearly down-sloping back. It is a powerful animal, weighing up to 80 kilograms (175 pounds). It is generally fawn in colour with a fleck of yellow and with ill-formed dark-brown spots on its body and legs.

The hyena lives in small matriarchal groups, called clans, which average eight or so in number. They hunt usually in packs but may sometimes be seen singly. They are looked upon as scavengers, only feeding off what others have killed, but they will also take their own prey, especially when they are in packs. They can be a real nuisance to leopards, whose kill they steal unless it has been dragged up into the safety of a tree.

Hyenas will eat almost anything. Their immensely powerful jaws and efficient digestive system allows them to consume bones as well as flesh, as their white droppings show. They hunt at night and will come close to safari camps looking for food even if it's only a pair of boots carelessly left outside a tent. They have been known to be attracted to such delicacies as the mud-flaps on vehicles.

Small Carnivores

Wild dog

This is another endangered species and, currently, only Kasungu reports the very occasional sighting. Previously, wild dogs were quite common and widespread. It is about the same size, and with some similarity to, the domesticated Alsatian dog. It should not be mistaken for a jackal because it has rounded ears and a patchy brown, black and golden coat. It lives and hunts in packs so

Above: The side-striped jackal usually hunts at night. Its pointed ears distinguish it from the wild dog.

its prey can be as large as a buffalo. It moves very fast and will usually outrun all but the cheetah. Man is probably its biggest enemy.

Side-striped jackal

Although called a side-striped jackal (distinguishing it from its black-backed cousin), the light and dark stripe on its otherwise grey back will probably not be seen at a distance. It has slightly pointed ears and, although similar in shape to the wild dog, it is overall significantly smaller. This jackal is only occasionally seen in Nkhotakota, Nyika, Liwonde, Majete and Lengwe. The chance of seeing one is enhanced by the fact that they hunt in the late evening and early morning as well as at night. Unlike the wild dog, they are mostly seen singly or in pairs. Their food is mainly small mammals and birds although they will also eat fruit.

Serval

The serval is believed to be present in all the parks and reserves except Lake Malawi and Majete. They are also occasionally seen in the high plateau areas. This cat has a shoulder height of rather more than 50 centimetres (20 inches). It has what may seem to be a disproportionately long body (80 centimetres/30 inches) and quite large ears. Its spotted coat makes it sometimes mistaken for a young leopard or cheetah. It hunts for its prey, rats and hares, mostly at night. Sightings will be largely by chance.

African wild cat

The wild cat has a similar distribution in Malawi to the serval. It is smaller than the serval and is not unlike a domestic cat in appearance. Its prey is much the same as that of the serval but is less likely to take a hare because if its smaller size.

Civet

About the size of a moderately sized dog, the civet has a shoulder height of about 40 centimetres (16 inches) but a long body, up to 90 centimetres (35 inches). It has a small pointed head and its coat is a mix of black and brown, spots, blotches and stripes. Civets are regularly seen in Liwonde and occasionally sighted in all the other parks and reserves. They may also be seen on some of the plateau areas.

Although they hunt by night, they start early and finish late so dusk and dawn may be the best time to see them. The civet will most often be seen singly but sometimes in pairs.

Large-spotted genet

Sometimes mistaken for the civet, the genet is much smaller, shorter legged and with more pointed ears. Their colouring is grey with rusty coloured spots. The genet's habitat and behaviour are much the same as the civet. There are regular sightings in Liwonde and Lake Malawi National Parks. All the other parks and reserves report genets except Majete.

Mongoose

Several species of mongoose occur in Malawi including the dwarf mongoose which is the smallest carnivore in southern Africa. Although all the species are similar in appearance they vary widely in size, colour, behaviour and habitat. Dwarf mongooses are only 35-40 centimetres (14-16 inches) in total length, dark brown in colour, favour open woodland or grassland, diurnal in habit and live in troops of up to thirty. On the other hand the bushy-tailed mongoose is 70 centimetres (28 inches) long, black, nocturnal, prefers rocky outcrops and acts in a solitary fashion. Other mongooses likely to be seen are the banded, slender and large-grey (also known as the Egyptian). Some of the easiest sightings will be in Nyika National Park although the slender mongoose is a common resident of Lake Malawi park and the banded mongoose is often to be seen in Liwonde. All the parks and reserves report mongoose sightings while other semi-wilderness areas, such as the Viphya, also support these animals.

Cape clawless otter

This otter is larger and much heavier than its spotted-necked cousin. Its general colour is similar but it has distinctive white fur under its head, throat and chest.

It tolerates muddier waters than the spotted-necked otter because it hunts by feel rather than by sight. Hence it is rather more widespread and found in Nyika and Nkhotakota as well as in Liwonde and Lake Malawi. It tends to hunt at sunrise and sunset and has a penchant for crabs. Otherwise its behaviour is much as the spotted-necked otter.

Spotted-necked otter

About the same length as the honey badger but far less bulky is the spotted-necked otter. Its upper parts are darkish brown shading to lighter brown under the body. It is attracted by the lake in the Lake Malawi National Park and by the Shire River in Liwonde. None of the other parks reports sightings. If present, it may well be located quite easily because it moves and feeds by day and makes a distinctive whistling sound. Its food is largely fish and frogs but it will also take small birds. These otters are usually in groups of up to six or more.

Honey badger

The honey badger is one of the most easily recognised of all the small carnivores. Its dark body appears to have an extra, silver-grey coat on the upper part of its back and head. Unlike the polecat or mongoose, its tail is short. The overall length of the honey badger may be up to a metre (thirty-nine inches). Honey badgers are occasionally seen in all the national parks and reserves except Lake Malawi.

Honey badgers are particularly fearless, even of man, and can be a nuisance around camps and villages. They will most often be seen singly but sometimes in pairs though rarely in groups.

Striped polecat (Zorilla)

Also known as the zorilla, the striped polecat will occasionally be seen in Kasungu and Liwonde. Its smell, for which it is well known, is a defence reaction and comes from a squirt of malodorous liquid ejected from its anal gland. It will have swung round to point its rear towards the enemy before spraying. It is otherwise easily recognised by its black and white stripes running down the length of its back. Its tail is predominantly white.

Nocturnal in habit and quite small (60-70 centimetres/24-27 inches), it is its white stripes that may reveal its presence. Polecats usually move singly or in pairs.

Antelope

Malawi is fortunate in retaining quite large numbers and a range of species of antelope. Because most tend to herd, sightings may often be of quite large groups. The rarity of lions reduces their natural predators, and

Above: Eland, the largest antelope, are stately and elegant. Opposite: A magnificent bull Kudu. This large antelope is found throughout Malawi.

patches of open savannah grassland can increase the frequency of sightings. The species range from the largest antelope, the eland, to the smallest, the blue duiker.

Eland

This is the largest of all antelopes. Some weigh up to 900 kilograms (almost 2000 pounds) and a bull's shoulder height is up to 1.7 metres (5.5 feet). Cows are slightly smaller and considerably less heavy. Both sexes have horns. Despite their size, eland are quite fast and agile. It is said that they can jump over two metres (six and a half feet).

The eland's fawn colour blends with the dry season grasslands and even when the fawn gives way to light grey, with age, they are usually sighted only because of their size. Close up, the eland will be seen to have a short dark mane and the older bulls have a pronounced dewlap.

Eland herds vary from 20 to over 60. The largest herds are likely to be seen in Nyika, where well over a hundred may be together. Other sightings should be in Nkhotakota and in Vwaza.

Kudu

Kudu are another large antelope and can be found in all Malawi's parks and reserves. Most likely sightings will be in the four most southerly parks and in Vwaza. These antelope are grey to reddish brown with between six and eight vertical stripes on their flanks. Perhaps their most distinctive feature is their large rounded ears which are pale red on the inside. The female is hornless but the bull supports elegant spiral horns.

They will usually be found in small herds of, at most, twelve or so but bulls may be seen singly. Kudu favour woodland areas, they are browsers rather than grazers, so they may often be hidden by stands of trees.

Nyala

The most northerly occurrence of this beautiful antelope in Africa is in Lengwe National Park where sightings may almost be guaranteed. They are not present in any other of the country's parks with the possible exception of Mwabvi. The grey bulls have large horns with a slight spiral but the females are without horns and are a chestnut colour. Both sexes have white vertical stripes on their flanks numbering anything from just three or four to up to twelve or fourteen. The nyala bull is rather smaller than the kudu and the cows are significantly smaller than the bulls. These antelope will often be seen from the hides at the water-holes in Lengwe.

Bushbuck

Bushbuck are present in all the parks although sightings in Kasungu, Lake Malawi and Mwabvi are not common. This antelope is only some 80 centimetres (30 inches) at the shoulder. A bull may weigh 45 kilograms (100 pounds) and the females are only two-thirds that mass. Males have short, straight and pointed horns. The females have no horns.

Bushbuck are darkish brown with white patches on the underside of the neck and flecks of white on the flanks. The underside of the tail is also white. Another recognition feature is the well developed rump which stands slightly higher than the shoulders.

The most likely places to find this antelope will be along rivers where there are woodlands. Bushbuck will usually be seen singly or in pairs.

Roan antelope

This is the second largest antelope and one of the most beautiful. Only the eland is larger and, unlike that antelope, which has a somewhat cow-like appearance, the roan is horse-like. Both sexes have characteristic swept-back horns and particularly large ears. Despite their name, they are grey-brown with only a slight reddish tinge. The head has pretty black and white markings.

Herds are usually small, up to ten or so, but occasionally larger groups will be seen. Sightings will often be near water because the roan antelope feeds on lush, well-watered grass if possible. Nyika and Vwaza have regular sightings; Kasungu, Liwonde and Nkhotakota also have small numbers.

Sable antelope

Not dissimilar to the roan antelope, the sable antelope also has wonderfully curving, swept-back horns just slightly more slender than the roan's. It is also a little smaller and

the bulls have a black coat with a distinctive sheen. Cows have brown coats. Both sexes have clear black and white markings. Herds may be up to thirty or more and the best sightings are in Nyika and Vwaza. Sable antelope have also been reported in Lengwe and Mwabvi.

Waterbuck

Also called the common waterbuck, this antelope is about the same size as the sable but often looks heavier, possibly because of its thick hindquarters. The waterbuck has a coarse grey-brown coat with longish hair especially round the head. The rump has a distinct white ring. Most notably, however, is the waterbuck bull's exceptionally long horns which have been recorded to reach as much as almost one metre (over three feet).

As their name indicates, they are usually associated with areas where water is readily available and they will wade into water to drink. They are gregarious and move in small herds. The younger bulls form bachelor herds. Vwaza, with its marsh areas, and Liwonde, along the Shire River, are two of the best places to see this antelope but there are also fairly frequent sightings in Lengwe.

Puku

Only Vwaza, Kasungu and, occasionally, Nyika report sightings of this medium sized and relatively rare antelope. It is golden-brown on the upper back with its colouring getting lighter, to almost white, on its underparts. Only the males have horns and these are quite short and ringed. Herds are small and best looked for near water or marsh.

Reedbuck

Reedbuck might be seen in all of Malawi's parks except Lake Malawi but there are regular sightings only in Nyika and Kasungu. This antelope is medium sized with the male having short forward-curving horns. It is grey-brown in colour with a yellowish tinge. Most often seen in pairs, the reedbuck, as its name suggests, prefers reed-beds but will also inhabit grassy areas, hence its presence on the Nyika Plateau. It is strongly territorial and this helps in locating the animals. It will usually be found in pairs or small herds and

Above: Impala are to be seen in most of Malawi's wildlife parks and reserves.

will make a loud whistling sound if its disturbed. As it runs off it appears to do so with a rocking movement and the short tail is curled up.

Lichtenstein's hartebeest

In Malawi, Lichtenstein's hartebeest is rare. Kasungu reports sightings but in the other parks where it is present (Nyika, Vwaza, Nkhotakota and Liwonde) they are only occasionally to be seen. The hartebeest has a rather sad expression, as though it had just had bad news. It has a distinctive darker colour, like a saddle on its back, but it is chiefly fawn with a yellowish tinge. Both sexes have short horns with a twist at the end. It is a medium-sized to large antelope with its shoulders higher than its hindquarters. Its habitat is savanna woodland and if seen it will usually be in a small herd.

Impala

This elegant antelope is not quite as widespread in Malawi as in many other southern Africa countries. All the same, there are regular sightings in Vwaza, Liwonde and Lengwe, with occasional reportings in Kasungu, Nkhotakota and Mwabvi.

Although medium sized, the impala is light in weight and obviously built for speed. They appear to live in a perpetual state of anxiety, always ready to sprint off. They are magnificent jumpers and can leap over eight metres (twenty-six feet) and to heights of three metres (ten feet). They will sometimes be seen demonstrating their agility for no apparent purpose other than the sheer enjoyment of leaping.

Impala are reddish-brown in colour with a sleek looking coat. From the rear, they can be recognised by a black streak down each buttock. The tail is white with a black stripe and, uniquely, they have a black tuft of hair behind the hind leg, just above the hoof. The males have lyre-shaped horns but the females are hornless.

Breeding herds and bachelor herds run separately and in quite large numbers. They avoid areas without cover so the habitats offered, especially by Liwonde and Vwaza, are ideal. In herds, one or two animals may be seen to be standing on watch while the rest of the herd grazes.

Above: The Nyika park is also a favourite of the rock-loving Klipspringer.

Livingstone's suni

The suni vies with the blue duiker as to which is the smallest of the antelopes but the latter just wins on weight. Both these tiny antelopes are only some 35 centimetres (14 inches) at the shoulder. Their diminutive size makes them difficult to see. The males have small, backward-sloping horns. Overall they are reddish-brown but the backs are flecked white. Close up they will be seen to have ears which are pink on the inside. When disturbed, they run off at a zigzag which compares with that of hares. Only in Lengwe are the suni commonly seen, usually in small family groups, although they are also present in the other three most southerly parks.

Klipspringer

This antelope is a regular in Nyika but only occasionally seen in the other parks. It is rather larger than the suni and distinctly more stocky. Its coarse hair is grey-brown with flecks of yellow. The male's horns are short, set forward and vertical. It is the only antelope to walk on the tips of its hoofs. It seems not to seek water but lives in rocky terrain where it exhibits all the agility of a mountain goat.

Oribi

Few sightings (in Liwonde and Kasungu) are reported of the oribi, an antelope about the same size as a klipspringer. It has a noticeably long neck and a black tuft of a tail. Its body colour is reddish-brown with the underparts being white. They have the rather unusual habit, when running away, of stopping to look back towards the perceived danger. The males have thin, vertical horns and both sexes have quite long, pointed ears.

Sharpe's grysbok

This grysbok is occasionally seen in all the parks except Nyika. Their overall colour appears grey although, when seen close up, there are mixtures of red-brown and white hairs. They are usually found singly and most movements are nocturnal.

Sharpe's grysbok have large ears but the male's horns are only some six centimetres (two and a half inches). Females do not have horns. The hindquarters look distinctly heavy.

Duiker

All three of southern Africa's duiker, the red, the blue and the common or grey duiker have a presence in Malawi, but only the last named is regularly seen. Red and blue duiker do occur in Nyika but the common duiker has been sighted in all the parks except Lake Malawi.

The blue duiker is the smallest antelope in southern Africa, only 35 centimetres (14 inches) to the shoulder and weighing just four kilograms (nine pounds). It gets its name from a grey-blue sheen to its dark-brown coat. The red duiker is 43 centimetres (17 inches) tall and weighs in at 14 kilograms (30 pounds). Against these tiny antelope, the common duiker is a relative giant with a shoulder height of 50 centimetres (20 inches) and a mass of about 20 kilograms (44 pounds).

All duikers prefer a habitat giving cover but, superficially, the common duiker seems particularly bold and only runs off, like a hare, when the 'enemy' gets very close. The best places to see the common duiker are Nyika, Vwaza and Nkhotakota where they may be seen singly or in pairs.

Other Mammals

Burchell's zebra

Zebra are odd-toed ungulates, an order of mammals which embraces rhinos, tapirs and horses. The zebra is of the horse family. Its black and white stripes are familiar but there are subtle differences between sub-species. Burchell's zebra (unlike Cape Mountain and Hartmann's zebra) may have shadow stripes overlaying the white stripe. Only Burchell's zebra are found naturally in Malawi.

Some of the zebra have an orange tinge to the white stripe and, on Nyika, the zebra often seem darker than is common. The stripes of Burchell's zebra continue under the belly but not all of the animals have stripes round the legs. Unlike others of the species these zebra have no dewlap.

Burchell's zebra weigh up to 340 kilograms (a third of a ton) and have immensely well developed and strong hindquarters. A kick from a zebra has serious consequences for any of its predators. Zebra have a strongly developed herding instinct and will even run with antelope. On Nyika, where there are horse safaris, zebra will happily run along-side the horses.

The best sightings are likely to be in Nyika, Kasungu and Liwonde. No sightings have been reported in the two most southerly parks. On Nyika Plateau, in the dry season, zebras may migrate to the warmth of the lower slopes.

Above: Lone buffalo can be especially dangerous. Those in Kasungu National Park are reputed to be particularly aggressive. Top: Zebra are common in Nyika National park.

Warthog

Generally described as Africa's most ugly mammal, this is a little unfair to an animal which can actually become a pet. The warthog is pig-like, with a shoulder height of about 70 centimetres (28 inches) and a weight of about 100 kilograms (220 pounds). Well fed, they can greatly exceed these averages. Warts on the face give it its name. There are two pairs on the male and one pair of smaller warts on the female. Adults have upward pointing, curved tusks.

The rather thin body hair thickens along the centre of the back and this tends to stand up when the animal is frightened. As it runs, the warthog's tuft-topped tail stands up like a marker flag. The warthog is usually seen in daylight when it is feeding on grass and roots. Small family or bachelor groups (known as sounders) are regularly seen in all the parks except Lake Malawi.

Bushpig

Slightly smaller than the warthog, the bushpig is much less common in Malawi although it is present in all parks. Its habitat is less open than the warthog, favouring woodland rather than open country. Seen from a distance it can be best distinguished from the warthog by its tail which hangs down when it runs rather than standing erect. Bushpigs are without tusks but males may develop facial warts. The hair on the face is light in colour. The bushpig sounders are usually of some six or so animals. Bushpigs are nocturnal, making sightings less likely.

Aardvark (Ant bear)

The aardvark, or ant bear, would probably not win a beauty contest in the animal world but it might get the prize for originality. It is often said to have the tail of a kangaroo at one end and the nose of a pig at the other. In between is a powerful body standing on short thick legs terminating in nails which are highly efficient digging instruments. The fully grown aardvark will be over a metre and a half (five feet) in length.

The body of the aardvark is only thinly covered in hair so that the predominant colour is that of the skin which itself takes on the colour of the soil in which it digs its burrows. It feeds on termites and ants but keeps under cover during daylight hours. All Malawi's

Below: Warthogs, distinguished by their 'marker flag' tails.

Above: The rock dassie or hyrax, is common in Malawi and is not confined to the game parks and reserves.

parks, except Lake Malawi, report occasional sightings.

Porcupine
The porcupine is a very large rodent, up to a metre (thirty-nine inches) in length. Its black and white quills make it easy to recognise. Although they have been sighted in all of Malawi's parks, they are infrequently seen because they are usually moving singly or in pairs and because they are nocturnal. During the day they hide away, perhaps in a rock crevice or in the burrows of aardvarks.

Pangolin
Described as looking like a small aardvark wearing armour, this mammal is easily recognised for its unique appearance. Its small pointed head and legs are covered by grey-brown scales while its back and long tail have proportionally large scales. If disturbed, it will curl itself into a ball with the points of the scales offering it protection. It is solitary and will probably only be seen at night when it comes out of its (or another animal's) burrow to feed on termites and ants. Although it is present in all of the country's parks, except Lake Malawi, it is only rarely sighted.

Rock dassie (Hyrax)
This interesting little creature looks like a large, over-fed hamster and it is often mistaken for a type of rodent. Amazingly, in evolutionary terms, it is a near relative of the elephant. In fact, it is only some 50 centimetres (20 inches) in total length. It has no tail and its other name is the hyrax.

It inhabits rocky areas and will often be seen peeping out of a rock crevice to satisfy its curiosity before scurrying away. By no means confined to the parks, many visitors to Nkopola Lodge on the southern lakeshore get their first sightings there. Almost all the parks report sightings with Lake Malawi National Park and Mwabvi Reserve being the most frequent.

Hare
Two hare sub-species, the red rock and the scrub hare, are the most likely to be seen in Malawi, with Nyika being the park where sightings are most frequent. The rare red rock hare (also called the red rock rabbit) has a slight red tinge to back and head, with black streaks. The more common scrub hare is grey with a white chest and belly. Both these types of hare are nocturnal.

Reptiles

Nile crocodile
In the past, Lake Malawi and the Shire River were home to very large numbers of the pre-historic reptile. Lake Malawi's history is full of horrific stories of man-eating crocodiles. There are still large numbers and culls were considered necessary in the Lower Shire Valley as recently as 2002.

It is possible to see crocodiles basking on sandbanks along the larger rivers, especially the Shire. Their apparent passivity, as they lie in the sun, sometimes with open mouths as they cool themselves, belies their speed and aggression on land and in water. The tail is all important in propelling the reptile through water and its main weapon in attack. It is also the edible part of the reptile.

Crocodiles will spend time in water completely submerged but will raise their nostrils and eyes above the water as they come up to breathe. They can, and do, travel long distances overland and can live without feeding for very considerable periods.

In Malawi, the easiest place to see crocodiles is along the Shire River as it flows through Liwonde National Park. A recent survey here discovered one specimen over five-and-a-half metres (nineteen feet) long, quite exceptional for a Nile crocodile. Crocodiles can be seen elsewhere in the Shire and very occasionally on rivers in Nkhotakota Wildlife Reserve, in Lake Malawi and in Majete.

Water monitor lizard
This lizard, which grows to over a metre (39 inches) is commonly seen in Vwaza, Kasungu, Nkhotakota, Lake Malawi and Liwonde. It keeps close to rivers and lakes which are its home. It is not easily frightened but poses no real threat to man. It can be seen moving slowly along river banks but has a more impressive speed if the occasion demands.

Birdlife and Bird Habitats

Many African countries claim to be a birdwatcher's paradise but Malawi's credentials in this field are especially impressive. Around six hundred and fifty different species have been identified with ten per cent not being seen in other parts of southern Africa. Rather more than eighty per cent of the recorded species breed in the country while the remainder are migratory, mostly from Europe with some from Asia.

The variety is wide, from the very large **Marabou stork** (over 150 cm/59 inches) to tiny birds like the **locust finch** (less than 10 cm/4 inches). One look at Malawi's geographical position and its range of environments quickly explains why this is so. The country's central position, close to the equator, puts it clearly on the route of those migratory birds which seek to exploit the conditions in contrasting hemispheres. The juxtaposition of mountains, plateaux and river plains, swamplands and lakes, cater for the habitat demands of all manner of birds. Malawi must certainly be a destination favoured by the true ornithologist as well as by those who are simply enthralled by the sight of such a colourful and extraordinary array in this relatively small country.

Although a particular species of bird is not usually confined to a single habitat, most species favour a particular haunt which satisfies its feeding, nesting and cover needs. Unlike many mammals, which need the protection of a game reserve, birds can be seen almost anywhere that the conditions are suitable. But it is in the national parks and reserves that the most natural habitats are found, hence they are often the first choice of those visitors to Malawi who wish to experience the winged wealth of the country. It is also in the parks that expert guiding should be available.

There is no single season of the year for birdwatching. However, to see the biggest range, which will include migrants, the period towards the close of the dry season, late September, to the end of the wet season, April, gives the greatest opportunities. This is, of course, the northern hemisphere's winter. Perhaps best of all are the months of November and December, before the rains set in at their heaviest and when the plumage of many birds is at its most colourful.

Around the Lake

Lake Malawi attracts a number of birds which favour either the water and islands or the particular vegetation of the shorelands. Pride of place must be given to the **African fish eagle**, Malawi's national bird. There are more concentrations of fish eagles here than anywhere else in the world. This magnificent bird, which has a black body with white head, neck and tail feathers, is easily sighted as it dives to take fish from just under the surface of the waters. If not seen, its loud cry will be heard as it perches on a waterside tree or skims over the lake.

Along the lakeshore, palms attract the **collared palm thrush** and **palm swifts**, while the mighty baobabs have their **mottled spinetails** with wonderfully swept-back wings. **Pied kingfishers** dive to take small fish and, where there are reeds, **golden** and **brown-throated weavers** can be seen. Very prominent, especially on the off-shore islands, are **whitebreasted cormorants**, although the **reed cormorant** is much less commonly seen. By far the most impressive bird, for its sheer size, found near the lake is the giant **Marabou stork**.

Wetlands

Vast numbers of birds inhabit Malawi's wetlands and riverine areas. Elephant Marsh, Lake Chilwa, Vwaza Marsh Wildlife Reserve and even the larger dambos, such as the Mpatsanjoka near Senga Bay, are rewarding haunts for birdwatchers.

Squacco and **greenbacked heron** inhabit Elephant Marsh, but the **rubybellied** or **rujousbellied heron** can be seen on the more accessible Mpatsanjoka dambo. **Hamerkops**, with their characteristic crests, feed in the

Opposite: The Marabou stork, one of Malawi's largest birds.

shallows of Lake Chilwa. **White pelicans** and **flamingos** are regularly sighted on Lake Chilwa and in Elephant Marsh. These great birds look most attractive in their breeding plumage when the, usually white, feathers of the body have a pink flush. Another big and beautiful bird of the dambos is the **crowned crane** but it is becoming rare.

Vwaza is noted for its duck and geese populations which include **whitefaced** and **knobbilled ducks** and **spurwinged geese**, as well as the smaller **Egyptian goose**.

The larger rivers, such as the Shire and the Bua, have their own specialities. The exposed sand cliffs near Chikwawa are home to **carmine bee-eaters**, known for their beautiful pale cinnamon underparts. **Giant kingfishers** are also seen along the Shire but the smaller **halfcollared kingfisher** is to be found mostly near heavily wooded river banks such as those in Nkhotakota Wildlife Reserve.

Brachystegia woodlands

These woodlands, also known as *miombo*, are the characteristic vegetation of much of Malawi. A number of bird species are seen only in these habitats and some of the best viewing can be had in the Dzalanyama Forest to the south-west of Lilongwe. A stay at the Forest Lodge there can be particularly rewarding.

Scimitar-billed wood hoopoes, with their extraordinarily curved bills, solitary **Souza's shrikes** and **Whyte's barbets** are seen here. **Boehm's flycatcher** is not seen elsewhere in southern Africa and two rarities are the **blue-head weaver** and **Stierling's woodpecker**. Another weaver bird, whose nest has a long spout and always looks just a little untidy, is the **redheaded weaver** found in the Dzalanyama Forest and elsewhere.

There are numerous species of brightly coloured sunbirds found in the *Brachystegia* woodlands. **Red and blue sunbirds**, the **greenheaded** and **Oustalet's sunbirds** are just three which are not usually seen in the rest of southern Africa. Of the pipits, the **wood pipit** is common but the lighter coloured **bushveld pipit** is a very rare visitor.

The **miombo rock thrush**, despite its name, is not confined to rocky areas of the woodlands but the **boulder chat** is often seen in the Mchinji area where there are rocky outcrops. Two visitors to these woodlands are the **European nightjar**, often seen near Thyolo in the wet season, and the **garden warbler**. A long distance and rare visitor is the **European blackcap** which keeps to altitudes above 300 metres (1000 feet).

Mixed savannah woodlands

Two national parks, Liwonde and Lengwe, provide this habitat. Just as the vegetation is mixed, so too one can expect to find a particularly wide variety of birdlife. Commonly found are **longtailed glossy starlings**, **hornbills** — both **redbilled** and **crowned** — and **whitebrowed sparrow-weavers**. More restricted is the attractive **Lilian's lovebird**, only seen in Liwonde. Where these woodlands are cut by rivers, **Pel's fishing owl** may be present. Again, Liwonde is the most likely place for a sighting.

Down in the Lower Shire Valley, and especially in Lengwe, is the **yellow-billed hornbill**. It is hardly ever seen outside this area but is quickly recognised by its especially large yellow bill. A rare summer visitor is the **hobby falcon** which hunts for small birds and bats at dusk. Another hunter is the rather larger **longcrested eagle**, a relatively common bird not only in the parks but also by the roadsides. During the day it may be seen perched on a tree but in the early morning it will be soaring high into the sky.

Rocket-tailed rollers are uncommon but worth looking out for as their blue under-parts catch the sun's light. Even more rare is the largest of the rollers, the **purple roller** — another pretty bird with mixed colours. At the opposite end of the scale of sightings is the **Mozambique nightjar**. It feeds from exposed sandy surfaces and even from dirt roads. Even more likely to be seen is the **Cape turtle dove**.

Evergreen forests

There are a few but important areas of evergreen forest which provide a different habitat for birds from the more common deciduous woodlands. Evergreen forest zones tend to be relatively small and distinct, such as those on Nyika and the Kalwe Forest near Nkhata Bay, as well as in the Thyolo and Mulanje area.

One of the species associated with these habitats but are not found elsewhere in

southern Africa is the **grey-olive bulbul**, seen especially on Nyika. Several other birds of the same family, **placid bulbuls, yellow-streaked bulbuls** and **stripecheeked bulbuls**, are also here in the evergreen forests. They are not especially easy to see but their whistling calls are distinct.

An uncommon bird is **Sharpe's akalat**. Not easy to see unless one gets a glimpse of its white belly, this bird is of the same family as the robin but is not seen in the rest of southern Africa. Neither is the **oliveflanked robin**, but it is quite likely to be sighted on the Viphya Plateau, in Nyika National Park and around Mulanje. Two other birds not seen in southern Africa outside Malawi are the **moustached green tinkerbird**, a member of the barbet family with a distinctive white moustache, and the **bartailed trogon**. The trogon is stunningly and beautifully coloured even down to its silver tail with black bars.

Another bird of the evergreens, which is something of a rarity and not easily seen, is the **bluemantled flycatcher**. On the other hand, the **green coucal** is not only more common but can be identified by its large yellow bill, green tail and white underbelly.

Above: Guinea fowl are almost always seen in small flocks. Top: Masked weaver birds are common residents in Malawi.

Above: White-fronted bee-eaters on the banks of the Shire River in Liwonde National Park.
Below: Long-toed lapwing.

Mountains and hills

The truly upland areas like Nyika and Mulanje clearly offer a distictive habitat but so to do the inselbergs that are scattered across the country. The inselbergs are home to a number of raptors which delight in the rocky vantage points these hills provide. Among these birds are the **black eagle**, the relatively common **lanner falcon** and the more rare **peregrine falcon**. The last named is most likely to be seen in the Mulanje area.

Among other inhabitants of the rocky inselbergs and other hills are the **rock** or **mountain cisticola**, the **largestriped pipit** and the **mocking chat**. The pipet has the habit of flying off into a tree when it's disturbed and pretending to be a branch. Mocking chats, like others in the same family, have distinctly different male and female colours.

Of the birds of the mountains, some are unique to their particular home areas in Malawi. On Nyika, **Denham's** (or **Stanley's**) **bustard**, the **red-winged francolin** and the **wattled crane** are in this category, although there have been sightings of the **bustard** on the Viphya Plateau and in the Kasungu

Above: Malawi, with its six hundred and fifty species, is a birdwatcher's delight. These enthusiasts are at the Luwawa Forest Lodge. Below: Flamingos are regular visitors to Lake Chilwa and Elephant Marsh.

National Park. All of these birds are attracted to Nyika's grasslands. On the more rocky parts of Nyika the **augur buzzard** is to be seen.

On Mulanje Mountain, the **common quail**, unfortunately, isn't common and the **red-tailed flufftail** is also rare but worth looking out for. The **Eurasian swift** is a visitor in summer but the **rock martin** is a resident.

Around and about town

As has been said, birds know no boundaries even when they are fiercely territorial. Not surprisingly, the larger towns such as Lilongwe and Blantyre have their own resident bird populations. For example, three owls are seen around the capital city. The **pearlspotted owl** and **Scops owl** are fairly common but the **giant eagle owl** can be seen near to its haunts in the Nature Sanctuary. Blantyre boasts the **crested barbet** and the **pennantwinged nightjar**. Showing no preference, the **sharpbilled honeyguide** may be seen in both cities.

The popularity of Malawi for birdwatching is well known. Apart from the very variable range of habitats which attracts such a wide

variety of species, the country has another attraction for those interested in sightings.

Malawi is relatively small and it is quite possible to visit a great number of different habitats to see the riches of birdlife even on a quite short stay in the country.

Lake Malawi's Fish

Lake Malawi is not just Africa's third largest, it is home to what is probably the largest number of fish species of any lake in the world. One has to say "probably" because it has rivals in Lakes Victoria and Tanganyika. Exactly how many different fish species inhabit Lake Malawi is difficult to say because the breeding habits of many fish, by which a species may be defined, are uncertain. It is estimated that there are over five hundred from ten families. Some authorities claim that the number of species may be closer to a thousand. Such figures, translated into comparative terms, would mean that there is a larger number of species in Lake Malawi than in all the freshwater lakes of Europe and North America put together.

The *Cichlidae* (cichlids) dominate and the lake is said to contain over thirty per cent of all known cichlid species. All but one per cent of over four hundred different cichlids are endemic to the lake. This high level of endemism, over ninety per cent across all species, is a particularly noteworthy feature.

Of the cichlid genera, ten are the small, highly coloured *mbuna* rock fish which frequently grace the aquariums of many a home in other parts of the world.

In the story of evolution, the *mbuna* have a special place. Their explosive speciation, the ability to evolve rapidly into large numbers of distinct species, has been compared with Charles Darwin's classic example of the finches of the Galapagos. Each species develops a harmony with its own unique part of the lake in terms of shelter and food. This exploitation and adaptation is referred to as adaptive radiation.

About thirty per cent of the lakeshore is rocky, the remainder being sandy with, in relatively small areas, patches of swamp or reed. It is in the rock areas, such as those of Cape Maclear and the Lake Malawi National Park that the *mbuna* have thrived and where the explosive speciation has taken place.

The level of the lake has changed over time. It is a matter of historic record that the waters dropped by over four metres (thirteen feet) in the latter half of the nineteenth century, only to rise again by over six metres during most of the last century. Over a longer time span, geological rather than historical, the lake's surface levels have fluctuated much more spectacularly. It is in the longer term changes of lake level that adaptive radiation has occurred as the fish were presented with different and separate habitats.

Despite the differences which define the various cichlid species, they have, in common, one remarkable characteristic: they are all mouth brooders. The female fish carries the eggs and fry in her mouth until the young are ready and able to look after their own needs. This ensures survival of a larger proportion of the offspring than might otherwise be the case. Only one of Lake Malawi's cichlids, the red-breast tilapia, does not conform to this practice.

The number of offspring produced depends on the size of the mother fish. Larger species may be able to carry hundreds of eggs while the tiny *mbuna's* eggs may scarcely reach double figures.

For visitors to the lake, it is not the size that matters. By any standard the *mbuna* are small; the largest are only 10-15 centimetres (4-6 inches). The fascination is not size but colour.

One of the largest of the *mbuna* is also the most colourful. These are the *Pseudotropheus zebra* which display colour polymorphism. That is, the species has more than one colouration. So great are the variations that some doubts have been expressed that these are indeed a single species; yet their breeding patterns have usually proved that they are.

The bright colours and endless pattern variations turn the waters of the lake into a colourful kaleidoscope wherever the *mbuna* flourish. There is an insatiable demand for these wonders of nature to fill the aquariums of homes around the world.

The colour variations are matched by a range of feeding habits among the *mbuna*. The food source is essentially the harvest of their rocky environment but while most feed off the algae on the rocks, subtly different feeding patterns are employed by different species thus reducing competition. Not only are different depths favoured by different species,

Above: The Lake's clear waters make 'fish-spotting' very easy.

but some will feed from underneath the rocks leaving others to graze on vertical faces with their bodies at right angles to the surfaces.

Of those cichlids which are not the same group as the *mbuna*, one is especially well known, not for its colour but for its taste. This is the chambo of the *Oreochromis* genus, a deep water fish which enjoys the reputation of being the best fish for eating of all the lake's vast number of species. It is difficult to find a restaurant menu in a Malawi hotel which doesn't feature chambo. This bream-like fish really does make an excellent meal but, sadly, overfishing of the lake has threatened its prime position. It will be a sad day for Malawian cuisine if it ever becomes a rarity at the dining table.

A non-cichlid fish, which is also favoured for eating, is the kampango. This is one of the many catfish found in the lake. The kampango, or *Bagrus meridionalis*, is a pedatory fish which constructs nests where sandy banks lie alongside rocky surfaces at depths of some 10 to 30 metres (30 to 100 feet). Although they are not mouth brooders, the male and female are highly protective of their offspring.

In the villages, it is not the chambo or smoked kampango that are on the menu but the *Engraulicypris sardella* or usipa. These small silver fish are to be seen spread on giant drying tables along the shore of the lake. Most fishing for the usipa is done at night when their vast shoals can be attracted to lights carried by the villagers' boats.

For the angler rather than the commercial fisherman, the prey is often *Opsaridium microlepis*, otherwise known as the mpasa or lake salmon. Like other salmon, its spawning pattern requires it to migrate up rivers flowing into the lake. Favoured are the large rivers north of Nkhotakota such as the Bua.

The unique fauna of Lake Malawi, with their unusual breeding habits and their gorgeous colours, to say nothing of their economic value, are a treasure which Malawi has to protect. Conservation is no longer an option; it is a necessity if the serious threat of overfishing is to be countered. Population pressures, changes in fishing practices and a shortage of alternative protein-rich food, conspire to aggravate the problem. Even in the so-called protected waters of Lake Malawi National Park, fishing continues without effective restriction. It is important that a solution is found without delay.

Vegetation

The pressures of a rapidly growing population, eager to obtain firewood and to clear the land for smallholdings, mean that Malawi retains little of its cover of natural vegetation. Even the important areas of forest reserves contain both indigenous and exotic trees. However, what one sees today is a modified version of the natural vegetation rather than something which is entirely man-made.

The greatest threat to the natural vegetation comes from indiscriminate, and often illegal, felling of trees to meet the insatiable demand for fuel wood by both the rural and the urban populations. This is a land where only four per cent of the people have access to electricity and few can easily afford even the cheapest of fuel oils for cooking. In addition to firewood, timber is required for building (often only the best is taken) while other trees fail to reach maturity as their bark is stripped away to make string.

It is a sad fact that visitors returning to the country after some years of absence almost always remark on the reduction in tree cover. Fortunately, Malawi's natural vegetation is dominated by woodlands and the country is favoured by a climate in which drought is rarely a severe problem. So much of southern Africa, seen from the air in the dry season, has a uniform parched-brown appearance. But Malawi stands out as a land having splashes of green in all seasons. To see Malawi's vegetation at its best, the period from January through to May is the ideal time of the year. For those areas which are famed for their wildflowers and orchids, the wet season and the weeks leading up to it, are often the optimum times.

Only in limited areas has man created an artificial vegetation cover on a large scale. However, the existence of plantations for sugar, tea and rubber have, here and there, altered the landscape. Thus, the tea gardens of Thyolo and Mulanje and the sugar plantations of Sucoma and Dwangwa have transformed large tracts of those districts.

Likewise, the forest reserves of plateau areas like Zomba are the creations of man and not of nature.

It would be possible to sub-divide Malawi's natural vegetation into a large number of different systems, but, for simplicity's sake, some six types can be recognised and described.

Brachystegia woodlands

These woodlands form the most widespread vegetation type in the whole country. The term *miombo* is also used as a shorthand for these woodlands, covering a great variety of trees of which the *Brachystegia* is the dominant.

The woodlands are mixed with a number of distinct trees rather than a monotony of a single species. Even among the *Brachystegia*, there are more than ten species. Additionally, other tree group such as the *Julbernardis*, *Uapaca* and *Monotes* are inter-mixed with *Brachystegia*. The tree types depend on local factors such as rainfall, altitude, drainage and type of soil — as well as on the impact man has had. At one time, almost three-quarters of the country could have been classified as *miombo*.

The trees are strictly deciduous but leaves are lost only towards the end of the dry season in September and October. Even then, they are without leaf for just a short time because the new leaves are ready to burst forth as the old fall. It is at this time, when the new leaves come through, that the *miombo* woodlands are at their prettiest. Indeed, such is the colourful display of the new foliage during this spring flush that it almost rivals that of the shoals of *mbuna* fish in Lake Malawi. Particularly brilliant are the crimsons and reds before the leaves take on their hues of dark green as they mature.

Most of the *Brachystegia* is what is known as open canopy. That is, the upper branches of adjacent trees do not touch. This allows sunlight to penetrate to give a ground cover. Two types of open canopy woodland are

Opposite: *Kigelia africana*, more popularly known as the sausage tree. This fine specimen is in Vwaza Wildlife Reserve.

Above: Beautiful acacias provide a modicum of shade.

recognised, the Msuku and the Thengo. Much of the true Msuku woodland, consisting *Brachystegia* and *Uapaca kirkiana* has been lost to fire and farming but a visit to Nkhotakota Wildlife Reserve will give a glimpse of what about one third of Malawi used to look like.

Thengo woodland is seen at its best in Kasungu National Park. There the short grass cover between the trees helps to provide a variety of habitat favouring a great range of fauna.

Closed canopy *Brachystegia* still covers parts of the Viphya Plateau in northern Malawi, but in the south of the country it has often lost the unequal battle with the development of plantations and pressures from a growing population.

Mixed savannah woodlands
The mixed savannah woodlands of Malawi are spread widely but found most often in the lower lying areas of the country such as the Shire Valley and the lakeshore regions. The grasslands of this savannah are most often tall and reed-like but vary according, largely, to soil type. The trees of this vegetation also are

varied; the species often decided by very local soil or climatic factors. Unlike the *Brachystegia* woodland in which the trees are scarcely ever leafless, those of the savannah woodland are without leaf for as much as half a year.

One species of tree, the *mopane*, flourishes in the warmer lowlands, such as those of the Shire Valley. Derived from the Bantu word for butterfly, the name serves to describe the leaf shape. An unusual characteristic of the *mopane's* leaves is that they twist during the day always to present their edges to the sun. Thus, they provide very little shade. To compensate for this somewhat anti-social behaviour, the leaves do provide food for animals when the savannah grasses have become parched. In Liwonde National Park, for example, the game finds the leaves to be a source of protein- and phosphorous-rich food. It is often in the *mopane* woodlands that the greatest concentrations of that oddity of the tree world, the baobab, are also found.

The semi-succulent baobab survives tropical high temperatures better than most other species. Although they appear to have their root systems at the top of the trunk (the upside down tree) the roots are actually extensive and water-seeking. The trunk is fibrous, allowing it to hold water, and the slightly shiny bark surface reduces water loss. All this resistance to drought, along with other characteristics, helps it have a long life — often many centuries. Rather like the comment that you never seem to see a baby pigeon, it is often said that a young baobab is a rare sight. It is also not often that one sees the baobab in leaf. Their branches are bare throughout almost all the dry season.

Baobabs are seen in many parts of the savannah woodlands with some especially fine specimens along the southern lakeshore. In Liwonde, the elephants sometimes eat the soft wood of the tree so ingesting the calcium it contains.

On the alluvial plains, the trees of the savannah include the large and spreading nsangu, the mtando and the so-called sausage tree (*Kigelia africana*). The nsangu has often survived where other trees have been felled, simply because of the shade it affords. It is common to see groups of people gathered under these trees during the heat of the day.

Kigelia africana has come to be called the sausage tree because of the enormous, sausage-like, fruit which hang from its branches by slender stalks. They can weigh up to 10 kilograms (22 pounds) and standing under this tree is to court real danger when the fruit is about to fall. Everything about the tree is large. Its flowers measure 10-15 centimetres (4-6 inches) across. Animals eat both the flowers and the seeds which spill from the fruit as it rots on the ground.

Extracts from the seeds have been made into creams which are said to have some curative effects on certain skin cancers. In the past, less sophisticated lotions were made to put on to skin burns.

Combretum-Acacia-Pilostigma woodlands
Much of this woodland has been lost to cultivation, especially to tobacco farms and smallholdings. Its natural homelands are the more fertile soils of the plateau of central Malawi, from the Bua River in a great swathe towards the capital, Lilongwe. This woodland type is also to be seen from the road leading up to the Livingstonia Mission along the Henga valley. Much of the old woodland is now replaced by cultivation or by tall, thin grass. The dominant trees include the *Acacia campylecantha*, which is favoured by deep soils, the *Combretum album* and the *Pilostigma thonningi*.

So much of this vegetation type has been destroyed that it may be best to visit the Lilongwe Nature Sanctuary to see just what the central plateau looked like in days long past.

Montane forest and grassland
Malawi has a number of mountains and high plateaux which rise above 1500 metres (5000 feet). The better known include Nyika, Viphya and Zomba Plateaux and the wonderful Mount Mulanje, east of Blantyre. Smaller areas, such as the Dedza Highlands and Ntchisi Mountain, are also distinguished by montane vegetation. Many of these areas have been selected as forest reserves and may have vast plantations which can supply the needs for fuel timber.

The natural vegetation of these uplands is montane forest and grasslands although there is dispute concerning the true natural balance between tree and grass cover. Many believe that, for example, the herbaceous vegetation of Nyika is a secondary cover succeeding the loss of woodland by fire. In all, the montane evergreen forests form only fifteen per cent of the total surface of these areas with the rest being grass and scrub.

Of the trees, and there are very many species, it is the Mulanje Cedar (*Widdringtonia wehytei*) which is king. Found naturally on the mountain which gives it its common name, the cedar is a truly magnificent tree. Although also found in neighbouring Mozambique and in Zimbabwe, the cedar is never as tall as in Malawi where it towers to 45 metres (150 feet). Its trunk, at the multi-stemmed base, may reach almost two metres (six feet) in diameter. The lower part of its straight trunk is bare of branches but the crown can form a canopy so thick that stands of the Mulanje cedar almost block out the sun's rays from the ground. Many of the cedars are draped with lichens giving them an eerie countenance such as was observed by Laurens van der Post in his book "Venture to the Interior".

Unfortunately, some of Mulanje Mountain's cedar have been lost to felling and it is in the more protected ravines that they are at their

best. More accessible are the planted cedars of the Zomba Plateau where they were introduced nearly one hundred years ago. Another easily visited domain of the Mulange cedar is on the Ntchisi ridge.

Nyika Plateau has an interesting small relic forest of *Juniperous procera*. In the shelter of the Uyagaya Valley, the forest is at the most southerly limit of the juniper. Some single trees are also to be seen around the high plateau. It is suggested that Nyika's trees are all that remains of vast juniper forests which once were common to this part of Africa but were lost as the climate became drier.

Nyika Plateau often surprises visitors because of its unique rolling grasslands and heath. There is no similar landscape in the whole of Africa. The total area of grass is 160,000 hectares (400,000 acres) supporting large numbers of grazing antelope and zebra. Together with a variety of grasses are herbaceous legumes, another good food source, and an ever increasing cover of bracken fern. The open vegetation of the plateau also provides excellent riding country; the horses from the stables run by Chelinda Lodge are unshod to protect the fragile ecosystem.

Swamps

Swamp vegetation, comprising reeds, sedges and sudd, is confined to areas of lagoons, lakes and riverine lowlands such as Elephant Marsh. There is a series of lagoons along the margins of Lake Malawi where a natural ridge runs parallel to the shoreline. The best known is the Chia Lagoon, north of Nkhotakota.

The Elephant Marsh and lakes such as Chilwa support dense aquatic vegetation which includes the floating fern (*Azola*) and sudd, tall mats of grass. As these plants grow they become so thick that it is almost impossible to force a small boat through the water. Palms also grow round these lake and swamp areas and these are used to make mats and palm wine.

Dambos

Dambo is the regional term for waterlogged stretches of river courses. These dry out as the rains stop. They are found on plateaux as well as in areas of lower altitude and support short grasslands together with geophytes and other herbs. Many visitors to Malawi will recognise the large dambo that is crossed by the road between Salima and Senga Bay.

Orchids and wildflowers

Malawi is not only justly famous for its very green landscapes, it is also renowned for its truly wonderful displays of orchids and wildflowers. Many of the wildflowers will be seen as spring arrives in October and November but the orchids are often at their flowering best during the rainy season.

Although wildflowers and flowering trees may be seen widely through the country it is the mountain areas of Nyika, Mulanje and Zomba that they and the orchids are seen in magnificent profusion. Man's activities have reduced their number and restricted their distribution on Zomba but Mulanje and Nyika remain largely unaffected.

In Malawi as a whole, almost 300 species of terrestrial and well over 100 epiphytic orchids have been recognised. The former grow out of the ground while the latter use the trunks of trees or the surface of rocks as their base.

On Mulanje, orchids can be found on treks up the mountain with varieties depending on altitude and habitat. In the forest areas, including near Likabula, epiphytic orchids are common while, on the more open grassy slopes, terrestrial varieties can be seen. But it is on Nyika that the orchids attract the *aficionado* anxious to view the ten or so species which are to be seen nowhere else in the world. These include the terrestrial *Dias miniata* and *Liparis nyikana*, an epiphytic.

The colours and delicacy of the flowers are beautiful. Each has its own attraction: bright yellow clusters of *Eulophia odontoglossa* in the grasslands, delicate white flowers of the epiphytic *Aerangis montana*, proud red *Disa erubescens carsonii* on the dambos. Fingira Rock, the Stone Age site has its own special species, the feathery white *Holothrix longiflora*. Nowhere else in this part of the world are there orchids so varied and in such numbers.

Malawi's wildflowers may not always be a match for the orchids in their form, but in

Opposite: A solitary baobab near Sucoma. The baobab is resistant to drought and can live for hundreds of years.

colour they do their best to compete. On Nyika, yellow carpets of everlasting flowers (*Helichrysum*) spring up through the burnt grass towards the end of the dry season. There is a 'forest' of protea (*Protea anglolensis*) inside the park along the road leading to Chelinda. *Oxalis chapmaniae*, with characteristic pink flowers, is one of several wildflowers endemic to Nyika.

Aloes are common to Nyika and Mulanje but one sub-species of the plant (*Aloe chabaudii var mlanjeana*) is a Mulanje speciality. Some of Mulanje's wildflowers will be easily recognised, none more so than the red hot pokers (*Kniphofia*) which stand out from the more subdued hues of the mountain's slopes. Colour is also added by the Mulanje iris (*Morea schimpei*), by the orange flowers of the Leonotis and the blues of the Lobelias. High up on Mulanje and flowering through the dry season is a variety of sunflowers (*Helichrysums*).

Malawi's vegetation mirrors the great variety of landscape, which is a distinguishing mark of the country. It is a fitting raiment for this most beautiful part of the African continent.

Bottom: Malawi's wet season brings a display of colourful and delicate flowers. Below: Colourful bougainvillea.

The Spectrum Guide

Series

High-quality, lavishly illustrated guides to exotic and exciting countries with essential information for the tourist or business traveller on getting around, the cultures, history, geography, flora, fauna and much more. With their many accurate and detailed maps, these guides are invaluable works of reference with a long 'shelf life.

Camerapix Publishers International
ABC Place, PO Box 45048, Nairobi, Kenya
Tel: 254-2 4448923/4/5   **Fax:** 254 2 4448926/7
Email: camerapix@iconnect.co.ke

6 Alston Road, Barnet, Herts EN5 4ET, UK
Tel: 020 8449 5503   **Fax:** 020 8449 8120
Email: camerapixuk@btinternet.com

INTERLINK BOOKS
An imprint of Interlink Publishing group, Inc.
www.interlinkbooks.com

Tastes of Malawi

Gourmet and food writer, Quentin Crewe, famously declared, "Africa does not provide much comfort for the greedy". A few might take issue with this view, and although Malawi lays no claim to fine eating, there are dishes of interest.

In hotels, lodges and safari camps, guests are presented with a choice of dishes which, apart from the fish, could be found almost anywhere. This is what constitutes the so-called 'international menu'. Unlike its neighbours in southern Africa, it is rare to find venison on offer and even less likely that crocodile tail or hippo meat will be on the menu. Much hotel food will have been imported, mainly from South Africa, and supplies of some produce are intermittent. The arrival of such exotics such as kippers will be celebrated and prominently featured.

In the private homes of the expatriate population and better-off Malawians, meals are often a mix of local and imported ingredients and there's a degree of initiative shown in adapting traditional dishes to western tastes. All the same there is often a nostalgic hankering after hard-to-get ingredients or foodstuffs. The arrival of, say, baked beans is duly given notice in the newspapers and the anxious wait is over.

Throughout the country, the basic crop is maize and it is *nsima* which is the staple diet of the bulk of the population. This porridge is the equivalent of *mieliemeal* in South Africa or *nshima* in Zambia. The ingredients are *ufa*, (maize flour) and water, although butter or margarine will be added by those who can afford such luxuries. Like any porridge anywhere, the quality is greatly dependent upon the cook's diligence in stirring the mixture throughout the preparation.

Nsima, eaten without meat or fish, is too bland to satisfy most tastes but vegetables or hot sauces make the dish more palatable. The ingenuity of the cook is tested with recipes for *ufa* crumpets, *ufa* pancakes and even *ufa* shortbread but all require additional ingredients beyond the reach of the average village family. In the villages, meat or fish are considered to be something of luxury items and *nsima* with chicken is often the fare for a Christmas dinner. A vegetable stew, perhaps with cassava and nuts, is a more likely accompaniment to the maize porridge.

Rice and potatoes are available as alternative or additional products to maize. The quality of rice, grown mostly in the Lower Shire Valley is not especially good but potatoes are often excellent. The areas around Dedza and the Zomba Plateau specialise in potato production. The roadside availabilty of excellent, freshly fried potato chips testifies to this.

A variety of vegetables is grown on smallholders' plots including yams, eggplants (aubergines), onions, spinach, a range of sweet potatoes (*mbatata*), green maize, Chinese cabbage (*mpiru*), and cocoyams (*koko*). Many farmers aim to produce a surplus which can be sold in the markets or along the roadside. Vegetable soups are made, sometimes with fish added, or the vegetables are eaten with the ubiquitous *nsima*.

Sugar cane is popular, chewed raw and the pulp discarded along the road. Malawians have developed a sweet tooth and refined sugar is also prized.

The country produces a variety of fruit, its range reflecting the climatic conditions of the plateaux and valleys. Much is of indifferent quality. Bananas are commonly grown but are often of poor quality and are better eaten cooked rather than raw. Tomatoes are seen in colourful displays in most markets. Avocados, guavas and mangoes are seasonally on the menu but pawpaws are available throughout much of the year.

The vegetable and fruit sections of the markets are fascinating for their variety of produce and, not least, for their very careful arrangements.

While beef and fish are available in the supermarkets, goats' meat is more widely favoured among the villagers and is easily come by. Chickens, usually sold live, are commonly seen for sale along the roadsides

Opposite: Bananas are commonly grown near Lake Malawi and in the Shire Valley.

Above: Village women employ mortar and pestle to turn their maize into *ufa*.

these fish are to be farmed in the future, supplies and prices may be greatly affected. Tiger fish are caught in the River Shire, especially in the area of Majete Wildlife Reserve. They are valued for their oily flesh but the smaller fish are considered too bony to make good eating. Larger specimens, say three kilograms (six pounds) or greater are usually barbecued. Lake salmon (*mpasa*), caught in the streams of Nkhotakota Wildlife Reserve are favourites with anglers.

Other sources of protein are the variety of edible insects which many Malawians see as delicacies. Flying ants, both black and white can, after frying, be eaten hot or cold. Locusts, grasshoppers and crickets are also on the menu while lake fly (*nkhungu*) is an exceptionally rich source of iron.

A 'delicacy' which will probably be declined by most visitors to Malawi, is dried mouse. Boys will often be seen selling the mice at the side of the road, the rodents carefully displayed on sticks. The whole, unskinned mouse is boiled in salt water, dried and eaten with salt. There have been recent scare stories of the mice being caught by poisoning but the sales go on. Like the roadside butchers' stalls, the mice on sticks are not the sort of sight to improve the average international visitor's desire for the next meal.

Many Malawian dishes may not seem very exciting to visitors but, if garnished with spices, the taste may be greatly improved. It is thought that the use of spices was influenced by the former Portuguese colony of neighbouring Mozambique and by the Arab slave traders of the nineteenth century. The most famous sauce in modern times is *Nali*, of legendary, volcanic heat.

Tea is produced in the Thyolo and Mulanje districts of south Malawi and Chombe tea comes from the Nkhata Bay area. Whatever its source, it is widely drunk. Small roadside stalls will often advertise themselves as 'tea rooms'. For something stronger, there is *wamasese*. Made, not surprisingly, from fermented maize, this homemade brew is not generally to the taste of most visitors to Malawi. However, it is nutritious and is commercially produced as *Chibuku*. Look for the sign 'Shake-shake' which is as much an instruction as an advertisement.

International travellers seem to prefer their

or in the street markets. Although a favourite dish with Malawians, many visitors find the birds tough and unpalatable.

By common consent, Malawi's fish can be excellent value and of the highest quality. With twenty per cent of its surface occupied by lakes, the country is not short of potential fishing grounds. Lakes Malawi, Malombe and, to a lesser extent Chilwa, provide the bulk of the catch but the streams flowing off the plateaux towards the lakes are also rich grounds. Unfortunately, overfishing is beginning to cause serious shortages and rising prices. Because fish provide the greater part of the average Malawian's protein intake the gravity of the situation is increased further.

Of all the edible fish species available, the *chambo* is almost everyone's favourite choice. This bream has white flesh and can be cooked in a variety of ways although it is most often grilled or fried. *Kampango*, a catfish, also white fleshed, is especially delicious when smoked. Smoked *kampango* is also made into a paté.

From the mountain streams, especially on the Nyika and Zomba Plateaux, come trout. If

Above: Unambiguous and amusing shop signs are common in Malawi. This one is at Phalombe.

'greens' and 'browns', a lager and a brown ale produced by Carlsberg in a giant brewery in Blantyre. The names come from the colour of the labels on the bottles. Rather stronger is the famous Malawi Gin and Tonic (MGT). The gin is a Malawian product with a distinctive, slightly scented and pleasing taste. Those who know their MGTs say that the accompanying tonic has to be Webb's.

Also popular are Malawi or rock shandies. The former is made with ginger beer, angostura bitters and soda water while lemonade replaces the ginger beer in the latter drink. CocaCola, Fanta and other soft drinks are readily available and very popular but it is always wise to check the bottle's metal cap. Any sign of a crease could be an indication that this is a re-filled, counterfeit bottle.

In the hotels and lodges, a modest selection of South African wines is usually available at reasonable prices. Any wines from elsewhere are likely to be expensive.

Many international visitors exclusively use the restaurants in the main hotels — coffee shops or à la carte. The latter offer some excellent three course meals for around K500. The coffee shops are simple and cheap with relatively quick service. They are often the choice at lunchtime for a sandwich and a coffee or beer. The prices are very reasonable.

There are a few independent restaurants, particularly in Lilongwe and Blantyre-Limbe, some offering specialised menus (such as Korean and Chinese). It is best to get advice locally to check which offerings are currently worth trying. The quality can sometimes be on a par with the better hotel restaurants. The widest choice is in Blantyre where one such restaurant, the Taj, runs a categorical advert in the classified columns of *The Nation*: "Miserable gits never come twice — you're safe at the Taj".

Simple meals like chicken and chips are available at basic outlets though the standard of the food and the hygiene are debatable.

Whatever your taste it is worth seeking out the unusual and appreciating the authentic taste of Malawi. An excellent innovation has been at Mvuu Safari Camp in Liwonde National Park. Guests are offered a night in a local village and meals can be taken with the villagers.

Activities

Using Lake Malawi

The calm, clear waters of Lake Malawi are a great lure and there is plenty of opportunity to experience the lake more closely — either on it or in it. The overriding concern when using the lake is bilharzia but common sense should prevent any problems. Activities should be restricted to areas of lowest risk — near the main hotels and lodges or away from the shore. The other concern is wildlife — hippos and crocodiles both live in the lake — but close encounters are unlikely.

The main lakeshore hotels and lodges have most activities on offer either directly or through specialist water-sports companies. Prices are not unreasonable and it is wise to confirm the cost before embarking. Advance booking is advisable but not always necessary. Though there is potentially much on offer, not necessarily everything will be available at the time you require it. Despite all these leisure activities, the most common sight on the lake is still that of a fisherman in a dugout canoe.

Lake Malawi's prevailing wind is south-easterly, the *mwera*. This blows strongest in July. During the build-up to the wet season, however, there is a change of direction and the more northerly *mpoto* takes over. Winds become variable and unpredictable through the rainy season (November to March). With such a vast lake, it is not surprising that, though rare, large storms and high swells (four to five metres/thirteen to sixteen feet) can occur.

Boat hire, pleasure trips and cruises

Boats of all sizes are available on Lake Malawi, offering simple individual hire, short pleasure trips or full cruises lasting some days.

Simple daytime hire is possible of every-thing from pedalos and canoes to outboard dinghies and sailing boats.

Kayaking is proving increasingly popular, particularly with the advent of the Kayak Africa operation in the Lake Malawi National Park. Sea-going kayaks are used to paddle to luxury camps on the deserted islands in the park.

The tide- and current-free waters make for good sailing. The Yachting Association of Malawi holds regattas and sailing championships, the highlight of which is the Lake Malawi Yachting Marathon every July. This international event consists of a series of daily stages, beginning in the south, and ending some eight days and 560 kilometres (350 miles) later in the north.

For a simple organised pleasure trip of up to a few hours there is a choice of destinations — places of interest along the shore, or small islands just offshore. Traditional wooden fishing boats or modern fibreglass speed boats are available, the latter considerably more expensive. There can be minimum or maximum numbers for these excursions and some include snorkelling or fishing along the way.

If only one pleasure trip is to be taken, it should be out to the Lake Malawi National Park. Brightly coloured fish are easily visible through the crystal clear water, and are eager to swarm round, and feed from, any hand placed in the water holding a piece of bread or biscuit. Young men wait on the beach at Cape Maclear and approach likely customers to go in their boats.

Leisurely cruises on larger boats can also be arranged from the main hotels — to last hours or days. Though there are scheduled trips by motor launch, the more interesting are again the sailing cruises. Catamarans can be chartered, complete with skipper. Daytime cruising can be complemented by diving, snorkelling or swimming and overnight beach camping. A new ocean-going catamaran is now operated by Danforth Yachting. From their guest house at Cape Maclear, everything from a sunset cruise to a full tour of Lake Malawi is offered aboard the *Mfasa*, which sleeps up to eight guests.

Perhaps the ultimate journey on the lake is on the *Ilala*, a large motorised vessel offering a scheduled ferry service up and down the lake. This is a functional ship much used by local people, but also offers passage and cabin accommodation to tourists.

Boat trips are also offered along the upper

Above: Water-sports of all sorts are catered for on Lake Malawi.

part of the River Shire, particularly through Liwonde National Park. These are primarily for game viewing and can be extremely successful in this regard as many animals are unperturbed by objects on the water. Boats set out from Liwonde township, heading north or sometimes from Lake Malawi.

Water-sports

Facilities for sailboarding, parasailing and water skiing are all available at the main lakeshore establishments and are relatively inexpensive. Experience is not required but basic tuition is available.

Diving and snorkelling

The clear, calm, warm, shark-free and tideless waters with abundant fish populations (around 500 species) make Lake Malawi a good place to dive. Visibility can reach 30 metres (100 feet) at the best times of year (August to December). Even simple snorkelling gives good results in the right places. Swimming with the fish is the favourite pastime at Cape Maclear's Otter Point.

The main dive centres are at Club Makokola, Cape Maclear, Senga Bay, Chintheche and

Nkhata Bay. One to six day courses are available with professional tuition and PADI certification. Alternatively, sailing tours can be taken to incorporate day or night dives.

Though equipment is available for hire it is best to bring your own mask, snorkel and flippers. A three millimetre wetsuit is recommended for the 22°C — 27°C waters. The lake surface's altitude of 474 metres (1555 feet) above sea level will require appropriate adjustment of decompression tables.

Otter Point and the eastern tip of West Thumbi Island have underwater trails worth investigating, though the fish can be seen everywhere.

Angling

As well as Lake Malawi, rivers, smaller lakes and reservoirs provide varied fishing opportunities. Light tackle will cover most situations and some equipment may be available for hire at the resorts, though it's always best to bring your own.

Lake Malawi

The majority of the 500 or so species in Lake Malawi are small tropical aquarium fish, *mbuna*. However, *sungwa* (perch), *ngumbo* (lake yellow-fish), *mpasa* (lake salmon), *sanjika* (smaller relative of lake salmon), *ncheni* (lake tiger), *kampango* (catfish) and *vundu* (catfish) offer interesting possibilities. In April the Angling Society of Malawi organises the Ultra-Light Tackle Tournament which attracts entrants from across southern Africa. In the south of the lake, Mangochi, White Rock and Boadzulu Island are favourite spots. Slightly further north, the river mouths near Salima and Mbenji Island offer the best possibilities.

Fishing is year-round but best between September and April.

Rivers

The best river fishing is usually off banks of reeds and heavy weed beds. The Bua River, running through the Nkhotakota Wildlife Reserve, is excellent for lake salmon (*mpasa*) with the Luweya, Lufira and North Rukuru not far behind.

In the Lower Shire River, below the Kapichira Falls on the southern boundary of the Majete Wildlife Reserve, tiger fish are abundant, joined further down by *vundu* and barbel as the river broadens. Heavier tackle and a boat are needed there.

Dry season fishing between May and November is possible in the Lower Shire River and requires no licence.

Highlands

The streams and dams of Zomba, Mulanje and Nyika are well stocked with rainbow trout. Only fly fishing is permitted, with flies tied on single hooks.

The season is September to April and licences can be obtained from Zomba Trout Farm, Likabula Forestry Office (Mulanje) or Chelinda Camp National Park Office (Nyika).

Horse Riding

Horseback safaris on Nyika Plateau are organised by The Nyika Safari Company. Though open to novices, some experience is an advantage. Not only is this an excellent way to explore this unique wilderness but it also allows closer encounters with the resident antelope and zebra. The horses are thoroughbred, part thoroughbred, part Boerperde and cross-breeds. All are between 14 and 16 hands, even tempered and well schooled. All tack is western Mclellan with saddles designed by the US cavalry giving comfort over long distances.

On Zomba Plateau is a residential dressage school. Straightforward accompanied rides around the plateau are possible but only by prior arrangement and with proof of riding experience.

A new horse-riding operation is currently being set up on the central lakeshore, north of Ngala Lodge.

Climbing, Hiking and Walking

Rock climbing is largely restricted to the Mulanje Massif where a number of little-used routes up the great granite faces offer experienced climbers a variety of challenges. The book *Guide to the Mulanje Massif* by Frank Eastwood includes details of these routes.

For the less adventurous there are plenty of fascinating and beautiful hikes and walks. Walks through all of the national parks and wildlife reserves are popular for game viewing but hiking is generally done in the cool, shady forests on the hills and plateaux.

Mulanje Massif again offers the greatest choice and has a network of huts for intrepid explorers to stay in. Marked paths offer a variety of routes and guides and/or porters can be hired cheaply. Mountain High Rangers is a new company which aims to offer uniformed guides, providing a more professional service.

Nyika Plateau is less rugged but walking is undoubtedly one of the best ways to explore this unique and wildlife-rich wilderness. There are marked trails for those prepared to hike and camp for a few days. They cover the various peaks and valleys whilst offering chances to encounter the animals in the park close at hand. It is advisable to use a guide.

Though not quite as high as Nyika, Viphya Plateau is now proving popular. Most of the area is forested by either plantation or indigenous woodland, including tropical rainforest. A new trail begins at Luwawa Forest Lodge, crosses the Viphya and descends the escarpment, arriving at Chintheche Inn on the lakeshore. The trek takes four days.

The serene forests, hills and streams of Zomba Plateau, and the views from it, offer another attraction for walkers.

Finally, a number of forest reserves around the country provide pleasant walks through shady environments, usually with excellent birdlife. The most popular are on the hills surrounding Blantyre.

Cycling

The change in scene over relatively short distances, and the varied terrain, make Malawi a good country for cycling. The generally good tar of the main roads allow for cycling tours over a few days, for example, along the lakeshore. More challenging mountain biking is provided in the forests and on the plateaux. Many of the newly privatised forest lodges offer mountain bikes for hire and there is an increasing number of trails to explore.

Other Sports

A number of old colonial clubs offer a range of sporting facilities. They are found in the main towns and also at the large agricultural estates.

Some of the golf courses have swarms of young men who will caddy and show you round the course as well as levelling off the 'greens' of sand for putting.

Most clubs have tennis courts though the surfaces may be poor. Swimming pools and squash courts are also sometimes available.

The clubhouses are the check-in points to arrange and pay for the facilities. These dark, cool buildings often have snooker tables, dart boards and well stocked bars.

Equipment may be available for hire but enthusiasts will prefer to bring their own.

Most hotels and lodges have swimming pools while a few also maintain tennis courts. Just three have squash courts — the Le Méridien Capital in Lilongwe, Luwawa Forest

Lodge on the Viphya Plateau and Club Makokola on the southern lakeshore. Also to be found at Club Makokola is the Mlambe golf course, the best in the country. The course is beautifully landscaped and hosts an annual Pro-Am Tournament in association with the PGA of South Africa.

Above: Mountain biking, as well as more leisurely cycling, are popular holiday pursuits in Malawi. Top: Trekking is increasing in popularity. The forest reserves, as here on Mulanje, provide ideal locations.

Crafts and Curios

The standard of hand-made souvenirs to be found in Malawi is extremely high. Wood carvings are the most admired and many items found throughout southern Africa originate in Malawi.

Wood

There is a massive selection of wood carvings available, from the purely ornamental to those items with a practical use.

The ornamental range from small animal figurines through medium sized human heads and masks to large standing figures. Practical pieces are also very attractive, incorporating intricate carvings. Much is available, including drinks mats, chess sets, goblets, vases, fruit bowls, tables, chairs and lamp standards. The larger pieces are usually 'collapsible' for easier transportation. Perhaps the most common and best known item is the 'chief's chair'. Each chair consists of just two pieces of wood. The smaller section is shaped like a very short, curved-handled paddle which forms both the seat and a prop to the back section. The curved back of the chair is much larger and also functions as the broad front base, sometimes forked into two legs. The two parts are assembled to form a chair by slotting the seat into the back so that the 'paddle handle' slips through a cut in the back piece to rest on the ground. The carvings on the back may depict animals, village scenes or even large sun motifs. Chief's chairs come in all sizes, even down to toy model versions. Those intended for seating are remarkably comfortable and sturdy, despite appearing as though they will either snap or topple over.

Most carvings are truly excellent and can be picked up relatively cheaply. The better carvings are in hardwoods such as mahogany and ebony. With the latter, a feature is usually made of the fact that soft pale outer wood surrounds the dark and dense core. Carvings in palm and walnut can also be found. Chief's chairs were traditionally made from strong *mpingo* wood but other woods are now also employed. Largely found in southern Malawi are decorative boxes made from Mulanje cedar wood. As well as being very durable and having rot-resisting properties, this wood retains its pleasant aromatic scent for a long time after cutting. It is also used for larger pieces of furniture.

Many vendors blatantly polish their pieces with dark shoe polish. This can be to darken softwood and give them the appearance of hardwood but many genuine hardwood articles will also be polished simply to improve the look. Scratching the underneath of any piece should reveal its true nature.

Stone

Soapstone carvings are less commonly found than wood. Most items are attractive small figurines. Mined in the Ntcheu district, the stone is soft and absorbent so care should be taken when handling it. Malachite is the other stone often found with similar, but even fewer and smaller pieces. This green mineral is harder than soapstone and can be highly polished so it is also used for jewellery.

Basketwork

Functional but well-made cane and raffia articles of straightforward design can also be found, though they can be difficult to transport without damage. Basketwork and use of grass is found in the form of mats (of all shapes and sizes) baskets and even tables and chairs. Intricate toy vehicles are made from these materials, and from wire.

Pottery and painting

Almost all of the quality pottery found in Malawi is produced by Paragon Ceramics at Dedza and now also at Nkhotakota. The items are functional more than ornamental with everything from plant pots to complete crockery sets. However, there is a wide range of decorative designs. Some show African village scenes and others simply use colourful patterns. For those keen to get their hands dirty, Paragon now offer residential pottery courses based at their new lakeside Nkhotakota pottery.

Local artists produce colourful paintings largely depicting local village life. The boldness of the style and colours is unmistakably African.

Buying and Bargaining

There are plenty of opportunities to pick up crafts and curios — mostly from street salesmen, many of whom have stalls set up. Victoria Avenue in Blantyre, the craft market outside the post office in Old Town Lilongwe, Senga Bay, the junction of the M10 and the S128 on the southern lakeshore and the back of the lakeshore hotels have the main concentrations of stalls. However, somebody will have something to sell at every point of interest to tourists. Even stationary cars will be surrounded and wooden carvings will be thrust through any open window without invitation.

All of the main stall concentrations offer a vast array of items. However, Blantyre is the place to buy cane and raffia pieces and Lilongwe has the widest selection of paintings. Around the country there are other specialisations. On the M3 between Zomba and Liwonde, hut after hut displays high quality 'chief's chairs' of all sizes and designs. The ultimate is, however, the Mua Mission on the M5 south of Salima. The wooden carvings there are quite fantastic—smooth and without blemish. They include a variety of three-dimensional village scenes made from single pieces of wood. These carvings are well worth a special trip though they are slightly more expensive than street stalls (prices are marked). Stalls along the M5 near Mua are stocked by work from 'graduates' of the mission.

Finally, there is the occasional high street curio shop for those wary of the authenticity of the items in the streets or not wishing to experience the pressures of bargaining. They are also useful to get an idea of prices to be paid, prior to venturing out to the stalls. The shop assistants will reassure you that polish has not been used on their items with the phrase: "No Kiwi!" Prices are close to those which can be achieved on the streets and there may even be a discount for quantity. Safari Curios on Glyn Jones Road in Blantyre has a good range while shops in the foyers of the main hotels also sell pieces. The Gangecraft

Above: Carved masks feature in many ceremonies and dances. Top: Malawi produces some of the finest carvings in Africa.

Above: Basketwork, practical or ornamental, is for sale throughout Malawi.

workshops can be visited at Bvumbwe on the M2 from Limbe to Thyolo. Perhaps the most impressive items are found in Africa Habit in Lilongwe's new Old Town Mall, which stocks carvings from Mua Mission of all sizes, including large pieces if furniture.

Whenever a purchase is being made in the street some form of bargaining will be involved. Some travellers dislike this but the discussions are invariably friendly and good-natured.

If selecting several items from a number of stalls close to each other, you should be able to make all your selections, gather them together and negotiate a single price. The only problem with this method is that, should you fail to achieve the price you want, all items will be 'lost' in one go.

Rather than setting a particular price, most curio sellers will ask what you are prepared to pay. It is probably better to insist they open the bidding but to have a rough idea in mind of what you should be charged (based on prices from a fixed-price shop). The most aggressive bargain hunters suggest that you should only ever pay one quarter of the initial asking price. However, this is rather excessive and a little unfair. With every

item hand-crafted, even the initial asking prices are generally quite reasonable for most visitors. A few minutes of negotiating is definitely worthwhile as the sellers will not really expect you to pay the full price. It is important not to lose sight of the true value of the items and the relative status of the average Malawian. It is easy to get sucked into the situation and become agitated over just a few *kwacha*. Items of clothing (even the ones you are currently wearing) can be bartered. This course of action will quickly be suggested to you should you claim to have no more cash than your last offer. Other currencies will also be accepted but be sure to check that your exchange rate is a good one.

For protection in transit it is a good idea to have goods wrapped. This can be done by the salesmen, usually expertly with brown paper and string. To avoid the disappointment of discovering once home that your purchase has been switched for an inferior copy, it is as well to keep an eye on the wrapping process.

Religion

Religion has played an important part in shaping Malawi over the last two centuries. Today, it has been estimated that seventy-five per cent of the people are Christian and some twenty per cent are Muslim. The traditional beliefs, chiefly animist, are largely gone although, like elsewhere in Africa, some of the old practices die hard and may sometimes be detected in the detail of otherwise orthodox worship.

The early excursions of the Portuguese into what was to become Malawi did not lead to any significant conversions to Christianity. Likewise, Arab traders did not bring with them the beliefs of Islam until the 1840s. Then, however, of the new religions, it was Islam that was the first to gain converts. As the Swahili Arabs raided the country for slaves and ivory, they found ready allies in tribes such as the Yao. Already involved in the tradition of domestic slavery and in trading in ivory, the Yao not only joined forces with the Arabs in their quest for slaves, but some began to adopt the Islamic faith and practices. This was more than just a matter of commercial convenience. The converts began to wear forms of Arab dress and to adapt their agricultural practices to ways learnt from the Swahili Arab slavers.

The connection between the slave trade and the Islamic faith can still be seen in the distribution of mosques and their concentration along the paths of the old slave trading routes. Thus, Muslims are found in their greatest numbers along the lakeshore and in villages on routes south of Lake Malawi. Towns like Nkhotakota are Muslim strongholds although by no means exclusively Islamic.

Christianity was a decade or so behind Islam in playing its part in Malawi's modern history. The coming of the Christian missionaries with Dr David Livingstone is a well-known story. No other event and no other single person has so influenced the shaping of the country over nearly two hundred years. The unlikely bedfellows of Christianity and commerce, Livingstone's goals, were to transform Malawi, not only in the second half of the 19th century but also throughout the 20th.

It was the Christian missionaries who led the way to the abolition of the slave trade and who introduced legitimate commerce and new agricultural practices. Most of all it was the mission schools in places such as Livingstonia, Bandawe and Likoma Island that helped to educate the people to a level unsurpassed in this part of Africa.

The benign influence of the work of the Christian missionaries, at first mostly from Scotland, was to be seen in the dampening down of the fires of inter-tribal wars which had led to the slaughter of tens of thousands in the early part of the 19th century. The harmony which can be witnessed now in 21st century among the many different tribes in Malawi is due in large measure to the early work of the missions.

The extraordinary Christian churches built by the missionaries remain as a testament to the faith and optimism of the early missionary-explorers. Perhaps the best known of these churches are St Peter's Cathedral on Likoma Island and St Michael and All Angels in Blantyre. That both were constructed without the employment of expert architects and builders makes them all the more remarkable.

Despite what might have been seen in the 19th century as an inevitable clash of interest between the adherents of Christianity and of Islam, there has been very little conflict. Muslims and Christians live side by side with little evident disagreement.

This unexpected harmony was seen as especially effective in events which led to the rejection of the regime of Dr Hastings Banda and to the establishment of the new democratic republic in the early 1990s. The newly elected President was Dr Baliki Muluzi, a Muslim, while Dr Banda had been an Elder of the Church of Scotland. But it wasn't only the difference in religion of the two presidents that was noteworthy.

The single most important event which sparked the overthrow of Dr Banda was the Catholic bishops' pastoral letter of 8 March 1992. Within a short time the voice of the

Above: A simple shelter serves as a church for a Catholic Mass near Monkey Bay. Below: The simple interior of the Livingstonia Mission Church.

Catholic Church had been joined not only by that of the Church of Central African Presbyterian (CCAP) but also by the Muslim Association of Malawi. Although secular and political groups also exerted their pressure for change, it is clear that the most telling influence came from the efforts of the combined faith communities.

Religion had been the driving force behind the abolition of slavery and inter-tribal strife. It had brought peace and education to what had been one of the most troubled regions of Africa in the 19th century. Now religion can claim to have played a leading role in Malawi's emergence as a truly democratic republic in the late 20th and early 21st centuries.

Le MERIDIEN
MALAWI

the way hotels should be

Music and Dance

It's hard to imagine any sub-Saharan African country where music and dance are not integral parts of the culture. So it is with Malawi. Although what might be experienced today is likely to have been modified from traditional forms, nonetheless, the old roots are still firmly embedded in the songs, music and dances.

Fifty years ago, the French anthropologist-geographer, Pierre Gourou, drew attention to the way that even agricultural productivity could be affected by the songs and music of the people. He cited the exceptional farming outputs of the Ngoni in the Dedza and Ncheu districts which led to unusually high population densities. These he attributed to the social organization and disciplined working practices of the Ngoni. In his book, *Les Pays Tropicaux*, Gourou wrote, "...the hardship of the toil (working the land) was softened by the pleasure of working together to the rhythm of songs and musical instruments."

Music, songs, chants and dances are appropriate to the occasion. What was used by the Ngoni to spur on their work in the fields was not the same as their *ngoma* war-dance which derived from their Zulu background. Each dance or song, and its accompanying music, varies with the circumstance in which it is performed and with individual tribal traditions.

In some cases there is a direct link between the music and witchcraft. In turn, the associated dances may be intended to assist in the healing processes of the 'traditional-' or witch-doctor or almost as a means whereby to intimidate the audience. An example of the curative dances is the *vimbuza* seen in North Malawi performed by the Tumbuka people. More sinister is the famous, or infamous, *gule wamkulu* (the big dance or mask dance) of the Chewa tribe. It is especially associated with the *nyau* secret society. This dance and the society took on a particular political significance in the 1990s.

Musical instruments differ less than do the songs and dances. Most are commonly found across the region of southern Africa.

Not surprisingly, the drum is ubiquitous. Small or large, the drum can be heard for miles across country summoning people to a village ceremony or festival. Again, it is the drum, of course, that also provides the basic rhythms for the dances.

As in the rest of southern Africa, the playing of the marimba or mambilira is becoming more popular, partly because it is attractive to the ears of visitors accustomed to western music. In fact, this xylophone-like instrument probably has its origins in Indonesia and was introduced to Africa, via Mozambique, two thousand years ago. Less likely to be seen is the hand-held *mbira* which is common in other parts of the region, especially in Zimbabwe. This little instrument, comprising metal strips or keys mounted on a wooden sounding board is technically related to the piano.

As in the rest of Africa, the use of a chrodophone or stringed instrument is now rare although it may have been common in the past. Only the single stringed fiddle (*zeze*) is to be seen occasionally. Dancers will often have bells or rattles, some attached to their costume, to create their own music.

If there are few instruments to accompany the various elaborate and story-telling dances, their lack is more than made up for by enthusiastic, even frenetic, chanting and singing. Most often the dancer or troupe of dancers will perform with a group of singers. The dances are almost always energetic and very physical. There is a touch of the acrobatic about some of them. The story-line may not be easy to follow and interpretations will vary but someone will usually be on hand to volunteer a very detailed explanation.

Dancers' and musicians' dress varies. Masks figure prominently with dancers. Straw may be the chief material of the costume or, sometimes, what seems to the observer a bizarre use is made of western dress. Soccer strips are now quite common with musicians and there is a touch of the military about some of the costumes. The latter is well illustrated in the *beni* dance seen among the Yao.

Above: The musicians are about to break into a dance!

Beni comes from the English "band". The Yao were recruited into the King's African Rifles from the regiment's inception at the beginning of the 20th century, serving with distinction both as soldiers and porters, especially in the Great War. The *beni* dance comes particularly from that era and the incongruous military overtones have their origins in the experience of the serving men. Over time, much has been added, and even more lost, but the semi-military dress remains as evidence of the *beni's* provenance.

Visitors to Malawi may well have the opportunity to witness something of the music and dance of the country as hotels increasingly invite local villagers to perform for guests. These after dinner shows will probably whet the appetite for more authentic performances. For an experience of something closer to the traditional culture, it may be necessary to visit a village when some sort of celebration is taking place. Hotels and lakeshore lodges may be able to arrange this although just turning up (to the call of the drums) will not usually cause offence, rather the visitor will be made welcome.

Music and weddings are inseparable. The authors once attended three weddings in a single day having been invited in just because they stopped to watch at the roadside. Attendance at church services is another way to become part of the audience for, or even to participate in, an exciting musical event. Even the traditional Catholic Mass is transformed when the congregation is in full voice.

There have been some successes in exploiting the African sense of rhythm and cultural history of music by adapting it to a more modern idiom. Some groups have performed in Europe and their audio-tapes often sell quite well. It has to be said, however, that what is described as 'modern' Malawi music owes as much to the Caribbean, to New Orleans and to the pop groups of Europe and America as it does to Malawi itself. This music is another example of globalization and it is to be hoped that the traditional musical and dance culture will not be the victim.

Coins, Currency Notes and Stamps

Before 1971, Malawi's currency reflected its colonial roots with coins such as the shilling and the florin. When decimal currency was introduced, the basic unit became the *kwacha* divided into one hundred *tambala*. *Kwacha* means dawn and *tambala* is Chichewa for cockerel so that one hundred cockerels are said to herald the dawn. If travelling in the region it is important to note that Zambia also uses the *kwacha* (ZK) but there isn't parity with the Malawi *kwacha* (MK).

Six currency notes at values of K200, K100, K50, K20, K10 and K5 are in circulation. It is a reflection of the impact of inflation in Malawi that in 1971 the highest denomination note was K50. All the notes more recently carry, not the portrait of the President as in the days of Banda's rule, but one of John Chilembwe who is seen as a freedom fighter against colonialism.

Pictures on the front of the notes tell something of the economy and culture of modern Malawi. The blue K200 note shows the famous 'bread basket' building of the Reserve Bank in Lilongwe. Capital Hill, Lilongwe, is shown on the red K100 note while the turquoise K50 note has a picture of Blantyre's Independence Arch. The lower denomination notes are particularly interesting. The mauve K20 note shows a tea plantation which has what is intended to represent Mount Mulanje in the background. 'Girls in Education' is the theme of the drawing on the brown K10 note and shows three girls seated under a tree reading. The smallest value currency note, a green K5, has a picture of women pounding maize with the intriguing title: 'Food Security'. Note sizes vary according to their value: the higher the value, the larger the note.

The disastrous fall in the value of the *kwacha* has led to most of the coins, except the *kwacha* pieces, being almost valueless and the visitor to Malawi will rarely have need to use them. It certainly isn't worth waiting for change if less than one *kwacha*. Even so there are still one *tambala* coins to be seen. These are worth less than one-hundredth of an English penny or fractionally more than one hundredth of an American cent.

The obverse of the coins carries either the President's head or the Malawi coat of arms. Various designs decorate the reverse of the coins. The one *tambala*, appropriately depicts a cockerel while the one *kwacha* shows Malawi's national bird, the fish eagle. Sometimes, the Malawi coat of arms is on the reverse if the President's head is on the obverse. Animals and crops are also employed to adorn coins.

Khobidi is the Chichewa word for coin and *ndalama* means money.

Some foreign currency notes are generally accepted in hotels. These include the British pound, the American dollar and the South African rand.

The postal services in Malawi have a long and honourable history. The mail runners, the *tenga-tenga*, used to make long and often dangerous journeys to carry mail and messages (and even officials) between the small towns. Often they would be carrying messages for the District Commissioners to various administrative centres.

A wonderful little museum, the Mtenga-tenga Postal Hut, is well worth a visit. It is described in the section on getting to the Zomba Plateau. It is on the main road between Zomba and Blantyre.

Some of the first stamps in use were those of the British South Africa Company with the company's coat of arms and the motto: Justice, Commerce, Freedom. These stamps were overprinted B.C.A. (British Central Africa) and with their value. Some of these stamps were of remarkably high value.

When the Protectorate of Nyasaland was created, and up to the time of Independence, the stamps usually, but not always, carried the portrait of the current sovereign of the colonial power, Great Britain. The head of the king or queen was most often in the corner of the stamp with some design taking up the greater part of the stamp's area. The design might be a map of the country or a picture of an animal or, say, a portrait of a soldier in the King's African Rifles. Some of the stamps were 'double-size', carried no portrait of the sovereign and showed scenes of the country

such as Monkey Bay and the Lake or tea pluckers and Mount Mulanje.

Today, the stamps' designs follow a pattern which is common to many countries. Thus, a variety of themed stamps, at all values, showing pictures of Malawi's birds were current in 2001. Various themes are selected from time to time, a new range of stamps often bringing in additional revenue from collectors. Seasonal stamps are usually printed for Christmas or a new selection is designed and printed to commemorate a particular event or anniversary.

Used stamps can sometimes be obtained from Malawi High Commissions, Embassies or Missions around the world.

Above: Malawi's currency notes and coins. Right top: Birds were the theme of Malawi's stamps in 2001. Right: Post boxes through the ages at Mtenga-tenga Postal Museum south of Zomba.

PART FIVE: BUSINESS MALAWI

The Economy

Despite an encouraging growth in Malawi's economy immediately after Independence (1964), by the early 1980s a full-blown recession was evident. Measures to counter this downturn met only limited success and the multi-party democracy of the post-Banda era has continued to struggle to find satisfactory solutions. With its lack of minerals there is no sound base for mining; manufacturing is limited by inadequate investment and skill shortages and tourism has, in the past, been all but ignored as a major player. Thus Malawi has had to rely on agriculture to prop up a structurally unsound economy.

Agriculture
The majority of the country's population (85 per cent) is rural and farming provides 90 per cent of employment. The emergence of a cash-driven agricultural economy really dates from the 1880s, from the missionaries' early gardens, and from the Scottish Moir brothers who introduced the concept of trade in agricultural goods. The experimental planting of a variety of crops by the missionaries soon distinguished between those with potential and those doomed to fail. Instrumental in these early crop plantings was John Buchanan. He and his brother, Robert, introduced sugar cane, tobacco, coffee and tea to what was then the Central African Protectorate. Cotton had already been planted by David Livingstone and it was seen as the alternative to coffee when that crop failed.

Today, the agricultural sector accounts for nearly 40 per cent of the Gross Domestic Product (GDP). This reliance on agriculture is, in no small measure, the reason for Malawi's present position as one of the world's poorest countries. The sector is only now beginning to put its house in order, repealing a variety of restrictive measures which had grown up under Dr Banda's regime. Much of this liberalisation has been directed towards giving the private sector greater freedom.

Agriculture in Malawi is a mix of large estates (plantations), essentially monocultural, and smallholder farming for both subsistence and cash crops. The estates have generally fared better than the smallholdings which have often suffered from unfair trading practices in which the middlemen cream off profits from the sale of cash crops giving little incentive to the small farmers to improve standards and productivity.

The smallholders have also found that competition from the large estates has made the growing of some of the otherwise most attractive export crops uneconomic on the scale that they can hope to achieve.

Malawi's climate is not unattractive to successful farming. Only in the occasional years of low rainfalls or, conversely, of exceptionally heavy downpours, is there any problem in yields or the viability of particular crops. Most of the smallholders' problems derive from poor practices, a shameful disregard of the opportunities for irrigation and, most of all, from the very small scale at which private farms operate. Many of the farms operated by the smallholders are less than half a hectare in size. As a consequence, farming remains scarcely above subsistence level with cash crops playing too small a part in the economy of the smallholders.

Most (95 per cent) of Malawi's farming is crop production. Livestock rearing is a very subordinate but growing sub-sector. Maize dominates, taking over 70 per cent of the cultivated area. Although this is the country's staple food crop, yields are low and, dependent upon rainfall in a particular year, planting varies. A dramatic fall in maize production in 1997 was the result of unusual climatic conditions. Other smallholder crops include sorgum, grown largely where rainfall amounts are less reliable, a variety of peas and beans, potatoes, cassava, rice and groundnuts. The last two named crops are important cash crops although the export of groundnuts has decreased significantly in recent years.

The major cash crops are those in which the estates have a commanding involvement. Tobacco, which has accounted for an incredible 70 per cent of foreign exchange earnings, is grown on estates and by small farmers. Higher quality leaf tobacco such as Burley tends to be harvested from the estates but even so the decline in world markets and consequent increasing competition has hit Malawi's exports to a degree which is little short of disastrous. Even the recent downturn in Zimbabwe's economy, also heavily dependent upon tobacco, has failed to save the day for Malawi. At this late hour, the Malawi government is finally accepting the need for radical diversification of the economy.

Cane sugar is grown chiefly on two large estates, one in the south of the country in the Lower Shire Valley and the other on the shore of Lake Malawi. Tea is important on estates in the Thyolo and Mulanje region south-east of Blantyre. As with tobacco, coffee, macadamia and cashew nuts and rubber are grown both on estates and by smallholders. Cotton is largely a smallholder crop with output very sensitive to fluctuating demand. Cattle ranching and poultry rearing are still underdeveloped but growing in importance.

For many years to come, agriculture will remain singly the most important sector of Malawi's economy in terms of its contribution to the GDP and to foreign exchange earnings and, most of all, to employment. Changes will undoubtedly occur. The programmes of privatisation of related activities, such as canning and seed and fertiliser production, are steps towards much needed reform.

Tobacco can no longer be relied upon to prop up the whole economy and alternatives will have to be found both within agriculture and outside it. Experiments in horticulture have been tried, with limited success but the search for new crops and new methodologies will continue. The utilisation of waters of Lake Malawi for irrigation purposes, allowing for double- or even triple-cropping is long overdue. The large scale cultivation of high-value tropical fruits and vegetables for the European markets must also be explored seriously.

Agro-Industry

Although highly dependent upon its agricultural base, the economy has failed fully to exploit the potential for agro-industries. Tobacco, sugar and tea, all estate products, have given rise to processing industries and these have had singular success. Bi-products from primary processing include ethanol, which goes to be blended with imported petrol, a confectionery industry, including soft drinks, and animal feedstuffs, especially seed cake from edible oil seeds.

Much processing is on a small scale, no more evident than in the milling of maize, the country's staple food crop. There are thousands of small-scale millers with primitive machinery. A common sight in the villages is the queue of women with their crop outside the local mill.

The small scale of these agro-industries mirrors farming practice and again there is scope for rationalisation and improvements in methods and distribution. There have been serious disincentives to the development of agro-industries. The dominance of the Press Corporation (Press Group) under Banda led to smaller companies operating under severe and unfair competition. The tax system, often in the form of double taxation on the import of capital goods such as machinery required for food processing, has not helped. Import liberalisation, too, has been seen as unfair competition at this critical stage in the country's economic development.

The dairy industry, poultry and meat processing are all in need of investment and improved distribution. Meat production is underdeveloped. There is a need for modern and more widely located abattoirs. A restrictive tax system has, in the past, held back both processed meats and poultry production. In the case of poultry, the import of feedstuffs has been expensive and, as a consequence, the import of frozen birds from Malawi's southern neighbours, especially Zimbabwe, has been seen as the cheaper alternative to home production.

The absence of a strong canning and packaging industry has held back a variety of agro-industries. These range from brewing and milk to meat and fruit. For a country so dependent upon agriculture it is often surprising to find that so much of its foodstuffs are imported. This is no more so than at the luxury or semi-luxury end of the market. The hotels catering for visiting foreigners rely heavily on imported food for their kitchens. As tourism develops, it is to be hoped that the consequent rise in demand for such goods will encourage more home production.

The future for Agriculture and Agro-Industries

Some progress has been made over the last few years in providing assistance and incentives to the agricultural sector. The setting up of a marketing organisation, the Agricultural and Marketing Corporation (ADMARC) has assisted in providing a rational marketing facility to the smallholder farmer.

There has been a general shift away from what had been a trend in the 1970s of smallholder land being bought by estates. This latter move, encouraged by the World Bank in the 1980s may, however, need reappraisal in the future if the problem of attendant unemployment can be solved. The enormous growth in the population over the last fifty years, without a concomitant increase in manufacturing or service industries, poses the question: what do the people do if they cannot farm? On the other hand, the absurdly small size of some of the smallholdings is holding back the modernisation of agriculture in Malawi.

Most recently, in common with other sectors in the economy, there has been a move towards privatisation. Some of the bodies administering funds to agriculture as well as government-run cattle ranches, fruit canning and seed production have been targets for the Privatisation Commission. The full effect of these changes has yet to be assessed.

The removal of subsidies for a range of agricultural inputs, most especially fertilisers, has been a mixed blessing. Overseas aid has cushioned the effect on the smallholder farmers but the long-term results will be seen in the future. In 1999-2000 over a quarter-of-a-million farmers benefited from the Agricultural Investment Programme (APIP) which provides fertilisers and seed while even more, nearly three million farms, received seed from the Starter Pack Scheme (SPS) which relies heavily on donor support from outside Malawi. As so often many fundamental problems remain unsolved, and even unexplored, while donors provide props.

Fishing

Despite its land-locked position in central Africa, Malawi has the vast resource of Lake Malawi. This is Africa's third largest lake and its fishing industry provides employment for perhaps some quarter of a million Malawians. Almost more important is the fact that 60 to 70 per cent of the animal based protein in Malawi's diet comes from fish.

As with agriculture, there are the same characteristics of smallness of scale of operation and outdated and inefficient practices. Despite the Lake Malawi's quite extraordinary abundance in terms of species, much of the fishing takes place close to the shore and in shallow lake Malombe. This is due largely to the fact that small craft, unsuitable for deep water fishing, are used. There has been little change in fishing practices over the last century.

While fishing is undoubtedly of importance to the Malawian diet and to the economy of Lake Malawi's littoral villages, its contribution to the economy as a whole is held back by lack of investment in the construction of larger vessels, in distribution, in canning, in refrigeration and in research. Over recent years there has been over-fishing especially for the well known chambo.

What has the potential for contributions to exports has become an industry under threat. This is mostly through the uncontrolled activities of the small fishermen rather than by commercial fishing. Maldeco is one of the very few major commercial operators.

Control and research are needed if the fishing industry is to play a part in reviving Malawi's economy. Fish farming has begun to develop but remains in its infancy and concentrates on replenishing the dwindling numbers of chambo. Yet again, as with irrigation and tourism, the great resource that is Lake Malawi has not been realised.

Some of the high plateau, notably Zomba and Nyika, are known for their sport fishing for trout. Perhaps there are opportunities for commercial fishing in the form of fish farms in these locations.

Forestry

If one asks any Malawian, returning to the country after an absence of some years, what he first notices he will almost always reply, "Where have all the trees gone?" The country is rapidly being deforested.

The reason for this state of affairs, a wholesale depletion of the once splendid forest cover, is not hard to find. It can be explained by the single fact that population growth has created a demand that cannot be met if the forests are to be safeguarded. Fuel wood, for cooking and for tobacco curing, is in such short supply that even the posts erected to carry telephone wires are not safe.

Many of the valuable hardwoods take forty or fifty years to mature and reforestation has hardly begun to redress the balance between felling and replanting. Where replanting has taken place it is often with non-indigenous trees that are faster growing, but the problem remains that more cutting takes place than planting. A national tree planting day was instituted, recently extended to become a tree planting week, but the solution probably lies in another sector of the economy, namely energy production and distribution. The (perceived) need for firewood must be challenged by alternatives.

As the tree cover reduces, there are problems of soil erosion and even flooding, especially near the escarpment edges. The reduction in tree cover over the last few decades is having a profoundly harmful effect on Malawi's environment and hence its economy.

What wood is cut but not burned goes to the construction industry and to the production of furniture and matches. The forests of Zomba provide timber for the construction industry and those of the Viphya Plateau are used for making plywood and other products. It is worth noting that wood is also the medium for most of Malawi's famous carvings. There is a certain irony in the fact that, in a country whose forests are regularly burnt, matches are an important product of the Zomba Plateau softwoods.

Energy

There are no known oil or gas reserves in Malawi but coal is mined. Recent research has suggested the possibility of oil or gas below Lake Malawi but, even if proved, the production difficulties and time lags are such that the country's economy over the next couple of decades is unlikely to be affected beyond what would arise from exploration. In the foreseeable future, oil will continue to be an import. Coal production from the Mchenga mine is comparatively small but yields are increasing after a degree of privatisation.

Almost all of Malawi's electricity comes from hydro-power. The most recent development has been the construction of a major hydro-electric power station at the Kapichira Falls on the Lower Shire river. This will go some way towards solving a problem that is revealed in the telling statistic that only four percent of Malawi's population has access to and use of electricity. The link between this fact and the depletion of the forests is self-evident. Among the rural population, that is the majority, the comparable figure for use and availability is usually accepted as being just one percent.

Recent liberalisation, part privatisation, has opened the energy industry door to private investment. A glance at Malawi's climate data and topography clearly shows that the country has significant potential for further development of hydro-electric power. The costs, however, will be large if this potential is to be realised because of the almost complete absence of a distribution infrastructure. The need for more electrical energy is clear but that is not the same as there being a proven demand. An industrial base, which might provide an eager market, is just not there. There is a classic "chicken and egg" problem here.

Mining

Apart from coal, mining and quarrying are limited to limestone and a few precious stones such as rubies and sapphires. The sector as a whole contributes less than one percent to the Gross National Product (GNP). Exploration suggests other minerals might be worth extracting, notably gold, uranium and potash. Alluvial gold deposits, recently discovered at Dwangwa, may prove workable but whether the kimberites at Rhumpi actually contain diamonds only time will tell. Bauxite, from Mulanje, and glass sands are also on the list of minerals which may have a future.

Manufacturing

Manufacturing industries, apart from those in agro-businesses, already discussed, play a small role in the country's overall economy. There are a number of reasons why this is so. Its land-locked position forces up transport costs. South Africa and Zimbabwe tend to dominate the sector in the southern African region. Malawi has to import over 60 percent of its industrial raw materials and capital goods. Energy supply is geographically limited and, above all, there is a very low level of domestic demand. The country is, after all, one of the poorest on the globe.

Manufacturing for the export market has been especially poorly financed while tobacco, sugar and tea were seen as the main foreign exchange earners. Now their fragility on world markets has been exposed, there is an urgent need to find substitutes both in manufacturing as well as in service industries such as tourism.

All too often it has been cheaper to import a vast range of goods rather than to manufacture them at home. Much of the legislation prior to the political changes of 1994 actually inhibited the growth of manufacturing. Fortunately many of the regulations have been repealed or reversed and privatisation has created a much more healthy climate for growth. It is to be hoped that recent exchange rate problems, illustrated by the massive fall in the value of the *kwacha*, will be temporary.

The need to reduce the drain on foreign exchange caused by imports suggests that import-substitution industries should be encouraged but, with a weak domestic market, a longer term solution must lie in developing export-led manufacturing. An example can be set by textiles — so often the salvation of a developing country's ailing economy. Cotton, almost exclusively a smallholder crop, can be expanded and a lead has already been taken by attracting investment from Taiwan and South Africa. The export base does, of course, need to be diversified (there is the lesson of tobacco) but at least this is a start.

Along with tourism, manufacturing industry, beyond the narrow confines of agro-industry, will surely be the way forward for growth in Malawi's developing economy.

Tourism

Until the fall of Dr Banda in 1994, tourism was, in some respects, positively discouraged. The dress laws and a general atmosphere of indifference to the industry by government held back development despite some valiant attempts by more enlightened officials to introduce professional marketing and training. "The Warm Heart of Africa" — a slogan that has stood the test of time because of its basic truth — was first coined in the 1980s but numbers of tourists were so small that talk of a tourist industry was wishful thinking. There was a strong reliance on "friends and family" visitors and upon the apartheid South African market (they had little choice in the region).

Since 1994 there has been a more encouraging climate for the industry but it has only been in the last few years that there has been official realisation that tourism has the potential to make a significant contribution to Malawi's foreign exchange earnings. The rapid decline in income from tobacco has brought the matter to a head and government is now committed to promote tourism as a major player on the economic scene. Just how resources will be directed towards this aim remains to be seen.

Investment is seen as critical but where funds are to be directed is still a matter for debate. There is a danger that concentration on improvement and extension of facilities will go ahead while marketing may be starved of funds Yet marketing is an essential ingredient of growth. Indeed, it is the necessary precursor. Plans to build new hotels, to create cultural villages and to promote eco-tourism will be likely to fail if marketing remains under-funded. With occupancy rates already at unhealthy low levels, the need for more beds is questionable unless hotel building is foreshadowed by vigorous marketing to international tourists.

Official visitor rates often fail to stand up to careful scrutiny. A majority of tourist establishments remain unregistered and do not, therefore, contribute to the tourist tax base. There is a shortage of real expertise in parts of both the public and private sectors of the industry, leading to misunderstandings about priorities. The establishment of a private sector body, the Malawi Tourism Association (MTA), and the employment of a European-based, but globally active, promotion and marketing company, Geo Group and Associates, operating as Malawi Tourism, have been steps in the right direction. However, both these bodies suffer from pitiful under-funding.

Despite some recent encouraging moves, there remains a lack of effective co-operation between government and the private sector. Until this is rectified, progress will be limited and the modest targets (ten per cent per annum) for increases in numbers of foreign tourists are unlikely to be achieved. Yet with better directed funding the target figure could be doubled, for no one doubts the potential is there. A way ahead may be for new investment to include a contribution to the marketing of Malawi as a tourist destination.

Communications

Effective communications, both physical and electronic, is a *sine qua non* for a developing economy. The transport infrastructure of Malawi is, in many ways, superior to some of its neighbours. The road network is generally good and the building of such links as the extended M18 from Mchinji to Nkhotakota is an example of sensible evolution.

The standard of the roads varies. At their best they are more than adequate for the traffic they carry. Most of the major roads are tarred but not always well maintained. A tarred road that is beginning to break up is worse than a dirt road. Unfortunately, damaged surfaces are too often left to deteriorate instead of being repaired quickly while the problem is limited. The establishment of a National Road Authority has yet to prove to be a step in the right direction.

There remain significant sections of strategic roads which are left to wither away. The collapse of the Dwambazi Bridge on the M5 north of Dwangwa is a case in point as was the M10 west of Monkey Bay. The replacement of the bridge is long overdue. Inadequate signposting remains a further, yet easily tackled, problem.

The railway network, once a particular pride of Malawi, plays only a small part in passenger transport but serves a useful role in freight carrying. If the Nacala line to the Indian Ocean becomes fully operational, it is estimated that import costs would fall dramatically. During the long Mozambique civil war, Malawi's land-locked position was highlighted by the doubling of transport costs for goods re-routed away from the war zone.

Air transport remains in a state of flux. The most positive move in recent times has been the establishment of an efficient charter network which plays a critically important part in tourism development. The national carrier, Air Malawi, provides regional and national services but has inadequate funds properly to develop either. National route schedules are changed with alarming frequency and at little notice. Investment is needed to allow time for services to bed-down and prove their attractiveness, especially to the tourist market which needs certainty. At a regional scale, Air Malawi, provides a useful operation linking the country with its neighbours but the experiments in intercontinental services (to the UK) with Air Zimbabwe and, later, with Virgin Atlantic, despite early successes, have not been wholly satisfactory.

Moves to privatise the national airline have met with resistance but it will surely be only a matter of time before it will be accepted as the only viable option. There is also scope for a radical rethink on the way in which the regional network operates. There is a complex system of code sharing but political considerations often freeze out more commercially attractive arrangements. An example occurred when Comair, a British Airways associate, was refused landing rights into Blantyre and promptly withdrew all its services to Malawi.

Telecommunications are developing rapidly. International direct dialling is almost universally available and the digitalisation of the telephone system is proceeding. Breakdowns in the system do occur but are less frequent than in the past. Cellular phones, based on the GSM standard, are generally reliable. Currently, there are two operators in the field; Celtel and Telekom Network Malawi (TNM).

The use of the internet has revolutionised international communications especially in the private sector. Government offices are comparatively slow in adopting this form of rapid and inexpensive communication perhaps because of a lack of training. The most widely used Internet Service Provider (ISP) is MalawiNet Ltd. This is a commercial company formed as a joint venture between the Malawi Posts and Telecommunications Corporation (MPTC) and the American USCOMNET Inc.

Postal services are better than in many of the countries neighbouring Malawi and the DHL courier service operates efficiently.

The introduction of a national television service, albeit with a very limited broadcast output, was a notable innovation in 1999. However, with so few Malawians being able to access electricity, let alone afford a television set, there will be little incentive for growth. Most of the larger hotels rely on satellite stations. Radio broadcasts are much more widely received and the BBC World Service has very recently begun to broadcast on FM frequencies in Lilongwe and Blantyre.

Opportunities and Investment

The climate is increasingly favourable for investment in a number of sectors of Malawi's economy. This fact arises from the avowed aim of government to attract foreign investment and from the real potential for growth in a significant number of economic activities. The country's political stability is also encouraging.

In recent years, the active encouragement of private investment by the state has been underpinned by moves to facilitate rather than to regulate. This has included the virtual elimination of price controls together with the withdrawal of import restrictions and their attendant licences. Although ever eager to attract large scale investment from overseas, the size of an investment is not restricted, small or large. Initially through the Malawi Investment Promotion Agency, the moves to attract both import and export-led activities have met with more success than sceptics believed possible. A variety of bodies such as the Malawi Development Corporation (MDC) and the Malawi Privatisation Commission act as catalysts for investment and, at the highest levels, government is not only sympathetic but positively welcoming.

In agriculture and agro-businesses the most obvious opportunities lie in the processing of farm products; maize, cassava, rice, fruit and vegetables, oilseed and rubber. If wheat growing can be encouraged in those areas with a favourable climate and soil, this is another crop which has significant attractions.

Meat production, milk and milk products, poultry and egg production give investment opportunities. Some of the estate products are already well catered for but bi-products from cane sugar and rubber are open to development.

Additionally, expansion of existing estate farming, preferably coupled with development of appropriate value-added integrated industrial growth, offers attractive propositions to foreign companies with expertise in these activities. Sugar, in particular, is a crop in which investment is sought.

One interesting agro-industry which is ripe for investment is the processing of tropical fruits for export and the home market. The most obvious here is the production of fruit juice concentrates, especially from oranges. A project which is at the examination stage is in Mwanza, in South Malawi, where most of the country's crop is grown. There is a need to raise the standards of fruit products coming off the farms but this is a matter of education in farming practices and not confined to fruit. Linked with the potential for irrigation from Lake Malawi, tropical fruit production and processing is one of the most exciting possibilities for future investment.

Cotton was once a major feature of Malawi's exports, the David Whitehead company being especially well known and respected in the United Kingdom. Production of cotton needs to be boosted with special attention to quality and yields but there is little doubt that this labour intensive rather than capital intensive industry, with relatively low skill requirements, could make an important contribution to Malawi's economy in the 21st century. There is considerable scope not only for expansion of raw cotton output but, particularly, for the manufacture of cotton goods, clothing, bed linen and soft furnishings. Cotton should be seen as a priority in Malawi's investment strategy.

The need for more pesticides and fertilisers is seemingly insatiable. Chemical fertilisers, especially sulphate and phosphate based, are particularly in demand. There are opportunities to couple these products with opportunities in the mining of phosphates, but other mining investment possibilities require more exploratory work.

Forestry, in the form of both afforestation and reforestation, invites investment. Here again there are clear links with parasitic industries such as wood products for the construction industry. It is noteworthy that the government plans to sell its holding in Leopard Matches because this is illustrative of opportunities arising from privatisation. Other examples include financial services (building society sector), airport catering and property development (MPICO holdings). Investors are being presented with a one-off chance to enter into areas of economic activity previously the preserve of government.

A parallel situation exists with the Press Corporation. Established in 1961 by Dr Banda (as Malawi Press Ltd) this was the mouthpiece and the breadwinner of the Malawi Congress Party. With a voracious appetite for growth, Press became one of the largest corporations in the whole of southern Africa. It still has interests in an exceptional number of sectors from mining to tourism. However, the Press Corporation is now keen to develop partnerships with foreign investors in many of its activities.

The fishing industry is expected to expand through the development of fish farming and the use of larger vessels capable of harvesting the deeper off-shore waters of Lake Malawi. There is a double opportunity here because tourism is also looking to the construction of cruise vessels to ply the lake.

The MDC and the Ministry of Tourism, on the look out for investors, have recently embarked on an EU-funded study of development opportunities, especially in hotel building. Two hurdles have to be cleared before these opportunities will be truly attractive. Firstly, the potential for international visitors has properly to be marketed, and funds released to do this. Secondly, the transport infrastructural support needs to be in place: better roads and more attractive international air connections to markets. On a different scale, there are very clear gaps in the provision of good class restaurants and in the car hire business. The latter is currently effectively almost unregulated and there is a perceived need for reliable car hire operators especially in the field of self-drive for tourists.

Power generation and distribution without which most other development will falter, has opportunities for investors at all scales. ESCOM, formerly a parastatal company with government owning 100 per cent of the shares, has converted to a limited incorporated company. The private sector is now able to play a role in generation, transmission and distribution. With so small a proportion of the population able to tap into the electricity network, the scope for investment is enormous whether it be in the manufacture of small diesel driven turbines or the development of regional and national grids.

The government's stated wish to privatise the national airline, currently offers one of the largest investment opportunities ever in Malawi. It is perhaps something of an indicator of the politics that overshadow this particular privatisation, that the contract, which Speedwing (British Airways consultancy division) had to advise on the future of Air Malawi, was prematurely curtailed.

A sector of the economy which cries out for investment from overseas is that prerequisite: training. One of the biggest handicaps to development of Malawi's economy is the low skill base from which it has to launch new activities. Particular sectors which might welcome the setting up of training schools are IT, tourism and catering, business management and electronics.

Finally a long neglected resource, water, offers opportunities for companies with interests and expertise in irrigation. There is no doubt whatsoever that this can be singly the most important innovation for the future of Malawi's agriculture which, for the foreseeable future, will remain the number one sector in the country's economy.

Finance

The financial services sector, a platform for the whole economy, is overseen by the Reserve Bank of Malawi. The Bank (established in 1965) is the supervisory authority for all financial services activities. With government, it has, since 1994, attempted to liberalise the sector including the sale of banks formerly owned by the State or State enterprises. An example of this broadening of ownership and acceptance of foreign investment into the sector occurred in 1999 when NEDCOR (South Africa) bought a controlling 75 per cent share in the Finance Corporation of Malawi (FINCOM) from the ADMARC subsidiary AIHC (ADMARC Investment Holding Company). In like manner, the largest commercial bank in the country, the National Bank of Malawi, now has seven per cent of its equity sold to the public.

The programmes of privatisation, the establishment of the Malawi Stock Exchange in 1995 and the passing of the Capital Markets Development Act have all been steps towards attracting foreign investment into the country. Foreign investment has come and gone in some enterprises since privatisation. The national network of buses and long distance coaches, for example, was taken over by the UK-based company Stagecoach but has now reverted to Malawi ownership with ADMARC owning 71 per cent of the newly formed company Shire Bus Lines. Such withdrawals by foreign companies should not necessarily be seen as failures.

The absence of established venture capital sponsors is partly compensated for by the provision of capital and long term funding which is available through MDC and the Investment and Development Bank of Malawi (INDEBANK). The latter is owned by a number of institutions including some which are state funded in European countries.

The largest, and most active, financial services in Malawi are those in the business of insurance. Dominant are Old Mutual (a southern African regional giant of a company) and the National Insurance Company of Malawi (NICO). The latter, is part owned by Press and MDC and has wide interests, especially in property. Many other small players in the field are off-shoots of United Kingdom insurance companies.

The accountancy profession is well represented with some internationally renowned companies such as Deloitte & Touche, KPMG and PricewaterhouseCoopers, in the field.

In many ways cash is king in Malawi. Business to business transactions are generally not affected but many day-to-day activities (in shops, petrol stations, etc.) there is no avoiding dealing in cash. Consequently, security becomes an attendant problem.

Bank accounts denominated in foreign (hard) currency are restricted to companies which actually earn foreign exchange. This includes most of the tourist industry.

On the periphery of financial services are numerous firms specialising in company law and a smaller number of real estate companies. In the latter category, Knight Frank, is the oldest and largest.

New investors into Malawi's economy would be well advised to seek assistance as they make their way through a labyrinth of financial regulations that, despite liberalisation, still have the propensity to trip up the unwary.

Incentives

A large number of policies have been put in place by government to encourage the private sector, including foreign investors, to play an active role in the economy. Implementation of some of the policies has been slow so that their true effect has yet to be seen. Anxious to see results, government has recently set up a Task Force, comprising both government and private sector representatives, to turn policy into practice.

Many of the government initiatives and the investment incentives which are outlined below are still in their infancy. No doubt some will fail to mature while other schemes will become operative as time goes on. It has to be accepted that Malawi's economy is in the early stages of its development and no one can say exactly what direction its evolution might take.

Many of the incentives have themselves evolved over the past decade since the Investment Promotion Act was passed in 1991. This established the Malawi Investment Promotion Agency (MIPA). Those shown below are operative at the time of writing.

General Incentives
- The corporate tax rate is 38 per cent for companies whose headquarters are in Malawi and 43 per cent for those whose head offices are outside Malawi.
- New investments between US$ 5 million and US$ 10 million are given the option of paying 15 per cent corporate tax indefinitely or taking a five-year tax holiday. Investments in excess of US$ 10 million have the option of paying 15 per cent corporate tax indefinitely or taking a ten-year tax holiday. If a foreign investment is involved, the foreign capital contribution should not be less than 30 per cent.
- There is no withholding tax on dividends.
- Tax allowances include: a 40 per cent allowance on new buildings and machinery; an additional 15 per cent allowance for investment in certain designated areas; up to 20 per cent allowance for used buildings and machinery; a 50 per cent allowance for approved training costs.
- Duty-free import of raw materials for the manufacturing industry.

- Duty-free import of heavy commercial vehicles (defined as those with a capacity of not less than ten tonnes).
- 100 per cent deduction for manufacturing company operating expenses in the first two years of operation.
- Indefinite loss carry forward to allow investing companies to take full advantage of tax allowances.

Fiscal Incentives
- To encourage the development of securities markets, through the Capital Market Development Act, there are no restrictions on issues of securities to the public nor are there restrictions on private placement of securities to Malawi residents. However, transfer of securities to non-residents should be registered with the Reserve Bank.

Free access to foreign exchange for investors for the purposes of paying for imports and transferring financial payments abroad. This free access includes:
- No licensing requirements for importing foreign exchange;
- Full repatriation of profits, dividends, investment capital and interest and principal payments for international loans;
- Unrestricted access to local financing facilities;
- Interest rates are market-based and no government controls on credit.

Export Incentives for Industries Manufacturing in Bond
- There is an export tax allowance equal to 12 per cent of export revenue for "non-traditional" exports.
- A transport tax allowance of 25 per cent is available on international transport costs, excluding "traditional" exports.
- No value added tax.
- No excise taxes on purchases of raw or packaging materials made in Malawi.
- There is a duty drawback on imports of raw materials or packaging made in Malawi.
- No duties on imports of capital equipment, raw materials or packaging materials.
- There is 100 per cent duty-free import on equipment and raw materials for companies engaged exclusively in horticultural products for export.

Export Incentives for Export Processing Zones
In 1995 Export Processing Zones (EPZ) were set up under the Investment Promotion Act. Certain incentives are available to companies operating in an EPZ. These include:
- No corporate tax.
- No withholding tax on dividends.
- No value added tax.
- No duty on capital equipment or on raw

materials.
- A transport tax allowance of 25 per cent for international transport costs.
- No excise taxes on purchases of raw materials and packing materials made in Malawi.

Investment Guarantees

As a signatory to a number of international treaties, Malawi provides protection for foreign investments. The main treaties are:
- Multilateral Investment Guarantee Agency (MIGA).
- International Centre for Settlement of Investment Disputes (ICSID).
- Bilateral Investment Protection and Promotion Agreements with a number of countries including China, Malaysia and Mauritius.

International Connections

Malawi has, since independence, had a very open mind about joining international organisations to further trade. Currently, Malawi is a member of:
- UN (United Nations)
- The Commonwealth
- SADC (Southern African Development Corporation)
- COMESA (Common Market for Eastern and Southern Africa)
- AU (African Union) — formerly OAU (Organisation of African Unity)
- IMF (International Monetary Fund)
- The World Bank

Malawi has trade agreements with:
- South Africa and Zimbabwe (bilateral trade agreements)
- Denmark, France, Kenya, the Netherlands, Norway, South Africa, Sweden, Switzerland and the United Kingdom (double taxation treaties)
- European Union (Lome Convention: preferential access to EU markets)
- GATT (General Agreement on Tariffs and Trade).

State, Parastatal and Private Organisations

The list below includes the more important organisations which investors may encounter.
- Agricultural Development and Marketing Corporation (ADMARC)
- Business Council
- Business Forum
- Electricity Supply Corporation of Malawi (ESCOM)
- Finance Corporation of Malawi (FINCOM)
- Independent Development Bank of Malawi (INDEBANK)
- Malawi Chamber of Commerce and Industry (MCCI)
- Malawi Development Corporation (MDC)
- Malawian Enterprise Trust
- Malawian Entrepreneurs Development Institute
- Malawi Export Promotion Council (MEPC)
- Malawinet Ltd
- Malawi Privatisation Commission
- Malawi Property Investment Co. Ltd. (MPICO Ltd)
- Malawi Telecom
- Ministry of Agriculture and Irrigation Development
- Ministry of Commerce and Industry
- Ministry of Finance
- Ministry of National Resources and Environmental Affairs
- Ministry of Tourism, Parks and Wildlife
- Ministry of Water Development
- National Economic Council
- National Insurance Company of Malawi (NICO)
- National Road Authority
- Reserve Bank of Malawi
- Small Enterprise Development Organisation

It must be pointed out that regulations and state institutions change from time to time, often far too frequently. Foreigners wishing to invest in or do business with Malawi will need to check the current situation.

PART SIX: FACTS AT YOUR FINGERTIPS

Visa and immigration requirements

A full valid passport is required for entry to Malawi though visitors from many countries do not need to arrange visas. Currently, citizens of the following countries do NOT need visas but will automatically receive a tourist pass for 30-days (or up to 3 months with proof of a later departure): Commonwealth countries (excluding India, Nigeria and Pakistan), European Union Countries, Iceland, Israel, Japan, Madagascar, Norway, San Marino and the USA. Since such regulations may be changed at any time, it is worthwhile for all nationals of these, as well as all other countries, to check with the nearest Malawian diplomatic mission, or the Deputy Chief Immigration Officer in Blantyre well in advance of travel. The official pre-requisite is for all travellers to have an onward ticket to a country to which they have the right of entry, or the cash resources to acquire one.

Health requirements

It is most important that travellers consult their doctor or a travel clinic to obtain the latest advice on immunisations.

At present, the following immunisations are usually advised before entering Malawi: polio, tetanus, typhoid fever and hepatitis A. Malaria prophylactics are also recommended. Yellow fever immunisation is not needed for Malawi, but an immunisation certificate is required if entering the country from the old yellow fever endemic zone (e.g. Zambia). Cholera and rabies are limited and vaccination is usually only recommended for those at particularly high risk.

Customs

International travellers over the age of 18 may import the following items free of duty: 200 cigarettes or 225 gm tobacco, 1 litre spirits, 1 litre beer and 1 litre wine, a reasonable quantity of consumable goods to meet the passenger's immediate needs while travelling within Malawi.

International flights

The following airlines serve Malawi: Air Malawi, British Airways, KLM, Kenya Airways, Air Zimbabwe, Ethiopian Airlines, South African Airways and Air Tanzania. Most international services are to and from Lilongwe International Airport, 26 kilometres north of the city, though some regional routes use Blantyre's Chileka Airport. Both airports have car hire, banks and tourism information.

Departure tax

When leaving the country by air, a tax of US$20 per person is levied. Vouchers are purchased in the airport entrance hall but must be paid for in US$ (currency which should be available in main bank branches).

Arrival by road

Malawi has road border points with all its neighbours: Zambia, Mozambique and Tanzania. Opening times should be 06.00-18.00.

Vehicle permits

Without a *carnet de passage*, a temporary import permit (TIP) is required to bring a vehicle into Malawi. These are obtained at border posts for a small fee.

Driver's licence

A full international driver's licence is required and a minimum age of 25 with 2 years driving experience may be asked for if hiring a car.

Road rules and signs

Malawians drive on the left and the use of safety belts is mandatory. There are two main speed limits — 80 kilometres (50 miles) per hour on main roads and 60 kilometres (38 miles) per hour in towns and villages. Seat belts must be worn in the front seats and red emergency triangles must be carried. The limited road signs indicate towns and distances but rarely road numbers. Signposts are not guaranteed even at major junctions so it is important to keep a close eye on the map to anticipate turnings.

Insurance

Third-party insurance is compulsory for all drivers. This can be purchased at border posts, or arranged through car hire companies.

Petrol and diesel

There is a good network of petrol stations covering all but the most remote rural areas.

Road conditions

The road network stretches for some 28,000 kilometres (17,500 miles), with major highways linking the main destinations. Roads are single carriageway and traffic volumes are low. However, the standard of the surfaces is variable and can be poor. The main towns and major routes have tarmac roads, though only the most recently built or upgraded roads have consistent surfaces. Older tarmac can be heavily potholed. Rural links and routes in national parks and wildlife reserves are dirt roads. Many can be quite acceptable but rains and surface water cause problems, particularly on slopes. When wet, roads become muddy skid pans; having dried, the remaining channels and potholes provide obstacles. Four-wheel drive is needed for the wet season on many of these roads, and even in the dry season some may be impassable by saloon car, due to low ground clearance.

Car hire
Hire cars are available but prices are high and standards are not all they should be. Most of the cars will have a few 'superficial' problems: cracked windows; creased wings; missing wing mirrors. It is worth checking out the vehicle — at least for a spare tyre, tool kit and red emergency triangles. The usual selection of car 'groups' is available. Air conditioning should be considered if driving on dirt roads to allow windows to be shut and keep the dust out. Hire is available on a 'per km' rate or with unlimited distance. If touring the country, it is easy to achieve the necessary average daily journeys (100 to 200 km) to make unlimited distance the most economic. Chauffeurs are also available at a not unreasonable charge, though costs increase if travelling away from the town of hire.

Public transport and taxis
In the main towns, a very small number of taxis operate, most easily found at the large hotels. For hitch-hikers there are numerous *matola* cars or pick-up trucks which pack themselves full of passengers for a small charge. These are either drivers doing the journey anyway (possibly returning from a delivery job) or they are purpose driven to collect passengers. These creaking, overloaded vehicles are cheap and quite common. Because of this form of transport, most people offering a lift to hitchhikers will expect a small payment. The bus network is quite extensive, and reasonably comfortable and efficient. Shire Bus Lines is the main operator, running everything from luxury long-distance coaches to local rural services. International coach routes connect Lilongwe and Blantyre with Lusaka, Harare and Johannesburg. (See Listings for bus companies). The *mv Ilala* is a passenger ferry boat operating on Lake Malawi. It travels between Monkey Bay in the south and Chilumba in the north, stopping regularly in between. The north-south journey takes approximately three days, with the round trip operating on a weekly schedule. Cabins are available and cars can be carried. Bookings can be made through Ulendo Safaris (see Listings). There is a limited rail network in Malawi, largely used for freight.

Domestic air services
Air Malawi's scheduled domestic services currently connect Lilongwe, Blantyre, Mzuzu, Karonga, and the southern lakeshore (Club Makokola). Proflight Air Services links the main towns with the lakeshore and the national parks. These are charter, not scheduled flights but there are regular departures and fixed prices for particular routes. Locations served include: Lilongwe, Salima (central lakeshore), Club Makokola (southern lakeshore), Mvuu (Liwonde National Park), Mzuzu, Chelinda (Nyika National Park), Likoma Island, Chintheche (northern lakeshore), and Mfuwe (Luangwa Valley, Zambia).

Currency
The Malawian currency is the *kwacha* (abbreviated to MK internationally, K or Kw locally) which is divided into 100 *tambala* (t). Since *kwacha* means 'dawn' and *tambala* 'cockerel' so 100 cockerels herald the dawn. Notes are available in K200, K100, K50, K20, K10 and K5 denominations, below which there are now only coins. The *kwacha* quartered in value relative to the pound sterling through 1994 and 1995 and suffered further slumps in 2000. Approximate exchange rates were as follows in 2002: 95K-£1; 68K-1US$; 6K — ZAR1.

Currency regulations
There is no limit on the amount of foreign currency which can be brought into the country though all should be declared on arrival to prevent any restriction on the same amount being taken out when departing. For Malawian currency, K200 is the current limit for export.

Banks
There is usually a choice of bank branches in the towns, open from 08.00 to 13.00 Monday to Friday. Mobile banks operate along the lakeshore and in more remote areas (check days and times of visits locally). For currency exchange, banks will accept traveller's cheques and notes of most major foreign currencies, though US dollars, South African rand and pounds sterling are favoured. Cashiers in the main hotels, and a small number of foreign exchange bureaux, offer similar services. Foreign currency notes can also be bought though they are in short supply and only available in the main towns after the daily exchange rate has been fixed.

Credit cards
Major hotels, restaurants and car hire companies do accept credit cards, but away from Blantyre, Lilongwe and the 'up-market' tourism industry,

their use is limited. Credit cards can also be used to draw cash in the main bank branches, though the process can take a day or more.

Government
Until 1994 Malawi was ruled as a single-party state by self-declared 'President for Life' Dr Hastings Kamuzu Banda. Multi-party elections for parliament and the Presidency now take place every five years. The current President is Dr Bakili Muluzi of the United Democratic Front (UDF). Muluzi and his party won the 1994 election and retained power in 1999.

The UDF government has embarked on a Poverty Alleviation Programme and aims to liberalise the economy to allow more open market operations. The establishment of the Malawi Stock Exchange, a privatisation programme, reduction of price controls and a flexible exchange rate policy are measures intended to counter the narrow export base and dependency on imported manufactured goods. It is hoped that creating an environment which favours the operation of private enterprise and encourages private investment will provide a boost to Malawi's economy.

Membership
International: Commonwealth, World Trade Organisation/General Agreement of Trade and Tariff (WTO/GATT); International Labour Organisation (ILO); International Monetary Fund (IMF); Non-aligned Movement; United Nations (UN); World Bank; World Health Organisation (WHO).

Regional: African Development Bank; Common Market for East and Southern Africa (COMESA); African Union (AU) (formerly Organisation of African Unity/OAU); Southern African Development Community (SADC).

Languages
The national language is Chewa (or Chichewa — literally 'language of the Chewa'), with Nyanja, Yao and Tumbuka (common in the north) the next most used local languages. However, English is the official language and is widely used, particularly in the commercial sector, as the primary language.

Religion
Eighty per cent of the population is Christian with the Church of Central Africa Presbyterian the strongest in the country. Muslims account for 13 per cent, squeezing indigenous beliefs to a small minority. Though the missionaries were responsible for some magnificent buildings, rural Malawians often worship with undimmed enthusiasm in simple open sided shelters. There is freedom of worship and the election of a Muslim president by the majority Christian electorate illustrates the lack of religious tension.

Business hours
Shops usually are open from 08.00 to 17.00 and are increasingly staying open through the traditional 12.00 to 13.00 lunchtime closing.

Security
Despite occasional high profile incidents, Malawi is a comparatively safe country and travellers rarely feel concerned about their own safety or the security of their belongings. Burglaries have increased and protection of premises is more noticeable but personal safety is rarely an issue for travellers. One or two township areas round Blantyre should be avoided and travel after nightfall is unwise, but the over-riding friendliness of the people shines through on most occasions.

Communications
Telephone: The telephone system in Malawi is rather poor and often frustrating. For those wishing to send faxes from Malawi it may be worth trying to sweet talk a local businessman to avoid the somewhat exorbitant charges made by the hotels. As well as the hotels, a small number of commercial outlets offer internet access and email. Local numbers are six digits with no area codes — Lilongwe numbers begin with a 7 and Blantyre's with 6. For the domestic operator dial 0 and for directory enquiries 191. The emergency number in Blantyre and Lilongwe only is 199. For International Direct Dialling, 101 is the prefix to dial out of the country and 265 to dial in. The international operator is on 102. Progress is now being made on the replacement of the old system with digital and electronic exchanges and mobile cellular 'phones have been introduced to the country in the last few years (numbers beginning with 8 or 9).

Post: There are post offices in most towns open Monday to Friday 07.30 to 12.00 and 13.00 to 17.00. Main hotel receptions also supply stamps and have a collection box for postcards and letters. The postal system is not especially efficient, particularly internationally. Postal addresses are usually simply PO Box or Private Bag numbers as there is no domestic delivery service. There is a *poste restante* service available in the main towns which allows visitors to receive mail. DHL is the only major international courier firm operating in Malawi and has offices in the main towns.

Media
Newspapers: *The Daily Times, The Nation, The Independent, The Malawi Times, The Malawi News, The Enquirer, Newsday.*

Radio stations: Malawi Broadcasting Company (on FM, MW and SW), BBC World

Service (SW and now also on FM), Voice of America (SW), a small number of independent FM stations.

TV: Malawi TV is very new and broadcasts for a limited time during the day. BBC World Service TV, CNN and M-Net are all received via satellite.

Energy

Supply is based on the 220/240 volts system, using "British type" square bayonet three-pin plugs.

Medical services

There are state hospitals of varying sizes in Malawi, the largest in the regional capitals. Medical practices and private hospitals can also be found in towns but only clinics in the rural areas. Health care and facilities can be at a basic level and ex-patriate residents usually travel to South Africa when in need of anything but the most straightforward medical care.

Medical insurance

Medical insurance should be purchased before arriving in Malawi. Emergency evacuation by air is now possible and this cover provides added peace of mind.

Chemists and pharmacies

It is worth carrying a simple sterile first aid kit (including syringes) as well as a full supply of any prescribed medicines as availability in Malawi is not guaranteed.

Liquor

For beers, Carlsberg is made locally under licence and their 'Green' (named simply after the colour of its label) is the most popular. The traditional brew from maize is sold as Chibuku. Spirits are also widely available, with gin and cane spirit made locally. The Malawi gin and tonic ('MGT') is a drink much loved by residents and visitors. Wines found are usually from South Africa and are quite reasonably priced. All liquor is available from supermarkets.

Tipping

Tipping is not a necessity and pressure is rarely unduly exerted. There is a service charge and tax on hotel and restaurant bills anyway.

Clubs

There is a handful of nightclubs in Lilongwe and Blantyre.

Daylight

Daylight varies by about an hour between winter (May to August), when there are around 11 hours of daylight, and summer (January to March), when there are 12 hours.

Time

Malawi time is Greenwich Mean Time plus two hours, the same Central African Time as South Africa. It is one hour ahead of Central European time, seven hours ahead of Eastern US time and 10 hours ahead of Western US time.

Climate

Malawi has three seasons:
May to August, cool and dry.
September to mid-November, hot and dry.
Mid-November to April, hot and wet.

ENGLISH-CHICHEWA

English	Chichewa
Meeting and greeting	
Hello	moni
Goodbye (when leaving someone)	tsalani bwino
Goodbye (when someone departs)	pitani bwino
Good day	zikomo
How are you?	muli bwanji?
I am fine	ndili bwino
Thank you very much	zikomo kwambiri
Good morning	mwadzuka bwanji?
Good night	gonani bwino
Please come in/Welcome	lowani
Where is the hotel?	Hotel ili kuti?
Please sit down (on the chair)	Khalani pampando
Where do you come from?	kodi kumudzi nkuti?
I come from . . .	Ndima chokera . . .ku..
What is your name?	Dzina lanu ndani?
My name is . . .	Dzina langa ndi . . .
Can you speak Chichewa?	Mumayankhula Chichewa
Only a little	Pang'ono
I want to learn more	Ndifuka kuphunzira
How do you find . . .?	Kodi . . . ?
I like it here	Ndikukukonda kuno
The weather is good	Nyengo ndiyabwino

English	Chichewa
Useful Words	
today	lero
tomorrow	mawa
now	tsopano
quickly	msanga
slowly	pang'onopang'ono
hospital	chipatala
police	polisi
friend	bwenzi
family	banja
Mr	Bambo
Mrs	Mayi
Miss	Mayi
I	ine
you	inu
she	iye
he	iye
we	ife
they	izo
what?	chiani?
who?	ndani?
when?	liti?
where?	kuti?
how?	bwanji
why?	chifukwa chiyani?
which?	chiti?
good	bwino

English	Chichewa
bad	ipa
beautiful	kukongola
money	ndalama
please	chonde
sorry	pepani
yes	inde
no	iyayi (ayi)
to/from	ku

English	Chichewa
Directions/emergency	
street/road	mseu
airport	bwalo andege
a little bit	pang'ono
a lot	zambiri
Go to the left	pita chakumanzere
Go to the right	pita chakumanja
Where are you going?	Mukupita kuti?
I am going to . . .	Ndikupita kuti . . .
Go straight	pita patsogolo
Please stop here	Chonde imani pano

English	Chichewa
Restaurants/shops/hotels	
hotel	hotel
room	chipinda
bed	kama/bedi
to eat	dya
to drink	mwa/imwa
to sleep	gona
to bathe	samba
to come	bwera
to go	pita
to stop	leka; letsa
to buy	gula
to sell	gulitsa
shop	sitolo
food	chakudya
coffee	khofi
tea	tiyi
beer	mowa
meat	nyama
fish	nsomba
bread	buledi
salt	mchere
matches	machesi
cold	wozizira
hot	tentha
I want	ndikufuna
I don't want	sindikufuna
What is this?	kodi ichi n'chiyani?
How much is it?	mumachita zingati?
Okay	chabwino
Excuse me	zikomo
Where is the toilet?	(Kodi) Chimbuzi chili kuti?
Where can I get a drink?	(Kodi) Chakumwa ndingachipeze kuti?
I won't take it, it's too expensive	Sindigula, mwadulitsa
Okay, I will buy it	Chabwino ndigula
Wait a minute	Dikirani pang'ono

In Brief

National Parks and Wildlife Reserves

Malawi has nine national parks and wildlife reserves located across its varied landscapes. Most are true wilderness areas which offer genuine and unique safari experiences. See also Part Four - Special Features.

Kasungu National Park
Size: 2316 sq km.
Geographical location: Central Malawi, its western edge running along the Zambian border. On the Central African Plateau.
Altitude: 1000 -1400 m above sea level.
Physical features: Undulating upland area intersected by rivers and dambos and punctuated by inselberg hills.
Vegetation: Mostly *miombo (Brachystegia)* woodland, with mixed open woodland on the valley slopes and grasses in the dambos.
Fauna: Baboon, vervet monkey, pangolin, porcupine, wild dog, honey badger, striped polecat, mongoose, genet, civet, spotted hyena, African wild cat, serval, lion, leopard, aardvark, elephant, rock dassie, Burchell's zebra, warthog, bushpig, hippopotamus, buffalo, kudu, bushbuck, roan, common waterbuck, puku, reedbuck, Lichtenstein's hartebeest, impala, klipspringer, oribi, Sharpe's grysbok, common (grey) duiker, water monitor lizard.
Visitor facilities: Lodge and camp beside Lifupa Dam run by Sunbird Hotels & Resorts.
Accessibility: Closest park to Lilongwe, very good graded road into the heart of the park (Lifupa) from the main M1 tar road.

Nkhotakota Wildlife Reserve
Size: 1802 sq km.
Geographical location: Central Malawi, covering the escarpment which descends from the Central African Plateau down to the Rift Valley.
Altitude: 500 -1600 m above sea level.
Physical features: The escarpment produces a rugged, occasionally steep, terrain with a few peaks. A number of rivers descend to the lake, including the Bua.
Vegetation: Predominantly *miombo (Brachystegia)* woodland with limited grassland and evergreen forest.
Fauna: Baboon, vervet monkey, blue monkey, pangolin, porcupine, side-striped jackal, clawless otter, honey badger, mongoose, genet, civet, spotted hyena, African wild cat, serval, lion, leopard, aardvark, elephant, Burchell's zebra, warthog, bushpig, hippopotamus, buffalo, eland, kudu, bushbuck, roan, sable, common waterbuck, reedbuck, Lichtenstein's hartebeest, impala, klipspringer, Sharpe's grysbok, common (grey) duiker, Nile crocodile, water monitor lizard.
Visitor facilities: Government camps only, with very limited facilities.
Accessibility: Though the M10 runs through the Reserve, this stretch is not tarred and, because it descends the escarpment, suffers badly from erosion by surface run-off during the rains. It is passable only with four-wheel drive.

Vwaza Marsh Wildlife Reserve
Size: 986 sq km.
Geographical location: North Malawi on the Central African Plateau just to the south west of the Nyika Plateau and bordering Zambia.
Altitude: 1000 -1600 m above sea level.
Physical features: Hills dominate the eastern side of the Reserve, providing tributaries to the Luwewe River. This drains the Vwaza Marsh in the north, flowing into the South Rukuru River which then runs along the Reserve's southern boundary, through Lake Kazuni in the south-east corner. West of the hills, the Reserve is flat alluvial land.
Vegetation: *Miombo, mopane* and *Combretum* woodland with grasses on the dambos and floodplains.
Fauna: Baboon, vervet monkey, pangolin, porcupine, honey badger, mongoose, genet, civet, spotted hyena, African wild cat, serval, lion, leopard, aardvark, elephant, rock dassie, Burchell's zebra, warthog, bushpig, hippopotamus, buffalo, eland, kudu, bushbuck, roan, common waterbuck, puku, reedbuck, Lichtenstein's hartebeest, impala, klipspringer, Sharpe's grysbok, common (grey) duiker, water monitor lizard.
Visitor facilities: Lake Kazuni Safari Camp provides luxury in en-suite reed huts, while the neighbouring Kazuni Camp offers self catering and camping facilities. Both are operated by The Nyika Safari Company.
Accessibility: Easy access to the Lake Kazuni entrance via a flat sandy road from Rumphi.

Nyika National Park
Size: 3134 sq km.
Geographical location: North Malawi, encompassing the Nyika Plateau which rises above the Central African Plateau. Part of its western boundary marks the border with Zambia.

Altitude: 500 -2500 m above sea level.

Physical features: A dramatic and unique high 'whaleback' plateau of rolling hills. Mountains and river valleys also feature and escarpments mark the descent from the plateau.

Vegetation: Montane grassland covers the main plateau, broken by pockets of evergreen forest. The escarpments below feature *miombo (Brachystegia)* woodland. Wildflowers carpet the plateau and with 120 species, Nyika is the richest orchid area in south-central Africa.

Fauna: Baboon, vervet monkey, blue monkey, pangolin, porcupine, side-striped jackal, clawless otter, honey badger, mongoose, genet, civet, spotted hyena, African wild cat, serval, lion, leopard, aardvark, elephant, rock dassie, Burchell's zebra, warthog, bushpig, hippopotamus, buffalo, eland, kudu, bushbuck, roan, puku, reedbuck, Lichtenstein's hartebeest, klipspringer, red duiker, blue duiker, common (grey) duiker.

Visitor facilities: The new log cabin Chelinda Lodge offers a stay in luxury while the original chalets of Chelinda Camp remain, including as a self-catering option. Camping is also possible. All accommodation is operated by The Nyika Safari Company.

Accessibility: Long and difficult road up to the plateau, particularly during the rainy season when it is cut by numerous channels and four-wheel drive is needed. There is an airstrip at Chelinda.

Liwonde National Park

Size: 548 sq km.

Geographical location: South Malawi alongside Lake Malombe and the upper Shire River within the Rift Valley.

Altitude: 200 -900 m above sea level.

Physical features: Liwonde is dominated by the broad Shire River, which runs north-south just less than a kilometre inside the park's western boundary. It also includes a part of Lake Malombe's south-eastern shore, with drainage lines running east-west into these two water bodies. Three groups of hills break up the alluvial plains.

Vegetation: A mix of woodlands including savannah and *mopane* on the higher ground and riverine forest alongside the watercourses. Grasslands occur on the floodplains and reed beds and water lilies by the river and in the lagoons.

Fauna: Baboon, vervet monkey, pangolin, porcupine, side-striped jackal, clawless otter, spotted-necked otter, honey badger, striped polecat, mongoose, genet, civet, spotted hyena, African wild cat, serval, leopard, lion, aardvark, elephant, Burchell's zebra, black rhinoceros, warthog, bushpig, hippopotamus, buffalo, kudu, bushbuck, roan, sable, common waterbuck, reedbuck, Lichtenstein's hartebeest, impala,

Livingstone's suni, klipspringer, oribi, Sharpe's grysbok, common (grey) duiker, Nile crocodile, water monitor lizard.

Visitor facilities: Mvuu Lodge provides an exclusive safari experience, its permanent en suite tents each have private balconies overlooking a lagoon off the Shire. Neighbouring Mvuu Camp is also on the river bank, offering self catering accommodation and camping. Central African Wilderness Safaris have established Mvuu over the last 10 years. Chinguni Lodge, among the hills in the south of the Park is a recent privatisation of a government cottage.

Accessibility: Lying just to the east of the M3, access is straightforward. Roads inside the park can be closed during the rains but river access is year-round. Mvuu Lodge is reached via a boat transfer across the Shire, having branched off the M3 at Ulongwe village. There is an airstrip at Mvuu.

Majete Wildlife Reserve

Size: 691 sq km.

Geographical Location: South Malawi at the western edge of the Rift Valley, stretching west from the Shire River at the transition from its middle to lower valley.

Altitude: 200 -900 m above sea level.

Physical features: The Shire River through Majete is marked by a dramatic series of falls and rapids. Elsewhere, the landscape is rugged with narrow valleys cutting between hills and ridges.

Vegetation: *Combretum* woodland in the eastern areas, changing to *miombo (Brachystegia)* in the west. Only narrow floodplains.

Fauna: Baboon, vervet monkey, pangolin, porcupine, side-striped jackal, honey badger, mongoose, civet, spotted hyena, leopard, aardvark, rock dassie, Burchell's zebra, warthog, bushpig, hippopotamus, kudu, bushbuck, common waterbuck, reedbuck, Livingstone's suni, klipspringer, Sharpe's grysbok, common (grey) duiker, Nile crocodile.

Visitor facilities: No facilities but camping is possible at old government sites. Majete Safari Lodge just outside the Reserve to the south, provides cabins alongside the river.

Accessibility: There is no access from the north. The road up from Chikwawa is good when graded. From Blantyre to Chikwawa, a series of hairpins characterise the road down the Thyolo escarpment to the Lower Shire Valley — but it is a tar road, passable throughout the year.

Lengwe National Park

Size: 887 sq km.

Geographical location: South Malawi in the Lower Shire section of the Rift Valley, its western boundary marks the border with Mozambique.

Altitude: 50 -400 m above sea level.

Physical features: Sandstone outcrops characterise

the rolling landscape to the west, but the terrain flattens eastwards to the Shire floodplain. A few seasonal rivers drain Lengwe eastwards.

Vegetation: Woodland on the western areas — *miombo (Brachystegia)* to the north and *mopane* to the south. *Acacia* and *Combretum* savannah and thicket to the east. A few dambos and stretches of riverine woodland.

Fauna: Baboon, vervet monkey, blue monkey, pangolin, porcupine, side-striped jackal, honey badger, mongoose, genet, civet, spotted hyena, African wild cat, serval, leopard, aardvark, rock dassie, warthog, bushpig, buffalo, kudu, nyala, bushbuck, sable, reedbuck, impala, Livingstone's suni, Sharpe's grysbok, common (grey) duiker.

Visitor facilities: Very limited facilities at the government-run Visitors Camp — chalets and camping.

Accessibility: Having descended the Thyolo escarpment from Blantyre (see Majete), the M1 continues along the floor of Lower Shire Valley. Final access roads through the sugar plantations are flat earth (though irrigation can create muddy skid pans).

Mwabvi Wildlife Reserve
Size: 135 sq km.
Geographical Location: South Malawi in the Lower Shire section of the Rift Valley, its western boundary marks the border with Mozambique and it is close to the southernmost tip of the country.
Altitude: 50 -400 m above sea level.
Physical features: A collection of hills to the south-east. Otherwise, a jumble of sandstone outcrops, ridges and hills, intersected by valleys of a small number of seasonal rivers and broader dambos.
Vegetation: Mix of *miombo*, *mopane*, *Acacia*/*Combretum* woodland, dambos and thicket. Some riverine forest along the watercourses.
Fauna: Baboon, vervet monkey, blue monkey, pangolin, porcupine, honey badger, mongoose, genet, civet, spotted hyena, African wild cat, serval, leopard, aardvark, rock dassie, warthog, bushpig, buffalo, kudu, nyala, bushbuck, sable, impala, Livingstone's suni, klipspringer, Sharpe's grysbok, red duiker, common (grey) duiker, water monitor lizard.
Visitor facilities: None.
Accessibility: Very difficult. The M1 along the Lower Shire Valley deteriorates southwards and is poor this far south. The final access roads are little used and not maintained.

Lake Malawi National Park
Size: 87 sq km.
Geographical location: South Malawi on the Nankumba Peninsula at the southern end of Lake Malawi.

Altitude: 400 -1100 m above sea level.
Physical features: The peninsula consists of rocky hills and a shoreline including sandy beaches. The park also incorporates 12 islands of similar terrain and the waters of Lake Malawi for 100 m off-shore.
Vegetation: *Miombo (Brachystegia)* and *Combretum*/*Acacia* woodland and baobabs on land. Green algae on submerged rocks, water-weeds on the sandy lake bed and phytoplankton in the water.
Fauna: Baboon, blue monkey, porcupine, clawless otter, spotted-necked otter, mongoose, civet, leopard, rock dassie, Burchell's zebra, bushpig, hippopotamus, kudu, bushbuck, klipspringer, Sharpe's grysbok, Nile crocodile, water monitor lizard.
Visitor facilities: Self catering rondavels or camping at Golden Sands Holiday Camp. Mumbo and Domwe Islands now have idyllic up-market camps run by Kayak Africa. There are alternative places to stay at Chembe village, which is completely surrounded by the park.
Accessibility: Usually easy but the road through the park to the lakeshore is undulating and can get damaged by surface run-off from the rains.

Waterfalls

Chelinda Falls
In the Nyika National Park, which is 129 km from Mzuzu in North Malawi. The Chelinda Falls are one of a series of falls and rapids as the Chelinda River descends the Nyika Plateau. The drop is just 10 m but this is a lovely spot on the plateau.

Chisanga Falls
In the Nyika National Park, which is 129 km from Mzuzu in North Malawi. Chisanga is a series of spectacular waterfalls and rapids seen as the North Rukuru River plunges 120 m over the western edge of the Nyika Plateau. The longest of the three main falls is 20 m and the whole series is set in evergreen riverine forest.

Manchewe Falls
At Livingstonia Mission in North Malawi, 125 km north of Mzuzu. These are the longest waterfalls in Malawi at 300 m, a sheer drop down the edge of the Rift Valley from the Khondowe Plateau into a gorge at the lakeshore.

Mandala Falls and Williams Falls
Both are on Zomba Plateau, 15 km or so from Zomba town. Both consist of a series of low rocky steps in the river with small pools below. The flow over the Mandala Falls has been affected by the expansion of the Mulunguzi Dam but both falls are in areas of lush vegetation and beautiful evergreen forest.

Nchenachena Falls and Zoa Falls
On the Ruo River in South Malawi at the border with Mozambique, 100 km south of Blantyre. The Ruo River remains quiet for much of the year but it is fed by streams from Mount Mulanje and soon after the start of the rains, its flow surges considerably. The flow over these two nearby falls is spectacular at this time of the year. Access is difficult, though a railway line runs to and alongside the Ruo River The recently re-furbished 'Presidential Train' can be chartered for this route.

Shire (Murchison) Cataracts
A series of falls, rapids and gorges along 20 -30 km of the Shire river as it descends to its lower valley in South Malawi. Best known are the beautiful Kapichira Falls, which blocked Livingstone's passage up the Shire. Most lie within the Majete Wildlife Reserve, 65 km southwest of Blantyre, though the northernmost Mpatamanga Gorge is usually accessed going west out of Blantyre for 50 km.

Wildlife Profile

Malawi has a wide range of species but population pressures have reduced the numbers of many of the mammals and reptiles. Those described in this profile may be seen although all sightings, as everywhere, will be partly a matter of luck. The parks and reserves named after each species report sightings but successful viewing is more likely in some parks than in others. For more details, see Part Four: Special Features.

The Chichewa name is shown in parentheses after the species' Latin name.

Mammals

PRIMATES (Order Primates)
Chacma baboon, Papio ursinus (Nyani): Largest primate, other than man, in southern Africa. Lives in groups (troops). Found in all Malawi's parks and reserves and elsewhere in Malawi. Prefers rocky habitats. The baboon is omnivorous.

Yellow baboon, Papio cynocephalus (Nyani): Very similar to the chacma baboon but smaller and with yellowish hair. Only seen in northern Malawi.

Vervet monkey, Cercopithecus aethiops (Pusi): Has long coarse hair with white rim round face. Lives in groups (troops). Male has characteristic bright blue scrotum. Mostly vegetarian. Seen in all parks and reserves and elsewhere.

Samango monkey, Cercopithecus mitis (Nchima): Better known as the blue monkey although it is predominantly brown. Seen largely in and around Lengwe, Nkhotakota and Nyika. Lives in small groups.

PANGOLINS (Order Pholidota)
Pangolin, Manis temminckii (Nkaka): Rather like a small aardvark but covered in scales. Curls itself into a ring if in danger. Rarely seen but in all parks except Lake Malawi.

HARES & RABBITS (Order Lagomorpha)
Scrub hare, Lepus saxatilis (Kalulu): Largely grey in colour. Nocturnal. Prefers habitats which afford cover. Widely distributed in Malawi.

Red rock rabbit, Pronolagus rupestris (Kalulu): Also known as Smith's Red Rock Rabbit and as the Red Rock Hare. Red-brown colour. Prefers rocky habitat. Nocturnal. Less common than the scrub hare.

RODENTS (Order Rodentia)
Porcupine, Hystrix africaeaustralis (Nungu): Can be up to a metre long. Characteristic long, black and white spines. Generally seen singly. Nocturnal. Seen in all parks.

CARNIVORES (Order Carnivora)
Side-striped jackal, Canis adustus (Nkhandwe): Distinguished by faint light and dark stripes running lengthwise along sides. Slightly pointed ears. Similar to small Alsatian dog. Not common in Malawi but may be seen in Nkhotakota, Nyika, Liwonde Majete and Lengwe. Hunts from dusk to dawn. Usually seen singly or in pairs.

Wild dog, Lycaon pictus (Mbulu): Very rare. Only in Kasungu are sightings possible. Has rounded ears and a mottled coat. About the size of an Alsatian dog. Hunts in packs and can run very fast.

Cape clawless otter, Aonyx capensis (Katumbu): A large otter which is found in Liwonde, Lake Malawi, Nyika and Nkhotakota. Moves in small groups, sometimes quite far from water.

Spotted-necked otter, Lutra maculicollis (Katumbu): Medium sized otter. Only likely to be seen in

Liwonde and Lake Malawi Parks. Moves in small groups, never far from water.

Honey badger, *Mellivora capensis* (Chiuli): Up to a metre long. Distinctive silver-grey upper coat. Can be quite aggressive. Seen occasionally in all the parks except Lake Malawi. Largely nocturnal.

Striped polecat, *Ictonyx striatus*: Black and white stripes lengthwise along body. Squirts foul-smelling liquid from anal gland at would-be aggressor. Nocturnal. Solitary. Found occasionally in Kasungu and Liwonde.

Banded mongoose, *Mungos mungo* (Msulu): Small (total length 60 cm) with distinctive brown-black transverse stripes on grey body. Seen especially in Liwonde.

Bushy-tailed mongoose, *Bdeogale crassicauda*: Medium sized mongoose (70 cm). Grey-black with black bushy tail. Found occasionally in all the parks but mainly where there are rocks

Large grey mongoose, *Herpestes ichneumon*: Also known as the Egyptian mongoose. Can be over one metre in total length. Black tip to tail. Seen usually near Lake Malawi and along banks of Shire and other rivers.

Slender mongoose, *Galerella sanguinea* (Nyenga): Small size, similar to banded mongoose. Seen in most of the parks as long as there is adequate cover.

Dwarf mongoose, *Helogale parvula*: Only 40 cm in total length. Diurnal. Favours rocky areas but seen in most of the parks and elsewhere.

Large-spotted genet, *Genetta tigrina* (Mwili): Long (1 m) slender body. Grey-white with rust coloured spots. Short legs and pointed ears. Mainly nocturnal. Seen in all parks except Majete.

Civet, *Civettictis civetta* (Fungwe): Like a medium-sized dog in build. Small head. Blotchy and striped body. Black markings on grey body. Hunts from sunset to sunrise. Regularly seen in Liwonde; occasionally in the other parks.

Spotted hyena, *Crocuta crocuta* (Fisi): Dog-like but hindquarters lower than shoulders. Immensely strong jaws. Nocturnal. Hunts in packs and will also steal kill from other predators. Seen in all the parks and in other remote areas of Malawi.

African wild cat, *Felis lybica* (Bvumbwe): Small cat, about the size of a domestic cat. Back of ears, behind hind legs and belly are distinct reddish-brown. Seen in all the parks except Lake Malawi and Majete.

Serval, *Felis serval* (Njuzi): Larger than a domestic cat and with long body. Black spots on yellowish body. Largely nocturnal. Seen in all the parks except Lake Malawi and Majete.

Lion, *Panthera leo* (Mkango): Large cat with fully adult males having mane. Lives in groups (prides) usually of six or more. To be seen in Nkhotakota, Kasungu, Vwaza and Nyika but not common. A pride may soon be relocated to Liwonde.

Leopard, *Panthera pardus* (Nyalugwe): Powerful cat rather smaller than lion. Characteristic black-brown rosettes (spots). May be seen in undergrowth or in trees during day. Hunts at night. Solitary. Relatively common in Malawi. Seen in all parks and some mountain areas.

AARDVARK (ant bear) (Order Tubulidentata)
Aardvark, *Orycteropus afer* (Godi): Unusual appearance. Pig-like, long snout. Arched back and short legs. Lives in burrows. Nocturnal. Seen in all parks except Lake Malawi.

ELEPHANT (Order Proboscidea)
African elephant, *Loxodonta africana* (Njobvu): Matriarchal herds with older males solitary. Very destructive in their eating habits. Also require vast quantities of water. Very poor sight but good hearing and sense of smell. Seen in Liwonde, Nkhotakota, Nyika, Vwaza and Kasungu.

HYRAXES (Order Hydracoidea)
Rock hyrax (dassies), *Procavia capensis* (Mbila): Rodent-like appearance, size of very large hamster. Actually it is near relative of the elephant. Found in many rocky areas in Malawi. Wrongly called rock rabbits but correctly known as hyraxes. Rock dassie is the name used in Malawi.

ODD-TOED UNGULATES (Order Perissodactyla)
Burchell's zebra, *Equus burchellii* (Mbidzi): Horse-like with well developed hindquarters. Black and white stripes with white stripe having shadow brown stripe superimposed. Strong herding instinct. Seen especially in Nyika, Liwonde and Kasungu.

Hook-lipped rhinoceros, *Diceros bicornis* (Chipembere): Rare. Massive mammal. Also called the black rhino. Two horns on face. Only in Liwonde where they have been relocated from South Africa but are now breeding.

EVEN-TOED UNGULATES (Order Artiodactyla)
Warthog, *Phacochoerus aethiopicus* (Njiri): Pig-like, with upward-pointing tusks. Males have two pairs of wart-like lumps on face; females have one pair. Small tail with tuft stands erect when the warthog runs. Diurnal. Lives in small family or bachelor groups (sounders). In all parks except Lake Malawi.

Bushpig, *Potamochoerus porcus* (Nguluwe): Smaller than warthog and no tusks or warts. Not common in Malawi but in all parks. Nocturnal. Live in small groups (sounders).

Hippopotamus, *Hippopotamus amphibius* (Mvuu): Very large, semi-aquatic mammal. Spends much of day in and under water. Grazes on land at night. Malawi has some of the largest concentrations in Africa. Seen in Shire River, Lake Malawi and various rivers, dams and ponds.

Buffalo, *Syncerus caffer* (Njati): Cattle-like mammals. Live in large herds. Can be dangerous especially if solitary. Most grazing is during the night. In all parks except Lake Malawi and Majete.

Eland, *Taurotragus oryx* (Nchefu): Largest of all antelopes. Cow-like appearance. Males and females have short, straight horns. Generally modest sized herds but can be very large. Found in Nyika, Vwaza and Nkhotakota.

Kudu, *Tragelaphus strepsiceros* (Ngoma): Large antelope distinguished by large ears the insides of which are pale red. Males have large, spiral horns. Females are hornless. Flanks have white stripes on light-brown body. Small herds. Found in southern parks and in Vwaza.

Nyala, *Tragelaphus angasii* (Boo): Males are large but females distinctly smaller. Both sexes have thin white stripes on body. Male is grey, female is brown. Only males have horns. These antelope are found in Lengwe (most northerly habitat in southern Africa) and in Mwabvi.

Bushbuck, *Tragelaphus scriptus* (Mbawala): Small antelope, brown in colour. Well developed rump stands higher than shoulders. Seen in all parks. Only the males have horns.

Roan antelope, *Hippotragus equinus* (Chilembwe): Second largest antelope. Grey in colour and both sexes have long beautifully curved horns. Usually in small herds. Found in Nyika, Vwaza, Kasungu, Liwonde and Nkhotakota.

Sable antelope, *Hippotragus niger* (Mphalapala): Large antelope with shiny black coat but belly is white and face has white markings. Females are less clearly black, rather a dark brown. Both sexes have wonderful, curved horns. The horns are smaller on the female. May be seen in Nyika, Vwaza, Lengwe and Mwabvi.

Waterbuck, *Kobus ellipsiprymnus* (Chuzu): Large antelope. Brown-grey coat has white ring round hindquarters. The male has very large horns sweeping forward. Seen in Liwonde, Lengwe and Vwaza.

Puku, *Kobus vardonii* (Nseula): Rare, medium-sized antelope. Golden-brown back with white under belly. Lyre-shaped horns only on the male. May be seen in Nyika, Kasungu and Vwaza.

Reedbuck, *Redunca arundinum* (Mphoyo): Medium-sized antelope. Brown with near-white under-parts. Only the male has horns, which curve outwards. May be seen in all parks except Lake Malawi.

Lichtenstein's hartebeest, *Sigmoceros lichtensteinii* (Nkhozi): Rare antelope in Malawi yet some relocated to South Africa in the 1990s. Shoulders are higher than hindquarters. Sad looking face. Brown with darker 'saddle'. Both sexes have characteristic Z-shaped horns. May be seen in Kasungu, Nkhotakota, Nyika, Vwaza and Liwonde.

Impala, *Aepyceros melampus* (Nswala): Medium-sized, elegant antelope with sleek brown coat lightening under belly. Only the males have long horns. Characteristic black stripe down buttocks. Seen in bachelor or breeding herds, often in large numbers. Seen in Kasungu, Liwonde, Vwaza, Nkhotakota, Nyika.

Livingstone's suni, *Neotragus moschatus* (Kadumba): Very small antelope. Reddish-brown colour. Only the males have backward-sloping horns. Rare in Malawi but seen in Lengwe.

Klipspringer, *Oreotragus oreotragus* (Chinkhoma): Stocky, small antelope. Appears to walk on tiptoe. Generally grey-brown. Males have short horns. Seen in Nyika but rare in other parks.

Oribi, *Ourebia ourebi* (Choe): Small antelope seen only rarely in Liwonde and Kasungu. Characteristic long, stretched neck. Rusty coloured but near-white under belly. Males have short horns.

Sharpe's grysbok, *Raphicerus sharpei* (Kasenye): Small antelope. Generally grey appearance. Large ears. Males have tiny horns. Seen in all parks except Nyika.

Red duiker, *Cephalophus natalensis* (Gwapi): Rare, very small antelope. May be seen in Nyika. Reddish brown coat. Both sexes have short backward-sloping horns.

Blue duiker, *Philantomba monticola* (Kaduma): Rare. Smallest antelope in southern Africa. Grey-brown with bluish sheen. Both sexes have short horns. May be seen in Nyika.

Common duiker, *Sylvicapra grimmia* (Gwapi): Small antelope. Grey-brown in colour. Rather prominent ears. Male has short slender horns. Seen in Nyika, Vwaza and Nkhotakota.

Birds

Malawi's famously rich birdlife is represented by seventy-nine families which comprise a total of six hundred and forty-nine species. A tenth of the species are not found in other parts of southern Africa and over eighty per cent of the species breed in Malawi.

Grebes: The **dabchick**, *Tachybaptus ruficollis*, is common throughout Malawi where there is water and cover. It favours dambos and marsh and can be seen in most of the parks.

Pelicans: Of the two pelicans in Malawi, the **pinkbacked pelican**, *Pelecanus rufescens*, is more common than the **White pelican** *(P. onocrolatus)*. Both may be found on marshlands and dambos.

Cormorants: Both the **whitebrested**, *Phalacrocorax carbo*, and the **reed cormorant** *(P. africanus)* are very common. The former is particularly to be seen around Lake Malawi while the latter tends to be along rivers such as the Shire in Liwonde.

Darters: The **darter**, *Anhinga melanogaster*, is most common on smaller stretches of water and marsh but not around Lake Malawi.

Herons, egrets, bitterns: Eighteen species of this family *Ardeidae*, are represented and widely distributed in Malawi. The most common are **squacco herons**, *Ardeola ralloides*, and the **cattle egret**, *Bubulcus ibis*.

Hamerkop: Very common, the **Hamerkop**, *Scopus umbretta*, is a builder of large nests. It is especially abundant around Lake Chilwa.

Storks: There are seven species of stork seen in the country. Only the **openbilled stork**, *Anastomus lamelligerus*, is very common and two, the **white stork**, *Ciconia ciconia*, and **Abdim's stork**, *C. abdimii*, are visitors.

Shoebill: Shoebills, *Balaeniceps rex*, are found near marshland in northern Malawi, including Nyika.

Ibises & spoonbills: Four ibises and the **African spoonbill**, *Platalea alba*, are found in Malawi. The **glossy ibis**, *Plegadis falcinellus*, is very common and **Hadeda ibises**, *Bostychia hagedash*, are residents of Liwonde.

Flamingos: Neither of the two species of visiting flamingo is common but the **greater flamingo**, *Phoedicopterus ruber*, is the more widespread. Lake Chilwa is a likely place for a sighting.

Ducks & geese: In a country with many open water surfaces, it is not surprising to find no less than 18 species of duck and goose. **Whitefaced ducks**, *Dendrocygna bicolor*, are the most common of all. Quite rare summer visitors include the **pintail**, *Anas acuta*, the **European shoveller**, *A. clypeata*, and the **tufted duck**, *Aythya fuligula*.

Secretary bird: The **secretary bird**, *Sagittarius serpentarius*, occasionally crosses the border into western Malawi from Zambia.

Vultures, harriers, eagles, hawks, etc.: The family *Accipitridae*, is represented by no less than 43 species including 15 eagle species. The **African fish eagle**, *Haliaeetus vocifer*, is Malawi's national bird and seen in large numbers near Lake Malawi. The most common vulture is the **whitebacked**, *Gyps africanus*, found in all the parks and reserves. **Little banded goshawks**, *Accipiter badius*, are seen in most woodlands.

Osprey: Osprey, *Pnndion haliaetus*, are a non-breeding species in Malawi but are seen on the Upper Shire River.

Falcons & kestrels: The family *Falconidae*, (13 species) is widespread although some species prefer acacia woodlands. A rare summer visitor is the **grey sooty falcon**, *Falco concolor*, seen in the south of the country. Much more common is **Dickinson's kestrel**, *F. dickinsoni*, which breeds in palm trees.

Francolins & quails: Common throughout Malawi is **Hildebrandt's francolin**, *Francolinus hildebrandti*, but most likely to be seen is the **rednecked Francolin**, *F. afer*, living in a variety of habitats. In total there are 11 species breeding in the country.

Guineafowls: Recognised by its blue neck and red cap, the **helmeted guineafowl**, *numida meleagris*, is very common but crested **guineafowls**, *Guttera pucherani*, are rare.

Buttonquails: Two buttonquails are resident in grassland areas. **Kurrichane buttonquail**, *Turnix sylvatica*, are more common than the **black-rumped buttonquail**, *T. hottentotta*.

Cranes: The **wattled crane**, *Grus carunculata*, and the **crowned crane**, *Balearica reulorum*, are not common but Vwaza Marsh may give a sighting.

Rails, crakes, flufftails, coots, etc.: There are 17 species of the family *Rallidae*. The most common include the **black crake**, *Amauromis flavirostris*, **moorhens**, *Gallinula chloropus*, and the **red-knobbed coot**, *Fulica cristata*. Dambos and marsh attract many of the species.

Finfoots: The **African finfoot**, *Podica senegalensis*, is found near rivers with wooded banks.

Bustards & korhaans: Stanley's (or Denham's) **bustard**, *Neotis denhami*, is found on the northern plateaux: Nyika and Viphya. The **blackbellied korhaan**, *Eupodotis melanogaster*, is in many of the parks and forest reserves.

Jacanas: The **African**, *Actophilornis africanus*, is much more common than the **lesser jacanas**, *Microparra capensis*. Both will be found in marshlands.

Painted snipes: The colourful painted **snipe**, *Rostratyla benghalensis*, not a true snipe, is seen near Lake Malawi and other water or swamp areas.

Plovers: There are 14 species of the family *Charadriidae*. The most common is **Kittlitz's plover**, *Charadrius pecuarius*, with its black mask across the eyes. Five of the plovers do not breed in Malawi. Of the **yellow-billed plovers**, the **wattled plover**, *Vanellus senegallus*, is quite common but the **whitecrowned plover**, *V. albiceps*, is a rarity.

Sandpipers, snipes, etc.: Twenty-one species of the family *Scolopacidae*, can be seen in Malawi. Only the **African snipe**, *Gallingo nigripennis*, breeds in the country. The remainder are summer visitors (late September to the end of March). The **common sandpiper**, *Tringa hypoleucos*, is widespread but most of these birds will be found only in marsh, dambo and mudflat areas.

Stilts & avocets: The **blackwinged stilt**, *Himantopus himantopus*, is more common than the **avocet**, *Recurvirostra avosetta*. The latter's strange upturned bill and black and white striped wings are its identification. Both are present in Liwonde.

Dikkops: Spotted, *Burhinus capensis*, and **water dikkops**, *B. vermiculatus*, breed in Malawi. Their large eyes are notable. Not often seen because they are largely nocturnal.

Coursers & pratincoles: Three **coursers** and three **pratincoles** represent this family *Glareolidae*. The pratincoles are shorter than the coursers which 'walk-tall' — a proud looking bird. **Redwinged pratincoles**, *Glareola pratincola*, are very common on both grass and wetlands. **Tremminck's courser**, *Cursorius temminckii*, seeks short grass and, at 20 cm, is the smallest of the coursers.

Gulls & terns: Of the family *Laridae*, in Malawi there are three gulls and five terns. The **greyheaded gull**, *Larus cirrocephalus*, is the most common but, in summer, the **whitewinged tern**, *Chlidonias hybridus*, is a frequent visitor to the dambos and marshes. A rarely seen visitor is the **lesser blackheaded gull**. *Larus fuscus*, which might be seen along the shores of Lake Malawi.

Skimmers: The **African skimmer**, *Rynchops flavirostris*, with its specially adapted bill for feeding in flight from the surface of water, is mostly seen in the Lower Shire Valley.

Sandgrouse: The **doublebanded sandgrouse**, *Pterocles bicinctus*, is another Lower Shire resident.

Pigeons & doves: There is no clear distinction between **doves** and **pigeons** but the family *Columbidae*, has thirteen representatives in the country; all breed in Malawi. The most common are **Cape turtle doves**, *Streptopelia capicola*, and the **emeraldspotted dove**, *Turtur tympanistria*. Well wooded areas, including evergreen forest, are the favoured habitats.

Parrots & lovebirds: Four of the family *Psittacida*, all exceptionally beautifully coloured, are seen in Malawi. **Lilian's lovebird**, *Agapornis lilanae*, is seen exclusively in Liwonde but the **parrots**: the **Cape** *Poicephalus robustus suahelicus*, the **brownheaded**, *P. cryptoxanthus* and **Meyer's parrot**, *P. meyeri*, are more widespread in woodland areas.

Louries: There are five resident **louries**. Two are not seen elsewhere in southern Africa: **Schalow's lourie**, *Tauraco schalowi*, and the **blackfaced lourie**, *Corythaixoides concolor*. Woodlands and forests are their habitats.

Cuckoos & coucals: This family *Cuculadae*, has twenty representative species in Malawi. The birds are not especially restricted by habitat. **Burchell's coucal**, *Ceuthmochares burchellii* and **Klaas's cuckoo**, *Chrysococcyx klaas* are the most common species. Klaas's cuckoo and the **emerald cuckoo**, *Chrysococcyx cupreus*, are beautifully coloured.

Barn owls: Barn owls, *Tyto alba*, are often seen near Blantyre. But the **grass owl**, *T. capensis*, favours the upland areas of Dedza and Mulanje.

Owls: Malawi has ten resident owl species. Some are seen round the towns but, as their names suggest, the **wood owl**, *Strix woodfordii*, is at home in evergreen forests while the **marsh owl**, *Asio capensis*, is seen in wetlands and riverine areas. The big grey **giant eagle owl** *(Bobo lacteus)* is to be found in evergreen forests.

Nightjars: Of the eight nightjars in Malawi, the most common are the **fierynecked nightjar**, *Caprimulgus pectoralis*, and the **Mozambique nightjar**, *C. fossii*. A migratory visitor, especially to the Thyolo district, is the **European nightjar**, *C. europaeus*.

Swifts & spinetails: The family Apodidae has two spinetail species and nine swifts in Malawi. All have wonderfully swept-back wings, feed on insects while in flight and seem reluctant ever to leave the air for a perch. Their powers of flight allow them to wander far from their habitats. The **mottled swift,** *Apus aequatorialis,* is one of the largest of the species. **Böhm's spinetail,** *Neafrapus boehmi,* favours the southern part of the country and the **scarce swift,** *Schoutedenapus myoptilus,* prefers high altitudes such as Nyika and Mulanje.

Mousebirds: Speckled mousebirds, *Colius striatus,* and **redfaced mousebirds,** *C. indicus,* are to be seen in woodland savannah.

Trogons: The wonderful colours of the **narina trogon,** *Apalodderma narina,* and the **bartailed trogon,** *A. vittatum,* make them two of the county's most beautiful birds. Both favour evergreen forest as their habitat.

Kingfishers: Nine species of the Halcyonidae family find Malawi's wealth of lakes and rivers an ideal habitat. However not all are fish eaters, for example, the **striped kingfisher** *(Halcyon chelicuti)* is an insectivore. One of the most attractive species is the **giant kingfisher** *(Ceryle maxima)* but the **malachite kingfisher** *(Alcedo cristata)* is probably the most brilliantly coloured.

Bee-eaters: There are three visiting bee-eaters and five resident species in the country. The most common visitor is the **European bee-eater,** *Merops apiaster,* and the **little bee-eater,** *M. pusillus,* is the most frequently seen resident. Bee-eaters find homes in a variety of habitats.

Rollers: Of the five rollers seen in Malawi, the most common is the **lilac-breasted roller,** *Coracias caudata,* seen in most woodland areas. In the summer months a common visitor is the **yellow billed broadbilled** or **cinnamon roller** *Eurystomus glaucurus.*

Hoopoes: Another woodland resident is the **hoopoe,** *Upupa epops.* Its splendid crest is raised when the bird is alarmed. It will usually be seen seeking insects on the ground with its long, curved bill.

Woodhoopoes: The **redbilled,** *Phoeniculus purpureus,* and the **scimitarbilled woodhoopoe,** *P. cyanomelas,* are widespread in all the woodlands. These birds look for insects on the trunks and branches of trees.

Hornbills: Eight **hornbills,** *Bucerotidae,* breed in Malawi. The **palebilled hornbill,** *Tockus pallidirostris,* is not seen elsewhere in southern Africa. All favour woodland but the **silvery-cheeked hornbill,** *Bycanistes brevis,* breeds in evergreen forest. The hornbills' flight includes much gliding.

Barbets: Almost half of the 12 barbet species *Capitonidae,* found in Malawi are not present in other parts of southern Africa. Related to the woodpecker, these are colourful birds. Only the **green tinker barbet,** *Pogoniulus simplex,* is confined to the south. The most common, and widespread, is the **yellowfronted tinker barbet,** *P. chrysoconus.*

Honeyguides: Honeyguides, *Indicatoridae,* got their name from some of the species' liking for the grubs and wax of bees' nests when they are broken into. They noisily fly around the nests, indicating the location. The **greater honeyguide,** *Indicator indicator,* exhibits this behaviour. Altogether, there are six species of honeyguide in Malawi, widely spread but most common in woodlands.

Woodpeckers: One of Malawi's seven **woodpecker species, Stierling's woodpecker** *Dendropicos steirlingi,* is not found elsewhere in southern Africa. It is seen at around 1000 metres (3250 feet) in the Dedza and Phirilongwe forests. The **cardinal woodpecker,** *D. fuscescens,* is the most common species and found throughout the country.

Broadbills: Widespread in sub-Saharan Africa, the **African broadbill,** *Smithornis capensis,* can be found in Malawi's evergreen forests and thickets.

Pittas: In much the same habitat as the broadbiill, the **African pitta,** *Pitta angolensis,* is rare in Malawi but might be seen in the months October to March.

Larks: Including the **finchlark,** there are six species of the family *Alaudidae,* in the country. One, unusually, is a winter visitor, the **dusky lark,** *Pinaocorys nigricans.* It prefers grasslands and might be seen between April and August.

Martins & swallows: No less than 22 species of Hirundiniae have been recorded in Malawi. Almost all occur thoughout the country. The most commonly seen is a visitor, the **European swallow,** *Hirundo rustica,* which is present during Europe's winter in all the parks and elsewhere. Two rarities are the **black saw-wing swallow,** *Psalidoprocne orientalis,* and the **greater striped swallow,** *Hirundo cucullata.* Both have been recorded in the Lower Shire Valley. The **common house martin,** *Delichon urbica,* with its blue upper parts, is a summer visitor.

Drongos: The **squaretailed drongo,** *Dicurus ludwigii,* and the **forktailed drongo,** *D. adsimilis,* are commonly seen in Lengwe National Park and elsewhere.

Orioles: Four oriole species can be seen in Malawi. All are predominently yellow, except the **greenheaded oriole,** *Oriolus chlorocephalus,* which has a green head and upperparts. It is most likely to be seen in the Thyolo area but the other species, including the visiting **European golden oriole,** *Oriolus oriolus,* are much more widespread in woodlands and forests.

Crows: The **pied crow,** *Corvus albus,* and the **whitenecked raven,** *C. albicollis,* breed in Malawi and can often be seen near settlements large and small.

Tits: Of the four tits found in Malawi, the most common is the **southern black tit,** *Parus niger,* which is native to all but the northern parts of the country. All four species can be found in mixed woodlands.

Penduline tits: Grey penduline tits, *Anthoscopus caroli,* are fairly common thoughout the country with similar habitats to the tits.

Creepers: The **spotted creeper's,** *salpornis spilonotus,* behaviour patterns are similar to that of a woodpecker. It is not always easy to spot but it is quite widespread in the *brachystegia* woodlands.

Babblers: Two of Malawi's three babblers are not seen in other parts of southern Africa. The most rare is the **mountain illadopsis,** *Malacocinchla pyyrrhoptera,* only seen in Nyika's evergreen forests.

Cuckooshrikes: The **whitebreasted,** *Coracina pectoralis,* and **black cuckooshrike,** *Campephega flava,* are widespread in mixed woodlands but the **grey cuckooshrike,** *Coracina caesia,* is a resident of the evergreen forests around Thyolo.

Bulbuls: Twelve **bulbuls,** *Pycnonotidae,* are common or fairly common in Malawi, but the **blackeyed bulbul,** *Pycnonotus barbatus,* is the most likely to be seen throughout the country. Half the bulbul species are not to be found in the rest of southern Africa. Most of the bulbuls are found in evergreen forests. Those at home in mountain areas, like Nyika, Zomba and Mulanje, include the **olivebreasted mountain bulbul** *Andropadus tephrolaemus,* and the **stripecheeked bulbul,** *A. milanjensis.*

Chats, robins, thrushes, etc.: No less than 30 species represent this family *Turdidae.* Spread across a great variety of habitats, the most common species include the **whitebrowed robin,** *Erythropygia leucophrys,* **Heuglin's robin,** *Cossypha heuglini* and the **kurrichane thrush,** *Turdus libonyana.*

Warblers: The family Sylviidae has as many as 58 species in Malawi. One of the most likely sightings will be of the **longbilled crombec,** *Sylvietta rufescens,* most often seen in pairs or bird parties. Other very common species are the **willow warbler,** *Phylloscopus trochilius* and the bleating **bush warbler,** *Camaroptera brachyura.* Most thrive in the woodland areas but the **African sedge warbler,** *Bradypterus baboecala* and the **blackbacked cisticola,** *Cisticola galactotes,* are found in marshlands and dambos such as Mpatsanjoka.

Flycatcher: The **Mozambique batis,** *Bias soror,* is perhaps the most common species of this family *Muscicapidae.* Woodlands, including evergreen forests, are the habitat. A rare species is the **vanga flycatcher,** *B. musicus* which might be sighted in or near Lengwe. In the north, the **collared flycatcher,** *Ficedula albicollis,* is not common but might be seen around Mzuzu in the summer. Altogether there are 20 species.

Tchagras and bush shrikes: The **puffback** *Dyoscopus cubla,* is very common and widespread but a more rewarding sighting might be of **Fülleborn's black boubou,** *Laniarius fuelleborni.* It keeps to high ground and Nyika's evergreen forests are a haunt.

Wagtails, pipits and longclaws: The most commonly seen of this family *Motacillidae,* is the **African pied wagtail,** *Motacilla aguimp.* It is widespread in the country and can often be seen near settlements. Of the other 14 species, the **yellowthroated longclaw,** *Macronyx croceus,* is common on the dambos and a summer visitor, the **yellow wagtail,** *Motacilla flava,* will be found where there is short grass or even bare ground.

Shrikes: Half of the six species of shrikes seen in Malawi are summer visitors. The most common visitor is the **redbacked shrike,** *Lanius collurio.* Of the shrikes breeding in Malawi, the most common is the **fiscal shrike,** *L. collaris,* which may forsake trees to perch on telegraph wires. It is often easy to spot because, even in trees, it does not seek cover.

Helmetshrikes: White, *Prion plumatis,* and **redbilled helmetshrikes,** *P. retzii,* both breed in Malawi. Very social birds, they will often be seen in groups. Both are widespread in the country, chiefly in woodlands or thicket.

Starlings: There are nine species of starling breeding in Malawi. The **slenderbilled redwinged starling,** *Onychognathus tenuirostris,* is not to be found elsewhere in southern Africa. It can be seen on the edges of evergreen forests on the Viphya and Nyika Plateaux. A common visitor in summer is the **plumcoloured starling,** *Cinnyricinclus leucogaster,* when it is widespread.

Oxpeckers: Two oxpeckers, the **yellowbilled,** *Buphagus africanus* and the **redbilled,** *B. erythrorhynchus,* breed in Malawi. Only likely sightings will be in the parks and reserves where they use their sharp claws to cling on to game animals to feed on flies and ticks.

Sunbirds: There are twenty sunbird species in Malawi. These wonderfully coloured birds occupy a variety of habitats but most prefer woodland and thicket. One of the prettiest is the **violet-backed sunbird,** *Anthreptes longuemarei,* most common in the north of the country. In the south, the **grey sunbird,** *Nectarinia veroxii,* is seen at Lengwe and generally in the Lower Shire Valley but is something of a rarity. The most common and widespread species is the **collared sunbird,** *Anthreptes collaris,* which can be seen in any tree habitat.

White-eyes: Yellow white-eye, *Zosterops senegalensis,* is common in all the parks. The tiny bird feeds on insects and nectar.

Weavers & queleas: There are 30 species of this family breeding in Malawi. The most common of the queleas is the **redbilled quelea,** *Quelea quelea.* Open acacia savannah woodland is its habitat. Other common birds of the family include the **yellowrumped widow,** *Eupledtes capensis* and two sparrows, the **greyheaded,** *Passer griseus* and the **yellowthroated sparrow,** *Petronia superciliaris.* Both the sparrows are found near settlement. The **spectacled weaver,** *Ploceus ocularis* and the **forest weaver,** *P. bicolor,* make nests with long entry spouts. The spectacled weaver is in all the parks.

Whydahs and widowfinches: The family *Viduidae* contributes six species to Malawi's bird population. The most common is the **pintailed whydah,** *Vidua macroura.* The male's exceptionally long tail is characteristic of the family. On the pintailed, it is slender but the **paradise whydah,** *V. paradisea* and **broadtailed paradise whydah,** *V. obtusa,* have spectacular broad tails. The last two named birds can be seen in most of the parks.

Pytilias, waxbills, mannikins, etc: Twenty-one species of the family *Estrildidae* occur in Malawi. The most likely to be seen are the **blue waxbill,** *Uraeginthus angolensis* and the **bronze mannikin,** *Spermestes cucullatus.* Both these birds can be seen in all the main parks. The blue waxbill is especially pretty with pale blue underparts.

Buntings, canaries, seedeaters: There are 13 species of the family Fringillidae. The **yelloweyed canary,** *Serinus mozambicus,* is the most common and seen in most of the parks. All of the species favour woodland habitats but the **cape bunting,** *Emberiza capensis,* likes rocky hillsides such as those near Dedza.

Reptiles

Schlegel's blind snake, *Typhlops schlegelii,* (Nthongo) Common but harmless. Bluish-grey but upperparts darker. Grows to 30-40 cm. Seen mostly from December to April.

African python, *Python sabae* (Nsato): Very large non-poisonous common python. Will give wounding bite. Up to four metres (thirteen feet). Found in Shire Valley and near Lake Malawi. Most active at night. Dark brown with lighter patches shading to white on underside. Will even attack young antelope.

Common house snake, *Boaedon fulignosus* (Chankhusa): Non-venomous and found mostly near human habitation. Just short of one metre (three feet). Brown-grey in colour with underside pinky-white.

Water snake, *Lycondonomorphus rufulus* (Chirumi): Non-venomous, harmless snake. Black or olive-brown with sheen. Underside is pinkish to redish-yellow. Up to 70 cm. Common throughout country but especially along parts of Lake Malawi and in mountain areas.

Western green snake, *Philothamnus irregularis* (Namasamba): Will bite but non-poisonous. Up to just under one metre. Quite common near water. Green on upperside and yellow underneath.

Eastern green snake, *Philothamnus hoplogaster* (Camasamba): Up to 75 cm. Non-venomous. Inhabits river and lake areas. Light to dark green. Underside yellowish. Will leap from tree to tree.

Boomslang, *Dispholidus typus* (Mbobo): Large (up to 170 cm) poisonous snake. Common in Malawi. Lives in trees. Young are grey-brown on upperside with light blue spots on dorsal scales. Adults have white underside with males being bright green and females olive-brown above.

Vine snake, *Thelotornis capensis* (Nalikukuti): Large poisonous snake (up to 140 cm). Found especially in savannah woodlands. Not easy to spot because it looks like a thin tree branch. Speckled head, green on top and with black spots. Head looks like a leaf. Underside of body is white but upperside is generally grey-brown with diagonal patches and flecks of black.

Tiger snake, *Telescopus semiannulatus semiannulatus* (Chiwa): Medium sized snake which will bite but is non-poisonous. Grows up to 75 cm. Yellow-rusty colour with dark bands down back. Common in Lake Malawi National Park, around the Lake and in the Lower Shire Valley.

Herald snake, *Crotaphopeltis hotamboeia* (Chisukhusa): Medium sized, non-poisonous but biting snake. Very common. More often seen at night in the rainy season. Green-grey colour with white underside.

Olive grass snake, *Psammophis sibilans* (Chidyamsana): Will bite but is generally harmless. Grows up to 130 cm and is common in grass and reed areas such as around Lake Chilwa. Slender build and body upperside is generally olive-brown. Underside is yellow-white.

Yellow-bellied sand snake, *Psammophis subtaeniatus* (Nsalulu): Not dangerous but quick moving. Grows to over one metre but very slender. Found in dry areas of the country. Underside is yellow. Upperparts are banded brown with sides largely yellowish-white.

Forest cobra, *Naja melanoleuca* (Mbadza): Large but slender snake. Up to 200 cm or more. Upperparts dark brown. Underside is yellow. Poisonous. Found in or near water and in upland areas such as Mulanje.

Mozambique spitting cobra, *Naja mossambica* (Mamba): Spits venom over 2.5 m rather than bites. Seems to aim at the eyes. Poisonous. Underside is yellow. Upper parts vary from green-brown to pink-brown. Common throughout Malawi.

Egyptian cobra, *Naja haje* (Mamba): Large and poisonous snake, 180 cm in length. Grey-black upperparts, underside is yellowish-white. Found in woodland areas. Hides in old termite mounds.

Black mamba, *Dendroaspis polyepis* (Songwe): Very large snake (up to 275 cm) but slender. Poisonous. Colour is more grey-brown than black. Underside is white. Common only in Lower Shire Valley and around Lake Malawi.

Puff-adder, *Bitis arietans* (Phiri): Grows to just under one metre. Common throughout the country and said to account for 80 to 90 per cent of all serious snake bites in Malawi. May be seen lying on road surfaces when it's cool. Yellow-brown to rust-brown with characteristic V-shaped black marks pointing to the tail.

Rhombic night adder, *Causus rhombeatus* (Kasambwe): Small snake (60 cm) but quite common in wetter areas. Poisonous but not dangerous. Mixed colours of grey, brown, green and yellow.

Burrowing viper, *Atractaspis bibroni* (Chigonakusa): Small snake up to 50 cm. Common in the wetter parts of the country. Poisonous. Darkish brown to almost black on upperside but white to dark brown on underside.

Nile crocodile, *Crocodylus niloticus* (Ng'ona): Still common in Shire River and in parts of Lake Malawi and larger rivers. Dangerous. Seen mostly in water or on river banks or lake beaches. Adults up to 4.5 m but, exceptionally, can be larger.

Water monitor, *Varanus niloticus:* Large lizard which reaches over one metre (39ins). Not dangerous unless cornered. Found close to rivers and lakes.

Animal Checklist

Mammals

INSECTIVORES
(Insectivora)
Elephant Shrew
Musk Shrew
Dwarf Shrew

BATS
(Chiroptera)
Straw-Coloured Fruit
Egyptian Fruit
Epauletted Fruit
Tomb
Leaf-Nosed
Slit-faced
Horseshoe
Vesper
Free-Tailed

PRIMATES
(Primates)
Chacma Baboon
Yellow Baboon
Vervet Monkey
Samango Monkey
Thick-tailed Bushbaby
Lesser Bushbaby

PANGOLINS
(Pholidota)
Pangolin

HARES & RABBITS
(Lagomorpha)
Scrub Hare
Red Rock Rabbit

RODENTS
(Rodentia)
Squirrel
Dormouse
Molerat
Porcupine
Cane-Rat
Pouched Mouse
Giant Rat
Fat Mouse
Climbing Mouse
Gerbil
Spiny Mouse
Rock Mouse
Water Rat
Single-Striped Mouse
Pygmy Mouse
House Mouse
Tree Mouse
Woodland Mouse
Grooved-Toothed Rat
Multimammate Mouse
House Rat
Vlei Rat

CARNIVORES
(Carnivora)
Side-Striped Jackal
Wild Dog
Cape Clawless Otter
Spotted-Necked Otter
Honey Badger
Striped Polecat
Banded Mongoose
Bushy-Tailed
Mongoose
Large Grey Mongoose
Slender Mongoose
Dwarf Mongoose
Large-Spotted Genet
Civet
Spotted Hyena
African Wild Cat
Serval
Lion
Leopard

AARDVARK
(Tubulidentata)
Aardvark

ELEPHANTS
(Proboscidea)
African Elephant

HYRAXES
(Hydracoidea)
Rock Hyrax (Dassie)

ODD-TOED UNGULATES
(Perissodactyla)
Burchell's Zebra
Hook-Lipped
Rhinoceros

EVEN-TOED UNGULATES
(Artiodactyla)
Warthog
Bushpig
Hippopotamus
Buffalo
Eland
Kudu
Nyala
Bushbuck
Roan Antelope
Sable Antelope
Waterbuck
Puku
Reedbuck
Lichtenstein's
  Hartebeest
Impala
Livingstone's Suni
Klipspringer
Oribi
Sharpe's Grysbok
Red Duiker
Blue Duiker
Common Duiker

Birds

GREBES
(Podicipedidae)
Dabchick

PELICANS
(Pelecanidae)
White Pelican
Pinkbacked Pelican

CORMORANTS
(Phalacrocoracidae)
Whitebreasted
  Cormorant
Reed Cormorant

DARTERS
(Anhingidae)
Darter

HERONS, EGRETS, BITTERNS
(Ardeidae)
Bittern
Little Bittern
Dwarf Bittern
Blackcrowned Night
  Heron
Whitebacked Night
  Heron
Squacco Heron
Madagascar Squacco
  Heron
Cattle Egret
Greenbacked Heron
Rufousbellied Heron
Black Egret
Great White Egret
Yellowbilled Egret
Little Egret
Grey Heron
Blackheaded Heron
Goliath Heron
Purple Heron

HAMERKOP
(Scopidae)
Hamerkop

STORKS
(Ciconiidae)
White Stork
Black Stork
Adbim's Stork
Woollynecked Stork
Saddlebilled Stork
Openbilled Stork
Marabou Stork
Yellowbilled Stork

SHOEBILL
(Balaenicipitidae)
Shoebill

IBISES & SPOONBILLS
(Plataleidae)
Sacred Ibis
Hadeda Ibis
Glossy Ibis
African Spoonbill

FLAMINGOS
(Phoenicopteridae)
Greater Flamingo
Lesser Flamingo

DUCKS & GEESE
(Anatidae)
Fulvous Duck
Whitefaced Duck
Egyptian Goose
Spurwinged Goose
Knobbilled Duck
Pygmy Duck
African Black Duck
Cape Teal
Yellowbilled Duck
Pintail
Redbilled Teal

Hottentot Teal
Garganey
European Shoveller
Southern Pochard
Tufted Duck
Maccoa Duck
Whitebacked Duck

SECRETARYBIRD
(Sagittariidae)
Secretarybird

**VULTURES,
HARRIERS, EAGLES,
HAWKS, ETC**
(Accipitridae)
Lappetfaced Vulture
Whiteheaded Vulture
Whitebacked Vulture
Hooded Vulture
Palmnut Vulture
Pallid Harrier
Montagu's Harrier
African Marsh Harrier
European Marsh
  Harrier
Gymnogene
Bateleur
Blackbreasted Snake
  Eagle
Brown Snake Eagle
Western Banded Snake
  Eagle
Black Sparrowhawk
Redbreasted
  Sparrowhawk
Ovambo Sparrowhawk
African Goshawk
Little Banded Goshawk
Little Sparrowhawk
Dark Chanting
  Goshawk
Gabar Goshawk
Lizard Buzzard
Augur Buzzard
Steppe Buzzard
Forest Buzzard
Longcrested Eagle
Crowned Eagle
Martial Eagle
African Hawk Eagle
Booted Eagle
Ayres' Eagle
Black Eagle
Tawny Eagle
Steppe Eagle
Lesser Spotted Eagle
Wahlberg's Eagle
African Fish Eagle
Yellowbilled Kite
Honey Buzzard

Cuckoo Hawk
Blackshouldered Kite
Bat Hawk

OSPREY
(Pandionidae)
Osprey

**FALCONS &
KESTRELS**
(Falconidae)
Lanner Falcon
Peregrine Falcon
Taita Falcon
African Hobby Falcon
Hobby Falcon
Sooty Falcon
Rednecked Falcon
Dickinson's Kestrel
Western Redfooted
  Kestrel Falcon
Eastern Redfooted
  Kestrel Falcon
Lesser Kestrel
Rock Kestrel
Grey Kestrel

**FRANCOLINS &
QUAILS**
(Phasianidae)
Coqui Francolin
Crested Francolin
Shelley's Francolin
Redwing Francolin
Hildebrandt's
  Francolin
Rednecked Francolin
Swainson's Francolin
Scaly Francolin
Common Quail
Harlequin Quail
Blue Quail

GUINEAFOWLS
(Numididae)
Helmeted Guineafowl
Crested Guineafowl

BUTTONQUAILS
(Turnicidae)
Kurrichane
  Buttonquail
Blackrumped
  Buttonquail

CRANES
(Gruidae)
Wattled Crane
Crowned Crane

**RAILS, CRAKES,
FLUFFTAILS,
COOTS, ETC.**
(Rallidae)
African Rail
Corncrake
African Crake
Ballion's Crake
Spotted Crake
Striped Crake
Black Crake
Buffspotted Flufftail
Redchested Flufftail
Longtoed Flufftail
Streakybreasted
  Flufftail
Striped Flufftail
Lesser Moorhen
Moorhen
Purple Gallinule
Lesser Gallinule
Redknobbed Coot

FINFOOTS
(Heliornithidae)
African Finfoot

**BUSTARDS &
KORHAANS**
(Otididae)
Stanley's Bustard
Blackbellied Bustard

JACANAS
(Jacanidae)
African Jacana
Lesser Jacana

PAINTED SNIPES
(Rostratulidae)
Painted Snipe

PLOVERS
(Charadriidae)
Blacksmith Plover
Lesser Blackwinged
  Plover
Crowned Plover
Longtoed Plover
Whitecrowned Plover
Wattled Plover
American Golden
  Plover
Grey Plover
Ringed Plover
Threebanded Plover
Kittlitz's Plover
Whitefronted Plover
Sand Plover
Caspian Plover

**SANDPIPERS,
SNIPES, ETC.**
(Scolopacidae)
Whimbrel
Curlew
Blacktailed Godwit
Bartailed Godwit
Greenshank
Marsh Sandpiper
Green Sandpiper
Common Sandpiper
Spotted Redshank
Redshank
Terek Sandpiper
Turnstone
Great Snipe
African Snipe
Common (European)
  Snipe
Curlew Sandpiper
Little Stint
Sanderling
Broadbilled Sandpiper
Ruff

STILTS & AVOCETS
(Recurvirostridae)
Blackwinged Stilt
Avocet

DIKKOPS
(Burhindae)
Spotted Dikkop
Water Dikkop

**COURSERS &
PRATINCOLES**
(Glareolidae)
Temminck's Courser
Threebanded Courser
Bronzewinged Courser
Redwinged Pratincole
Blackwinged
  Pratincole
Rock Pratincole

GULLS & TERNS
(Laridae)
Greyheaded Gull
Blackheaded Gull
Lesssser Blackbacked
  Gull
Gullbilled Tern
Common Tern
Sooty Tern
Whiskered Tern
Whitewinged Tern

SKIMMERS
(Rynchopidae)
African Skimmer

SANDGROUSE
(Pteroclididae)
Doublebanded
  Sandgrouse

PIGEONS & DOVES
(Columbidae)
Rameron Pigeon
Delegorgue's Pigeon
Pinkbreasted Turtle
  Dove
Redeyed Dove
Mourning Dove
Cape Turtle Dove
Laughing Dove
Namaqua Dove
Tambourine Dove
Bluespotted Dove
Emeraldspotted Dove
Cinnamon Dove
Green Pigeon

PARROTS &
LOVEBIRDS
(Psittacidae)
Cape Parrot
Brownheaded Parrot
Meyer's Parrot
Lilian's Lovebird

LOURIES
(Musophagidae)
Livingstone's Lourie
Purplecrested Lourie
Grey Lourie
Blackfaced Lourie

CUCKOOS &
COUCALS
(Cuculidae)
Great Spotted Cuckoo
Jacobin Cuckoo
Redchested Cuckoo
Black Cuckoo
African Cuckoo
European Cuckoo
Lesser Cuckoo
Madagascar Lesser
  Cuckoo
Thickbilled Cuckoo
Barred Cuckoo
Klaa's Cuckoo
Diederik Cuckoo
Emerald Cuckoo
Green Coucal
Black Coucal
Copperytailed Coucal
Senegal Coucal
Whitebrowed Coucal
Burchell's Coucal

BARN OWLS
(Tytonidae)
Barn Owl
Grass Owl

OWLS
(Strigidae)
Scops Owl
Whitefaced Owl
Cape Eagle Owl
Spotted Eagle Owl
Giant Eagle Owl
Pel's Fishing Owl
Pearlspotted Owl
Barred Owl
Wood Owl
Marsh Owl

NIGHTJARS
(Caprimulgidae)
European Nightjar
Fierynecked Nightjar
Mountain Nightjar
Freckled Nightjar
Mozambique Nightjar
Pennantwinged
  Nightjar

SWIFTS &
SPINETAILS
(Apodidae)
Scarce Swift
Mottled Spinetail
Böhm's Spinetail
Palm Swift
Alpine Swift
Mottled Swift
Black Swift
Eurasian Swift
Little Swift
Horus Swift
Whiterumped Swift

MOUSEBIRDS
(Coliidae)
Speckled Mousebird
Redfaced Mousebird

TROGONS
(Trogonidae)
Narina Trogon
Bartailed Trogon

KINGFISHERS
(Halcyonidae)
Giant Kingfisher
Pied Kingfisher
Halfcollared Kingfisher
Malachite Kingfisher
Pygmy Kingfisher
Woodland Kingfisher
Striped Kingfisher

Brownhooded
  Kingfisher
Greyhooded
  Kingfisher

BEE-EATERS
(Meropidae)
European Bee-eater
Bluecheeked Bee-eater
Olive Bee-eater
Carmine Bee-eater
Böhm's Bee-eater
Little Bee-eater
Whitefronted Bee-eater
Swallowtailed Bee-eater

ROLLERS
(Coraciidae)
European Roller
Lilacbreasted Roller
Racket-tailed Roller
Purple Roller
Broadbilled Roller

HOOPOES
(Upupidae)
Hoopoe

WOODHOOPOES
(Phoeniculidae)
Redbilled
  Woodhoopoes
Scimitarbilled
  Woodhoopoe

HORNBILLS
(Bucerotidae)
Grey Hornbill
Redbilled Hornbill
Yellowbilled Hornbill
Palebilled Hornbill
Crowned Hornbill
Trumpeter Hornbill
Silverycheeked Hornbill
Ground Hornbill

BARBETS
(Capitonidae)
Brownbreasted Barbet
Blackbacked Barbet
Blackcollared Barbet
Miombo Pied Barbet
White-eared Barbet
Green Barbet
Whyte's Barbet
Moustached Green
  Tinkerbird
Green Tinker Barbet
Yellowfronted Tinker
  Barbet
Goldenrumped Tinker
  Barbet
Crested Barbet

HONEYGUIDES
(Indicatoridae)
Scalythroated
  Honeyguide
Greater Honeyguide
Lesser Honeyguide
Eastern Honeyguide
Slenderbilled
  Honeyguide
Sharpbilled
  Honeyguide

WOODPECKERS
(Picidae)
Bennett's Woodpecker
Goldentailed
  Woodpecker
Little Spotted
  Woodpecker
Cardinal Woodpecker
Stierling's Woodpecker
Olive Woodpecker
Bearded Woodpecker

BROADBILLS
(Eurylaimidae)
African Broadbill

PITTAS
(Pittidae)
African Pitta

LARKS
(Alaudidae)
Rufousnaped Lark
Flappet Lark
Dusky Lark
Redcapped Lark
Chestnutbacked
  Finchlark
Fischer's Finchlark

MARTINS &
SWALLOWS
(Hirundinidae)
Banded Martin
European Sand Martin
Brownthroated Martin
European Swallow
Angola Swallow
Blue Swallow
Wiretailed Swallow
Whitethroated
  Swallow
Pearlbreasted Swallow
Redbreasted Swallow
Mosque Swallow
Redrumped Swallow
Greater Striped
  Swallow
Lesser Striped Swallow

Greyrumped Swallow
South African Cliff
  Swallow
Rock Martin
House Martin
Eastern Saw-wing
  Swallow
Black Saw-wing
  Swallow
Whiteheaded Saw-wing
  Swallow
Mascarene Martin

DRONGOS
(Dicruridae)
Squaretailed Drongo
Forktailed Drongo

ORIOLES
(Oriolidae)
European Golden Oriole
African Golden Oriole
Blackheaded Oriole
Greenheaded Oriole

CROWS
(Corvidae)
Pied Crow
Whitenecked Raven

TITS
(Paridae)
Northern Grey Tit
Southern Black Tit
Carp's Black Tit
Rufousbellied Tit

PENDULINE TITS
(Remizidae)
Grey Penduline Tits

CREEPERS
(Salpornithidae)
Spotted Creeper

BABBLERS
(Timaliidae)
Mountain Babbler
Mountain Illadopsis
Arrowmarked Babbler

CUCKOOSHRIKES
(Campephagidae)
Whitebreasted
  Cuckooshrike
Grey Cuckooshrike
Black Cuckooshrike

BULBULS
(Pycnonotidae)
Blackeyed Bulbul
Sombre Bulbul
Little Green Bulbul
Olivebreasted
  Mountain Bulbul
Stripecheeked Bulbul
Montane Bulbul
Yellowbellied Bulbul
Terrestrial Bulbul
Grey-olive Bulbul
Placid Bulbul
Yellowstreaked Bulbul
Yellowspotted Nicator

CHATS, ROBINS, THRUSHES, ETC.
(Turdidae)
Whinchat
Stonechat
European Wheatear
Capped Wheatear
Familiar Chat
Arnot's Chat
Mocking Chat
Miombo Rock Thrush
Boulder Chat
Rufous Bushchat
Whitebrowed Robin
Central Bearded
  Scrub Robin
Bearded Robin
Collared Palm Thrush
Cholo Alethe
Whitebreasted Alethe
Oliveflanked Robin
Sharpe's Akalat
Gunning's Robin
Starred Robin
Natal Robin
Cape Robin
Heuglin's Robin
Spot-throat Modulatrix
Thrush Nightingale
Mountain Thrush
Kurrichane Thrush
Spotted Thrush
Groundscraper Thrush
Orange Thrush

WARBLERS
(Sylviidae)
African Sedge Warbler
Eastern Forest
  Scrub Warbler
Longtailed Forest
  Scrub Warbler
Broadtailed Warbler
River Warbler
European Sedge

Warbler
European Marsh Warbler
European Reed Warbler
Great Reed Warbler
Basra Reed Warbler
African Marsh Warbler
Cape Reed Warbler
Yellow Warbler
Yellow Mountain
  Warbler
Moustached Warbler
Icterine Warbler
Olivetree Warbler
Garden Warbler
European Blackcap
Whitethroat
European Barred
  Warbler
Brown Warbler
Willow Warbler
Yellowthroated
  Warbler
Tawnyflanked Prinia
Redwinged Warbler
Barthroated Apalis
Rudd's Apalis
Whitewinged Apalis
Yellowbreasted Apalis
Chestnut-throated
  Apalis
Brownheaded Apalis
Blackheaded Apalis
Bleating Bush Warbler
Stierling's Barred
  Warbler
Yellowbellied
  Eremomela
Greencapped
  Eremomela
Burntnecked
  Eremomela
Redfaced Crombec
Redcapped Crombec
Longbilled Crombec
Yellowbreasted Hyliota
Mashona Hyliota
Redfaced Cisticola
Singing Cisticola
Trilling Cisticola
Mountain Cisticola
Lazy Cisticola
Rattling Cisticola
Tinkling Cisticola
Wailing Cisticola
Churring Cisticola
Blackbacked Cisticola
Croaking Cisticola
Neddicky
Shortwinged Cisticola
Fantailed Cisticola
Ayres' Cisticola

FLYCATCHERS
(Muscicapidae)
Spotted Flycatcher
Collared Flycatcher
Dusky Flycatcher
Bluegrey Flycatcher
Boehm's Flycatcher
Fantailed Flycatcher
Slaty Flycatcher
Black Flycatcher
Mousecoloured
  Flycatcher
Vanga Flycatcher
Cape Batis
Chinspot Batis
Mozambique Batis
Wattle-eyed Flycatcher
Livingstone's
  Flycatcher
Whitetailed Blue
  Flycatcher
Bluemantled
  Flycatcher
Whitetailed Flycatcher
Paradise Flycatcher

TCHAGRAS & BUSH SHRIKES
(Malaconotidae)
Brubru
Puffback
Marsh Tchagra
Threestreaked Tchagra
Blackcrowned Tchagra
Southern Boubou
Fülleborn's Black
  Boubou
Orangebreasted
  Bush Shrike
Blackfronted
  Bush Shrike
Olive Bush Shrike
Greyheaded
  Bush Shrike
Gorgeous Bush Shrike

WAGTAILS, PIPITS & LONGCLAWS
(Motacillidae)
Yellow Wagtail
Longtailed Wagtail
Grey Wagtail
African Pied Wagtail
White Wagtail
Grassveld Pipit
Plainbacked Pipit
Buffy Pipit
Wood Pipit
Jackson's Pipit
Bushveld Pipit
Tree Pipit

Striped Pipit
Yellowthroated
  Longclaw
Pinkthroated Longclaw

SHRIKES
(Laniidae)
Redbacked Shrike
Redtailed Shrike
Lesser Grey Shrike
Longtailed Shrike
Fiscal Shrike
Souza's Shrike

HELMETSHRIKES
(Prionopidae)
White Helmetshrike
Redbilled
  Helmetshrike

STARLINGS
(Sturnidae)
Waller's Redwinged
  Starling
Redwinged Starling
Slenderbilled
  Redwinged Starling
Lesser Blue-eared
  Glossy Starling
Greater Blue-eared
  Glossy Starling
Longtailed Glossy
  Starling
Plumcoloured Starling
Whitewinged Babbling
  Starling
Wattled Starling

OXPECKERS
(Buphagidae)
Yellowbilled Oxpecker
Redbilled Oxpecker

SUNBIRDS
(Nectariniidae)
Red and Blue Sunbird
Violetbacked Sunbird
Collared Sunbird
Olive Sunbird
Greenheaded Sunbird
Black Sunbird
Scarletchested Sunbird
Whitebellied Sunbird
Oustalet's Sunbird
Yellowbellied Sunbird
Greater Doublecollared
  Sunbird
Miombo Double-
  collared Sunbird
Eastern Doublecollared
  Sunbird

Shelley's Sunbird
Purplebanded Sunbird
Correry Sunbird
Grey Sunbird
Malachite Sunbird
Redtufted Malachite
  Sunbird
Bronze Sunbird

WHITE-EYES
(Zosteropidae)
Yellow White-eye

WEAVERS &
QUELEAS
(Ploceidae)
Thickbilled Weaver
Baglafecht Weaver
Bertram's Weaver
Yellow Weaver
Golden Weaver
Brownthroated Weaver
Lesser Masked Weaver
Masked Weaver
Spottedbacked Weaver
Forest Weaver
Spectacled Weaver
Oliveheaded Weaver
Redheaded Weaver
Cardinal Quelea
Redheaded Quelea
Redbilled Quelea
Red Bishop
Firecrowned Bishop
Yellowrumped Widow
Yellowbacked Widow
Redshouldered Widow
Mountain Marsh Widow
Whitewinged Widow
Redcollared Widow
Cuckoo Finch
Whitebrowed
  Sparrow-weaver
Chestnutmantled
  Sparrow-weaver
House Sparrow
Greyheaded Sparrow
Yellowthroated
  Sparrow

WHYDAHS AND
WIDOWFINCHES
(Viduidae)
Pintailed Whydah
Purple Widowfinch
Black Widowfinch
Steelblue Widowfinch
Paradise Whydah
Broadtailed Paradise
  Whydah

PYTILIAS,
WAXBILLS,
MANNIKINS, ETC
(Estrildidae)
Goldenbacked Pytilia
Melba Finch
Green Twinspot
Redfaced
  Crimsonwing
Redthroated Twinspot
Redbilled Firefinch
Bluebilled Firefinch
Jameson's Firefinch
Blue Waxbill
Grey Waxbill
East African Swee
Crimsonrumped
  Waxbill
Common Waxbill
Orangebreasted
  Waxbill
Quail Finch
Locust Finch
Bronze Mannikin
Redbacked Mannikin
Pied Mannikin
Cut-throat Finch

BUNTINGS,
CANARIES,
SEEDEATERS
(Fringillidae)
Cabanis's Bunting
Goldenbreasted
  Bunting
Rock Bunting
Cape Bunting
Yelloweyed Canary
Lemonbreasted Canary
Bully Canary
Cape Canary
African Citril
Streaky Canary
  (Seedeater)
Stripebreasted Canary
  (Seedeater)
Blackeared Canary
Oriole Finch

Amphibians, Reptiles and Fish

African Bullfrog
Grey Tree Frog
Schlegel's Blind Snake
Peter's Worm Snake
African Python
Common House Snake

Water Snake
Western Green Snake
File Snake
Eastern Green Snake
Common Egg Eater
Boomslang
Vine Snake
Tiger Snake
Herald Snake
Olive Grass Snake
Yellow-Bellied Sand
  Snake
Cape Centipede-Eater
Forest Cobra
Egyptian Cobra
Mozambique Spitting
  Cobra
Green Mamba
Black Mamba
Half-Banded Garter
  Snake
Puff Adder
Rhombic Night Adder
Snouted Night Adder
Burrowing Viper
Water Monitor
Nile Crocodile
Terrapin
Hinged Tortoise
African Mud Turtle
Binga
Catfish
Chambo
Mottled Eel
Elephant-snout Fish
Kampango
Mbuna
Minnow
Mpasa (Lake Salmon)
Ncheni
Sanjika
Sungwa
Tigerfish
Usipa
Utaka
Yellowfish

Demographic Profile

Population
At the 1998 census Malawi's population was 9.9 million with a growth rate of 2%. Because the country is relatively small (Zambia covers six times the area yet has a smaller population), this creates one of the highest densities in Africa of 105 per square kilometre (272 per square mile).

Languages
English is the official language and is widely used, particularly in the commercial sector, as the primary language. The national language is Chewa (or Chichewa — literally 'language of the Chewa'), with Nyanja, Yao and Tumbuka (common in the north) the next most used local languages.

Religion
Eighty per cent of the population is Christian with the Church of Central Africa Presbyterian the strongest in the country. Muslims account for 13 per cent, restricting indigenous beliefs to a small minority. There is freedom of worship.

Gazetteer

Figures shown below are distances in kilometres between major towns.

LILONGWE
Central Region.
Blantyre 311, Karonga 586, Kasungu 121, Mangochi 263, Mchinji 109, Mzuzu 360, Nkhotakota 191, Nsanje 490, Salima 98, Zomba 284. Alt: 1,050 metres. Pop: 505,200. Post Office. Hospital tel: 751 109. Police tel: 753 333. Emergency tel: 199. Petrol and diesel. Hotels, campsites. International airport.

BLANTYRE
Southern Region.
Karonga 822, Kasungu 432, Lilongwe 311, Mangochi 187, Mchinji 420, Mzuzu 596, Nkhotakota 369, Nsanje 179, Salima 264, Zomba 66. Alt: 1,050 metres. Pop: 506,700. Post Office. Hospital tel: 630 333. Police tel: 623 333. Emergency tel: 199. Petrol and diesel. Hotels, campsites. International airport.

ZOMBA
Southern Region.
Blantyre 66, Karonga 795, Kasungu 405, Lilongwe 284, Mangochi 121, Mchinji 393, Mzuzu 569, Nkhotakota 342, Nsanje 245, Salima 237.

Alt: 1,150 metres. Pop: 71,300. Post Office. Hospital tel: 523 266. Police tel: 522 333. Fire tel: 523 999. Petrol and diesel. Hotel, campsites.

MZUZU
Northern Region.
Blantyre 596, Karonga 226, Kasungu 240, Lilongwe 360, Mangochi 503, Mchinji 370, Nkhotakota 227, Nsanje 775, Salima 338, Zomba 569. Alt: 1,200 metres. Pop: 72,900. Post Office. Hospital tel: 332 888. Police tel: 332 333. Fire tel: 332 999. Petrol and diesel. Hotels, campsites. Airport.

MCHINJI
Central Region.
Blantyre 420, Karonga 596, Kasungu 131, Lilongwe 109, Mangochi 372, Mzuzu 370, Nkhotakota 257, Nsanje 599, Salima 207, Zomba 393. Alt: 1,200 metres. Pop: 61,400. Post Office. Hospital tel: 242 266. Police tel: 242 333. Fire tel: 242 333. Petrol and diesel.

Museums, Monuments and Historical Sites

Blantyre

Mandala House
Kaoshiung Road.
Said to be the oldest house in Malawi. Built in 1882, it was the headquarters of the Livingstonia Central African Company, now the African Lakes Corporation. It is possible to visit the house in normal office hours.

Old Boma
Victoria Avenue.
The original Town Hall in central Blantyre. One of the few old colonial buildings still remaining in the town. There is no admittance to the building.

St Michael and All Angels Church
Chileka Road.
The church was dedicated in 1891, the work of David Clement Scott who was a missionary. An incredible feat for someone with no training in architecture. Various connections with David Livingstone. Entry is free.

Museums of Malawi
Between central Blantyre and Limbe, Kasungu Crescent.
Exhibits inside and outside the museum tell the story of the country's culture and history. Officially open every day, including Sunday, 08.00 to 17.30. No entry fee but donations expected.

Heritage Centre
Limbe, near Shire Highlands Hotel.
Includes a small Transport Museum as well as the offices of the Malawi Wildlife Society and the Society of Malawi library. There is a well stocked shop. Open during the week 08.00-12.00 and 13.30-16.00 and between 08.30 and 12.00 on Saturday (library only open Monday afternoon and Friday morning, or by appointment).

Zomba

Old Parliament Buildings
To west of main road (M3).
The former Parliament and other old colonial buildings can be viewed only from the outside but they recall the importance of Zomba as the capital before the change to Lilongwe in the 1970s.

KAR Clocktower and Memorial
To west of main road (M3), near southern entrance to town.
At Cobbe Barracks, the clocktower is a memorial to the King's African Rifles (KAR), now the Malawi Rifles. It carries the interesting battle honours of the KAR. There is free access

Mikuyu Jail
Off the main road (M3), north of the town.
The old jail is about ten kilometres (six miles) out of Zomba. This was where many prominent citizens were incarcerated during the Banda regime. It now forms a memorial to its former inmates and is generally open to the public.

Mzuzu

Mzuzu Museum
M'Mbelwa Road.
This is a small museum devoted to telling the story of the North Malawi and its peoples. Much used by school children as an educational resource. Open every day except public holidays 07.30-12.00 and 13.00-17.00. No admission charge.

Central Malawi

Cave Paintings and Ancient Iron Kiln
Kasungu National Park.
Close to the Zambian border and north-west of Lifupa Lodge in the national park, this historical site dates from the late Stone Age and early Iron Age. Smelting continued up to the 1930s. Other historical sites are in the park. Open access once in the park. Entry to the park is US$5.

Kachere Tree
Kamuzu Academy.
The tree, now a national monument, is said to be where Dr Hastings Banda first received his education. The 'drum tree' was used to hang a drum which was beaten to call the children to their lessons. Open access.

Chencherere Rock Shelter
About 80 kilometres (50 miles) south of Lilongwe off the M1. The rock shelters contain geometric paintings of the Batwa people who hunted the area in Neolithic times.

Dedza Stone Age Paintings
Dedza Mountain.
These cave paintings were made by the Nyau, a secret society associated with witchcraft and prominent even in recent times. In addition to the paintings are strange markings in the caves. Open access.

North Malawi

Fingira Rock
Nyika Plateau.
The rock is a granite dome with a cave about half way up the eastern side. The cave was used as a shelter in Neolithic times and it also has Iron Age rock paintings in the form of geometric patterns. There is access through Nyika National Park. Entrance to the park is US$5.

Livingstonia Mission and Museum
Livingstonia Mission, Khondowe.
The mission includes a church and the Old Stone House which was formerly the home of Dr Robert Laws' family. Laws was one of David Livingstone's missionaries. There is also a museum in the Stone House. The exhibits tell a fascinating story of the early mission. Many of the items are priceless. The museum is open from 07.30 to 17.00 each day except Sunday when it opens at 13.30. Admission charge to the museum is K10.

War Graves
Karonga.
In the town cemetery are some graves dating from the 1914 Battle of Karonga in World War I between the forces from German East Africa (Tanzania) and British/Malawi troops. Open access.

South Malawi

Postal Museum
Namaka, between Zomba and Blantyre (M3).
Properly called the Mtenga-tenga Postal Hut, this little museum is a philatelist's delight. The exhibits tell the story of Malawi's postal services from colonial times. Generally open in office hours.

Chingwe's Hole
Zomba Plateau.
Well-like feature with a depth of about 20 metres (65 feet), the hole is said to be an ancient burial place where bodies were lowered into a cave by rope (chingwe). Open access to the site.

Fort Lister
Mount Mulanje.
The ruins of this fort are in the Lister Gap on the east side of Mount Mulanje. This was an anti-slave trade fort built in 1893. There are graves alongside. Open access.

Kapichira Falls
Majete Wildlife Reserve, Lower Shire Valley
These are the falls where, in 1859, David Livingstone was forced to abandon his voyage up the Shire River in his quest to reach Lake Malawi. Open access through Majete Wildlife Reserve. Entrance fee (to the reserve) US$5.

Livingstone Chapel
Lower Shire Valley
The chapel is a memorial to David Livingstone. Open access is through the Majete Safari Camp near to the Majete Reserve. It is in the grounds of, and owned by, the camp.

Lake Malawi

Queen Victoria Memorial
Mangochi
The memorial was erected in 1903 and is in the form of a clocktower. It is close to the town's bridge over the Shire River. Open access.

World War I Relic
Mangochi
A Hotchkiss gun taken from the lake patrol gunboat *Gwendolen* is all that remains to commemorate the first naval action of World War I. The gun is usually to be seen near to the clocktower (it has been temporarily housed in the museum). Open access.

mv Viphya Memorial
Mangochi.
The memorial is close to the clocktower and commemorates the loss of 145 lives on 30 July 1946 when the *mv Viphya* sank in Lake Malawi. Open access.

Lake Malawi Museum
Mangochi.
The museum is in the middle of the town. There is a broad range of exhibits, most of which show the history, including the natural history, of the lake. Open daily, no charge.

Lake Malawi National Park Museum
Lake Malawi National Park, Cape Maclear.
This little museum doubles as an environmental centre. It is just inside the park gate by the lake's shore. Open daily, no charge but access to the park is US$5.

Missionaries' Graves
Lake Malawi National Park.
Close to the gate of the Lake Malawi National Park is the site of the graves of four of Dr David Livingstone's missionaries who died in the 1870s. There is open access to the memorial crosses and plaque but there is a charge US$5 to enter the park.

KuNgoni Art and Craft Centre
Mua Mission.
The centre, opened in 1976, is part of the Mua Mission. It is possible to see very fine wood carvings and to visit the mission church. There is a shop selling the carvers' work. There is no charge. Normally open during the day.

Chamare Museum
Mua Mission.
This is the mission museum, opened in 1997. Exhibits, in three rooms, tell the story of the mission and celebrate three of the country's main tribes: the Yao, Chewa and Ngoni. A guided tour is charged at US$5. Unguided tours are not allowed. The museum is generally open during the day.

Livingstone Fig Tree
Nkhotakota.
The tree is inside the courtyard of St Anne's Mission in the centre of the village. This is where, in 1861, Dr David Livingstone failed in his attempt to negotiate the freeing of slaves and the abolition of slavery. Open access.

Bandawe Mission and Graves
Chintheche.
One of the failed sites of the original Livingstonia Mission. Set up by Dr Robert Laws in 1881 the Bandawe mission station has a church and a graveyard. Open access.

St Peter's Cathedral
Likoma Island.
The first mission of the island was established in the 1880s and work on the giant cathedral began in 1903. Interest lies in the size of the building, its construction materials and artefacts. Open access during the day.

Public Holidays

When a public holiday falls on a Saturday or Sunday, the following Monday becomes a holiday.

January 1:	New Year's Day
January 15:	John Chilembwe Day
March 3:	Martyr's Day
March/April*:	Good Friday/Easter Monday
May 1:	Labour Day
June 14:	Freedom Day
July 6:	Republic Day
October, second Monday:	Mother's Day
December 25:	Christmas Day
December 26:	Boxing Day

* no fixed date

Listings

Dialling Codes

Country Code: 265
Malawi has no area codes.
In July 2002 all Malawi's telephone numbers became 8 digits. Landlines gained the prefix 01 and cellphones 08 or 09. When dialling into Malawi from another country, the first 0 should NOT be dialled.

Air Charter Companies

Lilongwe
Proflight Air Services Ltd
PO Box 30728, Capital City
Tel: 01 754 717
Fax: 01 756 321
Email: proflight@malawi.net
www.zambiz.co.zm/proflight

Airlines

Blantyre
Air Malawi
Robins Road
PO Box 84
Tel: 01 620 811
Fax: 01 624 607/01 620 042

British Airways
Unit House
Victoria Avenue
PO Box 1225
Tel: 01 624 333/01 624 519
Fax: 01 623 221
Email:
malawi.1.info@britishairways.com

KLM Royal Dutch
Airlines
Mount Soche Hotel
PO Box 2136
Tel: 01 620 877/01 620 106
Fax: 01 622 449

South African Airways
Nico House
Haile Selassie Road
PO Box 672
Tel: 01 620 629/01 620 627
Fax: 01 620 027

Lilongwe
Air Tanzania
Centre House
PO Box 1118
Tel: 01 771 589

Air Zimbabwe
Arwa House
Private Bag 371
Tel: 01 771 430/01 773 583
Fax: 01 773 780

Ethiopian Airlines
Mitco House
PO Box 30427
Tel: 01 772 001/01 772 002
Fax: 01 772 013

Kenya Airways
Capital Hotel
PO Box 30818
Tel: 01 774 227/01 774 330
Fax: 01 774 293
Email: kenya-airways@malawi.net

Airports

Blantyre
Chileka Airport
Tel: 01 692 274/01 692 244

Lilongwe
Lilongwe International
Airport
Tel: 01 700 766

Mzuzu
Mzuzu Airport
Tel: 01 332 666

Banks

Blantyre
Commercial Bank
of Malawi
Victoria Avenue/Glyn
Jones Road
PO Box 1111
Tel: 01 620 144
Fax: 01 620 360
Email: combank@malawi.net

National Bank of Malawi
Victoria Avenue
PO Box 947
Tel: 01 620 199
Fax: 01 620 965

Lilongwe
Commercial Bank of
Malawi
African Unity Avenue
Capital City
PO Box 30386
Tel: 01 770 988
Fax: 01 773 493

Commercial Bank of Malawi
Kamuzu Procession Rd
Old Town
PO Box 522
Tel: 01 755 277
Fax: 01 755 728

National Bank of Malawi
Lingadzi House
Capital City
PO Box 30317
Tel: 01 770 322

National Bank of Malawi
Kamuzu Procession Rd
Old Town
Tel: 01 750 188

Mzuzu
Commercial Bank of Malawi
Orton Chewa Avenue
PO Box 104
Tel: 01 332 366
Fax: 01 332 574

National Bank of Malawi
Orton Chewa Avenue
PO Box 20 or 140
Tel: 01 332 500
Fax: 01 333 467

Zomba
Commercial Bank of Malawi
Kamuzu Highway
PO Box 302
Tel: 01 522 231
Fax: 01 522 088

National Bank of Malawi
Kamuzu Highway
PO Box 13
Tel: 01 522 788
Fax: 01 522 749

Boat Services

Liwonde
Waterline
PO Box 1641, Blantyre
Tel: 01 542 552
Fax: 01 542 552
Email: colin_sue@malawi.net
www.riversafarimalawi.com

Monkey Bay
Malawi Lake
Services Ltd
PO Box 15
Tel: 01 587 311
Fax: 01 587 359

Booksellers

Blantyre
Central Africana Ltd
Victoria Avenue
PO Box 631
Tel: 01 623 227
Fax: 01 620 533
Email: africana@sdnp.org.mw

Central Bookshops
Livingstone Avenue
PO Box 264
Tel: 01 623 535
Fax: 01 633 863
Email: hamidcbs@malawi.net

Times Bookshops Ltd
Private Bag 39
Tel: 01 670 000

Bus and Coach Companies

Blantyre
Shire Bus Lines
Masauko Chipembere
Highway
PO Box 176
Tel: 01 671 388
Fax: 01 670 038

Trans Zambezi Express
PO Box 1179
Tel: 01 623 262
Fax: 01 620 770
Email: transzam@iafrica.com

Translux International
Glyn Jones Rd/Hanover
Avenue
Tel: 01 621 910
Fax: 01 621 916

Lilongwe
Shire Bus Lines
PO Box 26
Tel: 01 756 226/01 726 334
Fax: 01 752 286

Mzuzu
Shire Bus Lines
Tel: 01 332 155
Fax: 01 332 364

Business Associations

Blantyre
Malawi Chamber of
Commerce and Industry
Chamber House
Chichiri Trade Fair
Grounds
PO Box 258
Tel: 01 671 198
Fax: 01 671 147

Malawi Development
Corporation (MDC)
MDC House
Glyn Jones Road
PO Box 566
Tel: 01 620 100
Fax: 01 620 584
Email: mdcgm@malawi.net

Malawi Export
Promotion Council
Delamere House
PO Box 1299
Tel: 01 620 499
Fax: 01 635 429
Email: mepco@malawi.net

Lilongwe
Malawi Investment
Promotion Agency
(MIPA)
Aquarius House
Private Bag 302
Capital City
Tel: 01 770 800
Fax: 01 771 781
Email:mipall@malawi.net

Car Hire

Blantyre
Avis
PO Box 51059, Limbe
Tel: 01 622 719/01 622 748
Fax: 01 672 429
Email: avis@malawi.net

Ceciliana Car Hire
PO Box 30184
Tel: 01 641 219/01 644 366
Fax: 01 640 255
Email: ceciliana@malawi.net
www.cecilianacarhiremalawi.com

Hertz Rent-A-Car
Tel: 01 674 516
Fax: 01 674 326
Email: hertz@malawi.net

Siku Car Hire
PO Box 51033, Limbe
Tel: 01 645 417/01 640 128

SS Rent-A-Car
PO Box 2282
Tel: 01 622 863/01 621 934
Fax: 01 625 074

U-Drive Car Rentals
Masauko Chipembere
Highway
PO Box 51280, Limbe
Tel: 01 645 966/01 642 382

Lilongwe
Afroma Rent-A-Car
Tel: 01 710 140
Fax: 01 712 236

Apex Rent-A-Car
PO Box 1132
Tel: 01 754 610/2/5
Email: apexrentacar@malawi.net

Avis
Tel: 01 750 530/01 750 756
Fax: 01 750 141
Email: avis@malawi.net

Boss Car Rentals
Private Bag 193
Tel: 01 753 816
Fax: 01 754 681

City Car Hire
Area 47
PO Box 31177
Tel: 01 761 550

Eagle Car Hire
PO Box 30700
Tel: 01 770 287

J&K Car Hire
Akulenje Arcade
Murray Road
PO Box 2142
Tel: 01 751 491/01 751 591
Fax: 01 750 642

Rainbow Car Hire
Off Chilambula Road
PO Box 975
Tel: 01 755 497/01 755 517
Fax: 01 752 958

Silver Car Hire
Off Chilambula Road
Tel: 01 753 156/01 752 335
Fax: 01 752 969
Email: tkmwale@sdnp.org.mw

Sputnik Car Hire
PO Box 2315
Tel: 01 761 563/01 771 013
Fax: 01 761 578
Email: sputnik@sdnp.org. mw

Zomba
Grand Prix Car Hire
PO Box 285
Tel: 01 522 598/01 522 101
Fax: 01 522 204
www.grandprixcarhiremalawi.com

Clubs and Societies

Blantyre
Angling Society
of Malawi
PO Box 744
Tel: 01 671 000
Fax: 01 671 151

Blantyre Sports Club
PO Box 245
Tel: 01 621 173/01 635 095

The Golf Union of
Malawi
PO Box 5319, Limbe
Tel: 01 633 007

Limbe Country Club
PO Box 5031
Limbe
Tel: 01 641 022

Mountain Club
of Malawi
PO Box 240
Tel: 01 634 436/01 635 259
Email: mcm@saints.merula.co.uk

The Society (Historical
and Scientific) of Malawi
PO Box 125

Wildlife Society
of Malawi
Heritage Centre
Churchill Road
Private Bag 578
Limbe
Tel: 01 643 502
Fax: 01 643 765
Email: wsm@malawi.net

Dwangwa
Kasasa Club
PO Box 46
Tel: 01 295 266
Fax: 01 295 242

Lilongwe
Lilongwe Golf Club
PO Box 160
Tel: 01 753 118/01 753 598

Mulanje
Mulanje Club
PO Box 59
Tel: 01 465 260

Mzuzu
Mzuzu Club
PO Box 45, Mzuzu
Tel: 01 335 040

Salima
Wildlife Action Group
PO Box 312
Tel: 01 263 143
Fax: 01 263 143
Email: safwag@africa-online.net
www.wag-malawi.org

Sucoma
Sucoma Club
Private Bag 50, Blantyre
Tel: 01 428 200
Fax: 01 428 244

Zomba
Zomba Gymkhana Club
PO Box 39
Tel: 01 522 275/01 523 111

Couriers

Blantyre
DHL
Delamare House
Victoria Avenue
Tel: 01 623 301/01 635 643
Fax: 01 620 631

Lilongwe
DHL
Centre House Arcade
City Centre
Tel: 01 772 366
Fax: 01 772 691

Zomba
DHL
Caltex Filling Station
next to Commercial Bank
Tel: 01 532 764

Mzuzu
DHL
Mzuzu Hotel
Tel: 01 334 390
Fax: 01 334 390

Crafts and Curios

Blantyre
Art of Africa
Tel: 01 633 158/08 829 364

Gangecraft
Chimwenya Estates
Bvumbwe
PO Box 5443, Limbe
Tel: 01 622 315
Fax: 01 652 553

Macoha
Tel: 01 643 466

Nica Arts & Crafts
Tel: 01 650 454

Safari Curios
Galaxy House
Glyn Jones Road
PO Box 1037
Tel: 01 631 947/01 620 164
Fax: 01 632 948

Dedza
Dedza Pottery
Paragon Ceramics Ltd
PO Box 54
Tel: 01 220 316
Fax: 01 220 391

Lilongwe
Gangecraft Art
Africa Shop
Capital Hotel

Mua Mission
KuNgoni Art &
Craft Centre
PO Box 41, Mtakataka
www.muamissionmalawi.com

Nkhotakota
Nkhotakota Pottery
Paragon Ceramics Ltd
PO Box 460

Foreign Diplomatic Missions

Lilongwe
American Embassy
Off Convention Drive
PO Box 30016
City Centre
Tel: 01 773 166

British High Commission
Off Convention Drive
PO Box 30042
City Centre
Tel: 01 772 400/01 772 550
Fax: 01 772 657
Email: blc@wiss.co.mw

German Embassy
Convention Drive
PO Box 30046
City Centre
Tel: 01 772 555
Fax: 01 770 250

Mozambique High
Commission
PO Box 30579
City Centre
Tel: 01 774 100

Royal Norwegian
Embassy
Arwa House
Private Bag B323
City Centre
Tel: 01 774 211/01 774 771
Fax: 01 772 845
Email: normwi@malawi.net

South African High
Commission
PO Box 30043
City Centre
Tel: 01 773 722

Zambian High
Commission
Off Convention Drive
PO Box 30138, City Centre
Tel: 01 772 100

Zimbabwe High
Commission
Off Independence Drive
PO Box 30187, City Centre
Tel: 01 774 988

Galleries

Blantyre
Central Africana Ltd
Victoria Avenue
PO Box 631
Tel: 01 623 227
Fax: 01 620 533
Email: africana@sdnp.org.mw

La Caverna Ltd
Chiperoni Warehouse
Churchill Road
Private Bag 554, Limbe
Tel: 01 643 039/01 642 376
Fax: 01 643 159

Government Offices and Ministries

Blantyre
Department of
Immigration
New Building Society
House
Victoria Avenue
PO Box 331
Tel: 01 623 777
Fax: 01 623 065

Department of
Meteorological Services
PO Box 2
Chileka
Tel: 01 692 333
Fax: 01 692 329
Email: malawimet@malawi.net

Department of Surveys
Chibisa House
Glyn Jones Road
PO Box 349
Tel: 01 623 722
Fax: 01 634 034

Lilongwe
Ministry of Agriculture
and Irrigation
PO Box 30134
Capital City
Tel: 01 788 444

Ministry of Commerce
and Industry
PO Box 30366
Capital City
Tel: 01 770 244

Ministry of Defence
Private Bag 339
Capital City

Ministry of Education,
Science and Technology
Private Bag 328
Capital City
Tel: 01 789 422

Ministry of Finance and
Economic Planning
PO Box 30049
Capital City
Tel: 01 789 355

Department of Forestry
PO Box 30048
Tel: 01 771 000
Fax: 01 774 268/01 771 812

Ministry of Foreign
Affairs and International
Co-operation
PO Box 30315, Capital City
Tel: 01 789 323

Ministry of Gender,
Youth and Community
Services
Private Bag 330
Capital City
Tel: 01 770 411

Ministry of Health and
Population
PO Box 30377, Capital City
Tel: 01 789 400

Ministry of Home Affairs
and Internal Security
Private Bag 331
Capital City
Tel: 01 789 309

Ministry of Information
Private Bag 310
Capital City
Tel: 01 773 233

Ministry of Labour and
Vocational Training
Private Bag 344
Capital City
Tel: 01 773 277

Ministry of Lands,
Housing, Physical
Planning and Surveys
PO Box 30548, Capital City
Tel: 01 774 766

Ministry of Local
Government and District
Administration
PO Box 30312, Capital City
Tel: 01 789 388

Ministry of Natural
Resources and
Environmental Affairs
Private Bag 309,
Capital City
Tel: 01 789 488

Ministry of Tourism,
Parks and Wildlife
Ex-French Embassy
Private Bag 326
Tel: 01 771 295/01 772 702
Fax: 01 770 650
Email: tourism@malawi.net

Ministry of Transport
and Public Works
Private Bag 322
Capital City
Tel: 01 789 377

Ministry of Water
Development
Private Bag 390
Capital City
Tel: 01 770 344

Horse Riding

Nyika National Park
The Nyika Safari
Company
PO Box 1006, Mzuzu
Tel: 01 330 180
Email: reservations@nyika.com
www.nyika.com

Zomba
Plateau Stables
PO Box 14
Tel: 01 522 143
Fax: 01 522 679

Hospitals

Balaka
Balaka Hospital
Tel: 01 545 344

Blantyre
Blantyre Adventist
Hospital
Kabula Road
Tel: 01 620 488
Fax: 01 623 293

Mwai Wathu Private
Hospital
Old Chileka Road
Tel: 01 622 999

Queen Elizabeth Central
Hospital
Chipatala Avenue
PO Box 95, Blantyre
Tel: 01 630 333
Fax: 01 631 353

Karonga
Karonga District Hospital
Tel: 01 362 211

Kasungu
Kasungu District
Hospital
Tel: 01 253 400

Ntcheu
Ntcheu District Hospital
Tel: 01 235 200

Lilongwe
Adventist Health Centre
PO Box 30416
Tel: 01 775 456

African Bible College
Community Health
Clinic
Tel: 01 761 670

City Centre Clinic
Tel: 01 772 164

Lilongwe Central
Hospital
Off Mzimba Street
PO Box 149
Tel: 01 753 555

Medical Rescue Services
(including Air Rescue)
Ufulu Road Clinic
PO Box 30666
Tel: 01 795 018

Liwonde
Machinga District
Hospital
Tel: 01 532 287

Mangochi
Mangochi Hospital
Tel: 01 584 344

Mulanje
Mulanje Hospital
Tel: 01 465 211

Mulanje Mission
Hospital
Tel: 01 465 344

Mzimba
Mzimba Hospital
Tel: 01 342 222

Mzuzu
Mzuzu Hospital
Tel: 01 332 888

Nkhata Bay
Nkhata Bay District
Hospital
Tel: 01 352 244

Nkhotakota
Nkhotakota Hospital
Tel: 01 292 277

St Anne's Hospital
Tel: 01 292 366

Nsanje
Nsanje District Hospital
Tel: 01 458 222

Salima
Salima Hospital
Tel: 01 261 277

Thyolo
Thyolo Hospital
Tel: 01 472 411

Zomba
Zomba Central Hospital
PO Box 21
Tel: 01 523 266

Hotels and Lodges

Blantyre
Alendo Hotel
Malawi Institute of Tourism
Chilembwe Road
PO Box 2673
Tel: 01 621 866
Fax: 01 621 923
Email: mit@malawi.net
www.alendohotelmalawi.com

Blantyre Sports Club
PO Box 245
Tel: 01 621 173/01 635 095

Doogle's Backpackers
Mulomba Place
Private Bag 346
Tel: 01 621 128
Fax: 01 621 128
Email: doogles@africa- online.net
www.doogleslodge.com

Le Méridien Malawi
(including Sunbird
Hotels & Resorts)
Central Reservations
PO Box 376
Tel: 01 620 071
Fax: 01 620 154
Email: lemeridienmw@sdnp.org.mw
Web:lemeridien-africa.com

Le Méridien Mount
Soche Hotel
Glyn Jones Road
PO Box 284
Tel: 01 620 588
Fax: 01 620 124
Email: msh@sndp.org.mw
Web: lemeridien-mountsoche.com

Limbe Country Club
PO Box 5031, Limbe
Tel: 01 641 022

Motel Paradise
PO Box 848
Tel: 01 623 338/01 623 278
Fax: 01 621 158

Namiwawa Lodge
PO Box 2542
Tel: 01 636 748/01 636 922

Nyambadwe Lodge
PO Box 30310
Tel: 01 633 551/01 635 849
Fax: 01 633 109

Protea Hotel Ryalls
PO Box 21
Tel: 01 620 955
Fax: 01 620 201
Email: ryalls@proteamalawi.com
www.proteahotels.co.za

Shire Highlands Hotel
PO Box 5204, Limbe
Tel: 01 640 055
Fax: 01 640 063
Email: blantyrehotels@sdnp.org.mw

Tumbuka Lodge
Corner Sharpe &
Chilembwe Roads
PO Box 2279
Tel: 01 620 489/01 633 489
Fax: 01 620 487
Email: tumbuka@malawi.net
www.tumbukalodgemalawi.com

Cape Maclear
Chembe Lodge
PO Box 187, Monkey Bay
Tel: 09 950 575/09 948 495
Email: info@chembelodge.com
www.chembelodge.com

Danforth Yachting
PO Box 2319, Lilongwe
Tel: 09 960 077
Fax: 09 960 707
Email: danforth@malawi.net
www.danforthyachting.com

Fat Monkeys
PO Box 182, Monkey Bay
Tel: 01 584 528
Fax: 01 584 528

Golden Sands
Holiday Camp
PO Box 48, Monkey Bay
Tel: 01 584 657
(Also through Ministry of
Tourism, Parks and
Wildlife)

Kayak Africa Camp
Chembe Village
Cape Maclear
PO Box 48, Monkey Bay
Tel: 01 584 456
Fax: 01 584 456

Kayak Africa
Reservations
1 Salford Road
Mowbray
Cape Town 7700
South Africa
Tel: +27 21 689 8123
Fax: +27 21 689 2149
Email: letsgo@kayakafrica.co.za
www.kayakafrica.co.za

Nswala Lodge
PO Box 121, Monkey Bay
Tel: 01 587 318
Email: nswalasafaris@malawi.net

Stevens' Resthouse
PO Box 21
Monkey Bay
Tel: 01 584 782

Chintheche
Chintheche Inn
PO Box 9
Tel: 01 357 211
Fax: 01 357 211
Email: info@wilderness.malawi.net
(Also through Central
African Wilderness
Safaris - see Tour and
Safari Companies)

Flame Tree Lodge
PO Box 150
Tel: 01 357 276

Kande Beach
PO Box 22
Nkhata Bay
Tel: 01 771 704
Fax: 01 771 939

Makuzi Beach
Private Bag 12
Tel: 01 357 296
Fax: 01 357 296
Email: makuzibeach@ sdnp.org.mw
www.makuzilodgemalawi.com

Nkhwazi Lodge
PO Box 120
Tel: 00 871 76 265 8745
Email: nkhwazi@inmarsat.francetelecom.fr
www.nkhwazilodgemalawi.com

Sambani Lodge
PO Box 89
Tel: 01 357 290/01 333 391
Fax: 01 333 391
Email: mzuni@sdnp.org.mw
www.sambanilodgemalawi.com

Dwangwa
Kasasa Club
PO Box 46
Tel: 01 295 266
Fax: 01 295 242

Ngala Lodge
PO Box 1456
Cape Town 8000
South Africa
Tel: +27 21 434 4654
Email: ngala@malawi.net
www.ngalabeachlodge.co.za

Dzalanyama
Dzalanyama Forest Lodge
PO Box 2140
Lilongwe
Tel: 01 757 120/01 754 303
Fax: 01 754 560
Email: landlake@africa-online.net
www.landlakemalawi.com

Karonga
Club Marina
PO Box 16
Tel: 01 362 391
Fax: 01 362 313

Kasungu
Kasungu Inn
Private Bag 19
Tel: 01 253 306
Fax: 01 253 306

Kasungu National Park
Sunbird Lifupa Lodge
Private Bag 62
Kasungu
Tel: 01 770 576/01 253 439
Fax: 01 771 273
Email: tdic@sdnp.org.mw

Lengwe National Park
Lengwe Main Gate
Camp
Ministry of Tourism,
Parks and Wildlife
Ex-French Embassy
Private Bag 326
Lilongwe
Tel: 01 771 295/01 772 702
Fax: 01 770 650
Email: tourism@malawi.net

Likoma Island
Kaya Mawa
PO Box 79
Tel: 00 871 761 684670
Fax: 00 871 761 684671
Email: KAY01@bushmail.net
www.kayamawa.com

Lilongwe
Capital City Motel
Off Youth Drive
PO Box 30454
Tel: 01 774 911/01 774 245
Fax: 01 774 245

Imperial Hotel
Private Bag A113
Tel: 01 752 201/09 930 454
Fax: 01 752 201
Email: imperial@eomw.net

Kalikuti Hotel
PO Box 703
Biwi Triangle
Tel: 01 725 570/01 726 172
Fax: 01 726 350

Kiboko Camp
Private Bag 295
Tel: 01 751 226/08 828 384
Fax: 01 754 978
Email: kiboko@malawi.net
www.kiboko-safaris.com

Le Méridien Capital Hotel
Chilembwe Road
City Centre
PO Box 30018
Tel: 01 773 388/01 774 080
Fax: 01 771 273
Email: chl@sdnp.org.mw
www.lemeridien-capital.com

Lilongwe Golf Club
PO Box 160
Tel: 01 753 118/01 753 598

Riverside Hotel
Tel: 01 750 511
Fax: 01 756 508
Email: riverside@malawi.net

Sunbird Lilongwe Hotel
Kamuzu Procession Rd
PO Box 44
Tel: 01 756 333
Fax: 01 756 580
Email: llh@sdnp.org.mw

Sunbird Lingadzi Inn
Chilambula Road
Capital City
PO Box 30367
Tel: 01 754 166/01 754 131
Fax: 01 754 129
Email: lingadzi@sdnp.org.mw

Livingstonia
Livingstonia Mission
PO Box 7, Livingstonia
Tel: 01 368 223

Liwonde National Park
Chinguni Hills Lodge
PO Box 318, Blantyre
Tel: 01 622 029
Fax: 01 624 312
Email: pirimiti@malawi.net

Hippo Lodge
Private Bag 4, Liwonde
Tel: 01 532 481
Fax: 01 532 276

Mvuu Wilderness Lodge
& Camp
PO Box 489, Lilongwe
Tel: 01 771 153/01 771 260
Fax: 01 771 397
Email: info@wilderness.malawi.net
www.classicsafaricamps.com/mvuu.htm

Majete Wildlife Reserve
Majete Safari Camp
PO Box 123, Chikwawa
Tel: 01 423 204

Mangochi
Baobab Resort
Tel: 01 587 259/09 916 007
www.angelfire.com/mt/starlake

Boadzulu Lakeshore Resort
PO Box 471
Tel: 01 584 725/01 584 570
Fax: 01 584 412
Email: boadzulu@africa-online.net
www.boadzuluresortmalawi.com

Club Makokola
PO Box 59
Tel: 01 584 244
Fax: 01 584 417
Email: clubmak@malawi.net
www.clubmak.com
(Also through Ulendo
Safaris - see Tour and
Safari Companies)

Holiday Motel
PO Box 338
Tel: 01 584 789

The K Lodge
Private Bag 16
Monkey Bay
Tel: 09 911 723
www.k-lodgemalawi.com

Martin's Beach Hotel
PO Box 584
Tel: 01 584 797

Mulangeni Holiday Resort
PO Box 442
Tel: 01 584 698
Fax: 01 584 768

Nanchengwa Lodge
PO Box 619
Tel: 08 830 062
Fax: 01 584 417

OK Motel
PO Box 401
Tel: 01 584 465

Palm Beach Resort
PO Box 46
Tel: 01 584 564
Fax: 01 584 798
Email: palmbeach@africa-online.net
www.palmbeach-mw.com

Sun N Sand
PO Box 333
Tel: 01 584 545
Fax: 01 584 723

Sun N Sand Central
Reservations
PO Box 51111, Limbe
Tel: 01 640 128/01 642 567
Fax: 01 644 202/01 641 806
Email: sunnsand@malawi.net

Sunbird Nkopola Lodge
PO Box 14
Tel: 01 584 444/01 584 802
Fax: 01 584 694
Email: nkopolal@sdnp.org.mw

Mulanje
CCAP Mission
Resthouse
PO Box 111
Tel: 01 465 262

Likhubula Forest Lodge
PO Box 361
Tel: 01 465 437
Email: likhubula@cholemalawi.com
www.cholemalawi.com/likhubula.html

Mulanje Motel
PO Box 203
Tel: 01 465 245

Mulanje Mountain Huts
Department of Forestry
Likabula Forest Station
PO Box 50
Tel: 01 465 218

Mulanje View Motel
PO Box 75
Tel: 01 465 348
Fax: 01 465 280

Mwabvi Wildlife Reserve
Mwabvi Camp
Ministry of Tourism,
Parks and Wildlife
Ex-French Embassy
Private Bag 326
Lilongwe
Tel: 01 771 295/01 772 702
Fax: 01 770 650
Email: tourism@malawi.net

Mzuzu
Makuzi Lodge
PO Box 422
Tel: 01 330 465
Email: polly_mzuzu@yahoo.co.uk
www.makuzilodgemalawi.com

Mzuzu Club
PO Box 45
Tel: 01 335 040

Mzuzu Tourist Lodge
PO Box 485
Tel: 01 332 177

Sunbird Mzuzu Hotel
PO Box 231
Tel: 01 332 622/01 332 575
Fax: 01 332 660
Email: mzh@sdnp.org.mw

Nkhotakota
Njobvu Safari Lodge
PO Box 388
Tel: 01 292 506
Fax: 01 292 460
Email: carole@birdsafaris.co.uk
www.birdsafaris.co.uk

Nkhotakota Pottery
PO Box 460
Tel: 01 292 444
Email: dedzapottery@africa-online.net
www.dedzapottery.com

Sani Beach Resort
PO Box 327

Nkhotakota Wildlife Reserve
Chipata, Bua and Wodzi
Camps
Ministry of Tourism,
Parks and Wildlife
Ex-French Embassy
Private Bag 326, Lilongwe
Tel: 01 771 295/01 772 702
Fax: 01 770 650
Email:tourism@malawi.net

Nkhata Bay
Chikale Beach Resort
PO Box 199
Tel: 01 352 338
Fax: 01 352 368
Email:cbrtours@malawi.net
www.chikaleresortmalawi.com

Njaya Lodge
Chikale Beach
PO Box 223
Tel: 01 352 342
Fax: 01 352 341
Email: njayalodge@compuserve.com
www.africanet.com/njaya/welcome.htm

Ntchisi
Ntchisi Forest Lodge
Private Bag 108
Lilongwe
Tel: 01 754 695/01 743 471
Fax: 01 754 584
Email: makomo@malawi.net
www.makomo.com

Nyika National Park
Chelinda Lodge & Camp
PO Box 1006, Mzuzu
Tel: 01 330 180
Email: reservations@nyika.com
www.nyika.com

Salima
Carolina Holiday Resort
PO Box 441
Tel: 01 263 220
Email: shelagh@malawi.net

Crystal Waters
Tel: 01 261 439

Kambiri Lakeshore Hotel
PO Box 16, Salima
Tel: 01 261 261/01 263 052
Fax: 01 263 152
Email: desco@malawi.net
www.kambiriresortmalawi.com

Le Méridien
Livingstonia Beach Hotel
PO Box 11
Tel: 01 263 444
Fax: 01 263 452
Email: lbh@sdnp.org.mw

Red Zebra Lodge
PO Box 123, Salima
Tel: 01 263 165
Fax: 01 263 407
Email: redzebras@malawi.net
www.lakemalawi.com

Safari Beach Lodge
PO Box 312
Tel: 01 263 143/09 912 238
Fax: 01 263 002/01 263 143
Email: safwag@africa-online.net
www.malawi-info.net

The Wheelhouse
PO Box 84, Salima
Tel: 01 261 485

Sucoma
Sucoma Club
Private Bag 50
Blantyre
Tel: 01 428 200
Fax: 01 428 244

Thyolo
Chawani Bungalow
Satemwa Estate
PO Box 15
Tel: 01 472 356
Fax: 01 472 368
Email: 113213.233@compuserve.com

Viphya Plateau
Luwawa Forest Lodge
Private Bag 43
Mzimba
Tel: 08 829 725/00 871
761 320897
Email: wardlow@malawi.net
www.plusdata.uklinux.net

Kasito Lodge
Department of Forestry
PO Box 30048, Lilongwe
Tel: 01 771 000
Fax: 01 774 268/01 771 812

Vwasa Marsh Wildlife Reserve
Kazuni Safari Camp
PO Box 1006, Mzuzu
Tel: 01 330 180
Email: reservations@nyika.com
www.nyika.com

Zomba
Ndindeya Motel
PO Box 527
Tel: 01 522 068

Zomba Plateau
Le Méridien
Ku Chawe Inn
PO Box 71
Tel: 01 514 211/514 74/79
Fax: 01 514 230
Email: kuchawe@sndp.org.mw

Zomba Forest Lodge
PO Box 2140
Lilongwe
Tel: 01 757 120/01 754 303
Fax: 01 754 560
Email: landlake@africa-online.net
www.landlakemalawi.com

Malawi Missions Abroad

Belgium
Rue de la Loi 15
1040 Brussels
Tel: +32 2 231 0980
Fax: +32 2 231 1066

Canada
7 Clemow Avenue
Ottawa
Ontario K1S 2A9
Tel: +1 613 236 8931/2
Fax: +1 613 236 1054
Email:malawi.highcommission@sympatico.ca

Ethiopia
Makanisa Road
PO Box 2316
Addis Ababa
Tel: +251 1 712 440
Fax: +251 1 710 490

France
20 rue Euler
4e Etage
75008 Paris
Tel: +33 1 4070 1846/
4720 2027
Fax: +33 1 4723 6248

Germany
Mainzerstrasse 124
53179 Bonn
Tel: +49 228 343 016
Fax: +49 228 340 619
Email:malawibonn@compuserve.com

Japan
3-12-9 Kami-Osaki
Kita Shinagawa
6-Chome
Shinagawa-Ku
Tokyo 141
Tel: +81 3 3449 3010
Fax: +81 3 3449 3220

Kenya
Westlands
Off Waiyaki Way
PO Box 30453
Nairobi
Tel: + 254 2 440 569
Fax: +254 2 440 568

Mozambique
Avenida Kenneth
Kaunda No.75
C.PP. 4148
Maputo
Tel: +258 1 491 468/492 047
Fax: +258 1 490 224/491 824

Namibia
56 Bismark Street
Private Bag 13254
Windhoek 900
Tel: +264 61 221 391/2
Fax: +264 61 227 056

South Africa
770 Government Avenue
PO Box 11172
Brooklyn
Pretoria 0011
Tel: +27 12 342 0146/342 1759
Fax: +27 12 342 0147

Tanzania
6th Floor
Nic Life House
PO Box 7616
Dar es Salaam
Tel: +255 22 113 239/113 240
Fax: +255 22 113 360

United Kingdom
33 Grosvenor Street
London
W1X 0DE
Tel: +44 20 7491 4172
Fax: +44 20 7491 9916
Email:kwacha@malawihighcomm.prestel.co.uk

United Nations
30th Floor
600 Third Avenue
New York, NY 10016
Tel: +1 212 949 0180/1
Fax: +1 212 599 5021
Email: mwiun@undp.org

United States of America
2408 Massachusetts Avenue NW
Washington DC 20008
Tel: +1 202 797 1007
Fax: +1 202 265 0976

Zambia
5th Floor
Woodgate House
Cairo Road
PO Box 50425, Lusaka
Tel: +260 1 228 296/228 297
Fax: +260 1 223 353

Zimbabwe
Chancery
42-44 Harare St
PO Box 321, Harare
Tel: +263 4 752 137/705 611
Fax: +263 4 705 604

Media

Blantyre
Blantyre Newspapers
Ginnery Corner
Private Bag 39
Tel: 01 671 566
Fax: 01 671 114

Central Africana Ltd
Victoria Avenue
PO Box 631
Tel: 01 623 227
Fax: 01 620 533
Email: africana@sdnp.org.mw

The Nation Publication Limited
PO Box 30408, Chichiri
Tel: 01 673 703/01 675 186
Fax: 01 674 343

Museums

Blantyre
Heritage Centre
Wildlife Society of Malawi
Churchill Road
Private Bag 578, Limbe
Tel: 01 643 502
Fax: 01 643 765
Email:wsm@malawi.net

Museum of Malawi
Kasungu Crescent
Chichiri
Tel: 01 672 001
(Also through Museums of Malawi)

Museums of Malawi
PO Box 30360
Tel: 01 675 448/01 671 857
Fax: 01 676 615
Email: museums@malawi.net

Cape Maclear
Lake Malawi Museum
PO Box 128, Mangochi
Tel: 01 584 346
(Also through Museums of Malawi)

Livingstonia
Old Stone House Museum
PO Box 7
Tel: 01 368 223

Mua Mission
Chamare Museum
PO Box 41, Mtakataka
www.muamissionmalawi.com

Mzuzu
Mzuzu Regional Museum
PO Box 138
Tel: 01 332 071
(Also through Museums of Malawi)

Namaka
Mtenga-tenga Museum
Tel: 01 534 306
(Also through Museums of Malawi)

Places of Interest

Blantyre
Carlsberg Brewery
PO Box 1050
Tel: 01 670 133

Paper Making Education Trust (PAMET)
Chilembwe Road
PO Box 1015
Tel: 01 623 895
Fax: 01 623 895

Tobacco Auction Floors
Auction Holdings Ltd
PO Box 5088, Limbe
Tel: 01 640 377

Dedza
Dedza Pottery
Paragon Ceramics
PO Box 54
Tel: 01 223 069
Fax: 01 223 131
Email: dedzapottery@africa-online.net
www.dedzapottery.com

Kamuzu Academy
Private Bag 1
Mtunthama
Tel: 01 253 488
Fax: 01 253 586

Lilongwe
Tobacco Auction Floors
Auction Holdings Ltd
PO Box 40035, Area 29
Tel: 01 710 377

Zomba
University of Malawi
PO Box 442
Tel: 01 522 622
Fax: 01 522 760

Rail Services

Blantyre
Malawi Railways Ltd
PO Box 5144, Limbe
Tel: 01 640 844

Tourist Information Offices (International)

Malawi Tourism
c/o Geo Group & Associates
4 Christian Fields
London
SW16 3JZ, UK
Tel: +44 115 982 1903
Fax: +44 115 981 9418
Email: enquiries@malawitourism.com
www.malawitourism.com

(See also Malawi Missions Abroad)

Tourist Information Offices (National)

Blantyre
Ministry of Tourism
Victoria Avenue
PO Box 402
Tel: 01 620 300
Fax: 01 620 947

Lilongwe
Malawi Tourism Association
Aquarius House
City Centre
PO Box 1044
Tel: 01 770 010
Fax: 01 770 131
Email:mta@malawi.net

Ministry of Tourism,
Parks and Wildlife
Ex-French Embassy
Private Bag 326
Tel: 01 771 295/01 772 702
Fax: 01 770 650
Email:tourism@malawi.net

Mangochi
Ministry of Tourism
Tel: 01 584 689

Mchinji
Ministry of Tourism
Tel: 01 242 296

Mzuzu
Ministry of Tourism
PO Box 848
Tel: 01 332 889
Fax: 01 332 389

Tour & Safari Companies

Blantyre
Jambo Africa
PO Box 2279
Tel: 01 635 356/01 633 489
Fax: 01 633 489
Email: jamboafrica@africa-online.net
www.jamboafricatoursmalawi.com

Lilongwe
Barefoot Safaris
Private Bag 357
Tel: 01 707 346/01 707 347
Fax: 01 754 519
Email: cpc@malawi.net

Central African
Wilderness Safaris
PO Box 489
Tel: 01 771 153/01 771 260
Fax: 01 771 397
Email: info@wilderness.malawi.net
www.wilderness-safarismalawi.com

Kiboko Safaris
Private Bag 295
Tel: 01 751 226
Fax: 01 754 978
Email: kiboko@malawi.net
www.kiboko-safaris.com

Land & Lake Safaris
PO Box 2140
Tel: 01 757 120/01 754 303
Fax: 01 754 560
Email: landlake@africa-online.net
www.landlakemalawi.com

Makomo Safaris
Private Bag 108
Tel: 01 754 695/01 754 584
Fax: 01 754 584
Email: makomo@malawi.net
www.makomo.com

Ulendo Safaris
Shop 1
Old Town Mall
Chilumbula Road
PO Box 30728
Tel: 01 754 950/01 754 926
Fax: 01 756 321
Email: reservations@ulendo.malawi.net
www.ulendosafaris.com

Travel Agents

Blantyre
Adventure Tours
PO Box 454
Tel: 01 671 095

AirTour and Travel
PO Box 112
Tel: 01 622 918/01 625 275
Fax: 01 620 270

AMI Travel
PO Box 838
Tel: 01 624 733
Fax: 01 670 240
Email: amitravel@sdnp.org.mw
www.amitravelmalawi.com

CBR Tours & Travel
Kapeni House
PO Box 1524
Tel: 01 620 226/01 633 297
Fax: 01 624 135
Email: cbrtours@malawi.net
www.cbrtoursmalawi.com

Galaxy Travel
PO Box 30741
Tel: 01 621 590/01 621 860
Fax: 01 622 592
Email: galaxytravels@wiss.co.mw
www.galaxytravelsmalawi.com

Interocean Travel
PO Box 5313
Limbe
Tel: 01 644 408
Fax: 01 641 142

Kabula Tours
PO Box 985
Tel: 01 644 009/01 644 376
Fax: 01 644 462

Lloyds Travel
PO Box 51380
Limbe
Tel: 01 652 113/01 644 512
Fax: 01 643 920

Royal Travel
PO Box 2385
Tel: 01 625 027
Fax: 01 623 512

Skylinks
Hanover House
Independence Drive
PO Box 560
Tel: 01 624 109/01 624 366
Fax: 01 636 518
Email: skylinks@malawi.net
www.skylinkstravelmalawi.com

Soche Tours & Travel
PO Box 2225
Tel: 01 620 777
Fax: 01 620 440
Email: sochetours@malawi.net
www.sochetourmalawi.com

Lilongwe
Atlas Tours & Travel
Arwa House
Private Bag 37
Tel: 01 771 430/01 773 583
Fax: 01 773 780

CBR Tours & Travel
Private Bag 414
Tel: 01 773 164/01 773 193
Fax: 01 773 192
Email: cbrtours@malawi.net
www.cbrtoursmalawi.com

Manica
PO Box 30320
Tel: 01 774 144/01 774 220
Fax: 01 771 958

Midland Travel Agency
PO Box 18
Tel: 01 756 310/01 756 147
Fax: 01 752 798
Email: midland@malawi.net
www.midlandtravelmalawi.com

Orbit Tours & Travel
PO Box 1615
Tel: 01 724 255/01 724 525
Fax: 01 726 237

Soche Tours & Travel
PO Box 30406
Tel: 01 772 377
Fax: 01 771 409
Email: sochetours@malawi.net
www.sochetourmalawi.com

Water Sports & Activities

Nkhata Bay
Aqua Africa
PO Box 209
Tel: 01 352 284
Fax: 01 352 284

Cape Maclear
Danforth Yachting
PO Box 2319, Lilongwe

Tel: 09 960 077
Fax: 09 960 707
Email: danforth@malawi.net
www.danforthyachting.com

Kayak Africa
1 Salford Road
Mowbray
Cape Town 7700
South Africa
Tel: +27 21 689 8123
Fax: +27 21 689 2149
Email: letsgo@kayakafrica.co.za
www.kayakafrica.co.za

Lake Divers
PO Box 182
Monkey Bay
Tel: 01 584 528

Mangochi
Rift Lake Charters
PO Box 284
Tel: 01 584 473
Fax: 01 584 576

Scuba Blue
Private Bag 18
Mangochi
Tel: 01 584 576
Fax: 01 584 576

Websites

For general and tourist information:

Africa Online
Web: www.africa-online.net

Forbes Report
Web: www.winne.com/
Malawi/index.htm

Malawi Business
Directory
Web: www.malawibiz.com

Malawi Directory
Web: www.zikomo.net

Malawi Guide
Web:
www.guide2malawi.com

Malawi Holiday
Web:
www.malawiholiday.com

Malawi Tourism
Web:
www.malawitourism.com

Bibliography

Birds of Malawi (1992), by Kenneth Newman et al., published by Southern Book Publishers, South Africa.

The Blantyre Handbook (1993), by Angela Sharp and Karen McDowall, published privately, Blantyre.

Britain and Malawi (1989), by John McCraken, published by Central Africana, Blantyre.

Chichewa Guide for Tourists (1995), by M Mangoche, published by Dzuka Publishing, Blantyre.

Commerce and Industry Handbook (1997), by Anthony Liouze et al., published by Central Africana, Blantyre.

Day Outings from Blantyre (1997), anon., published by Wildlife Society of Malawi, Blantyre.

Day Outings from Lilongwe (1991), by Judy Carter, published by Wildlife Society of Malawi, Blantyre.

Democracy With a Price: The History of Malawi since 1900 (1999), by Bakili Muluzi et al, published by Jhango Heinemann, Blantyre.

Early History of Malawi, The (1972), edited by Bridglal Pachai, published by Longman, London.

A Field Guide to the Butterflies of Malawi (1973), by J G Williams, published by Collins, London.

Field Guide to the Mammals of Southern Africa (1996), by C and T Stuart, published by Struik Publishers, Cape Town, South Africa.

A Guide to Malawi (1994), by David Stuart-Mogg, published by Central Africana, Blantyre.

A Guide to the Fishes of Lake Malawi National Park (1986), by Digby Lewis et al., WWF, Switzerland.

Guide to the Mulanje Massif (1988), by Frank Eastwood, published by Lorton Communications, Johannesburg.

An Introduction to the Common Snakes of Malawi (1989), by John Royle, published by Wildlife Society of Malawi, Blantyre.

Lady of the Lake (1991), by Vera Garland, published by Central Africana, Blantyre.

A Lady's Letters from Central Africa (reprinted 1991), by Jane Moir, published by Central Africana, Blantyre.

Lake Malawi's Resorts (1998), by Ted Sneed, published by Africonnections, Lilongwe.

Let Us Die for Africa (1999), by D D Phiri, published by Central Africana, Blantyre.

Livingstone (1973), by Tim Jeal, published by Heinemann, Oxford.

Livingstone's Lake (1966), by Oliver Ransford, published by John Murray, London.

Malawi (2001), by David Else, published by Lonely Planet, Melbourne.

Malawi A Geographical Study (1965), by John G Pike and Gerald T Rimmington, published by Oxford University Press, London.

Malawi A political and Economic History (1968) by John G Pike, published by Pall Mall Press, London.

The Malawi Cookbook (1985), by A Shaxon et al., Published by Dzuka Publishing, Blantyre.

Malawi Country Report (October 2000), published in Forbes Global Magazine, New York.

Malawi First (Periodical), published by Central Africana, Blantyre.

Malawi Wildlife, Parks and Reserves (1987), by Judy Carter, published by Macmillan, London.

Malawians to Remember — John Chilembwe (1976), by D D Phiri, published by Longmans, Malawi.

Nyala (Periodical), published by Wildlife Society of Malawi, Blantyre.

Reflections (Periodical), published by Central Africana, Blantyre.

Venture to the Interior (reprinted 1971), by Laurens van der Post, published by Penguin, London.

A Visitor's Guide to Nyika National Park, by Sigrid Johnson, published by Mbabzi Book Trust, Blantyre.

Wildflowers of Malawi (1975), by Audrey Moriarty, published by Purnell, South Africa.

Zomba Mountain — a Walkers' Guide (1975) by M and K Cundy, published privately, Malawi.

Index

(Illustrations are indicated in **bold**.)

A

aardvark (ant bear) 300, 301, 351-355, 363
acacia 46, 55, 122, 231, **238, 312,** 353, 357, 361
Addolorata Catholic Parish 196
Agricultural and Marketing Corporation (ADMARC) 338
African Development Bank 348
African Lakes Corporation 34, **36,** 70, 80 156, 369
African Union (AU) (formerly OAU Organisation of African Unity) 345, 348
agriculture 23, 38, 48, 192, 194, 261, 337-339, 342, 343, 345
air charters 274, 347, 372
airlines 14, 346, 372
airports 14, 16, 56-59, 66, 70, 87, 93, 100, 136, 217, 229, 255, 346, 350, 368, 372
All Saints Church 266
aloes 26, 281, 316
angling 118, 132, 145, 173, **323, 324**
Animal Checklist 363
antelope 115, 119, **145,** 150, 163, 188, 206, 281, 289, 290, 295, 298, 356, 363
anthem, national 27
ants 169, 300, 320
aquariums 245, 258, 308

B

baboon 87, 115, 119, 131, 142, 169, 206, 209, 247, 256, 281, **288**
Bakili Muluzi, Dr **43,** 348
Balaka 124, 181, 183, 186, 217, 220, 250, 375
Bamboo 192, 193
Bana Swamplands 261
Banda, Dr Hastings Kamuzu 13, 40, 41, 105, 329, 348, 369
Banda's tomb, Dr 65
Bandawe 33, 34, 151, 240, 262, 264, 268, 269, 329, 371
Bangula 213, 214
banks 60, 77, 78, 89, 94, 102, 222, 257, 343, 345, 346, 347, 372
bats 304, 363
Bembeke Hills 124
bilharzia 25, 26, 171, 224, 227, 232, 247, 256, 269, 322
bird, national **27,** 230, 303, 334, 357
birdlife 119, 131, 145, 147, 148, 149, 163, 169, **174,** 177, 189, 194, 206, 209, 214, 216, 281, 292, 303-307, 325, **335,** 357, 363
birds
  avocet 358, 364
  babbler 360, 366
  barbet 107, 359, 365
  barn owl 358, 365
  bee-eater 189, 359, 365
  bittern 357, 363
  broadbill 359, 365
  bulbul 116, 305, 360, 366

bunting 361, 367
bush shrike 360, 366
bustard 142, 358, 364
buttonquail 357, 364
buzzard 131, 201
canary 361, 367
chat 360, 366
cormorant **189, 230,** 357, 363
coot 357, 364
coucal 358, 365
courser 358, 364
crake 357, 364
crane 357, 364
creeper 360, 366
crow 360, 366
cuckoo 358, 365
cuckooshrike 360, 366
darter 357, 363
dikkop 358, 364
dove 358, 365
drongo 359, 366
duck 107, 177, 304, 357, 363
eagle 131, 149, 357, 364
  African fish 357
  Black 201
  Fish **27, 183,** 189, 214, 230, **238,** 245, 247, 257
  Long-crested 169
egret 131, 177, 281, 357, 363
falcon 149, 281, 304, 306, 357, 364
francolin 107, 357, 364
finfoot 358, 364
flamingo 177, 304, **307,** 357, 363
flufftail 357, 364
flycatcher 360, 366
geese 107, 304, 357, 363
grebe 357, 363
guineafowl **305,** 357, 364
gull 358, 364
hamerkop **174,** 177, 189, 245, 281, 303, 357, 363
harrier 357, 364
hawk 357, 364
helmetshrike 360, 367
heron 131, 149, 177, 189, 214, 357, 363
hoopoe 359, 365
honeyguide 359, 365
hornbill 359, 365
ibis 357, 363
jacana 358, 364
kestrel 357, 364
kingfisher 214, 245, 281, 359, 365
korhaan 358
lark 365
longclaw 360, 366, 367
lourie 358, 365
lovebird 358, 365
mannikin 361, 367
martin 359, 365
mousebird 359, 365
nightjar 116, 358, 365
oriole 360, 366
osprey 107, 357, 364
owl 116, 358, 365
oxpecker 360, 367
painted snipe 358, 364
penduline tit 360, 366
parrot 358, 365
pelican 177, 281, 357, 363
pigeon 358, 365
pipit 360, 366, 367
pitta 359, 365
plover 358, 364
pratincole 358, 364

pytilia 361, 367
quail 357, 364
quelea 361, 367
rail 357, 364
robin 360, 366
roller 359, 365
sandgrouse 358, 365
secretarybird 364
seedeater 361, 367
shoebill 357, 363
shrike 360, 367
skimmer 358, 364
spinetail 359, 365
starling 360, 367
stork 107, 149, 214, 357, 363
sunbird 107, 367
swallow 359, 365
swift 359, 365
tern 358, 364
tit 360, 366
thrush 360, 366
tchagra 360, 366
trogon 359, 365
vulture 289, 357, 364
wagtail 360, 366
warbler 360, 366
waxbill 361, 367
weaver 119, 245, 361, 367
white-eye 361, 367
whydah 361, 367
widowfinch 361, 367
woodhoopoe 359, 365
woodpecker 119, 359, 365
Black, Dr William 246
black rhino 188, 216, 280, 286, 352, 355
Blantyre 11, 14, 16, 17, 19, 22, 24, 31, 34, 38, 39, 43, 46, 48, 56, 58, 59, 63, **70,** 73, **74,** 75-77, **78,** 80, **81-83,** 86, 88, 89, 92, 93, 307, 368, 369, 372-375, 378, 379, 380
Blantyre's Independence Arch **83,** 334
Boating 322
British Central African Protectorate 34, 90
Buchanan, John 337
buffalo 13, **106,** 107, 116, 142, 143, 149, 150, 188, 206, 209, 281, 287, 288, 292, **299,** 351-353, 356, 363
Burgess, Col Brian 173, 174
burglaries 23, 348
bushbuck 116, 131, 141, 206, 209, 281, 296, 351-353, 356, 363
bushpig 142, 188, 206, 281, 300, 351-353, 356, 363
Business Council 345
Business Forum 345
Bvumbwe 78
Bwanje 250

C

Cameron, Colin 41
camping 22, **58, 93,** 145, 170, 173, 199, 200, 209, 216, 217, 226, 227, 243, 256, 264, 268, 272, 275, 282, 322, 351-353
campsites 21, 22, 140, 224, 368
canaries 361, 367
Cape Maclear 26, 34, **36,** 124, **240,** 242, 247, 322, 323, 376, 378, 379

car hire 16, 18, 57, 60, 66, 343, 346, 347, 373
cashewnuts 338
casino 56
Cathedral, St Peter's **274,** 329, 371
Central Lakeshore (see Salima)
Chamba 247
Chambe 201
Chawani Bungalow **190,** 192, 378
cheetah 280, 290-292
Chelinda 140-145, 316, 347, 352
Chelinda Camp 135, 140, **142,** 143, 145, 146, 324, 352
Chelinda Falls 353
Chembe 241, 243, **244,** 246, 353, 376
Chencherere 122
Chezi 118
Chia lagoon **260,** 262, 263, 265, **266,** 269, 315
Chichiri 80
Chimaliro Hills 100
Chinguni Hills 183, 188
Chikale Bay **272**
Chikalogwe Plains 188
Chikangawa 131
Chikwawa 203, 205, **206,** 209, 304, 352, 377
Chileka 16, 87, 186, 346, 372, 374
Chilembwe 356
Chilembwe Rising 39, 90
Chilenje 121
Chilomoni 76, 86
Chilumba 18, 156, 347
Chintheche 11, 14, 260-262, 264, **265,** 268, 269, 271, 274, 323, 325, 347, 371, 376
Chipoka 18, 254
Chiponde 14, 222
Chiradzulu 39, 163, 196
Chiradzulu Peak 171, 198
Chiromo 213
Chisanda Falls 145, 353
Chitakali 197, 198, 200
Chitimba Bay 153, 156
Chitipa 14, 157
Chiwi Hot Springs 268
Chongoni 122
Church of Central Africa Presbyterian 23
Civic Centre 80
climate 23, 46, 56, 88, 93, 100, 114, 120, 131, 135, 155, 159, 190, 195, 337, 340, 342, 349
Club Makokola 14, 25, 224, 228, **229,** 323, 325, 347, 377
coat of arms **27,** 334
Cobbe Barracks 90, 369
coffee 38, 46, 48, 57, 73-75, 93, 110, 137, 159, 190, 194, 196, 197, 263, **321,** 337, 350
COMESA 345, 348
common waterbuck 296, 351, 352
communications 341, 348
crafts and curios 374
credit cards 347, 348
crocodile 18, 116, 188, 189, 204, 212-214, 217, 218, 231, **232,** 245, **281, 283, 301,** 319, **322**
  Nile 301, 351-353, 362, 367
currency 334, 346
  foreign 334, 347
  notes and coins **335**
  regulations 334, 347
cycling 13, 132, 140, 325

D

Danforth Yachting 247
DB's Bistro 58
Dedza 11, 26, 46, 120, 122-124,
    249, 251, 265, 319, 326,
    332, 358, 359, 361, 374,
    379
Department of Surveys 16, 374
dialling codes 372
Domwe 143, 243, 244, 247, 353
Doogles 73, 375
Dowa 46, 100, 114
duiker 131, 145, 298, 356
    Blue 295, 298, 352, 356, 363
    Common (grey) 107, 141,
        150, 206, 241, 245, 281,
        298, 351, 352, 353, 356,
        363
    Red 145, 352, 353, 356, 363
Dwangwa 115, 116, 260, 262-
    264, 268, 311, 340, 341,
    373, 376
Dzalanyama 119, 376

E

Ekwendeni 136, 137
eland 116, 141, 150, 281, **295**,
    296, 351, 352, 356, 363
elephant 11, 45, 83, 106, 107,
    112, 115, 131, 142, 143,
    149-151, **178**, 188, 206,
    209, 213, 230, **238**, 285,
    286, 313, 363
Elephant Marsh 175, 194, 213,
    214, 216, 285, 303, 304,
    307, 315
ethanol 268, 338
even-toed ungulates 287, 355, 363
European Union (EU) 345
Electricity Supply Corporation
    (ESCOM) 345

F

fauna 5, 13, 132, 141, 201, 244,
    285, 309, 312, 351, 352,
    353
fern 119, 169, 171, 201, 315
Finance Corporation of Malawi
    (FINCOM) 345
fish **50, 182, 246, 267,** 367
    chambo 265
    kampango 324
    mbuna 245, 247, 280, 281,
        308, 311, 324
    mpasa 324
    ncheni 324
    ngumbo 324
    sanjika 324
    sungwa 281, 324
    tiger 281
    vundu 324
fishing 18, 23, 26, 48, 91, 105, 118,
    146, 173, 174, 183, 203,
    209, 219, **224**, 225, 232,
    238, 241, 247, 258, 260,
    265, 268, 270, 273, **309**,
    320, 322-324, 339, 342
flag, national 27
flora 5, 13, 119, 132, 141, 142,
    201, 245
Foot, Captain RN 34
Foreign diplomatic missions
    374
forest reserves
    Dzalanyama 118

Malawi's 168
Ntchisi 115
Zomba Plateau 168
Fort Lister 202
Fort Lister Gap 195, 201, 202

G

galleries 374
gazetteer 368
General Agreement of Trade and
    Tariff (GATT) 348, 345
golf course 233
gorge
    Luweya 45
    Mpatamanga 45, 210, 217, 354
    Mwabvi 216
    Narrow 216
    Njakwa 127
    Ruo 216
Gourou, Pierre 332
Government Offices 374
gwendolen, HMS 168

H

hares 107, 201, 292, 298, 354, 363
hartebeest 107
    Lichtenstein's 116, 297, 351,
        352, 356, 363
Henga Valley 153
Henderson, Henry 70
Heritage Centre 80, 217
highlands 119, 120, 128
    Dedza 100, 159
    Shire 159
    Viphya 127
hiking 13, 324
hippopotamus 18, 23, **103**, 107,
    116, 148, **149**, 150, **181**,
    187-189, 204, 212-214,
    217, 245, 258, **280, 283**,
    286, 287, 319, 322, 351-
    353, 356, 363
hitch-hiking 16
HIV (AIDS) 26
horse riding 13, **143**, 145, 173,
    262, 324, 375
hospitals 60, 90, 102, 123, 151,
    249, 368, 375
    Anglican 266
    Mulanje district 200
hot springs 266
    Chiwi 264, 268
hotels and lodges 375
hyena **66**, 87, 107, 119, 131, 145,
    169, 188, 280, 289-291
    spotted 142, **291**, 351, 352,
        353, 355, 363
hyrax 355, 363

I

impala 107, 150, 188, 206, **282**,
    297, 351-353, 356, 363
Imperial Tobacco Company 38
independence 13, 39, 40, 41, 64,
    88, **118**, 220, 270, 334,
    337, 345
    Arch 83, 162
Independence Development
    Bank of Malawi
    (INDEBANK) 343, 345
International Commonwealth
    348
International Labour
    Organisation (ILO) 348
International Monetary Fund
    (IMF) 348

insectivores 363
insects
    butterflies 169, 201, 312, 380
    mosquitoes 25, 135, 151,
        189, 240, 243, 247
    tsetse fly 25, 100, 107, 135,
        151, 240, 279
inselbergs **29**, 45, 100, **102**, 120,
    121, 124, **127**, 128, 131,
    170, 198, 217, 306
insurance 14, 343, 346
    Medical 349
islands
    Boadzulu **230**, 324
    Chisi 175
    Likoma 14, 18, 34, 156, 244,
        266, **274**, 275, 329, 347,
        371, 376
    Mbenji 324
    Namalenje 257, **258**, 259
    Thongwe 175
    West Thumbi 323

J

Jackal 107
Jackson, Jane 269
Jasi 207
James' Landing 213
Johnston, Fort 220, 222
Johnston, Harry 34, 37, 89, 90,
    220, 260
Jumbe 260
juniper 143, 144, 315

K

Kambiri point 256, 258
Kamuzu academy 11, 102, 108,
    110, 113, 369, 379
Kamuzu barrage 181, 182
Kapichira Falls 33, 45, 208, 209,
    211, 324, 339, 354, 370
Karonga 14, 31, **35**, 37, 39, 93,
    135, 147, 151, 156, 157,
    347, 368, 370, 375, 376
Kasankha Bay 243
Kasasa club 115
Kasasa Sugar Estate 261
Kasito Lodge 130
Kasungu 100, 102, 103, **106**, 107,
    109, 110, 112, 115, 120,
    128, 262, 279, 281, 285-
    289, 291, 293, 296-299,
    301, 375, 376
King's African Rifles 39, 50, **89**,
    90, 156, 333, 334, 369
Kirk, Dr 33
klipspringer 201, 281, **298**, 351,
    352, 353, 356, 363
Koma crocodile farm 225
Kota Kota 260, 266
kudu 116, 141, 150, 206, 209,
    216, 245, 281, **295**, 296,
    352, 353, 356, 363
KuNgoni Arts and Craft
    Centre 249, 248, 371
KuNgoni Waterfalls 248

L

La Caverna Art Gallery 79
Lakes
    Chilwa 88, 91, 159, 170, 171,
        174, **175**, 176, **177**, 214,
        303, 304, **307**, 357, 362
    Kauline **143**, 145

Kazuni 147, 148, **149**, 150, 351
Lifupa 105
Malombe 159, **182**, 183, 220,
    339, 352
language 23, 348, 368
    Chichewa 23, 30, 380
Laws, Dr Robert 33, 34, 151,
    155, 240, 268, 370, 371
Le Méridien Ku Chawe 89, 162,
    164, 167
Lengwe 159, 206, 304
leopard 66, **87**, **107**, **116**, 119,
    131, 141, **142**, 145, **150**,
    169, **188**, 206, 209, 257,
    280, 289, 290, 291, **292**,
    342, 351-353, 355, 363
libraries
    British Council 58
    Malawi 369
    National 64
    Old 79
    Malawi Wildlife Society's 82
lichen 169, 201, 313
Lifupa Lodge 57, 103, 105, 107,
    289, 369
Likabula (*Likhubula*) 197,199,
    200, 201-203, 315
Lilongwe 17, **20, 24, 42, 49, 53**, 55,
    56, 57-59, **60**, 61, 63, 64-
    66, **67**, 70, 77, 79, 87-89,
    92-94, **116, 121**, 304, 307,
    315, 322, 326, 328, 329, 334,
    335, 342, 372, 373, 379
Lilongwe Nature
    Sanctuary 66, 313
Limbe 46, 70-80, 82, **83**, 86, 159,
    163, 190, 198, 214, 229,
    321, 328, 369, 373-379,
    380
lion 13, **105**, 107, 116, 150, 188,
    216, **289**, 290, 293, 351,
    352, 355, 363
livestock 15, 23, 30, 48, 337
Livingstone, Charles 240
Livingstone, Dr David 5, 17, **31**,
    33, 34, 70, 80, 112, **119**,
    151, 155, 174, 208, 209,
    211, 213, 240, 260, 270,
    275, 285, 329, 337, 369,
    370
Livingstone, William Jervis 39
Livingstone's suni 206, 281,
    298, 352, 353, 356, 363
Livingstonia 40, 44, **45**, **145**,
    151, **153**, 154, 155, 156,
    329, 376, 379
Livingstonia Central African
    Company 369
Livingstonia Mission 11, **33**, 34,
    36, 136, 144, 151, **152**,
    153, **154**, **155**, 156, 208,
    240, 268, 269, 313, **330**,
    353, 370, 371, 376
Liwonde 181, **186**, 304, 375
Luchenza **196**, 197
Lunza 217
Luwawa 128, 130
Luwawa Falls **128**
Luwawa Forest Lodge 128, **130**,
    131, **132, 307**, 325, 378

M

Macadamia 337
Mackenzie, Bishop 33
Maclear, Sir Thomas 240
Madisi 102
Majete 207-209, **210**, 279, 352-355

Makanga 207
Makhanga 213, 214
malaria 24, 25, 33, 130, 151,
    189, 269, 346
Malawi Army Naval Unit 236
Malawi Development
    Corporation 82, 342, 345
Malawi Export Promotion
    Council 345
Malawi missions abroad 378
Malawi Telecom 345
Malawi Wildlife Society 80
Malawian Lake Service 236
Malosa 162, 171
Malosa Massif 179
mammals 363
Manchewe Falls 153, 353
Mandala 35, 36, 80, 81
Mangochi 11, 14, 31, 34, 162,
    164, 176, 178, 182, 183,
    220, 222, 223, 224-227,
    231, 236, 241, 246, 248,
    249, 254, 324, 375, 377,
    378, 379,379
Marka 14
Masongola 89
Mathiti gate 209, 211
matola 16, 17, 18, 347
Mchacha 194, 213
Mchesa 202
Mchinji 14, 102, 103, 109, 120,
    304, 341, 368, 379
Mfasa 322
Mfuwe 14, 119, 347
Mgawa 120
mice 119
Michuru 70, 73, 86
mining 337, 340, 342
Ministry of Agriculture and
    Irrigation Development
    345
Ministry of Commerce and
    Industry 345
Ministry of Finance 345
Ministry of National Resources
    and Environmental
    Affairs 345
Ministry of Tourism, Parks
    and Wildlife 21, 105,
    118, 282, 285, 345
Mkhulambe 201
Mkurumadzi 207
Mlozi 35, 37, 156, 157
Moir brothers John, Frederick
    34, 70, 80
monkey 66, 87, 115, 119, 131,
    163, 169, 194, 201, 227,
    230, 247, 281, 288
Monkey Bay 18, 224, 225, 226,
    231, 232, 236, 237, 238,
    240, 242, 243, 246, 248,
    249, 251, 330, 334, 341,
    347, 372, 376, 377, 380
mountain biking 146
mountains
    Bunda 121
    Chilenje 121
    Chongoni 121
    Chipata 116
    Dedza 120, 123
    Dedza-Kirk 249, 250, 251
    Dzalanyama 118
    Livingstone 156
    Malingu 127
    Malosa 179
    Mulanje 5, 13, 159, 163,
        170, 174, 176, 192, 195,

197, 198, 199, 200, 202,
    289, 307, 313, 354, 370
Mulanje Massif 46, 159, 195,
    197, 199-201, 203, 324, 380
Ndirande 73, 74
Nkhoma 121
Thyolo 194
Viphya 131, 133
Zomba 87, 89, 173, 380
Mountain Club of Malawi 203
Mountain High Rangers 203
Mpatsanjoka dambo 255
Mphonde 115, 262
Mponela 102
Mtanga 265
Mtenga-tenga Postal Hut 334
Mtunthama 108, 110
Mua Mission 217, 225, 228, 248,
    250, 251, 252, 327, 328,
    371, 374, 379
Mulanje Town 11, 26, 39, 47,
    159, 163, 174, 190, 194-
    199, 200-203, 304-306,
    311, 315, 316, 320, 324,
    325, 337, 340, 358-360,
    362, 373, 375, 377
Muloza 14, 196, 201, 202
Mulunguzi 88, 162, 170
Mulunguzi Dam 166, 172, 173,
    353
Mumbo 243, 244, 247, 353
Muona 194, 213
Murchison Cataracts 208
museums 378
    Chamare 251, 252, 371
    Lake Malawi 370
    Lake Malawi National 370
    Museum of Malawi 80
    Mzuzu 369
    Mtenga-tenga Postal 335
    Postal 370
Mvuu 14, 181-183, 186-189, 287,
    347, 352, 356
Mwala wa Mphini 245, 246
Mwanza 14, 207, 217, 342
Mzimba 30, 92, 131, 375
Mzuzu 11, 14, 16, 17, 19, 23, 48,
    56, 90, 92-95, 96, 100,
    102, 103, 109, 112, 127,
    128, 130, 131, 133, 135-
    137, 140, 147, 151, 156,
    254, 262, 270, 271, 347,
    353, 360, 368, 369, 372-
    375, 377, 379

N
Namadzi 164
Namaka 379
Nankhumba Hill 258, 259
Nankumba Peninsula 240
Nathenje 121
Nathenje Hills 121
National Motto 27
National Parks
    Kasungu 19, 33, 46, 57, 100,
        102-104, 105, 107, 110,
        260, 279, 290, 299, 306,
        312, 351, 369, 376
    Kruger 188
    Lake Malawi 45, 216, 226,
        238, 240, 242, 244, 245,
        277, 279, 281, 283, 293,
        301, 308, 309, 322, 353,
        355, 356, 361, 370, 380
    Lengwe 11, 45, 203, 205, 207,
        208, 211, 277, 279, 288,
        295, 304, 352, 359, 376

Liwonde 11, 14, 45, 107, 124,
    164, 177, 178, 180, 181,
    182, 183, 187, 188, 217,
    232, 250, 286, 289, 293,
    301, 304, 306, 312, 317,
    321, 323, 347, 352, 376
Majete 355, 356
Malawi 27, 116, 279, 285
Nyala 206
Nyika 11, 14, 46, 93, 135,
    136, 137, 142, 148, 279,
    283, 289, 293, 299, 305,
    347, 351, 353, 370, 375,
    377, 380
South Luangwa 119
National Economic Council 345
National Insurance Company 345
National Road Authority 345
Nchalo 211, 213
Nchenachena Falls 194, 354
Ncheu 332
Ndirande 70, 76, 86, 87
Newspapers 64, 348
N'gabu 213
Ngala Beach Lodge 115, 264
Ngondalo 171
Nguru-ya-Nawambe 105
Njuli 164
Nkalapia 128
Nkhata Bay 11, 18, 33, 44, 45,
    47, 49, 94, 133, 135, 147,
    243, 262, 265, 270, 272,
    273, 274, 304, 320, 323,
    375, 376, 377, 379
Nkhoma 121
Nkhotakota 11, 18, 31, 33, 34,
    100, 106, 109, 110, 112,
    115, 116, 260, 262, 263,
    265, 266, 269, 271, 274,
    281, 285, 286, 288, 289,
    292, 293, 295-297, 299,
    301, 309, 315, 326, 329,
    341, 354-356, 368, 371,
    374, 375, 377
Nsanje 38, 70, 213, 214, 368, 375
Ntcheu 124, 375
Ntchisi 46, 102, 110, 113, 114,
    115, 315, 377
Nyanja 23, 30, 31, 48, 348, 368
Nyika Plateau 46, 47, 127, 144,
    145, 153, 154, 280, 296,
    299, 315, 324, 332, 351,
    353, 360, 370
Nyika Safari Company 141

O
odd-toed ungulates 299, 355,
    363
orchid 26, 105, 123, 140, 142,
    169, 281, 311, 315, 352
    Terrestrial 142
    Wild 105, 123
oribi 107, 298, 351, 352, 356, 363
Otter Point 243, 244, 247, 323

P
pangolins 354, 363
people
    Batwa 30, 122, 369
    Chewa 22, 23, 30, 33, 40, 48,
        50, 251, 252, 332, 348,
        368, 371
    Lomwe 22, 48
    Maravi 22, 30
    Ngoni 22, 33, 34, 39, 48, 50,
        332, 371

Nkonde 37, 48
Nyanja 23, 30, 31, 48, 348, 368
Tonga 38, 48
Tumbuka 23, 30, 37, 48, 332,
    348, 368
Yao 22, 23, 31, 33, 37, 39, 48,
    50, 329, 332, 348, 368,
    371
Phalombe 46, 176, 195-199, 201,
    202, 321
Photography 26
Phwadzi 210
post office 58-61, 64, 77, 78, 89,
    94, 102, 110, 115, 156, 222,
    257, 269, 327, 348, 368
pottery 123, 164, 197, 248, 263,
    265, 326
    Dedza 59, 121, 123, 265, 374,
        379
    Nkhotakota 263, 326, 374,
        377
Presidential Train 354
Primates 288, 354, 363
Providential Industrial
    Mission (PIM) 39
Pwezi Rapids 153
puku 107, 296, 351, 352, 356, 363

R
rabbits 354, 355, 363
rail services 18, 379
railway 38, 118, 120, 181, 183,
    186, 188, 194, 195, 197,
    213, 220, 250, 254, 354
red hot pokers 201, 316
reedbuck 141, 142, 281, 296,
    351-353, 356, 363
religion 329, 330, 348, 368
reptiles 22, 201, 301, 354, 361,
    362, 367
Rhodes, Cecil 34
river
    Bua 102, 110, 115, 116, 262, 313
    Chivunde 71
    Domasi 162, 166, 171
    Dwangwa 260, 266
    Dwambazi 262
    Kaombe 115
    Kasitu 127, 131, 137, 151
    Lichenya 203
    Lifise 254
    Lilongwe 55, 57, 61, 118,
        119, 217
    Lingadzi 66
    Lower Shire 205, 324, 339, 353
    Luwewe 146
    Mudi 80
    Mulunguzi 162, 170, 172, 217
    Mwanza 203
    Mzimba 131
    Phalombe 195, 198
    Rovuma 33
    Ruo 197, 213, 354
    Shire 23, 33, 44, 45, 124, 159,
        168, 177-179, 181, 182,
        183, 187, 188, 189, 203,
        206-209, 210, 211, 212,
        213, 217, 220, 222, 232,
        281, 286, 287, 293, 296,
        301, 306, 323, 324, 352,
        354, 356, 362, 370
    Sombani 195
    Songwe 14, 157
    South Rukuru 127, 128, 137,
        145, 146, 147, 149, 150,
        152, 153, 351
    Thangadzi 216

Thuchila 197
Upper Shire 352, 357
Zambezi 34, 44
roan 141, **145**, 150, 281, 296, 351, 352
rock dassie (*hyrax*) 216, **238**, **300**, 301, 351-353, 355, 363
rodents 320, 354, 363
Roman Catholic Seminary 225
rubber 210, 338, 342
Rumphi 11, 135, **137**, **147**, 148, 151, 156, 351

S

Salima 11, 14, 31, 66, 112, **116**, 118, 220, 236, 241, 248, 251, 254-258, 262, 265, 269, 271, 315, 324, 327, 347, 368, 373, 375, 377
Sani Beach Resort (Njobvu Safari Lodge) 115
Sapitwa 46, 195
Scott, David Clement 80, 369
season
  cool dry (*masika*) 46
  hot dry (*malimwe*) 46
  hot wet (*dzinja*) 46
Senga Bay 11, **66**, 118, **218**, 246, 248, 251, **254**, 255-257, **258**, 303, 315, 323, 327
Shaka, King 33
Sharpe's akalat 305
Sharpe's grysbok 298, 351-353, 356, 363
Small Enterprise Development Organisation 345
sleeping sickness 25, 279
snakes (*see reptiles*)

Society of Malawi 82
Southern African Development Community (SADC) 348
sports clubs 21
  Blantyre 82, 203, 373, 375
  Limbe Country 82, 373, 375
  Sucoma 211
squash 232
Stamps 334, **335**
State House 164
Stevenson, Robert Louis 202
St Michael and All Angels Church **31**, **38**, **77**, 80, 329, 369
Stewart, James 70
Sucoma **212**, **315**, 377
Suni 206
swamps 175, 265, 315

T

table tennis 232, 233
taxis 16, 17, **66**, **87**, 347
tea 48, **130**, 159, 190, **191**, **192**, 194, 196-198, 200, 201, 214, **311**, **320**, **334**, 337, 340
The Legacy-Blantyre 73
Thyolo **190**, **191**, 375, 378
Thyolo escarpment 45, 194, 204, 214, 352, 353
Thyolo tea estates 192
tobacco 38, 46, 48, **66**, **74**, 82, **83**, 86, **99**, 100, 102, 105, 110, 115, 118, 131, 148, 159, 163, 190, **313**, 337, 338, 339, 340, 346, 379
Tour and Safari Companies 379
Tozer, Bishop 23
travel agents 379

U

Ulongwe 182, 183, 186, 352
United Democratic Front (UDF) 348
United Nations (UN) 345, 348

V

venus fly-trap 201
Viphya Plateau 11, **99**, 128, **132**, 378

W

Wardlow, George 132
warthog 107, 116, 119, 142, 150, 188, 206, 216, **300**, 351-353, 355, 356, 363
waterholes 206, **207**, **277**, 279, 283, 296
water sports 13, 219, 224, 227, **228**, 230, 232, 246, 247, 256, 259, 322, **323**, 379
Websites 379
Whyte's sunflower 201
wild dog 107
wildebeest 188
wildflowers 142, 170, 311, 315, 316, 352, 380
wildlife profile 354
wildlife reserves 15, 21, 23-25, 27, 100, 159, **279**, **285**, **324**, 347, 351, 377
  Lake Malawi 281
  Majete 33, 37, 159, 203, 205-207, **210**, 231, 281, 320, 324, 352, 354, 370, 377
  Mwabvi 45, 159, 213, 216, 279, 353, 377
  Nkhotakota 11, 45, 102, 110, **112**, 114, 115, **116**, **119**,

217, 262, 263, 264, 266, 279, 301, 304, 312, 320, 324, 351, 377
Vwaza Marsh 46, 93, 136, 146, **147**, **148**, **150**, 279, 303, 351, 378
Wildlife Society of Malawi 217, 380
Williams Falls 353
World Bank 348
World Trade Organisation (WTO) 345, 348

Y

Young's Bay 153, 156
Yachting 232

Z

Zaro pool 146, 150
zebra 107, **299**
  Burchell's 141, 188, 299, 351-353, 355, 363
Zoa Falls 194
Zomba 11, 16, 22, 26, 39, 48, **53**, 88, 89, **90**, 91, 159, **165**, **166**, **173**, 289, 311, 315, 324, 327, 334, **335**, 339, 373
Zomba Plateau 5, 11, 13, 19, 46, 88, 156, 159, **162**, 164, **165**, **167**-172, **174**, 179, 313, 315, 319, 320, 324, 325, 334, 339, 353, 370, 378

All pictures by **John Douglas** and **Kelly White** except the following:

Camerapix: Pages 27, 295, 306 (bottom)

Karl Amman: Page 298